Praise for *Wom*

"Martha Holstein has long been one of the best writers on the health care issues, politics, and ethics of aging. Her analysis in *Women in Late Life* is superb." —**Margaret Cruikshank, University of Maine; author of *Learning to Be Old***

"Martha Holstein advances a brilliant interpretation of the challenges faced by women in old age, effectively deploying a feminist lens to illumine multiple social inequalities shaped, particularly, by gender and social class." —**Frida Kerner Furman, DePaul University**

"Reading this book makes me excited to teach Sociology of Aging again. Martha Holstein accomplishes here what no other book in the field offers by offering a comprehensive interdisciplinary text that is part personal and community narrative, part social science and ethics of aging, and part feminist gerontology. I know that my students will appreciate being invited into this well-researched conversation with noted gerontologist and ethicist Martha Holstein, who has been 'thinking about these issues for a long time,' and it shows." —**Meika Loe, Colgate University; author of *Aging Our Way***

"Martha Holstein has written a highly intelligent work that blends extraordinary scholarship with personal experience through a critical gerontological and feminist framework. This book is pertinent for all women and men to embrace (rather than evade) age as a valued 'work in progress.'" —**Marcia Spira, Loyola University Chicago**

"*Women in Late Life* is a profound contribution to feminist scholarship and critical gerontology, vividly portraying the intersectionality of ageism, sexism, ableism, classism, and power; and critiquing gerontological paradigms of successful and productive aging influenced by our societal values of independence and privatization. The book is a remarkable blend of the personal and the political, relying on women's voices and individual biographies intersecting with the scholarly evidence base on gender and aging. The reader will savor the deep wisdom and insights embedded in Holstein's eloquent writing and find the book hard to put down. This book is a gift in the finest sense of the word." —**Nancy Hooyman, University of Washington**

"It is critical that those of us who work with older women read Martha Holstein's book. It will help build empathy and understanding of the many societal factors, including ageism, that have come together to form the expectations and structures in which older women live their lives." —**Robyn L. Golden, Director of Health and Aging, Rush University Medical Center**

Diversity and Aging
Series Editor: Toni Calasanti, Virginia Tech

The elder population is not only growing in size, but also becoming more diverse—including differences in gender, race, ethnicity, class, and sexuality—and the experiences of aging people can vary dramatically. Books in this series explore this diversity, focusing on the ways that these social inequalities, along with ageism, shape experiences of growing old. The series will illustrate the challenges and opportunities that diversity and aging present for society, both now and in the future.

Facing Age: Women Growing Older in Anti-Aging Culture by Laura Hurd Clarke
As the Leaves Turn Gold: Asian Americans and Aging by Bandana Purkayastha, Miho Iwata, Shweta Majumdar, Ranita Ray, and Trisha Tiamzon
Women in Late Life: Critical Perspectives on Gender and Age by Martha Holstein

Women in Late Life

Critical Perspectives on Gender and Age

Martha Holstein

ROWMAN & LITTLEFIELD
Lanham • Boulder • New York • London

Published by Rowman & Littlefield
A wholly owned subsidiary of The Rowman & Littlefield Publishing Group, Inc.
4501 Forbes Boulevard, Suite 200, Lanham, Maryland 20706
www.rowman.com

Unit A, Whitacre Mews, 26-34 Stannary Street, London SE11 4AB, United Kingdom

British Library Cataloguing in Publication Information Available

Library of Congress Cataloging-in-Publication Data
Holstein, Martha.
Women in late life : critical perspectives on gender and age / Martha Holstein.
pages cm. — (Diversity and aging)
Includes bibliographical references and index.
ISBN 978-1-4422-2286-1 (cloth : alk. paper) — ISBN 978-1-4422-2287-8 (pbk. : alk.
paper) — ISBN 978-1-4422-2288-5 (electronic)
1. Older women. 2. Aging. 3. Ageism. 4. Sexism. I. Title.
HQ1061.H576 2015
305.26'2—dc23
2014046660

Printed in the United States of America

*To my daughters Jennifer and Julie Holstein and my granddaughter Ila
Belle Holstein-Rosen
My hopes for an ever-better future for women and girls.*

Contents

Acknowledgments   ix

Introduction   1

The Women of Mayslake   25

Part I: The Body and Beyond

1 What Do You See When You Look at Me?: Women, Aging, and Our Bodies   37

2 Ageism: You're Only as Old as You Feel and Other Fictions   63

3 The "New" Old Age: From Productive Aging to Anti-Aging and Everything in Between   91

4 Disruptions and Repair: Identity and Chronic Illness   117

Part II: Aging Women in Contemporary Society

5 A Looming Dystopia: Feminism, Aging, and Community-Based Long-Term Care   147

6 Retirement: In Pursuit of Women's Economic Security   175

7 Beyond Rational Control: Reflections on End-of-Life Care   205

Part III: I'm an Old Lady and Damn Proud of It (Maggie Kuhn)

8 Resistance and Change: Where to from Here?   235

References   263

Contents

Index   291

About the Author   303

Acknowledgments

Getting the chance to say thank you to all who have helped me along the way is one of the great pleasures of writing a book like this one in which almost every woman I spoke to became a source from whom I learned something that I needed to know. I can't list them all, but I am grateful for the many, many conversations I had about a sometimes difficult subject—one's own aging in an often inhospitable society.

When this book was still a dream, something that I knew I wanted to do but wasn't sure how I would carve out the time to do so, Marilyn Hennessey, then the president of the Retirement Research Foundation (RRF), said that she thought a board member might be interested in my project. She pursued the idea and to my everlasting appreciation, I received a grant from RRF that helped me start this project while still working full time. So my first thank you goes to Marilyn and, following her retirement, her successor at RRF, Irene Frye, and my program officer, Julie Kaufman, who had infinite patience with me as I fell behind my schedule because of another book project. Without the generous and timely support of RRF, I am not sure I would be writing these words today.

My second thank you goes to the philosophy department at Loyola University, Chicago, where I taught part-time for a number of years. Through its auspices I had library privileges, a place to work, and generous colleagues with whom to talk. Again, without those privileges, I would not have been able to do the research that a book of this sort requires.

My third thank you goes to the wonderful "women of Mayslake" whom I mention often throughout the book and will introduce in a brief essay de-

ix

voted specifically to them that follows the introduction. For now, I will simply say that for almost three years we have talked and laughed and gotten angry when that seemed to be necessary. They taught me a great deal while cheering me on when I seemed to be flagging. I have also been fortunate to have the chance to colead a series of discussions called "Exploring Our Aging Selves" for women over sixty at my synagogue in Evanston, Illinois. Despite differences in backgrounds from the women at Mayslake, there was agreement that we need to be informed, politically engaged, and accepting of what it means to become older (not all were ready to accept the term "old") in our society today.

Other grateful thanks go to friends and colleagues who reviewed chapters, providing me with much appreciated and needed feedback, and also listened to me as I tried to sort through my thinking and the arguments that I was making. Those conversations were invaluable, but so too was the moral support when I needed it. So a very special thank you to Phyllis Mitzen, Linda Zises, Ellyce Anapolsky, Adele Meyer, Karen Nisely Long, Madelyn Iris, Nancy Hooyman, Anne Rosen, Larry Polivka, Marcia Spira, Ellyn Banks, and Nicole Gotthoff for their generosity and help.

My daughters, Jennifer and Julie Holstein, asked me pertinent questions, supported my work, and let me be when I visited them in Los Angeles and New York and popped open my computer when the need to work overtook me. But they also gave me many weekends of simple pleasures away from work. My granddaughter, Ila Belle Holstein-Rosen, while interested, supportive, and enthusiastic, thought the book might be a little boring and wanted to know if it would have any pictures, but she is just nine and already is giving hints of future activism. While I have dedicated this book to Jennifer, Julie, and Ila as the present and the future hope for a more decent society, I am also pleased to acknowledge the support and encouragement of my sons-in-law, Noah Rosen and Adam Rosenblatt, who checked in to see how I was doing, welcomed me to their homes, and offered assurances when it all seemed to be too overwhelming. My grandsons, Jonah Rosenblatt and Miles Holstein-Rosen, are too young to have had too much interest in my work, but I hope that one day they will become men who notice and address in their own lives issues that affect women (and many men, too).

In a group of one, I thank Toni Calasanti, the editor of the series of which this book is a part, for her responsiveness and encouragement and for her thoughtful, thorough, and respectful readings and editorial comments. Every writer deserves an editor like Toni. I trust that the book has benefitted greatly from Toni's dedication and knowledge. As I write these words, I anticipate the continued support of Sarah Stanton, my editor at Rowman & Littlefield, who has calmly accepted my lengthening deadline and has always responded kindly and quickly to my questions. I am, often to my dismay, an obsessive rather than an efficient writer, and so everything took longer than I thought it would.

I thank the following for their permission to use portions of previously published work: Chapter 5: "A Looming Dystopia: Feminism, Aging and Community-Based Long-Term Care" is reprinted with permission from University of Toronto Press (http://www.utpjournals.com). doi:10.2979/intjfemappbio.6.2.6. It originally appeared in the *International Journal of Feminist Approaches to Bioethics* 6 (2). I note that it has been partly revised for this book.

An edited and revised version of chapter 5, titled, "A Looming Dystopia: Feminism, Social Justice, and Community-Based Long-Term Care, appeared in Michael Reisch, ed., *The Routledge International Handbook of Social Justice*, 409–23, published in 2014 by Routledge.

While substantially rewritten for this publication, portions of chapter 6, "Retirement: In Pursuit of Women's Economic Security," appeared in an earlier article, "The 'Crises' in Retirement Security: Social Security Is the Answer, Not the Problem," published in the *John Marshall Law Review* 46 (3): 719–47. Research assistance for that article was provided by Kristin Pavele who appeared as the second author in the law review article.

Similarly, chapter 7, "Beyond Rational Control: Reflections on End-of Life-Care," appeared as a chapter with the same name in *Ethics, Aging, and Society: The Critical Turn*, written collaboratively with Jennifer Parks and Mark Waymack, both of Loyola University, who have given their permission for its use. It was published by the Springer Publishing Company. The chapter itself has been substantially revised for this publication.

Introduction

I've been thinking about this book for more than a decade and actively working on it for the past two years. Perhaps it is fortuitous that I didn't get the chance to do so until I reached my seventies; much has changed for me and I imagine for other women as we enter this decade. We may worry more about our health than in the past, about making ends meet financially, about the experience of inhabiting an aging body and how others "read" our bodies, and about what it means to live a good life in the face of these changes. We may move toward old age unpracticed or uneasy or even with dread. Unlike little girls trying on their mother's makeup or high-heeled shoes, we don't prospectively identify with old age, a practice that might ease our way (de Beauvoir 1973). We also know, whether we think about it consciously or not, that we live in a culture that seems most at ease with dichotomous images of late life—either vigorous and ever young individuals who are busily engaged or like "that," that is, frail, uninvolved, and with little to contribute beyond tending to one's grandchildren. We rarely see representations that look like us, however it is that we look. In this cultural ambience, we may respond by trying to evade "old" as if it need not happen to us, or we narrow our worlds to protect and manage our identity. Neither of these responses are good ones, but they are understandable in our deeply ageist society.

In what will be a recurring theme in this book, I argue that such evasion comes at considerable social, material, and existential cost. Molly Andrews (1999) maintains that when old women affirm that they are young people in old-looking bodies (the mask), they are voicing a "desperate plea for personal exceptionalism, which challenges, not the ageist stereotype, but rather its

1

application to themselves" (306). As a result, we often neither own our old age nor define it on our own terms. It is thus more difficult to find within it the potential for rich developmental possibilities. Further, in the current political environment, to adopt a now-familiar stance of agelessness or an extended midlife is to wittingly or unwittingly collaborate with efforts to undercut the public support that so many of us need to live our late lives with dignity.

To accept our own aging does not mean a radical rupture with our past selves; we are always all the ages we have ever been (Segal 2013). Poet Linda Pastan (2014) captures this confusion in her striking poem "Any Woman." After asserting that she isn't the "crinkled face" she sees in the mirror today or the "young and frowning" face she sees in photos of the past, she reflects on someone offering a seat on the bus, realizing that the "only one standing" is her (146). Because we were once young and learned then to judge old negatively, the internalized ageism that persists urges us to identify with our younger and hence more desirable selves. It takes particular effort to understand and see how and why we do this and how it does a disservice to what we are now.

There are so many ironies to growing old when we may feel so young. I wonder, for example, if like me, other women suddenly see themselves, like participant-observers, as unwittingly conforming to common stereotypes about old age like needing help with our new phone or fumbling for coins in our purse or being unable to rise from a crouched position without some leverage. These experiences tell me that when we are old, we will always be a pale imitation of our younger selves, like a twelve-minute-a-mile runner when seen in the context of four-minute milers. We may be proud that we can easily touch our toes doing a yoga stretch, but the next minute that aching hip joint reminds us that we are not forty anymore. Thus, I have come to believe that as long as we let the standards of our younger years prevail, a common strategy in the "new old age," we will lose (see chapter 3). I take from Molly Andrews (1999) this affirmation: "We must be able to call our old people old, acknowledge all the challenges and the possibility that their advanced years embody" (311). We may have more to offer society as an acknowledged old person than as a second-class midlife one hidden in an old body.

My goals in this book are simple, although reaching them is far more complex. I write from a critical and feminist perspective, which means that I question, challenge, contest, and resist the status quo (Ray 1999). My first goal is to consider how women experience late life as uniquely shaped by their life course and by contemporary cultural norms and political ideologies. Our lives are profoundly situated. Because age, like gender, is a social category that affects our status and our everyday interactions with others, much of what I will discuss is applicable to men as well as women. My focus, however, will primarily be on old women. In part that is because I am one, and as a feminist writer, my own experiences and those of other women are critical sources of knowing, inviting contradictions, complexities, and ambiguities. But it is also because women face particular difficulties that derive from the intersection of age and gender across their life spans (Ridgeway 2011). The implications of the inequalities that result are apparent in many aspects of a woman's life—economic insecurity, her devalued body, the consequences of her caregiving responsibilities, and her experience of chronic illness. Ageism and sexism are "embedded in social institutions" and "expressed in everyday interactions" (Hatch 2005, 21) and so they matter greatly in women's day-to-day lives.

I turn to the "new aging" that I will discuss in chapter 3 as an example of how ageism and sexism matter. The new aging exhorts us to age successfully. It assumes that this goal is individually achievable and so open to all of us. But this assumption is erroneous. While postmodernism may celebrate freedom, we are not entirely free as long as we have a gender and an age and as long as we live in a particular culture, at a particular time in history, and in a particular political climate. Thus, throughout this book, I will call attention to history, context, and our individual biographies, that is, those factors that open or foreclose late-life possibilities for us. The unequal power that marks the relationships between individuals and groups (Calasanti, Slevin, and King 2007), most often rooted in age, gender, class and race, become manifest in the basic structures of society such as work and the family that disadvantage the subordinated group. As such they challenge our ability to live comfortably—psychologically, existentially, morally, and practically—in old age. Thus simple measures like replacing "myths" about old age with "realities" or insisting that the old are really young people in old bodies (see chapter 2) cannot root out societal ageism as long as the unequal power relations between men and women, the young and the old, and, I add, the ill and the healthy, the affluent and the poor, are not disrupted.

These worrisome features of our society suggest the book's second goal. By revealing our strengths as women and possible fractures in the social and political context, I look for opportunities to resist what harms us and thus create the potential for change. One of the most enduring of feminist projects, notes Ruth Ray (2004), is to "identify the inequities and the social structures that justify and perpetuate them and to work toward equity at the concrete level" (112). This aim means honoring and supporting our advantages while actively working to address the disadvantages that are beyond our individual control.

THEMES

Basic to these explorations are three themes. The first is the observation that old age is a biological reality but also an inescapably embedded experience. We arrive in late life shaped by the multiple influences we've experienced across our lifetimes. And we are old in a particular social, cultural, and political context that makes certain ideas, policies, and practices more possible and palatable than others (Rodgers 2011). As a result, rather than being wholly or even primarily under our own control, late life is heavily laden with the weight of our past and the contemporary context. Recognizing the weighty influences on our old age, we can better understand why some people have so much more freedom than others to choose how to live (Ray 2004).

Given the intersecting and persistent inequalities that old women face, the second theme addresses the problems that emerge when economic elites and organized business interests, that is, people of privilege, play an outsized role in setting public agendas, a power that marginalizes interest groups and the average citizen and voter (Polivka 2012; Gilens and Page 2014). Thus, feminist standpoint theory would remind us that where we stand influences what we see (Harding 2003); standing in the corner office offers a very different perspective on what is possible than standing in the broom closet. "Who one is affects the way one thinks about society—what issues will be salient, how one conceptualizes and interrelates them, what policies and practice will seem benign, and what sorts of changes seem urgent. . . . One's moral outlook is not independent of one's identity and one's identity is not independent of one's position in the world" (Meyers 2001, 39). As a result, many issues that affect old women are neither understood nor acknowledged and so are left unaddressed. Try to imagine the contrasting worldviews of the dually eligible (Medicare and Medicaid) seventy-two-year-old woman resident of an affordable senior housing complex with the tall, white-haired, seventy-two-year-old CEO of a major financial institution. Consider the words of the women of Mayslake (see essay of that title) when they talk about class and how perceptions about them are so inflected by generalized ideas related to one's class position.

The third theme, as touched upon above, is a commitment to reclaiming "old" as a valued and important time in human life. Taking her words to heart, I see with the late professor and writer Carolyn Heilbrun (1997) that late life is the "last gift of time" when we have the chance to free ourselves from the expectations of others, including the insidious goal to be "not old" (Hurd 1999; Biggs et al. 2006).

SOURCES

To achieve the book's goals, I turn to social and biological research, to fiction, to poetry, to writings by women of a "certain age," to formal and informal conversations with women, and also to my own experiences as a seventy-three-year-old who has spent the past forty-plus years working in the field of gerontology. I integrate my own thoughts and feelings not because I represent any particular group but because reflexivity is an important element in feminist scholarship. I hope that my feelings and experiences can help inform our thinking about late life. Together these sources will offer a wide lens from which to view women's experiences as we become and are old. I have been lucky to have occupied an interdisciplinary space for most of my career and will continue to occupy it for what follows.

METHODOLOGICAL DEPARTURES

Scientifically replicable experiments across the spectrum of traditional social and biological sciences have taught us much about aging and old age, but their methodologies have limited the problems addressed, the questions asked, and the kind of knowledge that counts. Traditional methodologies can, for example, explain what causes wrinkles but not what those wrinkles mean to the woman who has them in a particular culture at a particular historical moment and even for a certain age cohort. They can document the income and related inequalities that exist in society but miss exploring what it means to live on the downside of the income ledger. Further, without an explicit social justice framework, they evade naming these inequalities as social injustices that have identifiable causes that can be remedied. Thus, while I will rely on traditional research for the questions that demand that approach, I will turn primarily to critical gerontology and feminist scholarship that calls for multiple sources of knowing, commitments to ameliorating oppressions, and interrogating what we, as researchers, choose to investigate. I will amplify these approaches below.

PERSONAL AND CONCEPTUAL FRAMEWORKS

Moral Perception

When I teach ethics, I always ask my students to think about issues that they identify as ethically problematic but which might not be even noticed by a person of another race or gender or religion. Feminist philosopher Diana Meyers (1997a) emphasizes the importance not only of moral perception (what we see and notice as morally problematic) but, in particular, of heterodox moral perceptions as essential to righting wrongs. It we fail to identify what we see as a wrong, we do not act to remedy it. This stance is relevant for the issues that this book addresses. Often the absence of a critical perspective, a commitment to question the directions in which we are going, permits reinforcement of a problematic status quo. A simple example makes this point. As I discuss in chapter 3, successful and productive aging in its many manifestations became the take-off point for a vast research enterprise that in thirty or forty years normalized positive thinking about late life. But, building on earlier scholarship (e.g., Katz 2000; Holstein and Minkler 2003), I shall argue, it did so uncritically. It didn't, for example, consider its unintended consequences like its link to the emergent neoliberal political agenda or the exclusiveness of its claims. Instead, it took for granted that what was needed was evidence of what we might do to age "successfully" or to be productive without asking if those goals or even that language were the ones we ought to be seeking and using. Heterodox moral perceptions would have raised questions about their worthiness as normative goals from their very beginning, and a critical perspective would have suggested wariness about dichotomous labels and the necessity of broadening the discussion to involve those who would be most affected by the normative claims.

In addition to questioning what appears to be taken for granted, this project is a vehicle to explore my own values and commitments and even more importantly to encourage readers to do the same. Feminist works welcome the personal. Exploring our own subjectivity is a research method (Miller 1999). Such writing, Ray (1999) observes, "when done carefully, succeeds in contesting the established systems of power, authority, and knowledge-making in academe" (176). Margaret Gullette (1997) maintains that telling our own stories, what she calls age autobiographies, allows us to distinguish our stories from the dominant ones upheld by culture, a topic to which I will return in the concluding chapter. Thus, I want us—reader and writer—to be fully "age conscious," in Ruth Ray's (2004) words, and to explore our own attitudes toward aging and late life and also to understand how we see the respective responsibilities of individuals, families, communities, and government in helping to assure the possibilities for a good life in old age.

The Personal

I write from a particular standpoint that influences the topics I choose to write about and what evidence I find compelling. I think all researchers and writers start from some particular place, including the belief that one's work can be value free. As a feminist I see differently from others not because of my sex as such but because material and historical conditions, linked to my gender, have given me a particular vantage point from which to view the world (Holstein and Minkler 2007). It is thus important for you, the reader, to know my value orientation and my commitments, and to consider how that vantage point has influenced my thinking.

Most basically, I believe in collective responsibility for helping to make life livable for all. I am a progressive who maintains that demonizing government harms all but the most affluent. I write as an interdisciplinary scholar with primary training in the humanities, a teacher but also a mother, a grandmother, a sister, and a friend. The humanities, for example, grounds my comfort with complexity and ambiguity, and my social commitments remind me that many roles I play, while done willingly, are often unchosen and that life often trumps plans. I am neither affluent nor in danger of going without food or a roof over my head. I rely heavily on Social Security and savings, but know I have backup support. My daughter said recently, "We have your back," a gift that many really low-income women do not have.

Aging so far has been gentle with me. I face no important limits, although I can't climb hills with the same ease or walk as far and as fast as I once did. I ache at times where I never ached before. I have read much about loneliness as older women watch their friends and family move away or become ill and die. I have lost several friends to death, and my world is poorer as a result, but so far, my life feels very rich. I am lucky in that I find great comfort in

my Chicago home (in a high-rise) with my view of Lake Michigan, access-
ible walking paths, friends nearby, and my books, making it a place in which
I can imagine remaining even if and when I have mobility limitations.

What I Worry About

I worry about what will happen if I need long-term care services; if I do, my
money will be gone in a very short time. I, who am white, well educated, and
in relatively good health, can slip off the edge if the value of my savings
plummets, if I trip on the ice and break my hip, or if there is a retrenchment
in Social Security or Medicare or Medicaid that I may need to rely on if I
become disabled and require assistance with daily living. I worry about the
economic and social inequalities that old women face as disadvantages accumulate over their lifetimes (O'Rand 1996; Dannefer 2003). I worry about the
social marginalization of old women in public places and often in their own
families. I worry about the narrowing role that any but the most affluent now
play in political life (Gilens and Page 2014). Thus, I worry about the power
of elites to set the public agenda based on their commitments to individualism, the unregulated free market, and the limited state since it disadvantages
old women, women and men of color, and all other individuals whom the
market served poorly. I worry about our country's collapsing social ties and
the fracturing of the bonds that have historically connected us as a community (Rodgers 2011). I worry too about the premium placed on wealth, activity, speed, beauty, athletic prowess, and other ephemeral (except perhaps for
wealth) aspects of human life, seen as individual achievements. Each of these
worrisome issues matters for how women experience their old age and sustain the arguments made in each chapter.

Frameworks: Critical Gerontology and Feminism

Both feminism and critical gerontology take into account the importance of
context across the life span and invite subjective experiences and narrative as
sources of knowledge. They are engaged and at times disruptive, have explicit concerns about class, gender, ethnicity, and power, and accept ambiguity
and complexity while inviting a wide range of questions that are not subject
to traditional scientific and detached investigations. Context, for example, is
not intrusive but essential to understanding.

Feminists and critical gerontologists are committed to social action that
removes barriers to fuller, freer, and less problematic lives for women in old

age. They link personal experience and structural inequities and use what is learned as openings for collective change (Estes, Biggs, and Phillipson 2003, 148). To be critical is to make a commitment not just to understand the social construction of aging but to change it, to raise questions about "what everyone knows," to consider the unintended consequences of very worthy goals. Philosopher Richard Bernstein (1992) said it well: the role of the critic is to "analyze the present and to reveal its fractures and instabilities and the ways in which it at once limits us and points to the transgressions of those limits" (162).

Both critical gerontology, which encompasses both the humanities and the political economy of aging (Ovrebo and Minkler 1996), and feminist scholarship ask us to be aware of values in our choices of research topics and approach. Can they make a difference? Because these approaches often seek understanding rather than generalizable information, they expect—indeed welcome—complexity and ambiguity as particularly suitable to understanding the experience of aging. Novels, for example, do not "prove" anything about being an old woman, but they awaken us to particular experiences about aging from the inside. As such, they are conduits to encourage the not-yet-old to enter the worlds of the old, thereby fostering interactions that can decrease marginalization. To become known is one way to counter stereotyping and devaluation (Waxman 2010).

They encourage a fruitful integration of structure, agency, critique, and reform that rests on a social justice perspective. They encourage attention to the gendered workplace, the broad disparities in access to social goods like adequate health care, and clean, safe environments as formative elements in our experience of old age. They ask: How do we overcome, or resist, or bow to the difficulties that we face, that is, how do we exercise agency, which we do despite the many constraints we face?

Feminist thinking as I am using the term deepens our understanding about the particular circumstances of women in our society. By understanding how gender frames social relationships and how these arrangements play out in the family and in work, we can see how the effects of this framing last into our oldest years. The fundamental potency of the gender frame explicates the interlocking systems of oppression that contribute to the "precarious situation of older women and their treatment through public policy" (Estes, Biggs, and Phillipson 2003). Policies like Social Security, for example, which is constructed on the normative work histories of men and the traditional family, disadvantages many old and single women (see chapter 6).

I use a simple example to elucidate the differences between traditional and critical and feminist approaches. In giving the motivation for their early work on productive aging, Bass, Caro, and Chen (1993) cite the words of Elsie Frank, the seventy-nine-year-old president of the Massachusetts Association for Older Americans, who argued that older people should not be excluded from society, that they should have an active voice in decisions that affect their lives, and that they should have access to the power necessary to achieve those ends. In her talk, she maintained that policies should focus on a "vigorous, empowered and productive old age" (4). While the goals she sought were broad ones, the response quickly narrowed to productivity, especially monetized productivity. From the urgent words of an aging advocate, it quickly became the subject of academic study. Rather than seizing on the wish to actively participate in the decisions that affected her life, study turned to how to increase volunteer roles and paid work without exploring why Ms. Frank and other women like her were marginalized and were in effect sidelined from political participation. Recent research has made it abundantly clear that neither interest groups nor individuals have an influence over policy agendas set by business and political elites (Gilens and Page 2014), nor do these groups demonstrate an empathic response to people unlike them (Goleman 2013). A critical, feminist approach to the issues Ms. Frank raised would have brought together women to tell their stories of exclusion and perhaps their successes in overcoming it. It would have taken the adage that the personal is the political to move outside the circle and see what needed to be changed to remediate the problems identified. It would have sought the broadest possible agenda for examining her concerns and would not have turned almost immediately to efforts to increase productive roles of old women in society without asking questions about the environment in which productivity was to occur. It would ask whose ends productivity served or what definitions, if any, suited the issues raised. I suggest that this is how feminist and critical scholarship differs from traditional scientific scholarship.

UNDERSTANDING TODAY'S SOCIAL, POLITICAL, AND CULTURAL CONTEXT

As the above suggests, both feminism and critical gerontology consider context as critical to our experiences in old age. Context is wide ranging. It includes cultural norms and values, the likelihood of us being economically secure at different points in our lives, the advantages and disadvantages that accumulate across a lifetime, and our opportunities to have a voice in making the policies that will directly affect our lives. Context helps to explain why so many women resist following Gray Panther founder Maggie Kuhn's advice to ask for a loving arm when we can no longer rely on our own balance. It helps to account for why so many old women resist the label of "old." The influence of context serves as an important counterweight to the popular assumptions about individual responsibility for just about everything that happens to us. Being old is an intimate but also a very public experience. It also demonstrably captures the effects of the seismic shifts that have occurred in American society over the past thirty or so years. Many of us are retiring and living for many years beyond retirement. We are the beneficiaries of medical advances, cleaner environments, and greater knowledge of what we need to do to keep ourselves as healthy as possible. Slim, trim grandmothers on the elliptical trainer or jumping hurdles are more popularly featured than chubby grandmas baking cookies or sitting on their recliners with their swollen feet elevated. The evolution of these representations of aging is not accidental. Since the late 1970s, as the West moved into a period variously labeled "high modernity" or "postmodernity," the old certainties related to retirement and the traditional responses to perceived need began to dissolve. Into this void entered new and often problematic ideas generally labeled the "new aging" or the "third age," the subject of chapter 3.

This changing cultural context of aging is situated in a broader context dominated by the ideology and practical manifestations of neoliberalism, which maintains that "human well-being can best be advanced by the maximization of entrepreneurial freedoms within a framework characterized by private property rights, individual liberty, free markets and free trade" (Harvey 2006, 145). It is about enhancing corporate control of the state, primarily through regulatory, trade, and labor policies and privatizating formerly public roles such as welfare and warfare. It calls for low taxes on wealth and high incomes while encouraging the deregulation of the financial sector (personal communication with L. Polivka, March 31, 2014). A politics that focused on deficit reduction and austerity in regard to public spending also marked the neoliberal agenda. What it stands for has become so rhetorically familiar that it almost seems normal and natural rather than what it has become—an ideology maintained by elites, generally across party lines, who translate their understanding of what works for them into policy norms. Their power to do so is considerable since elected officials have succeeded in weakening intermediary structures like unions and NGOs, strengthening the role of capital and the financial sector, and weakening government, the likely source of remedy for the problems the market cannot or does not address. The result is wage stagnation and even wage decline and accelerated inequality, facts that will influence generations of future retirees. Originating in the conservative economics and politics of the 1970s, this ideological context has become the foundation of national policy (Polivka 2012).

This ideology and its adherents among elite decision makers have had major responsibility for many changes that are worrisome if the goal is a more equal and secure society. Robert Hudson (2007) refers to the pivotal decade of the 1980s as marked by decentralization, individualization, and privatization where individual responsibility is elevated to a primary value. The result:

> Assessment of blame rather than the distribution of risk in addressing the "bad things" that can happen to people in modern society, and the fundamental loss of security brought on by catastrophic events that overwhelm the resources that individuals acting alone can bring to their misfortune. (2)

The 1980s, a decade that will appear frequently in these pages, was a critical one for women and also for older people more generally. Almost as soon as women gained new opportunities, they began to see that opportunities alone were not enough. The 1980s marked the time when women took on serious careers but found that a national child-care entitlement was not on the public agenda and that having a home and children was entirely a personal problem. Women still earn 77 percent of men's income (Polivka 2012). Instead of adapting the workplace so that it responded to normative expectations for women, women adopted the styles of men, from clothing to long working hours, and if they did not adopt these styles, advancement was slowed or blocked—the infamous glass ceiling (Collins 2009). This nagging problem of women and work is a consistent thread in women's disadvantaged status. The women who made their career steps in the 1980s are nearing retirement or already retired. They (or we) are watching their daughters face the same difficulties they faced as career and home and working out and so many other obligations, chosen or unchosen, mark their lives.

The ideology of neoliberalism offers some useful clues to the origin of the changes that threaten women's well-being today. Primary concerns center on efforts to change Social Security, the subject of chapter 6. A further concern is the continued attack on public spending for health and social services driven by the politics of austerity. This attack originated in the 1970s but continues today. From President Carter on, the policy of the United States has been lower taxes, decreased public spending, financial deregulation, and pro-market trade policies (Polivka 2012). In his 1998 State of the Union message, President Clinton proclaimed that the era of big government was over. Welfare reform is a good example of how the retreat of the state took place even under a Democratic president. President Obama has not been very different in that he has not lent support to labor union priorities, was willing to put Social Security "on the table," and did not address the "too big to fail" banks.

This dominant ideology, which shows few signs of abating (Polivka 2012), is apt to influence other policies that are critical for women's well-being, like Medicare and publicly funded long-term care services that I look at in chapter 5. In 1965, when it passed, if Medicare had been sensitive to the universality of dependency and the exploitation of women family members as caregivers, no matter how lovingly that care was given, perhaps the Medicare program would have included a long-term care benefit. Threats to turn Medicaid into a block grant are also potentially threatening to women's well-being since there is no guarantee that a block grant would meet shifting needs.

With the policy debate so tilted toward austerity, with the growing attacks on the public sector, including programs like Social Security, Medicare, and Medicaid (Polivka 2012), we can see how much has already changed from the time when the old were a favored constituency. Thus, as their most favored status slips, the future security of anyone without a substantial private income is threatened. Yet the irony is that the very success of age-based entitlements that have lifted so many of the old above the poverty line has now become the justification for reducing benefits. As I argue in chapter 6, the repercussions of benefit cuts and further erosions of safety-net programs would have deeply detrimental effects on women. Yet if not the state, then who will tackle the problems of income erosion, threats to access to and quality of health care, limited affordable housing, and parsimonious public long-term care benefits?

While power was moving into the hands of the economic elite as early as the late 1970s, that power is consolidating. It matters to old women that agenda setting is in the hands of people very different from themselves. A clear example is this—when President Obama established a deficit reduction commission, he appointed as its cochairs two men—Erskine Bowles and former senator Alan Simpson—both of whom are millionaires and critics of Social Security. From their vantage point, the lives of low-income women are most likely quite opaque, and perhaps even more significant is the research suggesting that those with the most social power "pay scant attention to those with little power," and thus inconvenient truths about them are also dismissed (Goleman 2013). The late political philosopher Iris Marion Young (1990) noted that while theories of justice most often focus on distribution, the important background questions are who defines the problems and who makes the allocation decisions. Wealth translates into political power; the ability to define problems gives the people with that power substantial influence over what actually occurs. As noted above, with the "popular classes" poorly represented in the political process, it is hard to see where change will originate. As Larry Polivka (2012) observes, "The neoliberal model will not achieve equitable or sustainable growth and its continued policy dominance will only continue to erode economic security" (135). Each of us will have to consider our responses to the results that flow from this dominance of economic and policy elites.

The ability to see from a woman's perspective in public life has been limited, though we have seen some powerful voices raised about some women's issues like rape in the military. We have not, however, found a spokeswoman for important issues such as the need for a stronger public-sector response to women's caregiving responsibilities (see chapter 5). Nor have we heard a strong reaction to the male executives of the Business Roundtable who asserted that the best way to prepare for retirement is to save more (Carpenter 2013; see chapter 6) although the Lilly Ledbetter bill at least touches upon pay inequities. Recalling the importance of moral perception as the stimulus to social action, we can see how the absence of strong advocates for women in positions of power can mean that social ills are not highlighted and brought to public attention. Without this occurring, how can we discover "heretofore unacknowledged kinds of wrongs" (Meyers 1997a, 197)?

As will become clear in the remainder of this book, assertions and policy recommendations that do not consider gender, such as proposing an increase in the retirement age for Social Security, blinds us to the differential impact this action will have on women. Similarly, when advocates for the "new old age" assume greater affluence and individual assertiveness of the "baby boom" generation, they are speaking of the relatively privileged. When Chris Gilleard and Paul Higgs (2011) assert that this generation will not be the pensioners of the past, they may be making a valid observation, but not for the reasons they claim. Instead it may be that we are witnessing the deinstitutionalization of retirement as the social welfare state shrinks even further (Phillipson 1998; Estes, Biggs, and Phillipson 2003; Polivka and Estes 2009; see chapter 6). As neoliberalism policies show no signs of weakening, individuals and families will become increasingly responsible for their lifelong safety and security.

In this mix of individualism, personal responsibility, and a limited state, it should be no surprise that being old was an outlier. As noted above, one way to remedy that was to stress how old age was really just an extension of midlife, so ceding to the more powerful generation the norms by which the old were to be judged. Far better but also far more difficult is to reclaim old age but to do so on our own terms. In the next section, I defend this position that will appear throughout the book in varied contexts.

The Importance of Accepting "Old"

I open with a question my daughter asked me: What do you mean by "old"? I continue to attach importance to chronology, starting at about sixty-five or seventy. I do not think of chronology as demarcating certain roles, behaviors, or universal attributes. Neither do I assume we are all alike once we pass sixty-five or seventy. Nor do I assume that age is the most important feature of our lives. But it is also not irrelevant. It marks a time when our body's changes are more prominent than before, no matter how healthy we are and when our perspective on time alters. We see it among our contemporaries as they become ill and die, assume roles as caregivers for spouses and partners, or speak more often about unexpected bodily changes. For me, being seventy-three is very different from being forty-five or even fifty-five; I walk more slowly and am less agile than I once was, but, above all, it is my foreshortened future that gives an urgency to the decisions and choices that I face. Moments become more precious. We have had life experiences that also distinguish us from a fifty-year-old, which gives new dimension to our lives. We may also feel an unexpected sense of freedom at the same time that societal ageism may make us self-conscious about our bodies or the way that we move. Although we may resent marginalization when we are ignored, we also have less need for certain kinds of recognition. As poet and novelist Rosellen Brown (2014) aptly puts it:

> Being free—or freer—of the temptation to be preoccupied by questions of reputation is a little like the way so many postmenopausal women are pleas-

antly surprised that sex has a new piquancy once it's not overshadowed by the
dangers of pregnancy and the exhaustion of early motherhood. (45)

By now, it has become common to hear repeated assertions that seventy is the new fifty or that age scarcely matters, that we are indeed ageless. Societal ageism elicits this kind of need to separate ourselves from the negative stereotypes as long as the years often sit relatively lightly on us. That remedy, however, may temporarily protect our identity and self-confidence, worthy and important goals, but it will do nothing to remedy ageism.

Thus, I will argue that as tempting as it may be to assert that seventy is the new fifty, it is inevitably a failing strategy, a topic to which I will return in chapter 2. For now, I raise a few questions: How will we feel about ourselves when (and I say when, not if) we begin to resemble the stereotypes? Will we punish ourselves for not trying harder? Will our sense of self-worth be harmed? In the meantime we will have lost the opportunity to gracefully move ourselves into the next phase of our lives and the wonderful freedom that can accompany it (assuming we are relatively secure economically and not overwhelmed by physical or mental difficulties). Being sixty-five or seventy or older is a privilege that deserves our respect and not our denigration. To accept our age with pride does not mean that we don't sometimes feel "youthful"; we are, as noted above, simultaneously seventy-five and forty and sixty-three. There is continuity and there is change; we are the same but we are also different as we make adaptations to changes.

Yet neither gerontology nor consumer culture encourages such integration. Instead it often instructs us to resist change, whether through cosmetic products and procedures or gym workouts or other strategies intended to elicit the young self thought to be hidden behind the mask of aging (see chapters 1 and 3). Why would we join in the denigration of who we are and encourage younger women to believe that they need not ever look old? By so doing, we encourage a prejudicial view about their future selves and our own selves as our bodies move further from valued norms. Another generation thus absorbs the notion that old is unacceptable and so pursues a lifestyle and values that are no longer suitable, a probable threat to personal identity. We cede power to a younger generation to assign the values of a good life that suits them more than it suits us (Biggs et al. 2006). Further, by denying age we actually call attention to its salience and give undue honor to those who seem to have evaded signs of decline (Brown 2014) instead of recalling

Maya Angelou's observation that "all great achievements require time" (Krysl 2014, 103).

By calling attention to the existential condition of being an old woman, I recognize that there is great diversity among those of us who are old, but diversity exists at all ages and we do not try, for example, to eliminate middle age or youth by saying that one can't make meaningful generalizations. To be old is not to conform to stereotypes or to limit our freedom to be what we want to be. Perhaps a more reflexive probing of what is important to us now will reveal new opportunities and permit us to treasure the time we have left. It is a plea for flexibility in defining what old age ought to be about, not the drive to be "not old," which narrows our choices and urges us to conform to standards set by those much younger than we are. My goal, then, is for us old women to define what old age is about to us and to give it meaning not by denying but by embracing it. In the last chapter I will explore how we might do this, how we might broaden the vision of what it means to be an old woman so that we are not either cuddly and incompetent or a ski-jumping grandmother with a lithe and unmarked body.

LITERATURE ABOUT WOMEN AND AGING: A BRIEF REVIEW

For a variety of reasons, old women, understood through feminist lenses, have not been well attended in gerontology or women's or gender studies. But this situation is beginning to change, slowly. This book fits into a relatively new but, I am happy to say, growing interdisciplinary literature on gender and aging. I'd like to mention a few recent books in whose tradition I see this work fitting. Academic studies of women and aging, such as *Age Matters: Realigning Feminist Thinking*, edited by Toni Calasanti and Kathleen Slevin (2006), have urged us to think beyond menopause. They ask us to consider how age and gender are both about power relations and intimately involved in forging social inequalities that play out in almost all aspects of women's lives. Their earlier work, *Gender, Social Inequalities, and Aging* (2001), is among the first academic studies to call attention to the damaging implications of efforts to mask chronological age and to deny our age through an assertion of and a commitment to "agelessness" and to systematically examine how gender and age influence almost every aspect of our lives. In the United Kingdom, the works of Miriam Bernard, Judith Phillips, Linda Machin, and Val Harding Davis (2000), *Women Ageing: Changing Identities, Challenging Norms*, offers a well-developed conceptual framework that is critical, feminist, and life course in approach, which they follow with an excursion into many aspects of women's lives. Paying specific attention to women, Margaret Cruikshank (2009), in *Learning to Be Old: Gender, Culture, and Aging*, passionately and credibly asks us to affirm age by challenging the factors that harm women, like ageism and medicalization, that limit our ability to make our own way and instead define what it means to be old for ourselves. Feminist work elevates the voices of those whom contemporary society marginalizes so that we can hear their voices rather than the dominant voices of privilege. In cultural studies and literature, the works of Margaret Gullette (1997, 2004, 2011), Kathleen Woodward (1991, 1999), and Ruth Ray (1996, 1999, 2004) provide deep insights into the cultural roots and persistence of ageism while also looking at emancipatory possibilities for women who are old. Meredith Minkler and Carroll Estes (1991, 1999) have persistently called attention to the structural and institutional factors that ground women's inequality while proposing ways to address those inequalities. While not specifically interested in gender, Tom Cole (1992) and Harry (Rick) Moody (1994) have, for the past thirty years, challenged us to consider the limited norms now upheld for late life, which close rather than open doors to a fuller life and do not ask us to evade our own aging.

Two recent books, more popular in orientation but offering thoroughly argued indictments of the efforts to see only the positive aspects of aging, are Susan Jacoby's *Never Say Die: The Myth and Marketing of the New Old Age* (2011) and Lynne Segal's *Out of Time: The Pleasures and Perils of Ageing* (2013). Segal and Jacoby, both realists, challenge the ideas that we can somehow live without experiencing the physical changes that come with age or, in Lynne Segal's words, "unburdened by the actual signs of ageing" (18). Susan Jacoby notes that as long as the dominant images of the old are of happy, sprightly couples seemingly without a care in the world, the need for social policy protections seems indefensible. She worries, as I do, that the risk of focusing so strongly on the positive undermines the needs that are very present among so many old people. While neither of these books looks exclusively at women, both note that the older we get, the more women there are, and it is women who most often need social and other supports. I am not sure quite how to categorize Lillian Rubin's (2007) *60 on Up: The Truth about Aging in the Twenty-First Century*; it is a relentlessly realistic account of old age by a writer and a sociologist who was herself in her eighties when she wrote her book. As you will see in the following chapters, I have appreciated her blunt and sharp observations based on interviews and her own experiences. Similarly, women writers reflecting on their own experience, like Doris Grumbach's (1991) *Coming into the End Zone*, an account of the seventieth year, and Carolyn Heilbrun's (1997) *The Last Gift of Time: Life beyond Sixty*, offer candid observations of professionally successful women, one who has little good to say about turning seventy and the other who finds much to value in later life. Heilbrun, also a successful academic, sadly chose to take her own life while she still could (see Gullette 2011 for an account of Heilbrun's suicide).

I also find especially valuable the work of women who identify primarily as writers. The quotes above from the fine anthology *A Story Larger Than My Own*, edited by Jane Burroway (2014), demonstrate how the reflexive voices of women who are themselves old but also novelists and poets can express many of the elusive and perhaps inexpressible feelings that so many women experience.

In addition to these works, there is an emergent literature by feminist philosophers. The one exemplary book-length study is *Mother Time: Women, Aging and Ethics*, edited by Margret Urban Walker (1999c) (in the interests of full disclosure, I have a chapter in that book). While feminist ethicists have carved out an expanding role in rethinking conventional ethical approaches so that they take into account the issues and approaches directly relevant to women's lives, aging has not so far been a major focus. I call special attention to social ethicist Frida Kerner Furman's (1997) wonderful ethnography, *Facing the Mirror: Older Women and Beauty Shop Culture*, which not only brings us the painful but reflective voices of old Jewish women she observed and interviewed but also is a powerful exemplar of feminist analysis.

CHAPTER OVERVIEW

Part I, "The Body and Beyond," opens with "What Do You See When You Look at Me? Women, Aging, and Our Bodies." Focusing on the intimate and personal experiences of women as their embodied selves move about in a culture that devalues them, it asks: What does it feel like to look in the mirror and see a face and a body that doesn't look as we have come to think of ourselves, a body that rarely meets the shapes and abilities that consumer culture and the beauty industry uphold as available to all of us if we use the abundant tools now available? Given that consumer culture both reflects and advances certain images and assigns primary responsibility to us individually to meet the new norms, we can easily experience shame, humiliation, and blame if we fail to measure up.

I argue that our bodies are texts that are commonly read in singular ways that distort the complexities of the mature selves we see as central to our identity. This distortion often leads women to try to manage their identities so that others see them as they see themselves. I also note that realism, often tinged with sadness and regret, is a familiar way that many women come to accept their aging bodies. Thus, I argue that while women vary greatly in how they view the limitations of their aging bodies and the nefarious forms of ageism that often marginalize us, many women have come to both accept and laugh, albeit sardonically, at how we look. I further argue that bodies are both material and constructed and that they matter in multiple ways—morally, politically and socially—a reason why it is so important to attend to the ways in which our bodies are represented.

In chapter 2, "Ageism: You're Only as Old as You Feel and Other Fictions," the focus moves to how others see and interpret our appearance, that is, our oldness, in ways that are negatively consequential. We may maintain that we are only as old as we feel, but to a society rife with ageism, we are as old as we look and as old as stereotypes define us. Bearing in mind that the body is a text that others interpret, I consider the consequences of generally negative readings on how we see ourselves, how we are simultaneously hypervisible but also invisible and often marginalized as a result of this paradox. My aim is to show the many ways in which ageism plays out in society and why resisting it is far more complex than countering myths with realities or elevating positive ideas about old age. It needs to be addressed at a very fundamental level—the inequalities that derive from social relations of power, for example, between men and women and young and old (Calasanti 2007; also see above).

Ageism happens when salespeople ignore us, when we receive less than good service at restaurants, and, more significantly, when we are not referred for certain medical treatments or when we are unable to find work. Societal ageism, I suggest, is the only "ism" that has become so naturalized and normalized that it rarely leads to challenges. Jokes on television and on greeting cards are accepted in ways that comparable comments about race or sex would not be.

In chapter 3, "The 'New' Old Age: From Productive Aging to Anti-Aging and Everything in Between," I focus on the emergence of academic and popular narratives about late life that establish an ideal self that continues to enact midlife norms. The successful ager is productive, independent, healthy, and not a burden on society. She achieves success by her own efforts without regard to her individual biography or the social-political-cultural context in which she lives. That context in which individualism, performativity, and the weakening of the social ties that once bound us together as a community (Rodgers 2011; Dionne 2012) as well as the loosening of life-course boundaries provide a comfortable setting for the new aging.

New cultural norms associated with productivity, engagement, and continued good health have led many women to strive, often with considerable effort and even harm to themselves, to remain in the category of the "not old" given the greater power and rewards associated with being young rather than being old. I further argue that the almost unstinted, upbeat character of the new aging rhetoric, combined with its individualistic assumptions, serves as an unwitting ally in the neoliberal agenda to undercut social and income support programs. If the predominant image of women in later life shows them as busy, productive, and hardly looking older than fifty, what can possibly be the reasons to exempt them from work or to provide social or other supports? This unintended consequence of the new aging might turn out to be among the most problematic to women's opportunities to have a safe and secure old age.

Chapter 4, "Disruptions and Repair: Identity and Chronic Illness," addresses a topic that does not fit easily with the upbeat rhetoric of the new aging. Starting from the assumption that meaning is critical at every life stage, this chapter's goal is to explore the cultural and other impediments to finding meaning that women who are chronically impaired face. They must confront a culture that would prefer to shunt decline aside and box it into the abject "fourth" age, a time when our bodies become increasingly unreliable and our agency threatened. I argue that the binary between the "third" and the "fourth" ages ought to be ruptured and that the goal should be the valuing of the whole of life in all its manifestations, not only when it is physically strong. To act as if we can evade chronic illness is to reinforce already powerful cultural fears about bodily suffering and old age, fears that further marginalize the people who live with debilitating conditions (Morell 2003) while blinding us to their hopes, dreams, and struggles. Chronic illness is very much with us, and it affects more women than men since we both live longer and are more likely to live with osteoarthritis and other limiting conditions. Already devalued because of our appearance and judged for not aging "successfully," chronic illness deepens our exclusion by situating us in the fourth age.

Part II, "Aging Women in Contemporary Society," opens with the chapter "A Looming Dystopia: Feminism, Aging, and Community-Based Long-Term Care." Locating the situation of the chronically impaired older woman in the context of historic changes in how we understand obligation, citizenship, community, and society, this chapter projects thirty years into the future to imagine what it will be like if we continue on our current trajectory. The chapter opens with a historic account of how the very notion of society and collective obligations dissipated into many fragments. One result has been the erosion of social responsibility to people who need some form of assistance with day-to-day life, especially old women. They must rely on family members, most often women, and if their income is low enough, they can hope for some care provision from the public sector. Yet the successes of neoliberalism and its disdain for government all directly affect the care we are likely to receive when we need assistance. In contrast to neoliberalism, feminists offer rich accounts of dependency, vulnerability, and autonomy, which establish a moral foundation for a very different way of thinking about care.

Resource allocation to older people is increasingly contested (Estes, Biggs, and Phillipson 2003). To analyze the dystopic future, I identify the troubling warning signs, project them into the future by thirty years, and explore how that will affect older women. I will take the warnings as I see them and suggest ways to mitigate the potential for grave harms that can result using a variety of sources to build a case for an alternative future.

To compound the threats to our security as old women, the next chapter in this part, "Retirement: In Pursuit of Women's Economic Security," explores the ways in which the major transformations that started to unfold in the late 1970s introduced elements of increasing risk for old women, many of whom had faced economic and other challenges throughout their lives. For most older women, Social Security is the essential element in their retirement portfolio. Despite rumors to the contrary, nearly half of all older women live within 200 percent of the poverty line; their average Social Security payment is about $1,200 a month (Harrington, Meyer, and Estes 2009). Large numbers of older people, especially women, cannot makes ends meet, as demonstrated by the Elder Economic Security Initiative (Wider Opportunities for Women 2013). The "Elder Standard," which seeks to replace the official poverty line with a more accurate measure of income adequacy, clearly demonstrates that older people, especially those who are renters and live alone, do not have enough income to make it, even keeping to a bare-bones budget. The other two legs—pensions and savings—that the creators of the Social Security system envisioned as essential for a secure retirement are not only collapsing but were never as available to women as to men (Institute for Women's Policy Research 2011). And now, as "entitlement reform," that is, reductions in lifetime benefits, is on the political table as a negotiating tool in the pursuit of deficit reduction, women's possibilities for a relatively secure old age are further threatened. I argue that the threats women now face have far more to do with their gender and the gender roles they played at home and in the workplace than their lack of financial responsibility. The further erosion of retirement security demonstrates the implications of the "great risk shift" discussed above.

At the same time, the future sustainability of Social Security requires action, but that action does not require benefit cuts. Elite opposition to the payroll tax, their preference for private solutions, and their ultimate aim of fully privatizing Social Security means that revenue enhancement is off the table, even though average Americans are willing to pay higher payroll taxes to assure the future stability of the program they know that they can rely on.

The last chapter in this part, "Beyond Rational Control: Reflections on End-of-Life Care," addresses a particularly difficult topic—the experience of loss and death in contemporary American society. My interest in this chapter is to challenge the now dominant ideas of what it means to "die with dignity" while proposing a broader array of values that might bring more people closer to the kind of death they say they want. I consider the impediments to achieving a "good death" and suggest ways to overcome those barriers. I challenge the assumption that rational control over decision making, while important, cannot carry the burden assigned to it. I argue that sources of change lie in medical education and training, the difficulties associated with death in the hospital, the culture of medicine, and the limits of advance care planning. Even when people have executed documents and chosen a surrogate, those actions often make little difference in the care that they receive at the end of life. I tell the story of my friend Susan's death from metastatic breast cancer in 2002 as a way to reflect on what may be of particular importance to the person who is dying.

For the book's last part, I borrow my title from Maggie Kuhn, the founder of the Gray Panthers, "I'm an Old Lady and Damn Proud of It." In the single chapter "Resistance and Change: Where to from Here?" that comprises this part, I will adopt a "power gaze" (a modification of the oppositional gaze suggested by bell hooks for African American women), and propose strategies for old women to engage in organized efforts in microcommunities and in larger arenas to confront persistent societal ageism and their own often inadvertent acceptance of social norms that make them "less than." How might old women adopt and adjust this "power gaze" to their own situations? How can we gain a place at the table so that we offer a countervoice to the agenda set by predominantly male elites? It will offer a preamble for a "call to action" to build an older women's movement.

The Women of Mayslake

Often in this book, I refer to the "women of Mayslake." I have been meeting and talking with them about issues that affect women as they age for almost three years. While not designed as a formal research project, our conversations have been personally and professionally enriching. I consider it a privilege that they have shared so much with me. These women—Mary, Lee, Audrey, Carol, and Jan (they requested that their real names be used)—are self-selected and range in age from sixty-nine to ninety-one. They responded to a short article in *The Acorn*, Mayslake's in-house newsletter, that invited women to participate in conversations about what it means to be an aging woman in our society today. The group started with twelve women and then narrowed to six and then five. Early on, some withdrew because they expected informational sessions rather than the wide-ranging discussions that we actually had. Later, others withdrew because of poor health. The remaining five women, the core group, are dependable, enthusiastic about participating, and unhesitating in making their opinions very clear. As the group's convener, I raised issues, stayed engaged with the women, and took their words as significant contributions to what I know about being an old woman in today's society. As Ruth Ray (1999) once observed, "One of the most significant contributions of the feminist movement in and out of academe has been the validation of personal knowledge and experience" (175). As I reviewed my notes, for example, I was particularly struck by the importance of class in their experiential worlds.

MAYSLAKE: THE PLACE

Mayslake is an affordable independent-living retirement community in Oak-brook, a western suburb of Chicago. It has 630 apartments primarily targeted for low- and moderate-income residents. While there are a small number of market-rate apartments at Mayslake, the majority of units are subsidized. To be accepted for an affordable unit, an individual must be over sixty-two and have an income below $26,000. They pay 30 percent of their income for rent. Many residents rely primarily on a modest Social Security check for their income. The average age is eighty. Founded by the Franciscans in 1963, it has a sprawling campus and a warm and welcoming environment. It is bright and airy with many comfortable seating areas that I actually see people using. Unlike my visits to more upscale retirement communities, I never come away from Mayslake feeling somewhat sad.

THE WOMEN

Of the five women in the core group, Carol is the youngest at sixty-nine, and Mary the oldest at ninety-one. Only Jan, now seventy-one, is currently married; three years ago, she met and married another Mayslake resident, a man whom she initially knew in grade school. While his health is fragile, she describes herself as "very happily married" after prior bad experiences with marriage, including violence. Proudly getting her cosmetologist license at eighteen, she continues to cut, style, and color hair at Mayslake and insists that "when I go gray, then I am old." She cared for her parents, had her own salon, obtained a real-estate license, watched her husband awaken from what appeared to be a permanent coma, and exudes self-confidence. She speaks eloquently about love—the need to be receptive in order to give and receive love. Jan has no children.

Mary describes herself as an "Iowa farm girl," born at home, a tomboy and always ready to stand up for herself. She worked in secretarial positions and, with her husband, built the home in which they lived for sixty-five years. The mother of five, grandmother of twelve, and great-grandmother of two, she goes away with the "girls," has a warm and loving relationship with them, and is the beneficiary of pedicures from her granddaughter. Her husband, who died very recently, had dementia and congestive heart failure and lived in an assisted-living facility. Mary is optimistic, enthusiastic, loving the life she is living at ninety-one and totally comfortable with her freedom to live just as she wishes to. Here's a picture of Mary that I treasure: for someone (me) who threw out all her shorts, one summer day Mary arrived at our meeting in bermuda shorts, a comfortable top, an attractive necklace, and sandals—and looked fabulous.

Lee is seventy-nine. She is adopted and had a difficult childhood, including emotional abuse. She "flunked the third grade" and was not invited back after a year in college the first time she tried it. But she did go on to complete a degree in fashion and merchandising and also complete associate's and bachelor's degrees. After a variety of jobs and hospitalizations for alcoholism, Lee married, worked for an insurance agency, and did factory assembly work. A central part of her life, which she talks about openly, has been her struggle with drugs that led her to set up a guardianship for her daughter and finally to her major career activity—substance abuse/addiction counseling— and the proud affirmation that she has been thirty years in recovery. Lee moved to Mayslake six years ago with her husband after their house was foreclosed on but has since divorced. Coming to Mayslake "was the best thing I ever did. Living here has broadened my life and provided me with a safety net." While important for many residents, for Lee the friendships she has formed at Mayslake have given her something she never had before— close relationships. "I had no concept of how to relate to people." Regretting the people that she never got to know, she now speaks often about being more open and trusting than she ever was, reflecting the developmental potential of late life. Lee has one daughter, who lives with her family in Alabama. A visit this past Christmas to her daughter's home was not a successful one.

Carol, at sixty-nine, is the youngest in the group. She left a bad marriage in which she described herself as having no identity, a cipher doing what others expected of her. Her marriage devastated her. Her husband returned from serving in Vietnam, suffered from PTSD, did not work steadily, and was abusive. She thus left her marriage with no money and no skills and suffering from depression; "I just wanted to be free." Freedom is a prominent identifying feature in her life. At last, she asserts, "I am free to be me." She arrived at Mayslake after a complex, ten-year journey that fortuitously was exactly what she needed. Depressed and without resources, she found her way into two sequential shared living arrangements that gave her a place to live but, very significantly, warm friendships and, in time, a new extended family. Now, at Mayslake, "I found happiness, love, and peace from my church family, friends, and many activities . . . to me sixty-nine is just a number." Carol has an estranged relationship with her daughter and no contact with her son. She sees her grandchildren regularly. Once uncomfortable at being with all those old people, they now come to stay with her at Mayslake. Carol told a wonderful story about her high school reunion that occurred in fall 2011. She was determined to show those "boys" who ignored her that she was now a confident and attractive woman. She carefully shopped for her dress, had her makeup done, and proudly arrived at the reunion. She felt great, but none of the boys showed up.

Audrey is seventy-nine and has been at Mayslake for six years, a place she purposely selected for its activities, ambience, and services. The mother of four children, whom she sees (and cooks for) regularly, she also faced the tragic loss of a grandson who was killed in an accident when he was twelve. Audrey comes from a food family. She worked in her family's restaurant and then held the position of director of nutritional services at Loretto Hospital, a job that she loved but needed to leave for health reasons. To look at Audrey and to hear her talk, it would be impossible to know that some years ago she had both a heart attack and colon cancer, for which she refused chemotherapy. When she retired from Loretto, she used a small annuity to travel, often as part of a large group that she put together; on a cruise to Alaska that she organized, she was accompanied by fifty-two friends and family. She counts herself fortunate in the life she has been able to lead that continues at Mayslake. "This is a great life. It's wonderful to let go of 'oughts.'"

GLEANINGS

What a group they have turned out to be. I have come to rely on their input, their passion, their humor, their reliability, and their support. They have discussed nearly every topic in the book and have also read and critiqued chapters. Above all, I have come to value their friendship and encouragement. While I refer to them often in the book, I'd like to highlight elements of our discussions that are so revealing but found an insufficient place in the book.

One issue was their awareness of class and how they saw it influencing how they were seen and treated. Carol told the story of meeting a woman when she was out walking in the very affluent neighborhood near Mayslake. They struck up a conversation, and the woman invited her for coffee. When Carol wanted to reciprocate, she invited the woman to Mayslake. The woman never spoke to her again. Living at Mayslake, Carol believed, stigmatized her, and the other women agreed. Thus, as much as she and the other women loved living at Mayslake, especially valuing their feelings of safety and security, they felt judged and looked down upon by their more affluent neighbors. "People with money perceive us as dumb, stupid, and don't see us as we are." They make us feel "ashamed, incompetent" (Audrey). Their recurrent use of the term "stupid" to describe how they thought others saw them was one I never heard among more affluent women. To them, while their apartments were modest in size and the food pretty basic, they never had to worry about having a place to call home that was clean, comfortable, and safe, a minimum foundation on which to build a life. What may never have been a concern for those neighbors across the road—a place to live that was both affordable and pleasing to them—was a prominent feature of their lives. They valued the strong networks of mutual support that they had built at Mayslake that were invisible to their more affluent neighbors, who, most likely, had the ability to buy the support that they needed. They were thus able to feel that they were dependent on no one, a myth that can alter perceptions of others who need assistance for which they turn to the state. They then become "burdens" on society while the more affluent can maintain their "independence."

Class is so often an invisible dimension in our society. An example—one day, I was talking to another woman, probably in her seventies, whom I know only from a yoga class. She lives in an affluent Chicago suburb and comes across as a warm and comfortable person, a former schoolteacher. When I mentioned the women of Mayslake to her and the fact that the average monthly Social Security check that many women relied on for the bulk of their income was $1,200, her look was one of amazement. These women are invisible to her, as they may also be to so many who advocate for individual responsibility to age "successfully" (see chapter 3) or those who assume raising the Social Security retirement age will be nonconsequential (see chapter 6).

When we discussed the practical implications of ageism, they had experiences familiar to many old women—stores not offering enough clothing that suits them or salespeople avoiding them. They disliked being called "granny" and resented it when people spoke to them in patronizing terms, greeting them with "Hi, sweetheart," or calling them "young lady." People always seemed to be in a hurry and so lacked patience with them. Old women, Audrey noted, are cast aside. Assistive devices further stigmatized them, and so did any demonstration that they needed any help; thus, they tried to avoid showing that they needed assistance and acknowledged how hard it was to face people around them who were deteriorating. Jan, who used a cane following back surgery, thought that it was a visual symbol of needing help, which she insisted she did not need. Lee, who has COPD and so cannot walk very fast, thought she was seen as inept and that people treated her as if she were incompetent. Yet after overcoming resistance, she accepted a ride in a wheelchair at the airport and found that it was just fine to accept the help.

Confirming research, they felt that others saw them as burdens, that younger people did not realize that they had spent time working and it was now their chance to do nothing or only what they chose to do. They felt invisible—seen but not seen, recipients of blank stares and glances that suggested they were stupid. Often they felt sad and sometimes bitter that people did not really know them or even want to know them but that the responses of others mattered—the more they were treated as old, the more they felt old and the more they questioned their own competence, a particularly ironic fear given their vitality and social/political awareness. To protect themselves, they often narrowed their worlds to avoid being judged negatively (see chapter 2). "No wonder people don't want to see themselves as old; they've spent their whole lives saying they won't be like that"; yet they acknowledged that they too internalized ageism, demonstrated by their insistence that they were not like "them," those women who didn't leave their apartments or keep up with the news or participate in any activities.

While all the women had strong self-images, these images were besieged by how others seemed to see them. To counter ageism, Audrey suggested that they "negotiate stereotypes" and try to create an impression of themselves as different. While Jan's response to manifestations of ageism was this—"strong women don't let it matter when others knock them down," Mary "just lets it go" and attributes ageist responses to the ignorance of others.

The women regularly spoke about wanting to remind those young people who viewed them negatively that they too will be old one day. We "foreshadow" what they will be, Lee observed. In a comparative exercise in which they described how they thought others saw them and how they saw themselves, with the exception of Jan, the gap was very wide. Lee thought that people saw her as needing support, as a person who could be ignored, slow, a burden, as someone consuming space and resources. In contrast, she saw herself as having much to offer, as being a person with intrinsic worth and value, patient, respectful, fun, still learning and growing, independent, and politically relevant. She described her growth as "peeling away the onion" and being like "a lion roaring" as she tries to free herself from what people think about her and what she was in her past. Thus, age has brought her greater honesty, spiritual connectedness, and the wish not "to be a character but to have character." She'd like young people to know that slow doesn't mean stupid and that she would like to be heard when she speaks. "It took me a long time to become the person I am today, but I am still in progress. Don't treat me like a child."

Mary thought that people saw her as shy and quiet, a person who waited to be approached, but she saw herself as strong physically and mentally and privileged to have a positive outlook, as a good friend when people got to know her, and as accepting of what has happened in her life. Capable, independent, and healthy were her further descriptors, aided by her friends, family, and her faith. Mary, the most optimistic of the women, did not feel disrespected because she was no longer productive or useful. She did, however, find it hard to understand how "old I am; age doesn't mean anything to me." To that I add that while she doesn't specifically identify with her age, the way of life she claims—the freedom—at ninety-one is possible because she is ninety-one and not fifty or even sixty.

Audrey's assessment of how others saw her was as grandma, an old lady, inactive, slow, in the way, not useful, out of sync with the times, dumb, nonproductive, a nuisance, and a financial drain. In contrast, she saw herself as caring, loving, hopeful, cooperative, helpful, active, curious, inclusive, generous, capable, loyal, and faithful. She also has had time to be more introspective and unfortunately has "twenty-twenty vision about the past," a source of some regrets. Yet she is clear that one can't go back and redo what she now regrets "since we wouldn't be able to bring about what we've learned." Her message to the world is what goes around comes around, be faithful to yourself and others, maintain a positive attitude, and rise above negativity. Love life in all its aspects.

Jan had no doubt that people saw her as accomplished, with high standards and a stern manner, a very confident person. She redirected criticism to young people and the throw-away society. Her self-assessment was that she was impatient, was smart but not arrogant, honest and open, and spiritually connected, a very important element to her self-identification, as became clear once when the talk turned to faith and the absence thereof. She strode out of the room. Her faith tells her that she is not in control of everything. Though she traveled a "long, hard road," she feels that she's accomplished her goals and lives every day as if it were her last. She's comfortable and at peace. Whatever happens, let it happen. The desire to accomplish more is gone, in contrast to when she was younger, where she set ever-higher goals, a message that she would like to transmit to younger people.

Carol thought that younger people saw her as a senior but one who could still function. She accepts the aging process and so mocks the TV ads for the miracle products that "will keep us from getting old." She loves the freedom to "be me," emotionally intelligent, thoughtful, and with goals. She calmly accepts the limits she faces and lives according to her abilities. And she wants to remind all young people that "someday you too will get older."

When I asked if images of aging affected how they saw themselves, Lee had a direct response, "I never did like how I looked, but it is hard not to get caught up in all those images." That said, the women enjoyed mocking the images of women in magazines who looked like nobody they knew and certainly not themselves. They laughed at their wrinkled upper arms and thighs and avoided certain kinds of clothing. Yet Audrey liked to see older women on TV when they looked good. She noted that when she did not wear makeup she felt like an old lady. Makeup, she said, offers some protection from devaluation. Despite living in bodies that were generally devalued, they felt more comfortable "in their skin" than they did when they were younger and enjoyed the freedom of worrying less about their appearance. Let it all go, a few women stated, and gain confidence not from how one looks but from the close relationships that one has. It's good not to have to keep up a façade. Aware of the double standard, they observed that guys can get sloppy, but women can't.

When we talked about what was good about aging, they stressed freedom, above all freedom from stress and worry, and more time to pursue their own interests and to make new friends. They do not want to answer to anyone. Thus, it is not surprising that they resent the imposition of expectations like productivity, which "co-opted the chance for multiple voices." They adopted something of a group motto, "I don't do cultural scripts." Not living by directives was one of the great pleasures of being old. They valued their "acute awareness of the world" and their "intense desire to know." They saw happiness as a choice and took pleasure in the now. Contentment was a prevailing feeling. They felt that they were in charge of handling what happened to them. But there was also a sense of loss. While able to do without, that didn't mean that they were fully able to accept losses.

Most are comfortable with the past that they cannot change, but as I listened to them, I was regularly amazed at the difficulties some of them had lived through and seemingly overcome. Emotional and physical abuse, marriage to difficult and violent men, mental and physical health problems, estrangement from children, and the need to let go of a wished-for idyllic relationship with these children. I was particularly moved when Carol described her exit from an abusive marriage when she was "stripped of everything." The supportive environment at Mayslake has made up for some of those losses. Their view of a good day was when they accomplished something, made something better.

These women were ardently political; they followed the news closely and argued issues fervently. Our discussions about politics, about which we unexpectedly agreed (DuPage County, where Mayslake is located and where most residents spent their adult lives, is commonly seen as one of the most conservative of the collar counties that ring Cook County), were intense and very informed. Above all, they wanted a way to be found to take away worries about money. They argued that Social Security penalized them because they stayed at home for many years when raising their children, that socially valued work received no recognition, and that when they wanted to return to the workforce, no one wanted them. They favored a guaranteed income and urged support for working mothers. But they were also tired. We have fought too many battles and now sometimes it is easier to withdraw.

MAYSLAKE

The women all valued living at Mayslake. They appreciated the choices of activities, the security of the environment, the people with whom they shared not only age but also similar backgrounds. They liked the generational companionship of living at Mayslake, the ability to remember parts of the past that are not known to younger people. They particularly enjoyed the freedom to choose what they wanted to do and loved not having structured lives, something that they lived with for too long. "We live the way we want to live." Most find other ways to be with younger people. For some, the chance to be outrageous and get away with it was a privilege of age. Carol and Lee were particularly sensitive to class distinctions both within Mayslake and outside in the community. They attributed the lack of respect they sometimes experienced from people serving them as class based. All the women would like to see a more formal support program so that they can know when a neighbor or neighbors need help. They cherish the concept of neighbors helping neighbors and worry about residents who do not let themselves be known. They wished that everyone had the same sense of safety that Mayslake gives to them.

Because they are so aware of the negative stereotypes that exist about people like them, they would like to create opportunities for multigenerational interactions. They talked of setting up intergenerational panels at Mayslake so that each generation could recognize and address the stereotypical impressions that they had of people unlike themselves, to penetrate beyond the message of appearance. They were eager for a political system that recognized what they had already contributed and what everyone needed in terms of safety and security, recurring words in what they loved about Mayslake. They offer strong testimonials to the value of this kind of living.

I close by affirming that these women—the women of Mayslake—are just what they say they are. They are kind, smart, politically aware, appreciative of what they have, and indulging in what they see as an earned freedom. To their words, I add these words from Rabbi Abraham Joshua Heschel, since I think they reflect what these women have made of their aging.

> May I suggest that man's [*sic*] potential for change and growth is much greater than we are willing to admit and that old age be regarded not as the age of stagnation but as the age of opportunities for inner growth. . . . The years of old age may enable us to attain the high values we failed to sense, the insights we have missed, and the wisdom we ignored. They are indeed formative years, rich in possibilities to unlearn the follies of a lifetime, to see through in-bred self-deceptions, to deepen understanding and compassion, to widen the horizons of honesty, to refine the sense of fairness. (from *To Grow in Wisdom*, 1961)

Part I

The Body and Beyond

Chapter One

What Do You See When You Look at Me?

Women, Aging, and Our Bodies

Personal worth becomes tied up with our ability to match up to approved models of fitness and slimness, whatever our age. (Segal 2013, 175)

From the time we are little girls, we absorb, it seems by osmosis, the cultural preoccupation with how we look. When she was seven, Ila, my very, very slim granddaughter, asked her pediatrician if she could have one or two treats a day. When she and my daughter were leaving, the pediatrician reminded her to have only one treat a day. Ila asked my daughter, "Does she think I'm fat?" She is already aware that she has a body, which she and others will judge against socially constructed ideals of feminine beauty. Although she does not yet know it, her body will be an "evaluative marker" of her social worth and hence its devaluation a potential threat to her self-esteem (Calasanti and Slevin 2001). Self-worth for women is embodied in a way that it is not for men (McMullin and Cairney 2004). She will soon learn that to grow up female in our society is to assume that how others perceive our bodies and how we perceive our attractiveness in our own cultural context matters (Fey-Yensan, McCormick, and English 2002). Ila is already sensing the potency of judgment by others and by herself despite her parents' efforts to mitigate body consciousness.

Thus, by the time we reach seventy or eighty or ninety, we have experienced a lifetime of judgments that reflect the hierarchical and relational

37

ordering of power and privilege in our society. So when I look in the mirror
and the face looking back at me often looks unfamiliar, that is, old, it is likely
that I bring with me not only images of my younger face (and body) but also
years of experiencing and reacting to judgments about how I looked. While I
don't want to change the face that I see in the mirror through cosmetic
procedures or surgery, I think nostalgically of that younger and more vibrant
face, a face that reflected my younger and more vibrant body. A friend once
said, "When I look in the mirror I have to remind myself that it is me, not my
mother, that I am looking at." My decision not to intervene to alter my
appearance does not mean that I either accept it fully or that it doesn't
influence how I feel and act with others, especially with those who are much
younger than I am. This happens because age frames our social relationships
(Rubin 2007), and in contemporary society the aging face is hardly the normatively desired one (Furman 1997). Nor does the unimproved aging body
measure up against the toned, slim, agile, that is, youthful and abled body
encoded in popular representations in ads and other media. By violating
normative standards, old (and "unimproved") women invite negative judgments, judgments that the gospel of self-control, which holds that how we
look as we age is up to us (Calasanti 2007) reinforces. Thus blame, including
self-blame, often accompanies negative judgments (Calasanti and Slevin
2006; M. Walker 2008; Holstein and Minkler 2003; Rowe and Kahn 1987).

The body is implicated in our sense of self and our ability to feel comfortable in disparate settings. It is the marker that provokes ageist responses that
result in exclusions from valued social and other goods (Furman 1997; Hurd
Clarke 2011; see chapter 2). As a result, many women often try to distinguish
between their subjective experience of self, which is the feeling of inner
youthfulness or agelessness, and the outer, visible self that fails to meet the
test of attractiveness (Featherstone and Hepworth 1991; Hurd Clarke 2011),
a topic to which I will return later in the chapter.

In this chapter, my interest is the experiential body, what it means to be an
embodied woman in an inhospitable environment where being a woman and
old puts us on the "wrong" side of familiar binaries. After exploring the
complexities of understanding the body and considering the major physical
changes that so often come with aging, I will explore how bodies matter
personally, morally, and politically. Moving next to considering the recurring—but nongeneralizable—themes that occur in women's talk about their
aging bodies, I will reflect on my own experiences both as illustrative and in
recognition that "personal struggles and experiences offer an important

touchstone for academic theorizing" (Twigg 2004, 62). Ground-up under-standings have long been part of the feminist project. As will become clear, I have no grand narrative to offer about how women interpret, assess, and respond to conflicting messages about their bodies. We may accept our bod-ies or complain about them; we may do little to change them, or we may go to great lengths to "improve" them; we may wholeheartedly buy into consu-mer culture, or we may scorn it. But I think it is safe to say that we are very aware of how we are changing and how these changes are rarely socially valued. Our varied responses are often contingent on context, age, class, race, and other social locations. Research generally offers snapshots, albeit often taken over time, that contrast with the shifting and evolving nature of how we do or do not come to terms with our aging bodies, how we experience them in different contexts, and how we respond to how others treat us. This multi-dimensional process is far more complex than the ads for youth-enhancing face creams suggest. Further, the general inattention to class in this country means that few studies specifically consider how income differentials and the life experiences that result from these differences are reflected in women's assessment of and attitude toward their bodies (Dumas, LaBerge, and Straka 2005). Yet "the intersection of social locations" (Calasanti and Slevin 2001) notably affects our bodies; historic inequalities, for example, may lead to early impairments or to lined faces and heavier bodies. As I will discuss below, class also matters in the avenues we can use to manage our identities, and thus it influences how others see us. As cosmetic surgeries, for example, become increasingly normalized and touted as signals of boldness and pride (Brooks 2004), class is an important variable.

In this, the first of three interrelated chapters that explore the cultural and societal impediments to becoming and being a self-affirming and proud old woman, I raise a question to which I will return—how do we unintentionally partake in our own devaluation by accepting standards that have us looking backward rather than creating new standards that suit us as we are now? When and if we feel shame about how we look, a feeling that consumer culture reinforces, perhaps we can remember all the places our bodies have been and all the experiences they have had and practice what bell hooks calls the "oppositional stare" (as cited by Furman 1997) and affirm Gray Panthers founder Maggie Kuhn's assertion that she is an old lady and damn proud of it, all the while recognizing that "aging is ultimately not optional" (Twigg 2004, 63).

A caveat, I will only indirectly allude to Foucault's ideas about surveillance, discipline, and control of the body as interpreted by feminist philosopher Sanda Bartky (1990). As will become clear in the next section, contra Foucault and other radical culture critics, I do not think we can evade physiology but to attend to it does not imply that aging is a medical problem soluble by individual medical interventions (Estes and Binney 1991). While I value the contributions that medicine can make to our well-being, I am sympathetic to Christopher Faircloth's (2003) observation that "medicine is part of a totalizing regime to 'manage' bodies through normalization" (5), with women's bodies particularly subject to such intense efforts. Today, however, drug ads for "low-T" or erectile dysfunction suggest that men are now also the subject of pharmacological and medical attention for reasons that parallel regimes of beauty and health optimization that consumer culture markets to women (see chapter 3).

THE BODY: A COMPLEX UNDERSTANDING

I see the body as constructed and material. Both matter in the "crucial complexity of growing old" (Falcus 2012, 1384). I start with a very simple observation—only, I think, in the eyes of a young child is the body seen without attaching multiple meanings to it. My four-year-old grandson sees my gray hair. To him that marks me as old, but he seems to attach no value, good or bad, to that label. So when I am with him the only bodily concern I have is getting up from the floor after playing with him. But because most of the people we come into contact with as well as the society in which we live are not four-year-olds, our bodies are given meanings in culture (Gullette 2004). Our slower or less-than-graceful stride may be caused by physical problems in our hip joints at the same time that they are culturally interpreted. Culture teaches us to feel badly about the signs of aging that might be the first gray hair at thirty-five and urges us to be watchful for any signs of incipient lines or other telltale signs of aging (Twigg 2004; Gullette 1997). And, as I shall discuss more fully in chapter 3, consumer culture builds on our discomfort by giving us both the message and the tools to turn our bodies into self-improvement projects.

Yet no matter what we do, we will not skip old age and leap from an extended midlife to death unmarked by physical and/or mental changes; age-related changes are real (Gillick 2006; Scannell 2006), but to note the obvious, age-related changes are not identified only with old age (think puberty), although the changes in late life are the ones most likely to be devalued. Moreover, at any age, changes may limit us by forcing us to move slowly or keeping us from climbing long, steep hills, as happened to me, at the same time that they also open ways to think about our lives and give us opportunities that we might not otherwise have had. Lee, a member of our Mayslake group, who has COPD, notices how her pace allows her to notice things she never saw before. Consider the burgeoning of illness narratives as examples of how change often provokes valued self-reflection (Bury 1982; Charmaz 1987; Toombs 1995; Hurd Clarke and Bennett 2012) (see chapter 4).

To integrate the constructed and the body as experienced, I offer Cheryl Laz's (2003) suggestion that bodies are discursive—shaped, represented, and constructed—while they are also phenomenologically experienced; we humans are "organic creatures with bodies," that is, with muscles, tissue, blood, and nerves (5040). We can neither will away old age by maintaining that it's all a social construction (Andrews 1999), nor can we assume that the manifestations of those aches and pains or other indications of age such as lined faces have no social meanings. So while all life stages are socially constructed, their boundaries are permeable and are necessarily linked to our physical and mental capacities. Toddlers and teenagers are socially constructed categories, but we do not deny that they are grounded in physical changes. The goal, it seems to me, is not to deny that old age and the old body exists but to find ways to alter the meanings that are attached to it and to affirm our individual identity without denying that dominant cultural norms insinuate themselves into our self-understanding. Defending a concept of identity, which recognizes that social constructs of gender and age have power and infiltrate our self-understandings, I argue, with Meyers (2001), that this often-perceived alienation between social identification and one's sense of self is a provocation for the critical reflection that is the foundation for emancipatory social criticism. To support our personal identity when we occupy subordinated positions calls upon us to find and speak in our own voice.

As moral agents, we can work toward choosing how to respond to physiological changes to and cultural readings of our bodies. To do so amid the clamor of multiple voices calls for what Diana Meyers (2002) calls autonomy competence, a skill set that helps us to mediate among interpretations of our bodies, our physical capacities, our values and goals, our social locations, our resources, the relationships of which we are a part, and our physical environment. Through this mediation, we can arrive at decisions that "preserve our integrity, tell the world who we are, or reflect motivations that we find desirable" (Holstein, Parks, and Waymack 2011, 21).

This mediation process occurs when women try to maintain socially desirable, youthful bodies while wondering why this struggle is important. It happens when they color their hair or seek other interventions, perhaps for jobs, but feel inauthentic when they do so (Hurd Clarke 2001). These dilemmas are familiar to many women and raise this question: should we risk losing self-esteem because of the social responses to what our body is becoming, or do we try to mask the aging process by adopting multiple interventions (Calasanti 2005)? Autonomy competency, a skill that takes particular nurturing in the oppressive circumstances in which many women mature, once developed can liberate us from the dominant cultural meanings assigned to our aging bodies without, however, disrupting the underlying age and gender relations that frame these negative assessments, the much tougher task and a topic to which I will return in chapter 8. As moral agents, the goal is to at least pose the question of what a wise woman should do and seek to answer it as best we can, knowing that few answers are for all times.

There are times, however, when the balance between physical changes and cultural constructions can be addressed by others. From disability studies, we learn that often society and not our disability handicaps us (Putnam 2002; Freund 2001). The environmental context in which we age and live our daily lives can limit our activities and reinforce stigma. I use a simple example as illustrative. In a recent excursion to the theater, to reach the exit, I had to walk down several relatively steep steps without a handrail. Like many women my age, I know that my balance is not as good as it once was, and so I walk down stairs carefully and hesitantly. If anyone noticed my hesitance, I suspect it would have been interpreted accordingly and probably not in my favor. In this momentary scenario, I had to take into account my physical limitations and my awareness that I was confirming existing stereotypes and so opening myself to negative judgments while recognizing that the problem could have been easily solved if the theater had installed handrails. That contextual feature is thus a complicating but easily resolvable element in how we experience our bodies.

In sum, then, neither the materialist nor the constructionist view taken alone can explain how women experience their embodied selves. My physical body limits the discourses that are possible for me (Twigg 2004, 63), yet it is also possible that "biological limits can be stretched and cultural representations modified" (Holstein, Parks, and Waymack 2011, 57). It means that physical changes by themselves do not cause ageism and the negative experiences aging bodies provoke, but "it is the meaning we give to these changes that matter" (Calasanti 2005, 9). And it means that the cultivation of autonomy competency, and the ability to speak in our own voices, will help us negotiate these complexities while we monitor and call attention to the length of traffic lights and curb cuts and handrails in theaters.

THE BIOLOGICAL BODY

Most of us, in our sixties or seventies, begin to notice what our bodies can no longer easily do. I was once a regular hiker, but today when I plan a long walk (not even a vigorous hike) I often prepare for it with an ibuprofen to keep my legs from hurting. When I was forty I never thought about the possibility of pain accompanying my walking. I assume that my body will continue to change in ways that I will find distressing since they may limit favored activities. For most of us, resiliency will diminish. Today we might scale a mountain or at least climb a flight of stairs; tomorrow even one step might be too much. We will relate differently to our bodies as our vulnerabilities deepen, leading us to approach social interactions and movement differently. The once-taken-for-granted body is infused with new risks and uncertainties. Over time, we will lose functional cells and tissues, our organs will become less efficient, and our reserve capacities will decline (Hillyer 1998). We will heal less quickly and lose muscle mass and lung capacity. Cellular damage will accelerate (Hayflick 1994); joints might stiffen. These changes are not disease, but they force us to modify our behaviors, like no longer carrying baggage that must be tossed into the overhead bins on planes because of diminished physical strength. For women in particular, what we have long taken for granted becomes problematic; without estrogen, for example, older women often find sexual intercourse painful. This new "fact" of their lives is not life threatening, but it requires a reassessment of one's interactions with partners and decisions about possible medical interventions. Instead of a habitual body that we might ignore, we gain an attention-demanding body. Some changes like osteoporosis are more severe and may limit the most common tasks we perform, such as cooking and shopping. These physical limitations are associated with aging and will be chronic and recurrent (Hillyer 1998). They will happen to us despite diet regimens, lots of green tea, and exercise.

Aging will also change our physical appearance. When basal metabolism slows down, lean body tissue decreases and fat increases. Our shape changes (Chrisler and Ghiz 1993). The skin on our faces and necks becomes drier and flakier, and it wrinkles and loosens. The passage of time leaves its mark. As sociologist Andrew Blaikie (1999) observes, "Each of us is engaged in a losing battle with the ravages of time" (86). We may be able to retard the process, and we certainly can affect its outward manifestations through simple procedures like hair dyes to the more complex surgical and chemical overhauls. But, as Florida Scott-Maxwell (1968), writing in her eighties, reminds us, "nothing in us works well, our bodies have become unreliable" (35). Other older women writers like Doris Grumbach (1991) and Carolyn Heilbrun (1997) candidly describe aging bodies that no longer perform as they once did. We may feel eighteen years old sitting in the park—but eighty when we rise. Stiff joints, balance, vision problems, and even weakness suddenly remind us that we are no longer eighteen.

As I explore these many issues, I do it with awareness that inequities in our starting positions affect our biological bodies as much as they affect our economic security and family status. As we move through adulthood, the effects of our starting inequalities—based on race, ethnicity, and class, to name just a few—worsen and leave us very different from one another in old age and also different physically and often mentally from our younger selves. We are the product—and sometimes the unwilling victim—of our own history, especially its material conditions, which have always mattered, but they matter today more than they did thirty or forty years ago. I say this because the individualism that now dominates our culture (see introduction) has contributed to the erosion of the once-strong ties (neighborhoods, social clubs, language of community, bowling leagues) that bound us together in many different ways (Dionne 2012). Hence, just as the material conditions that have shaped our lives worsen as we enter old age (Dannefer 2003; O'Rand 1996), we now can have fewer expectations of social remedy than we might have had fifty or sixty years ago (Hacker 2007; Rodgers 2011; Dionne 2012).

THEMES: HOW BODIES MATTER

Bodies matter, most simply, because how we see our bodies and how others interpret them inform our relationships with individuals and with institutions. My body is "what I *am* in relation to objects and others" (Diprose 1995, 209). Sociologist Lillian Rubin (2007) observes that our sense of self and personal identity is "formed and sharpened in the context of . . . social interaction[s]" (Rubin 2007, 46), an observation that I analyze more fully in the next chapter. Thus, our bodies affect us daily; they challenge or affirm our self-worth and our moral standing in the diverse communities of which we are a part. Social ethicist Frida Furman (1997) reminds us that we cannot understand "who women are as socio-moral beings apart from the reality of their embodiment" (5). As age provokes devaluation, we may face humiliation, the obverse of dignity, an essential element in maintaining a valued sense of self (Margalit 1996).

The body is thus morally important; it affects our "moral standing in later life"—the "respect, recognition, and concern that a person elicits from others in her community, the responsibilities exacted from and owed to her, and her own sense of value, selfhood, and responsibility" (M. Walker 1999c, 2). We face threats to our moral standing when our bodies trigger ageist responses, as discussed in chapter 2, that diminish our social participation or when patronizing speech threatens our sense of self or when we feel and express "disgust" at the way an older woman's body, including our own, looks (Furman 1997; Brooks 2004; Vares 2009). Each time our moral standing is threatened, so too is our possibility for acting autonomously. In writing a few years ago about age, gender, and the moral life, my colleagues (Holstein, Parks, and Waymack 2011) and I suggest that:

> If the development of one's self or identity is tied to the body, and we gain a sense of ownership over the body through the development of autonomy competency, then the significance of embodied experience becomes clear. Our *external* experience of our bodies . . . informs our *internal* development of autonomy competency, and vice versa. We are not simply selves, then, but embodied selves; and the ways in which we are embodied affect the development of our autonomy and the ownership of our bodies. (Holstein, Parks, and Waymack 2011, 48)

Since appearance has traditionally been the source of our social capital, that is, our access to desired goods and relationships, we cannot easily ignore the judgments our embodiment provokes (Furman 1997; Vares 2009). How different our responses to our weight would be if we lived in the time of Rubens, when fleshy bodies prevailed, or if the time ever came when young women went to the beauty counter asking for brown spots, a vision that the cofounder of the Older Women's League, Tish Sommers, offered many years ago.

Bodies matter because aging (not just being old) is about living through the process of physical change, which often leads to greater physical vulnerability, a particular problem in a cultural milieu where "successful aging" is a normative expectation (see chapter 3). It may be that the minute we adjust to some change, another one is upon us. We often move from having an "abled" body to a "disabled" one, thus uniting in one body three devalued statuses—gender, age, and disability.

Bodies matter in yet another significant way that I shall also address more fully in chapter 3. As anthropologist Sharon Kaufman (2011) observes, health promotion and the pursuit of "optimal health" have become meaningful social practices, and the pressure to take advantage of newer and newer strategies to achieve those ends escalates as failure to care for the self is "understood as a moral transgression" (citing Crawford 2004; Calasanti 2005; Hepworth 1995; see chapter 3). The existence and promotion of these possibilities project us further and further into defining new "late-life somatic ideals" (Kaufman 2011, 231) that go beyond what we look like and pressure us to measure up to ideals that are increasingly normalized. This pursuit of the optimal can result in a widening gap between the affluent, who have the resources to seek these ends, and those who do not (Dumas, Laberge, and Straka 2005). It will create another arena in which inequality deepens, a topic to which I will return below. For more affluent women, who have both the free time and the resources, body maintenance can become a consuming activity (Faircloth 2003). Gym memberships seem almost de rigueur for women with adequate resources.

Bodies also matter politically. If it is possible by dint of our own efforts to have an ever-youthful self, we can be blamed if our bodies "fail" us and so make us burdens on society. By holding us accountable, policymakers can justify a reduced social response (M. Walker 1999c; Calasanti 2005; Segal 2013; chapter 3). For marketing professionals, this commitment to the perpetually youthful self opens an arena for an exploding array of anti-aging products. The unintended collusion of old women in this mythology reinforces the agendas of both policymakers and marketing professionals. Blamed personally for the condition of our bodies and used as a tool politically, these new oppressions overlap and intersect with the familiar and interlocking oppressions of gender, race, and class.

WOMEN TALK ABOUT THEIR BODIES

Sociologist Cheryl Laz (2003) notes that it is striking how frequently adults in a research project about age talked about their bodies, their body parts, and their physical abilities and activities. It seems that in almost every conversation I have with my contemporaries, some item about the body comes up. These issues run the gamut from clothing that doesn't look the same as it once did to dissatisfaction with weight or distressing physical limitations. It seems as if women's relationship to their aging bodies is a recurring theme when in the company of peers. It is also a theme in fiction, an often neglected source of insight, especially as it can demonstrate the "crucial complexity of growing old" because novels and short stories embrace contradictions and often gain their aesthetic sense from doing so (Chivers 2003, x). Fiction also reminds us why grand narratives about women and their bodies are apt to omit what is often most important.

Women's conversations about their bodies say much about their fears and their awareness that others read their bodies stereotypically (see chapter 2). As a result, women frequently talk about not "going gray" and sometimes about cosmetic surgeries as ways to intercept the cultural prejudices about the old body (Slevin 2010; Hurd Clarke 2011). Yet, they may also touch upon strategies to insinuate new ideas into the cultural miasma especially if and when they feel conflicted about anti-aging interventions. It is hard to evade the cultural standards about beauty and femininity, and it is easy to feel defeated by the changes brought about by advancing age. Thus, women may negotiate between pride in what they do and who they are at the same time that they negatively judge their bodies, especially their weight and gray hair (Bordo 1993; Winterich 2007). I arrived at a dinner party about a year ago and a guest—about my age and from a similar background, with strong feminist and activist commitments—looked very different from the last time I had seen her—her hair was now a flaming red. Without being asked, she commented that this color was a slight aberration, but there was no way "I'd let my hair go gray." The support around the table was nearly universal. "Many more white, heterosexual, middle-class women associated gray hair with aging . . . and did not question the cultural assumption that women should hide their gray hair . . . they reject gray hair because they associate looking old as negative" (Winterich 2007, 62). For the late Nora Ephron, "hair dye has changed everything, but it almost never gets the credit" since it at least temporarily succeeds in "stopping the clock" (2011, 36). Jan, a seven-

ty-one-year-old member of our Mayslake group and a cosmetologist, observes that "when I let myself go gray, I'll be old." In her multiple studies
about women and their bodies, Laura Hurd Clarke (2011) finds that gray hair
is a significant expression of a "person's age, social class, ethnic affiliation,
gender, political inclinations and sexual preferences" (53). Since women
recognize that gray hair is a major trigger for social devaluation and obsolescence, is dying their hair a form of self-protection and perhaps a practical
necessity like a job? Or is it a sign of collusion with oppressive social relations? Or is it primarily a matter of cost and time? My mother, for example,
whose hair turned gray in her thirties, never colored her hair and spoke out
quite firmly against doing so. I think I absorbed that attitude and to it added
what I considered my feminist and my gerontological commitments—how
could I erase my gray and still argue that we need to own our age? Clearly
other feminist gerontologists (I offer no names) do not share my view.

Some do more. One friend whom I had not seen in over a decade (still in
her fifties) greeted me at a conference with the news that she had had a
facelift and other cosmetic surgery. Another friend is considering it. Cosmetic surgery has become increasingly normalized in the past few decades as
deregulation and commercialization has unleashed advertising that markets
such surgery as safe and minimally invasive (Brooks 2004). Articles in popular magazines highlight its positive results far more often than its negative
ones while elevating surgery as a sign of progress and technological skill. It
is one more element in the self-project of bodily perfection (Elliott 2003). It
is also the vehicle that women often use to reconcile the incompatibility
between what they look like and what they feel like (Hurd Clarke and Griffin
2008; Coupland 2009), a topic often referred to as the "mask of aging" that I
will consider later in the chapter.

Women may express despair about their appearance (Furman 1997; Hurd
Clarke 2011). One woman in Frida Kerner Furman's ethnographic study of
women in beauty shop culture said, "The face, the face, I am ashamed of"
(Furman 1997, 12). They may feel this despair even when defining themselves as "not old" by virtue of their remaining physical capacities (Hurd
Clarke 2011). One result of becoming "old" is shame for failure to meet the
"disciplinary practices of femininity" (Bartky 1999) much of which focuses
on the body.

Yet women do far more than despair. As they complain about parts of
their bodies—those puckered thighs and fleshy upper arms and those extra
pounds—they often do so with sardonic laughter that also greets the photo-

graphs of "older" women featured on the pages of AARP's magazine, *Modern Maturity*, who look like nobody they know. Laughter both binds them to one another and "pokes fun at our society's unrealistic expectations that women remain forever the icons of youthful beauty and sexuality" (Furman 1997, 38). The best laugh that we have had in more than two years of meetings occurred at Mayslake when Lee described her experience one day when wearing shorts. She looked down and was startled by her puckered thighs but couldn't figure out what to do to hide them so that they would be less noticeable. She improvised by trying to hold her hands and arms in front of her thighs, not exactly a comfortable solution.

The women of Mayslake did more than laugh at their own bodies, which seemed far less important to them than other features of their lives like their curiosity and engagement. Thus, they actively rejected the beauty norms they saw in magazines and on television. They know that they don't conform to normative ideals of beauty and, most importantly, don't expect themselves to do so. None of the women hated their bodies or their appearance. Expressing pride in how they looked, they seemed to have no desire to radically remake themselves, although they indulged on occasion in whimsical clothing like boldly patterned socks and bright red shoes. Yet the women of Mayslake are protected in much of their daily lives from negative judgments about their appearance since they live in a homogeneous retirement community. So we laugh and feel pride in who we are at the same times that we have difficulty in accepting what we look like. "I despair of ever being able to reconcile my overall sense of well-being, self-confidence, achievement, and pleasure in the richness of the present with the image I see in the mirror" (Sobchack 1999, 200).

Women may also express an increasing defiance about responding to social expectations—including spousal criticisms—about their bodies (Tunaley, Walsh, and Nicolson 1999). There is also hope because, contra Fukuyama, who argued that history was at an end, that is not so. When cultural norms defined women as frail and fragile, middle- and upper-class women were effectively denied higher education or were negatively labeled "blue stockings," doomed never to marry or have children. Poor women, however, worked without professionals worrying about the effects on their bodies. Also more affirmatively, we are not wholly subject, in Foucault's terms, to the disciplinary practices society tries to impose on us. Despite everything, we are also agents; we can and do make choices about how we will regard our bodies. Our new and aged body thus gives us a chance to rethink our self-understandings and commitments (Meyers 2003) despite the social pressures to conform to youthful ideals.

The British writer Penelope Lively (2012), herself in her midseventies, captures the aging body brilliantly in her novel *How It All Began*. Charlotte Rainsford, also in her midseventies, was mugged. In the process, her hip was shattered. After observing that "old age is not for wimps," she goes on to say:

> Of course before the hip there was the knee, and the back, but that was mere degeneration, no malign external interference. The knee. The back. And the cataracts. And those twinges in the left shoulder and the varicose veins and the phlebitis and having to get up at least once every night to pee and the fits of irritation at people who leave inaudible messages on the answerphone. Time was, long ago, pain occasionally struck—toothache, ear infection, cricked neck—and one made a great fuss, affronted. For years now, pain has been a constant companion, cozily there in bed with one in the morning, keeping pace all day, coyly retreating perhaps for a while only to come romping back: here I am, remember me? Ah, old age. The twilight years—that delicate phrase. Twilight my foot—roaring dawn of a new life, more like the one you didn't know about. We all avert our eyes, and then—wham! you're in there too, wondering how the hell this can have happened, and maybe it is an early circle of hell and here come the gleeful devils with their pitchforks, stabbing and prodding. (7)

But, as Charlotte affirms, despite all that, "life goes on in parallel—real life, good life with all its gifts and graces." (7)

Lively's writing is free of the current rhetoric that we live in an "ageless" culture. Charlotte does not assume that age is irrelevant, a state of mind that we can modify, rather than something we experience in our bodies and our psyches (Biggs, Phillipson, Money, and Leach 2006). Stella, a sixty-five-year-old retired anthropologist in another of Lively's novels, *Spiderweb* (1998), observes, "If you have been a beauty, ageing must be intolerable. . . . The process is bad enough as it is—the ebbing away of possibilities, the awful tyranny of the body—but for those who lose their very trade mark, it is savage. No wonder . . . elderly actresses take to the bottle" (85).

Other women writers, like Doris Grumbach (1991), a noted critic and novelist, in discussing her own aging as she turned seventy, do so with a fierce realism. She notes that her body is no longer "a good servant that will obey my orders. . . . I am always in fear of slipping, stumbling, and being hurt when I fall. . . . My once-firm, reliable body, quick to command and as quick to respond, now moves in slow motion, dry to the touch, weary, lax, unresponsive" (80, 81). Women's talk about their bodies is an important reminder that we exert less individual control than contemporary ideas about successful aging, as outlined by Rowe and Kahn (1987) and to be addressed in chapter 3, for example, suggest we do.

IDENTITY MANAGEMENT

Because we live in an ageist culture, even if we are reasonably comfortable with our own bodies and appearance, we may try to manage our identity as a way to reconcile how we see ourselves and how we assume others see us. I think of identity management (Featherstone and Hepworth 1991; Biggs 1997) not singularly as a way to pretend we are unchanged or that we are ageless or eternally youthful but also as a way to reveal ourselves as we see ourselves. Some, of course, manage their identity by trying to conform to the new mythic ideals about growing old without aging. These women experienced a painful split between their subjective sense of self and the outer shell that was their body. This division was the foundation for the development of theories called "masks of aging." The "mask" is created by the physical processes of aging that prevent the inner and, to many, the youthful self from participating in the freedom that the condition of postmodernity, with its fragmentation and disruption of identity, makes possible. The goal, then, is to see how we might peel away or override that mask so that we can experiment with new identities that postmodernism and consumer culture make possible (Featherstone and Hepworth 1991). To overcome the constraints of appearance, the theory postulates, older women may seek to manage their identities by engaging in consumer practices that alter their outer appearance so that they can reconcile it with their inner youthful self. In this view, we do whatever we can so that the outer, visible self does not thwart expression of the inner and more youthful self.

Psychologist Simon Biggs (1997) proposes another way to understand the mask of aging. Also interested in identity management and postmodernism, for Biggs the mask or masquerade allows us to negotiate our sense of personal integration and complexity in a society that seems unable to see beyond our appearance. Hence, partaking in appearance-altering activities makes sense as a way to protect the integrated, mature self from the devaluation that stereotyping promotes. Both masking and masquerade, however, commit older women (and men) to active participation in consumer culture. Thus, when we use makeup or hair coloring or choose certain styles of clothing or hairstyles or more invasive appearance-altering actions, we may be trying to override the messages that our appearance communicates.

Masking or masquerade is at once understandable and deeply troubling. No one, I would imagine, wants our appearance to be the measure of who we are, although for women this assessment is a familiar one. Altering our appearance to conform happens at all ages (think of teenage girls), although, as noted above, class plays a strong role in how we respond. As we get older and more distant from socially valued norms, the judgments become more encompassing and our complexities are further obscured. I return to Diana Meyers's (2002) question—what is a courageous woman to do?—do we protect ourselves from misogynist interpretations by bowing to them, or do we refuse to conform?

There are roughly four, not entirely discrete, approaches that women adopt to cope with a body that may threaten their identity and marginalize them socially. These approaches reflect different personalities and coping styles and often mirror diversity and material and social circumstances (Dumas, Laberge, and Straka 2005). We can simply say, "Who cares?" and move on with our lives. This response may lead to social marginalization and exclusion, but that may be a price one is willing to pay to stop striving for a goal that is ever more elusive. Laura Hurd Clarke (2001) labels such women "realists." They pragmatically accept how age has altered their bodies and do not see a separation between their outer and inner selves. Second, we might adopt a full panoply of beauty and exercise routines in an effort to manage our identity so that we can, at least for a while, avoid encompassing and often totalizing judgments about us. These women often feel trapped in their aging bodies, which do not reflect how they see themselves and limit their participation in socially desirable activities (Hurd Clarke 2001). Their aim is to reconcile the incompatibility between what they look like and what they feel like (Hurd Clarke and Griffin 2008; Coupland 2009). By so doing, they can at least for a time expand their social capital. The message communicated by this approach to identity management is that if we "strive hard, pay enough attention, remain sufficiently vigilant, we can grow old free from the standard signs of aging" (Segal 2013, 175), an achievement that offers at least temporary protection from devaluation. The third option is a minimalist one. Women who adopt this approach are not immune from social evaluations of their bodies and their implications but limit their investment in beauty and body work. They may resent the inducements of the beauty industry and the crusade for an unmarked body but still want to "keep up appearances," or they may simply lack both resources for and interest in these inducements. Women on limited incomes, as noted above, can neither afford the biweekly "blow-outs" that Nora Ephron (2006) describes or their class position has historically discouraged a sustained preoccupation with appearance. The fourth approach includes women who resist the very idea of "keeping up appearances." While wanting recognition for a self that transcends their appearance, as in the longing of the women of Mayslake, these women may dye their hair or engage in some minor masking activities (Hurd Clarke 2001).

Class is a key variable in how women manage their bodies as they become less socially valued (Dumas, Laberge, and Straka 2005). Women with limited incomes do not say "Who cares?" because they are willing to accept marginalization. They want the self that they know and value to break through the barrier of their appearance, but they have few resources—and often little tolerance—to partake in consumer culture. Class influences their worldview and shapes their options. While more limited than affluent women in seeking bodily makeovers, their realism about what is possible and their history of limited means relieves them of the struggle more affluent women may undergo. The women of Mayslake, for example, resist the demeaning judgments that they believe others are making about them based on their appearance, but they do not, even if they wanted to, have the choice to engage in the practices Nora Ephron described or that I see in a noted television newswoman who seems to grow younger and younger.

In what follows, I speak now of the six women who have been members of our Mayslake group for more than two years. For them, identity management is important. As the women discussed the painful dichotomy between how they see themselves and how they think others see them, they found no easy path to reconcile this dichotomy. They sought not mastery over their appearance but mastery over how others perceived them. This distinction is critical. They saw themselves as mature, complex, and experienced individuals, an identity that their outer appearance belied but one that they could claim among their peers and friends who recognized and acknowledged their complexities. They also felt that in a different context where the power relationships were different, they would be less likely to be seen as they see themselves. Context is a central element in how they see themselves, just as I feel differently the first day of the semester, when I face forty eighteen- to twenty-year-olds compared to when I am with my contemporaries.

The numerous interventions that consumer culture makes available to more affluent women were impossible for the Mayslake group, and even if they could afford them, they had no illusions that it would matter greatly. They found it comical that older women dressed or adopted hairstyles that were far better suited to much younger women. The assumption apparent in fitness and wellness programs, that if only we try hard enough we can avoid the common signs of aging, seemed illusory to them. They didn't want to be those women, yet they wanted the respect that they assumed other women, perhaps their age peers, were able to obtain by body improvement projects. Like other women who have low incomes, while they rejected popular role models, they often still had a "disturbed body image" (Fey-Yensan, McCormick, and English 2002, 69). No one, it seems, wants to be "fat," even as the images of iconic women become thinner and thinner.

I thus reaffirm that class or, more broadly, social location shapes our values and our goals. The goal to somehow bypass or overcome the changes wrought by time, wholly by our own efforts, ignores how inequalities across our lives are implicated not only in our ability to manage our appearance but in our interest in such vigilance.

For the more affluent women that Nora Ephron (2006) writes about, however, consumer repair and remedy (hair dyes, Botox, microdermabrasion, hair washes and blow-outs—twice a week) were eagerly used to try to mask the changes in their appearance that they did not like. For these women, the mask served a double purpose: a form of resistance to the totalizing—and negative—meaning of old and an affirmation of a continued and familiar identity based on appearance. So we women in our sixties, seventies, and beyond may do what we can to control the impression we make on others, to try to manipulate how others interpret our bodies.

REFLECTIONS ON BODIES

The irony is that no matter what we do, few of us can or do meet the standards that represent the normative body now extended far into late life. Undeniably, some of us are living longer and are in better health than previous generations, but that does not mean we are unburdened by age. Nor does it mean that our current status is a permanent one; change will come whether it is sudden or gradual (Lamb 2014). Yet to maintain this belief that we can live unburdened by age has an undeniable appeal. I am not like "that." The mythology of the ever-young offers temporary protection from negative stereotyping and lets young women affirm that they will never be like "that" (i.e., unattractive, ungainly, and to some, abject) and gives many decision makers allies in their commitment to individual responsibility.

In the long run, however, it is a failing strategy. Old women's status is not so easily altered no matter how hard they try to be "not old" because they will still differ from the dominant group (Cruikshank 2009) since age brings with it physical and other liabilities that cannot be ignored. My body simply does not—and cannot—look or move like that of my daughters who are in their forties even if I dyed my hair, had a face lift, and spent hours in the gym. It also is ultimately a failing strategy for young women. By believing that they can grow old without aging (Katz 2001–2002), they develop prejudices against their future selves. How will they feel about themselves when they too have loose flesh under their arms or a less-than-firm jawline? If they believe that they won't be like "that," it is unlikely that they will find reasons to empathize and respond to women who are like "that," nor is it likely that they will support public policies to mitigate the burdens of age. What young women today may not realize is that prior generations also believed that they would not be "like that" (Jönson 2013).

Thus, many older women face a conundrum; the more we discipline our bodies through careful eating and exercise and the cosmetic preparations we try to resist but often don't, the more we cooperate in a "culturally meaningful set of values" (Reischer and Koo 2004, 300) that ultimately will betray us. Women have reported, and I can echo that feeling, that they know they are participating in a giant sales pitch, but it is still persuasive and motivates action, at least among those women who can afford active participation in consumer culture. As Laura Hurd Clarke (2011) concludes from her studies on women and embodied appearance:

> Even the self-identified feminists who articulated awareness of the critiques of idealized feminine attractiveness and the power of media imagery were not immune to negative body image. These women conveyed a poignant and deeply personal struggle between their intellectual rejection of misogynist beauty culture, their internalized ageism and sexism and the social realities of nonconformity. (65)

Because a very particularistic body imagery is pervasive and because consumer culture has discovered the gray market (Minkler 1991; Katz 2001–2002; Calasanti 2007), if we are interested and most often if we are also relatively affluent, endless interventions are available that allow us to maintain a more youthful appearance even if we are unable to forestall aging indefinitely (Calasanti, Slevin, and King 2006, 15) (see chapter 3). Advertising inundates us with messages that nurture our dissatisfaction with how we look and feel while instructing us about how we can—and should—improve our appearance through available interventions, including diets, exercise, cosmetics, and surgery. In addition to the profits these activities generate, they subtly promise us that we need not develop visible signs of aging. This mythology lends support to a particularistic and prejudicial view of what is possible and, from its perspective, desirable for most of us in old age. Its individualistic and upbeat focus obscures the realities of the aging body, ignores class and the effects of lifelong health care and other disparities, substitutes personal responsibility for well-being over social action, reinforces the medicalization and surveillance of the body (can "it," whatever it is, be fixed or prevented?), and displaces ageism so that it is primarily directed at those who "failed" to age in these mythic ways. It leaves few openings to respect the "vicissitudes of aging" (Cole 1992) or the disabled body and so adds to the burdens of being old (Rubin 2007).

Advertising, which is an integral part of modern culture, reinforces and builds upon the dissatisfactions that women already experience as the result of marginalization and internalized ageism. While we harbor those dissatisfactions, advertising reinforces the belief that our "natural" appearance is inherently flawed and inadequate. Already susceptible to its blandishments and aware of the cultural importance attached to our appearance, we are often not hard to convince that interventions from simple creams to makeup or other more invasive procedures will overcome the "sin of aging" (Wolf 1991, 95)—labeled "age terrorism" (Pearlman 1993)—and promise us a younger self. (See chapter 3 for a further discussion of advertising.)

PERSONAL REFLECTIONS

As I think about my own aging body and appearance more generally, I compare myself, to use an apt phrase from Maria Lugones (1987), to a world traveler. To be a world traveler has to do with the "desire and ability to explore reality wearing the other's shoes" (Bordo 1993, 287). In this case, the other's shoes are also mine as I try to become fully at home in this evolving body. It is familiar because it is roughly the same size and shape that it has been for most of my adult life; it is strange because stripped bare, I sag in places I never sagged before and it hurts where it never hurt before.

I am still surprised when the bus driver lowers the steps of the bus or someone offers me a seat. In everyday life, I am treated in response to that visible body. My surprise when I am treated like an old person suggests that I probably do not see myself as I am seen. I find that out when the outside world communicates its interpretations to me in ways that are out of my control. No matter how hard I may try, I still will look old. My body generates meanings that far transcend the actual physical manifestations of age that beset me (Woodward 1999). These meanings say as much about the society in which I live as they say about me.

I try to reconcile the dualism between the negative and positive poles of aging. I recognize that my lived body both limits and opens me to new opportunities like sitting on a hillside in Scotland while my daughter completed a steep hill walk that I could not do. I still can do most of what I want to do. I will continue walking and will even seek hills, which are hard to find in the Chicago area, but I will not try to emulate what I once did easily. This is what negotiating my aging self means to me.

I am neither reduced to my body nor wholly defined by it, but I cannot act as if it doesn't matter. I and other women my age thus face some difficult tasks—to find ways to resist internalizing the negative readings that are most often associated with an aging body while not denying that I am aging and that my body is not what it once was. It is difficult to simultaneously accept my own aging and resist the cultural conventions that don't describe me (Twigg 2004) without creating a dichotomy between "me" and "them."

I ask myself how I wanted to fit, if at all, with the new cultural demands on body maintenance and the beauty ideology of consumer culture. I'm still careful about what I eat despite sometimes wanting to just let go and eat whatever I'd like. I think about what writer Carolyn Heilbrun (1997) said about becoming fifty—I decided not to try to be thin anymore. I haven't gotten there yet; the reasons are health but also vanity. Sometimes, however, I imagine what it would be like to become a bigger person who takes up more space—a role usually reserved for men—in part to avoid the stereotype of the "little old lady" that fits my size so well.

My goal is to reach a place where women like me can define what it means to be old so that we can own the label proudly. I feel a nagging anger at all the hyperbole about looking young and an equal anger at the poorly dressed, poorly coiffed, and poorly fit bodies that appear, for example, on greeting cards. I feel anger at the pressure to control my body in certain ways and to assume if I don't meet normative expectations that I am somehow to blame. At times I am rebellious, at times uncomfortable, and at other times neutral. I borrow an apt description from Nancy Miller (1999), who speaks of aging as a "project of coming to terms with a face and a body in process—as an emotional effort, as oscillation that moves between the mirrored poles of acceptance and refusal" (4).

CONCLUSION

I reaffirm that "the body we experience is always mediated by constructs, associations, images of a cultural nature" (Bordo 1993, 35). These originate in a society that has transformed "chronological, biological based age," that which makes my hair gray and my skin thin, "into social and cultural signs" (Laws 1995, 113) that are almost universally negative. Hence, older women, coming of age and living in the sociocultural environment of our times, often feel like "moral failures, weighted down by guilt, shame or the experience of insufficiency; for having wrinkles or not being thin enough" (Furman 1997, 167). We are marked in ways that neither pride about reaching this age nor resistance to being influenced by the opinions of others can erase. To be so marked is to be "othered," to be seen not as an individual but part of a category labeled "old."

Yet I am surprised by how well so many of us seem to do if we are not too burdened by financial difficulties and the profound losses that accompany late life. As women get older and as their bodies continue to change, they may start to emphasize the "self" over the body as a way of "negotiating the loss of physical attractiveness and functional abilities that occurs in later life" (Hurd 2001, 460). In her conversations with older women and men, Lillian Rubin (2007), herself in her eighties, noticed this acceptance. They told her that they still had energy but "it sure as hell isn't forty" when "I didn't have the pain that's with me most of the time now. And if my body didn't remind me that I am closing in on sixty, the mirror does" (14). But, as Rubin observes, "reality doesn't sell" (15), the identical retort that Ken Dychtwald, a guru of the new aging, gave me more than a quarter of a century ago when I argued for a balanced representation of old age.

From so many women, I heard about the longing to be seen as mature, experienced individuals who are also old. We know we are far more than our aging bodies. But it is hard, after all, to escape all those negative images. We too grew up with them. Ironically, we learned them when we were in the privileged position of being young. The views may thus persist even when we have lost that privileged perspective. In this way how we learned to think about age, and the judgments that we make about it differ, for example, from those we make and internalize about sex or race. They are, as I noted, the source of discrimination against our future aging selves. So I practice, with friends, declaring myself "old." Frida Furman (1997) observed that "the acceptance of an older body—heavier, slower, sometimes sagging, not infrequently sporting a lined face and graying hair—is not automatic. Rather, it is achieved through processes of resistance against the dominant culture that denigrates women's older bodies as it makes them invisible" (15). There may be important lessons to be learned from women who have always resisted or from women who had neither the time nor the resources to discipline their bodies to meet socially constructed norms. If women have, throughout their lives, been subject to multiple oppressions, having an "old" body may hardly rank among the worst of those oppressions. Many years ago, I heard a talk that I don't think was ever published, by an African American gerontologist. She commented that old African American women willingly accepted help from others feeling that they have earned it; now it was time for others to care for them. This may also be so for appearance.

There is little doubt that as we try to integrate and accept changes that are happening to us, our ability to do so is encumbered by how those changes are interpreted, politicized, and seen in a particular cultural context. Thus, discovering how to live proudly, even defiantly, with the ambiguities of an aging body is both a personal and a societal necessity if our marginalization and exclusion is to be mitigated. We have, for example, learned from disability studies, that altering our environments can go a long way toward easing the problematic effects of physical or other limitations. The effects are significant and addressed in chapter 4. We will never be free of social and cultural norms, but we can contribute to shaping them. I and other women need to find a comfortable place for ourselves as socially shaped but also autonomous individuals. Exercising our autonomy competency in groups is a good starting place (see chapter 8).

I think we must also acknowledge and accept that learning to be old is a work in progress. A simple illustration—I have been thinking about this issue for a long time, have consistently resisted coloring my hair, perhaps missing the frivolity of going purple, or doing anything more than using basic make-up. Yet a few days into a brief vacation with my daughters and their families, I looked in the mirror and was ready to do whatever I could to make me look less old. Back home I am reasonably comfortable again, but it was a visceral reminder that there will be setbacks and surprises in the path to acceptance. Acceptance, however, does not absolve me from responsibilities to do what I can, within my means, to live as healthfully as possible, but I do not have the responsibility to try to maintain a body best suited for a woman thirty or more years younger, especially if that demands constant and often expensive attention. We cannot be morally expected to do what is not possible for us (Flanagan 1991), yet, as I note throughout this book, we experience moral blame when we do not meet such standards (M. Walker 1999c). I do not mean to suggest that we should be absolutely free from "appraisal and objectification since this may arguably be a natural element in our human relationships." We cannot and ought not be entirely free of norms (Holstein, Parks, and Waymack 2011, 57). We do, however, need to be liberated from the moral blame that ensues when we are held accountable, on paltry evidence, for societal problems, like budgetary deficits or inattention to problems of children, that they (we) did not create (A. Walker 2012). These many complexities do not, however, detract from the essential tasks for all women—to find ways to challenge normative claims about how we should look and act and to disrupt the assignment to categories that mask our diversity, a topic to which I will return in chapter 8.

While we engage in these efforts, often in conversation with other women, we may also succeed in liberating ourselves from the most damaging elements of our socialization and marginalization. This task would be so much easier if there were many different representations of old women that infused our culture, but those images are absent, which makes the adaptation to our aging bodies that much harder. It is also made harder by the tightrope we walk as we try to manage our identities at the same time as we reject collaboration with a political agenda that upholds the "mythic self" as justification for limited social support, a topic which I address more fully in chapter 3. More immediately, the body is the most visible locus of exclusionary practices that constitute societal ageism, which we experience in multiple ways (see chapter 2). My gray hair marks and categorizes me in ways that are dependent upon the particular prevailing assumptions of the times. Fifty years ago, the standard assumption maintained that people like me were dependent; today the assumptions have changed, and we are seen as independent and indeed, hardly different from a middle-aged person (see chapter 3).

I have offered a complex story of aging women and our bodies. For most of us, we will have to learn that the face in the mirror is our face and that what we once did may no longer be possible for us. I just came in from a walk. It is very cold in Chicago, and the streets have patches of snow and ice. I like to push myself to walk as fast as I can, but when I need to walk across one of those patches, I practically tiptoe through it to avoid slipping. I am relatively at ease with my body on a personal level, despite bouts of nonrecognition, and uneasy on a social level. I can guess how I am read, and I don't like it. I wonder how my attitude toward my face and body in the mirror would change if those readings were more affirming. In chapter 8, I will take up the topic of resistance, not resistance to aging but rather to the ways in which my body and that of other older women is totalized and universalized so that my identity as a full and complex person is lost. How do we challenge the "ageist gaze" (Falcus 2012, 1396) or the gaze of youth (Twigg 2004) to reveal our complexity and our understanding of our own aging bodies? How, in Molly Andrews's terms (1999), can we be ageful and proud?

Chapter Two

Ageism

You're Only as Old as You Feel and Other Fictions

Why do they think I don't know anything? (Iva Brown, a woman in her eighties)

Sometimes it seems as if we'll do anything to avoid being old. We insist and we are repeatedly told that we are only "as old as we feel" or that we are "young at heart" or that age is irrelevant to our lives. The now familiar refrain is that "seventy is the new forty." When waitpersons call us "young lady," they assume they are flattering us, as do strangers who say, "You must be sisters," when they see us with our grown daughters. These expressions are all understandable disavowals of old age (Segal 2013) in an ageist society that judges and often penalizes us for being old. They are also ageist and signal an internalized ageism normalized and naturalized in our society. Thus, citing Neugarten and Moore, Glenda Laws (1995) observes that we often move in our lifetimes from being the oppressor to becoming the oppressed as our age and related power shifts.

Ageism is a persistent and generally unacknowledged prejudice against the old that functions through systems of inequality that privilege the young at the expense of the old (Calasanti, Slevin, and King 2006). Often passing unnoticed and thus unremarked upon, ageism saturates our culture, deepening the barriers to comfortable ownership of our older selves, contributing to discrimination in the workplace and in the clinic, affixing blame for medical and other conditions that have their roots in lifelong inequalities, limiting the public roles and public recognition that are open to us, and often blinding policymakers to their ageist assumptions when they construct old age as a problem of enormous magnitude—the silver tsunami and the cause of generational inequities—that justifies the neoliberal agenda that Margaret Gullette (2011) calls "violence by budget" (37).

Yet compared to sexism or racism, ageism evokes little public concern. It persists in part because there are few, if any, consequences for holding, expressing, and even enacting negative views or actions. It has become a common way of thinking shared even by the old themselves as witnessed by their adoption of age-denying strategies. It is a prejudice without visible and visceral opponents, socially condoned and institutionalized (T. Nelson 2005). Americans, notes social psychologist Todd Nelson (2002), have limited tolerance for older people and few reservations about the negative feelings they harbor. They might welcome the old as kindly and indulgent grandparents (if they were not depicted as ogres) but not as the voice one had to hear in the back of the room at a public meeting.

Ageism persists because it is built into social structures and laws and other relations among individuals and groups so that the "not old" are more powerful than the old. Because gender and class intersect with age, women may be particularly harmed. Ageism also persists because many professionals, who are committed to improving the lives of those who are old, contribute to it by upholding norms as represented by "successful aging" best suited for a fifty-year-old rather than a seventy-year-old (see chapter 3; Calasanti and Slevin 2006). Ageism persists because differences reflected in departures for the normatively valued are invested with negative judgments about people and their categorical location.

THE FAMILIAR

Sitting by my window at my laptop, looking out at Lake Michigan on this very cold but very bright day, I simultaneously am all the ages I've ever been. Novelist Marisa Silver (2013) put it this way: "You never stop being one thing when you became another" (262). *Then* and *now* coalesce; continuity and change work in tandem. Age is neither deniable nor all inclusive, and identity in old age is complex. Ageism denies us this complexity by reducing us to generalized ideas about what we are and should be. So when I venture outside to the often busy paths along Lake Michigan, if anyone pays attention to me, the *now* is what matters. I am placed into the category of "old," and my body, as noted in chapter 1, becomes "a language for representation" transformed into "social and cultural signs" (Laws 1995, 113, 114). These signs signal common inferences about a person like me, which will most likely be about my expected *incapabilites* (Lewis, Medvedev, and Seponski 2011). I often internalize these stereotypes because I already hold them since I was once in the privileged position of being young and because I am influenced by how I think others see me in a process identified as "reflected appraisal" (McMullin and Cairney 2004, 77; Rubin 2007).

On the lakeside path, however, ageist responses such as discounting, marginalization, and exclusion do not usually invade my sense of who I am and what matters to me. No one is keeping me off the path, and there are no designated paths for slow walkers. This nonchalant attitude becomes more problematic in spaces where equal recognition, which is socially bestowed, is necessary for effectiveness or when biased attitudes and age prejudice reinforce discriminatory practices, as evident in the workplace. Nor can we be nonchalant when we are tacitly and sometimes explicitly blamed for having needs over which we are assumed to have control and which "burden" society (see chapters 3 and 6).

In the remainder of this chapter, I will explore the manifestations of societal ageism, its stubborn persistence, and potential strategies for mitigating it, a topic that I will address further in chapter 8. I will seek, for example, to understand why Iva Brown, a bright, articulate, informed but somewhat bent over and slower-moving woman in her eighties, had to painfully pose the question in the epigraph. That question is one of many she could have asked that seem to have been inspired solely by her age as announced by her appearance. She might have asked why she is treated paternalistically in medical settings or not offered certain referrals, or why TSA agents or waitpersons, for example, spoke to her as if her intelligence had somehow evaporated along with her erect posture, or why so many legislators, pundits, and other people of influence see her as burdening society, or why no respectful representation in film or on television resembles her at all. In each case the answer is ageism, which harms those of us who are old through disrespect, devaluation, marginalization, moral blame, and reduced opportunities while the perpetrators of these harms rarely, if ever, experience any negative consequences while often gaining advantages such as protecting their privileged place in the job market. As I shall discuss below, unintentional perpetrators are themselves often sixty or seventy or eighty.

AGEISM: DEFINED

At the outset, I used common descriptors of ageism, terms like prejudice, discrimination, and exclusions, that result from and reinforce the systems of inequality that help to explain ageism's stubborn persistence. I now extend that analysis because understanding how those systems of inequality work and manifest themselves, I suspect, is the only way to work toward ameliorating them.

In an early and prominent definition, Robert Butler (1969), the first director of the National Institute on Aging, described what he labeled as ageism as "systematic stereotyping of, and discrimination against, people because they are old, just as racism and sexism discriminate on the basis of skin color and gender" (243). Note that Butler importantly combined stereotyping and discrimination. Stereotyping is part of social life; hence, it can also be affirming, such as stereotypes about the work ethic of certain ethnic groups. Ageism, in contrast, always involves exclusionary behavior, which hinders or prevents participation in social networks such as work, certain status groups, and often families. It is in these groups that the distribution of resources and privileges becomes apparent (Calasanti 2007).

Prejudice against and exclusion of the old is not new despite its relatively recent naming and the romantic, albeit unrealistic images of what once was, that is, happy, multigenerational families living together where the oldest members were highly regarded. More realistically, with industrialization and other major social and economic changes in the nineteenth and early twentieth centuries, old people became increasingly irrelevant and so also marginalized (T. Nelson 2005). Families may have continued sharing living accommodations not because they necessarily wanted to but because resource constraints made it essential (Haber 1983; T. Nelson 2005).

Ageism, as a societal phenomenon, is based on age relations (Calasanti 2005, 8). Age relations have three dimensions: age is a *social organizing principle*, age groups *gain identities and power* in relation to one another, and age relations *intersect with other power relations* (Calasanti and Slevin 2006, 5; italics in the original). These relations are hierarchical (the young preferred over the old) and reflect differences in resources, power, and status. They also serve as cultural resources that people use to "construct identities, invoke norms, and justify particular arrangements" (Jönson 2013, 199). As such, they influence our self-concept, shape our opportunities and material circumstances, and contribute to multiple inequalities in opportunities for satisfying work, social recognition, and power. The resulting marginalization, exploitation, and powerlessness are oppressive and hence an important target for feminist analysis and action. Specifically, as "an embodied form of oppression" (Laws 1995, 114), ageist practices are inseparable from the bodies that become the markers of who will be excluded (Calasanti 2005) and thus help to explain women's striving to be "not old," as described in chapter 1.

In her study of persisting gender inequalities despite the many advances that women have made, feminist sociologist Cecilia Ridgeway (2011) observes that such inequalities are *categorical*—they reinscribe themselves "in new forms of social and economic organization as these forms emerge in society." The key to disruption, in her assessment, will be found in asking *how* and not *why* these inequalities have persisted (4). Thus, the question that I will touch upon later in the chapter and explore more fully in chapter 8 is this one: Can these hierarchical relations of power and status be disrupted, and if so, how?

While ageism has been compared to sexism and racism, there are important differences. Ageism, for example, is the only "ism" from which none of us is exempt if we live long enough. Ironically, this means that younger people, when they resist seeing themselves in the old women they see daily on the street or on the bus or in the restaurant, begin to nurture prejudice that will harm them when they are older (Hurd Clark 2011). Butler (1975) thus notes that "ageism allows the younger generation to see older people as different from themselves; thus, they subtly cease to identify with their elders as human beings" (12). So rather than embrace what we have viewed negatively for much of our lives, we distance ourselves from those who are visibly disabled, and we see ourselves as exceptions to those old people (Hurd 1999; Minichiello, Browne, and Kendig 2000), an option not available for race or gender. We who are old then become collaborators in the continued devaluation of and prejudice against "old." This collaboration helps to explain the variety of protective practices, addressed in chapter 1, that women use to establish their difference from the visibly old (Hurd 1999), a temporary personal strategy that cannot ameliorate the underlying ageism.

AGEISM NORMALIZED

Ageism is also the only "ism" that seems to exist in a realm that is free of negative fallout or consequences for those generally privileged by age (and other statuses) who casually assume their assumptions about the old are universal. Consisting of naturalized and normalized stereotypes—slow, incompetent, cranky, greedy, demanding, unattractive, sexless—it denigrates all older people but especially women (Gullette 2011). Repeatedly reinforced, the discriminatory stereotypes become what everyone knows with or without awareness on the part of the perpetrator. No public figure, for example, is reprimanded or loses his or her job for being ageist. Further, given that ageism is reflected in a wide range of exclusionary practices, the lack of public censure permits the continuation of such practices. They, too, may become normalized and hence invisible.

An example. Shortly after the tragic shooting of teenager Trayvon Martin by George Zimmerman, a neighborhood watch volunteer, a segment of Jon Stewart's *The Daily Show* featured a seventy-one-year-old couple whose address Spike Lee had erroneously tweeted as that of Zimmerman. Stewart described them as "cute," assumed that Spike Lee's apologetic "tweet" for giving out the wrong address was not in their realm of technological competence, and so suggested that messages to them be sent via their grandchildren. He implied that their retirement to Florida meant that they had dropped out of the contemporary world. He made these assumptions without meeting or speaking to the couple. Stewart's culturally normative prejudices are such that "holders of the prejudice don't even notice its enactment, because it is normal; it feels like business as usual to them" (M. Walker 1998b, 181). His casual ageism suggests how such prejudices are reproduced for adoption by the next generation. As a representative figure for the liberal young, Stewart reinforced familiar stereotypes that "legitimate behaviors and limit the possibility for imagining and acting on alternative realities" (Angus and Reeve 2006, 141). These stereotypes have become so normal that any objection to them seems silly or even improper or odd (M. Walker 1998b). Moral outrage is missing. In contrast, it is unlikely that belittling comments about race or gender would have passed unnoticed. White students, for example, may feel free to say that they don't want to work with old people when they would not feel as free to make a similar statement, for example, about people of color (Nancy Hooyman, personal communication, March 17, 2014).

While Jon Stewart's ageism is distressing, ask yourself about stereotypes you may carry about that old lady you see pushing her grocery cart, especially if she is fifty pounds overweight, slow to unload her groceries onto the conveyor and even slower to pay, and, by the way, wearing gray, baggy sweats. And if we are old ourselves, do we insist that we are different because we see ourselves as slim, well dressed, and "youthful"? We're not that overweight woman in baggy sweats; hence the stereotypes don't apply to us! The irony is not that stereotypes have disappeared but that, for a time, some of us may be able to keep ourselves from identifying with the negative images.

Stewart's ageism is joined by the relaxed attitude that many have toward mocking greeting cards that portray old people in particularly unflattering ways. Friends who would not tolerate racist or sexist greeting cards defend silly and prejudicial birthday cards about old people. Like all stereotypes, these images and comments on greeting cards have elements of truth to them that seem to make them acceptable. They continue to be bought, which also communicates a message of acceptability. Thus, ageism appears to be a legitimate form of oppression (Minichiello, Browne, and Kendig 2000) whose stubborn persistence, despite multiple efforts to dislodge it, highlights its power.

BRIEFLY NOTED: BODILY MARKERS AS A TRIGGER OF DISCRIMINATORY STEREOTYPING

For the individual, ageist responses are triggered by the devalued aging body (see chapter 1). When people look at us, they see not our hearts or our brains but our hair and our noses and our weight (see chapter 1). Today the "normal" human condition in our culture is youthful, active, and independent. It is speedy and technologically savvy. It is often impatient and committed to multitasking. Margaret Gullette (2004) describes it as the "speed-up" culture (30). Since the aging body deviates from these standards, it is less than "the fully, or naturally, or normally human" (M. Walker 1998b, 198) and so ripe for negative judgments. I'm in pretty good shape, and think I would pass muster as a reasonably well put-together seventy-three-year old. Yet as my outer body becomes "biologically and socially old" (Turner 1995, 250), I continue to be surprised when I am treated in response to that visible body. I regularly look at other women my age, especially if they are more substantially built than I am (i.e., taller and heavier) and with hair that is not liberally sprinkled with gray and wonder whether TSA agents would talk to them in the patronizing language with which they often talk to me.

AGEISM AND EVERYDAY LIFE

While our personal experiences with ageism vary with the contexts in which we find ourselves and the roles that we seek to play, older people can describe instances when they were treated, for example, disrespectfully, without attributing it to ageism. Such acknowledgment would mean accepting that they are old, an identification that they often fiercely resist (Hurd 1999). The practices and consequences of ageism are as diverse as everyday life since we encounter it in restaurants, at cosmetic counters, in gyms, in the health care system, in the media, and in the workplace. We are caught in the puzzling predicament of being simultaneously invisible and hypervisible. Our bodies make us stand out, but once we are seen, we become invisible. Feminist scholar Lynne Segal (2013) notes that we must face the challenge of holding onto some "sense of who we are even though we feel increasingly invisible" (1). Often ignored at meetings, we may protect ourselves by avoiding situations where we may encounter such marginalization. We also encounter ageism in physically and mentally hurtful ways when we are the victims of elder abuse and neglect. And while we may not always be aware of it, it is present in the often disrespectful ways political operatives treat residents of retirement communities (Leibovitch 2013) or tacitly blame older people for events beyond their control. An example is the "hanging chads" problem in the Bush-Gore vote count in 2000. Commentators regularly noted how many older people voted in the polling places where the "hanging chads" made the vote count problematic, as if the problem would not have occurred if the polling place had been on a college campus.

We may be most immediately familiar with ageism at the micro level as the result of age grading since it determines when we start school or get a driver's license or register to vote. These divisions are embedded in the social structures of our society. Age grading, which does not equate with age prejudice, may be exclusionary without intention. I use this example—it is only in the past twenty years or so that the possibilities for lifetime learning have gained attention. As ideas about old age changed, so did the notion that education was not just for the young. Age grading in terms of housing can be both advantageous or problematic; it can represent a comfortable way to live for women who have low incomes as it is for the women of Mayslake, but it can also be isolating and serve to reify the "us" and "them" dichotomy. Sunbelt and other retirement communities for the more affluent separate not only the young and the old but the old as consumers of certain lifestyles and the old as needy and sedentary (Laws 1995). As much as the postmodern dream for lessening age grading and for creating a free-flowing, age-irrelevant society, age grading, often with detrimental effects, persists (Bauman 1992; Blaikie 1999; Gilleard and Higgs 2000; Katz 2001–2002).

Ageism involves petty annoyances like being talked to as if we have the intelligence of a baboon (no insult to the baboon intended). It is manifest when people speak with great deliberation and in shorter sentences than they do with others, an experience that is often humiliating. I am reminded of the ticket agent at the Amtrak counter who slowly and deliberately told me not to lose the ticket that she just handed me because, if I do, I'll have to buy another one. Humiliation is among the most painful of social wrongs (Margalit 1996), yet old women experience it when they are treated, in Iva Brown's words, as if they don't know anything. We may feel humiliated because we are held individually responsible for not meeting normative ideals of health, which we may ourselves have internalized. Thus, ageism also harms because it reflects the unequal power in our society. Cultural meanings, after all, are not achieved by democratic consensus; they have "social and political origins and consequences, in private and public realms alike" (Fox and Lears 1993, 4).

Older women have described themselves as feeling like nuisances when salespeople in shops avoided them: "They don't want to see you coming" (Minichiello, Browne, and Kendig 2000). They noted that in restaurants they do not get the same kind of service and respect that they once did (Horton et al. 2008). Paternalistic or discounting behavior and language occurs regularly. Recently, a hospital ultrasound technician said to me, "Come this way, sweetheart," an experience that was instantly recognizable by the women of Mayslake, who also described servers and salespeople asking, "And what would you like, young lady?" Insisting that they mean only to be kind, such service providers fail to hear the condescension in their words. To treat anyone with patronizing speech reduces that person to childlike status by the powerful adult. Implicit in calling old women "young lady" is that age is a deficit and thus necessary to deny through flattery. Patronizing speech denies us our adult status (Cruikshank 2009). I ask, is it a sign of respect or due regard to call anyone "sweetheart" or "young lady" if she is older than ten? In contrast, Mary, the oldest member of our Mayslake group, takes such language as a compliment, as some old women might take demeaning birthday cards as funny. I suspect such responses mean that she has been acculturated and came of age in a society that was profoundly sexist and ageist and so does not react to language that denies age. She knows she is old (at ninety-one a hard fact to deny), but she accepts the language as flattering because it taps into the possibility that maybe she is not really old.

AGEISM AND PROFESSIONAL ENCOUNTERS

Ageism is manifest in medical encounters, in social services, and in long-term care, three of the most important areas where old women encounter prominent societal institutions. Care work, in particular, demonstrates how care providers who are not old assume that the older people they are caring for have "fewer needs than they themselves expect to have as care users in the future" (Jönson 2013, 200). The golden rule is nonoperative (e.g., do unto others as you would have them do unto you) in part because age relations hinders the establishment of relationships of equality. Below, I highlight by example a few ways in which ageism is often most apparent.

Medical Care

While the situation has undoubtedly improved since Samuel Shem (1978) described medical students' responses to old patients who would not die—GOMERs, or "Get Out of My Emergency Room"—physicians may share with the rest of the population ageist attitudes toward the aging body, often extended to the person herself (Reyes-Ortiz 1997). "That autonomy is the guiding principle of health care—that dependency is to be eschewed and hidden because it is embarrassing and undignified has ageist (not to mention ableist) implications" (Holstein, Parks, and Waymack 2011, 175). Old patients are often time consuming, have multiple chronic conditions, and are often accompanied by family members. Often referrals are not made and certain treatment options not offered. A cautionary note here—I am not advocating unlimited treatment, and I support a careful definition and assessment of potential benefits, but limited referrals for mental health services is an example where treatment can make a substantial difference. Yet depression is often left untreated because the possibilities for treatment are underestimated (Pasupathi and Lockenhoff 2002). It is worth, however, being alert to claims of ageism that may be otherwise explained. Robert and Rosalie Kane (2005) ask—is it age alone that leads to a particular medical decision about screening, referral, or treatment? Physicians may blame basic, treatable conditions on age and not offer the treatments they would offer a younger person. Mary from Mayslake recalled a time when, in her early seventies, her blood pressure became problematic. Her doctor's response was, "What do you expect at your age?" Mary never saw that doctor again. If this occurs once, you can think it is just that particular doctor. But when it is a recurring pattern—for you and for others—then one can see it as ageism. In its research, the International Longevity Center (ILC) at Columbia University (Anti-aging Task Force 2006) found that this kind of treatment was not atypical, a pattern that has been documented by others (Hajjar 2002). We can, however, discern the patronizing speech observed in the "tone, simplicity, or brevity of the communication. . . . Compared to young patients, old patients are addressed with less respect and less patience, given less precise information, and asked fewer open-ended questions" (Cruikshank 2009, 145). Doctors, for example, "tend to be less egalitarian, patient, respectful, engaged and optimistic with older patients" (Minichiello, Browne, and Kendig 2000, 255).

Enrollment of older people in clinical trials for both prescription drugs and treatments is limited (US Senate Special Committee on Aging 2003; Hutchins et al. 1999). The reason often given is that their conditions are so complex, the very reason that participation in such trials may be so valuable, a fact that is not obvious when the younger body is accepted as normative. Inevitably, the issue of spending on care for old people raises the issue of whether certain medical treatments ought to be explicitly rationed on the basis of age, a proposal that philosopher Daniel Callahan (1987) has made in a number of books and articles. Callahan would argue that after a certain age, roughly eighty-five, no life-extending treatments ought to be offered. Kane and Kane (2005), among other critics (Binstock and Post 1992), suggest that such rationing seems tied into concepts of worthiness linked to Medicare spending. They conclude, however, "that no matter how one cuts it, they seem to meet the criterion that they discriminate against people because of age alone" (52). Yet the irony is that today biomedicine is moving in the opposite direction as it normalizes many advanced therapies no matter the person's age (Kaufman 2006; see chapter 7). What is less clear at this point is the issue of class. Do "dual eligibles" (Medicare and Medicaid recipients) get the same treatment options as people with Medicare and a private supplemental policy?

Long-Term Care

In long-term care, as states move increasingly toward home and community-based care (see chapter 5), what younger people with disabilities find unacceptable is often taken for granted as acceptable for older people, especially the nursing home as a place of residence (Kane and Kane 2005). In long-term care, privacy is virtually nonexistent; a knock on the door means "I'm coming in" rather than "May I come in?" (Ray 2008). Care tends to be defined narrowly in that its relational qualities are downplayed and quality of care replaces efforts to improve quality of life (Tronto 1993; Glenn 2000; Kane 2001). Staying out of the nursing home takes priority over broad goals such as mobility and social participation. Older women, the primary recipients of care at home, often find themselves in a situation where deeply personal care is rendered mechanically or when they must accept help from their family members, most often daughters, because there is no other option (see chapter 5). While the absence of adequate public options is a primary reason that choices are so limited, it also sends a tacit message about the value of late life, what some describe as the fourth age.

Social Services

When receiving care in their homes for nonmedical but essential services, women are open to the charge of burdening society by virtue of their needs. It is no surprise that women experience this charge more often than men. Women are more numerous than men in late life, they are often widowed and so do not have a spouse to care for them, and they generally lack the resources to pay for private assistance (Gullette 2011). In care situations, they may become, in Margaret Walker's (1998b) terms, "diminished" subjects, the cause of lesser respect, concern, compassion, or reciprocity (194). The way old women are treated in these settings also reflects existing power relationships, given professional control over resources and definitions of the problem. Some patients are often referred to as "difficult" or even toxic, reflecting a problem to be managed rather than a chance to understand the situation from the recipients' perspective. Social-service programs rely on a relatively narrow view of autonomy that is limited to choice from preexisting options that often are meaningless to recipients. In contrast, as philosopher George Agich (1995) frames it, actual autonomy is not primarily about specific or nodal decisions but rather about the ability to live in habitual ways, a goal that care plans and limited resources make particularly difficult to achieve for most people.

In some cases, treatment might be paternalistic "even if people are, in fact, capable of assessing their own goals and making their own choices" (M. Walker 1998b, 195). Care provision does not demand moral regard or recognizing the person as being "like me." Care providers may have a hard time seeing that the recipients of care are an "extension of [their] future selves . . . rather [they are seen] as totally apart" from the person providing care (Andrews 1999, 303). We construct separation—an "us" and a "them"—and imagine that we need not ever become "them." In the summer of 2013, the concept of burden became a political strategy in the endless war against "Obamacare" as ads showed young people complaining that they were being forced to buy health insurance so that older, sicker people—and, by implication, people who did not plan responsibly for their futures—could get subsidies. This construction of burden is part of the larger message that aging itself is a problem.

AGEISM AND WORK

The workplace is a primary site of ageist practices (Laws 1995), thus women have a hard time reentering the workforce should they lose their jobs or drop out to provide care or for other reasons. Managers often see older workers as "too costly, too inflexible and too difficult to train" (Minichiello, Browne, and Kendig 2000, citing Imel 1996). Women often face discriminatory practices based on their aging appearances rather than performance (McMullin and Berger 2006). Hence, more women than men try to systematically alter their appearance in an effort to overcome this bias. If I were looking for a new job today, I might consider not only masking my early jobs on my resume in order to hide my age but also covering the gray in my hair. Seeking a more youthful appearance is considered necessary in the marketplace and a source of power for women who see it as a route to achievement, economic gain, and wider opportunities. To assume that surgical or other cosmetic interventions like Botox are important and even necessary to keep or get a job symbolizes the economic and social control of consumer culture and of youth over age and is an indictment of the culture that makes this even a possibility (McMullin and Berger 2006).

Discrimination in the workforce may best be understood as involving both sex and age, with women encountering more discrimination than men and older workers more discrimination than younger workers. Thus, it is fair to argue that "sexism and ageism combine to reduce older women's job opportunities" (McMullin and Berger 2006) at the same time that policymakers are advocating for raising the Social Security retirement age because older people are presumed to be healthier and therefore able to work longer (see chapter 6).

OTHER SITES OF AGEISM

Ageism is reflected in how the media represents old women (Kessler, Rakoczy, and Staudinger 2004; Cruikshank 2009) and in ads (Calasanti 2007; Robinson, Gustafson, and Popovich 2008), and in how we are *not* represented in fashion magazines or clothing design (Twigg 2008; Lewis, Medvedev, and Seponski 2011). Media images generally offer two dichotomous images of older women. We are doddering, silly, frail, and meddlesome, or we are sleek, sexy, and bossy. Rarely do the media show us images that realistically feature women who are complex, reflective, and engaged in varied roles. A caveat—my friends tell me to watch shows like *Modern Family*, where the characters are more ordinary and familiar. In general, however, less than 2 percent of prime-time television characters are over sixty-five (Anti-aging Task Force 2006, 12, citing Donlon, Ashman, and Levy 2005). Given that television is a major source of representations in American life, the absence of diverse older women is a lost opportunity for broadening perspectives about women in late life.

Clothing may seem like a minor matter, but as Twigg (2008) points out, "clothes are the key mediators between the body and the social world" (160). Clothing communicates messages about gender, race, class, age, era, our attitudes toward our own bodies, and even political persuasion. Among older women, how many of us want a choice between baggy, multicolored print tops made of some unknown fabric and cleavage-revealing T-shirts? Few of us want to be "mutton dressed like lamb." Perhaps I exaggerate, but while skinny jeans and low-rise pants may not suit our bodies or our styles, neither do the baggy "mommy jeans" that replace them. If I, a relatively small person, shop carefully for elbow-length sleeves and skirts that touch my knees, it is possible to dress in a way that projects a relatively accurate image of whom I see myself to be; but if one is larger, that becomes increasingly problematic.

AGEISM AND PUBLIC POLICY

Ageism also plays a part in politics. How often, for example, have we heard about the high costs of the last year of life? Commonly, the implication is that it was somehow the user's fault, yet the issue is generally far more nuanced. Considerable responsibility rests with the medical care system and in the complexity and even normativity of advanced treatment options (Kaufman 2006). Thus, the physical realities of late life often become the locus of blame by policymakers who do not see themselves as one day being similarly situated. Thus, ageism gains strength from the distorted and evasive assumption that we will not be like that, that we will somehow not "let ourselves go," that we will maintain a high level of fitness, that we will not need to have our beds made or our meals prepared, or that we can simply pay someone to do it. Ageism means that inequalities originating earlier in life and thus influence who would be in a wheelchair and who on the ski slope at eighty will not be remedied, a consequence of the individualistic ideology that holds us responsible for how we age (Calasanti, Slevin, and King 2006). When ageism intersects with other inequalities, it makes sense that the eighty-two-year-old millionaire legislator will not identity with—and therefore try to help—his eighty-two-year-old contemporary—a woman whose home care services plummeted from twenty hours to ten hours a week when she was enrolled in a Medicaid managed-care program (Bernstein 2014). Individuals who are privileged by virtue of age or gender or class have no reason to see and thus resist ageist perspectives, especially when maintaining them serves the individuals' interests (Bytheway 1995).

Ageism has justified opposite policy positions. In the first half of the century, it legitimated policy interventions based on a compassionate view of the needy old (Binstock 1983), what feminist Barbara MacDonald (1991, with Cynthia Rich) described as "exploitation by compassion." Today, blame—for allowing themselves to have health or financial needs and for "busting the budget"—has replaced compassion and serves as a justification for reducing expenditures directed toward old people (Katz and Calasanti 2014; Hepworth 1995) (see the introduction and chapter 6). British political economist Alan Walker (2012) labels the ageist assumption that an aging population will result in explosive costs an "evidence free zone" (816). He further challenges the underlying narrative that supports the new ageism—a homogeneous vision of older people as financial consumers of precious health resources who deprive children and other citizens. We see this claim manifest whenever policymakers or pundits appeal to the dependency ratio, as if the shrinking of working age to retired individuals clinched the afford-ability argument; yet challenges to the use of that ratio (Binstock 1992) question its disregard for the increase in women's labor-force participation and the decline in the size of the younger population. It is further manifest in political assumptions about the political power of a unified bloc of older voters, a view challenged in both the United Kingdom and the United States (Binstock 2000, 2012; A. Walker 2012).

The generational equity debate, discussed in chapter 6, constructs the equity debate as between old and young people, where the young are paying the price for the exaggerated attention to the old. This argument, initially constructed "as a front for a neoconservative campaign against the welfare state" (A. Walker 2012, 815) found in the old a more convenient scapegoat than, for example, the tax expenditures that serve the more affluent. The contemporary rhetoric of generational inequities ignores important causes of childhood poverty and continues to blame programs for the old. At the same time, its advocates further reduce the budget for programs that actually help kids, like SNAP (food stamps). The media nonetheless continues to fuel the conflict between old and young (Jacoby 2011; A. Walker 2012). As dis-cussed elsewhere in this book, ageist assumptions, although not the only reason, thus justify and fuel the neoliberal agenda, a combustible mix if one worries about the future of being an old woman in this society. The con-structed idea of generational conflict reflects the role of scapegoating, an-other particularly insidious manifestation of ageism (Gullette 2011; see chap-ter 6). It is an essential element in the retreat from the social safety net that has and will continue to undercut the fundamental need that we all share for safety and security.

AGEISM, IDENTITY, AND SOCIAL RECOGNITION

Ageism thus matters in countless ways. What I have recounted in the previ-ous sections is more easily documented than the subtle harms that are exis-tential, psychological, and moral. A common concern, for example, that many of us share is the wish to be our own person, to know who we are and what matters to us and to have other people respect those qualities in us. For this to happen, social recognition is essential. The absence of respect and recognition is what Iva Brown felt. To be our own person means that we recognize our capacities and limitations and that we are able to "enact [our] introspective understanding of [our] 'true' selves in [our] everyday lives" (Meyers 2002, 11–12). It also means that others acknowledge our identities and self-conceptions. The need to struggle for such recognition is a particularly damaging consequence of ageism, which is exclusionary by definition. It denies us acknowledgment for identities we value.

A friend, then in her seventies, a member of her church's finance committee and with long experience in nonprofit organizations, commented that when she made a point it was passed over; if a younger (especially male) member of the committee made a similar point, everyone listened. In a recent interview, Supreme Court Justice Ruth Bader Ginsburg (Liptak 2014) recalled that when she was the only woman on the court, her comments were passed over in judicial conferences, in this case an example of sexism but a clear parallel to ageist behavior. Such gendered, ageist responses may tacitly bar us from full participation in groups to which we might wish to belong. A sense of belonging, as Abraham Maslow (1943) defines it, is a basic human need. Without it, it becomes more difficult to see ourselves as capable of effective action, which in turn further erodes our capacity for autonomous moral agency (Mackenzie 2000). Moreover, If we cannot gain recognition for what we know, for how we present ourselves, our ability to enact valued parts of our identity is limited, which in turn narrows our scope of action and blocks our access to valuable social roles, often leading to avoidance of certain activities in order to protect self-esteem (Horton et al. 2008). Almost casual insults like my friend experienced can accumulate and lead us to withdraw from situations where such experiences are likely. We may disengage not because we want to but because engagement can threaten our senses of worthiness, an ironic rebuttal to the demands of the new aging for engagement (see chapter 3). Women have, by necessity, developed strong self-defense mechanisms to protect themselves from such insults (Whitbourne and Sneed 2002b), but the price is steep—a narrowing world.

In response, we may opt to behave in ways that reflect stereotypes (Whitbourne and Sneed 2002b) or we may restrict our activities to places where we feel most fully ourselves and where that self is respected. That's one reason the grandmother role is such a comforting one. In this context, women confirm existing stereotypes; when we do so, we are more apt to be liked—another reason that our worlds may narrow (Cuddy, Norton, and Fiske 2005). Grandmas, like women in the 1950s, belong on pedestals and not in Congress or in the boardroom or on a solo hike in Costa Rica.

Because a dominant theme in American society is the importance of choice and individual responsibility, older women can become entangled in a web of self-blame if they do not get the recognition they think they deserve. We may then take responsibility for our exclusion rather than locate the difficulty in the ageism that permits others to marginalize us. In one qualitative study looking at the effects of ageism, Queniart and Charpentier (2012) found that older women respondents understood, if tacitly so, that old age was a process that "structures every dimension of their lives: their identity as a woman and their positions and role in society, a position that is all too often on the margins or peripheral to social action and engagement" (995).

This difficulty parallels the problems that women have faced historically because we live in a male-dominated culture. Such dominance limited our ability to remake our lives on our own terms by damaging our capacities for agency (Meyers 2002; Furman 1997; M. Walker 1998b). Now that ability can be thwarted by efforts, ironically, to improve our status, but only if we meet new culturally normative standards (see chapter 3). The downside, as I shall argue in the next chapter, is that these new norms are best suited for middle-class, white women with ample leisure and the ability and will to choose activity over other valued ways to live.

In writing about her own aging, feminist philosopher Sandra Bartky (1999) identifies one by one the parts of herself that no longer receive affirmation. She sees old age as a series of losses and notes specifically the loss of social and intellectual networks, the increasing irrelevance of our knowledge, and the "loss of the admiring gaze" (67). Her sense of what is worthy in her identity is bound up with how its relevant parts are reinforced or undermined in different social spheres. Bartky's concept of loss encompasses her whole self and has little relationship to her physical condition.

THE DENIAL OF AGE: RESISTING OR REINFORCING AGEISM?

Despite the language of the "new" aging that is the subject of the next chapter and its optimistic picture of what aging can and should be like, being old is still the less powerful and hence the less desirable status in comparison with being young. Cecilia Ridgeway's (2011) comment about gender that "difference easily becomes inequality" holds for age as well. Thus, the "new aging" that I will discuss in the next chapter seeks to efface difference by espousing a conception of late life as basically a continuation of midlife. In this way, it is assumed that the grounds for ageism will be deconstructed for most people who are old and reserved for those who are different by virtue of their disabilities. These new aims have migrated from the academy to the media and to consumer industries and so have been adopted by many women as a way to situate themselves in the "not old," that is, the devalued category. The result is that they resist ageism as represented by negative stereotyping by denying that they fit that devalued category (Queniart and Charpentier 2012; Minichiello, Browne, and Kendig 2000). This plea for personal exceptionalism does not confront or eliminate ageist stereotypes but denies their application to themselves (Andrews 1999). The words are familiar: I am not like "them"—that is, the familiar stereotypes. Internalizing ageist attitudes and assumptions, age deniers identify old people who act and look "old" in stereotypical ways as different from me because of my relative youthfulness and good health (Horton et al. 2008). The label "old woman" belongs to someone they have not yet become—a person who has slowed down, who is inactive, bored, and isolated (Queniart and Charpentier 2012; Mayslake May 13, 2013). It means that I am okay only if I am like someone younger, that is, an idealized younger person who takes care of herself, keeps up, stays active, and never forgets a name. As Andrews (1999) comments, the best result is that one has made an exception of oneself, "which is based on an illusion and which leaves intact the larger structure of oppression" (307).

Yet the phenomenon is both common and understandable given the ageist culture in which we live. The women at Mayslake (July 8, 2012, and July 22, 2013) avidly distanced themselves from old people who sit in rocking chairs; "We are busy, involved, informed (all accurate); we don't sit in our rooms." We are not like the women who live in the past, who lack interests and are waiting to die, who don't pay at least some attention to how they look. They reject images that evoke bodily and mental deterioration despite the health problems that they have. The goal is to prevent others from "seeing them as old and treating them as old" (Minichiello, Browne, and Kendig 2000, 273). These efforts suggest how marginalization and the "tension between personal and structural identity" push people to adopt coping strategies so that they can "continue to live and develop in circumstances not of their own choosing" (Biggs 2004, 46). "The need to deny old age is at the heart of ageism" (Calasanti, Slevin, and King 2006, 16). In the words of writer Susan Jacoby (2011), such denial represents "submission, not resistance, to cultural prejudice" (11). If I respond to the old and ugly version of my seventy-three-year-old self by getting a face-lift or liposuction, I am embracing the story of old and ugly rather than resisting it. Yet, in all fairness, I note that there is also the possibility that should I choose to take advantage of such practices, I am potentially expanding the range of what a seventy-three-year-old woman can look like and thus perhaps the roles she can play (Lindemann Nelson 1999). My own view, however, suggests that the face-lift as resistance fails because it leaves the "old is ugly" position intact; it reinforces the idea that beauty is the measure of worth; and it is itself only a temporary solution, for even face-lifts go only so far in altering our aging faces. It also reinforces the idea that our appearance tells a fair story of who we are. One cannot vitiate an oppression by leaving it in place so that it applies to others in the oppressed group.

A corollary to the notion that one is not old is the insistence that old people "like us" are, in fact, "young" (Calasanti 2008, 155), often designated with the phrase "young at heart." This affirmation of agelessness or youthfulness assumes we can transcend age, a goal that is the "product of a society which tells us that age—old age—is something to be transcended if at all possible" (Andrews 1999, 301). If one can't change the power of binaries—young is better than old—then claiming to belong to the valued category is a sensible, albeit problematic, strategy. Hence, the now familiar adages are often voiced—seventy is the new fifty, or you are only as old as you feel; age is irrelevant. Rather than understanding the "ageless self" as a reflection of continuity with one's past, of being oneself and recognizing oneself as one ages (Atchely 1987; Kaufman 1987), the affirmation of agelessness becomes an active form of age denial. In this way of thinking, ageism can be erased by eliminating the category of old age until such time as denial is no longer possible. If I don't feel old, then I am not old.

Thus, while it is understandable as a personal strategy, age denial is also ultimately a failing one. It does not protect one from discrimination based on age, or if it does, it is only for a narrow window of time and then at great cost and so available for only the more affluent. It costs us in other ways. Think of the herculean efforts it takes to monitor oneself for signs of oldness and to act when they appear; think of the potential for self-blame if our efforts to be "not old" fail (Hurd 1999; Minichiello, Browne, and Kendig 2000; Jönson 2013; Queniart and Charpentier 2012). Imagine the struggle one faces to exempt oneself from the group in which others place us.

My concern—and a reason why I am so uneasy with the "third" age and "fourth" age distinction that I discuss in chapter 5—is that the struggle to be "not old" is also a struggle in opposition to our probable future selves. If being "not old" is the success story, what happens when we can no longer make that claim even to ourselves? The precarious ledge on which women walk as they seek to be "not old" leaves no option but a precipitous fall when a stroke or dementia or severe arthritis makes it impossible to enact the prescribed lifestyles. We are perpetually at risk for jeopardizing our moral standing in the community (M. Walker 1998b) because the moral community constructed by the third- and fourth-age distinctions excludes the already old.

For all the extraordinary and fit ninety-year-olds that the media present to us or the images of a sixty-eight-year-old Hillary Rodham Clinton considering a presidential bid, discrimination is not eradicated. After several decades (see chapter 3) of popular and academic attention to successful aging and related concepts, negative stereotypes remain, and anomalies remain just that—anomalies and not a challenge to stereotypes. Blame escalates while ageism remains. In the absence of a sustained "structural critique" (Andrews 1999, 305) that exposes how ageism operates, it will persist. By denying the old "their rightful category," notes Molly Andrews, "we do not remedy the problems perpetrated by an ageist society" (311). Instead we help perpetuate them. At the same time, these commitments to agelessness obscure challenges that often accompany late life and efface the strengths that may be particularly suited to the old.

Efforts to be seen as not old also don't work very well. We may change our appearance, dress in unique clothing, and get great haircuts, but none of those makes us fifty again. My friend, now eighty, loves to wear outrageously bold socks and to leap onto the bus, but she wryly comments that "people still jump up to give me a seat," which she insists on refusing. When we can embrace old age, we can still wear bold socks and wildly colored sneakers because we like them and not because we think it will give us youthful credibility. Being young is not the only way to have a good life (Mayslake, July 2014). It limits our opportunities to be "free to be me," as Carol, a member of our Mayslake group, sees as one of the privileges of being in her sixties.

What if we aimed at living fully as an old person as we transitioned into late life, smiled when offered a seat, and thanked the person who grabbed our arm as we started to slide on the icy sidewalk? The aim to be perpetually young is falsely optimistic and tends to erase what is unique and important about being old. In an important sense, it creates a new essentialism, the central feature of which is refusal to define oneself as old (Queniart and Charpentier 2012). I will touch upon more sustained efforts to challenge ageism later in this chapter and then more fully in the concluding chapter.

DECONSTRUCTING AGEISM

In defining ageism and describing how it works, I relied on the analysis of age relations developed by feminist scholars (see citations above) since that explanation emerges from observable phenomena in the everyday world and, as such, gives us a way to begin to deconstruct it by rupturing or at least lessening the power that is vested in different age locations. A valued status endows one with power, and difference assigned to age or gender or other categorical features of individual lives is the source of that power. Thus, while the new aging has sought to erase difference, as discussed above, its way of doing so—by situating old people as just like younger people only older, a topic I will return to in the next chapter, may have had limited successes without really deconstructing how ageism works.

We can understand how ageism operates by considering how it plays a role in maintaining the valued status of in-groups. Stereotypes signal who is part of the "in-group," membership in which establishes a desired sense of belonging, trust, and self-esteem but also of power. "In-group" members, whatever the unifying element, rely on categorization and sharp contrasts that preserve binaries (e.g, young-old) to protect the self and preserve the power relationships that uphold the first side of the binary. Stereotypes are thus a source of both inclusion and exclusion. The "privileged position of one group relies on the disadvantaged position of another" (Calasanti and Slevin 2001, 3) since it offers specific advantages like success in the job market. Cognitive shortcuts, based on cultural representations of older people, preserve one's in-group status. As a result, members "may treat stereotyped groups, including older people, in particularly pre-emptory ways, to maintain power hierarchies with older people toward the bottom" (Cuddy and Fiske 2002, 16).

Difference is a central feature of today's understanding of the world. Difference may be lodged in biological or other definable facts or in the environments in which we live, but its meanings are socially constructed. They matter most when the differences also reflect differences in power. The environments in which we live tend to be inhospitable to old people. Traffic lights may not give us enough time to get across the street, and so drivers blame us for being slow and old. Or, as Anita Silver (1999) suggests, if everyone used a wheelchair to get around, the meanings attached to mobility-limiting disability would change. Thus, our environments reinforce the ageist stereotypes that already narrow our worlds. If we live in the suburbs or in cities without good public transportation and we no longer drive because we can't afford a car or because our vision is no longer acute enough for driving, we inadvertently contribute to the stereotypes that blame us for becoming so cloistered. We live in a culture defined by the able-bodied—the "normal"— and the slim and fit, an odd claim given the prevalence of obesity in our culture. Dualistic thinking, as typically conceived, assesses difference against a normative standard. Thus, old age is deviant when judged against this standard, which is based on youth. Similarly, male is the normal, female the other; beauty takes priority over ugly and activity over sedentary. This way of conceiving difference assigns power in defining what is good and desirable to the "normal" and limits and often denies older women their own voice, thus tilting social power from old to young people. What would happen if we saw difference in relational terms, in which there is no standard of normality and the differences between age groups can each be taken on their own terms? The goal is to be at seventy what is possible for us then and not what was possible for us at fifty (Scannell 2006). Why measure ourselves against a norm that we will, most likely, be less able to meet than women who are really fifty?

Other explanations move from *how* to *why*. A basic psychological explanation, for example, is that distancing provides a means of managing fears— of death and of losing beauty, youth, and strength (Grefe 2011). This theoretical approach, labeled "terror management," lets the young elevate their differences from the old as a protective device (Greenberg, Schimel, and Mertens 2002, 37). We may also wish to protect ourselves from accepting the transience of youth and beauty and strength. If we can attribute "letting oneself go" and other signs of aging to personal failings, then whatever negative judgments we make become acceptable since those changes won't happen to us. We won't "let ourselves go" or permit "oldness" to take over our bodies. Notions of personal control and individual responsibility thus fuel ageism in ways that work less well with characteristics like gender and race, over which we have no control.

Ageism is regularly reinforced in the arts and cultural imagery. Think of Shakespeare's tragedy *King Lear* or the comedy *As You Like It*, where aging is mocked, although those plays are so much more than that. Children's stories and fairy tales, Disney films and cartoons, and other popular media often transform old women into witches and hags, ugly and sexless. Images of loving grandmothers also appear, but they too have a stereotypical appearance—chubby, gray haired, not beautiful by the reigning stereotypes of beauty, and sexless (see Woodward 1991). They do not look like the House minority leader, Nancy Pelosi, or former secretary of state Madeleine Albright, both grandmothers. They don't look like me. Hence, unappealing images, both the cause and the effect of stereotypes, are not hard to find. Are these images cause or effect? Or are they both cause *and* effect? Given that these images are produced by those who are a part of a society in which ageism is deeply rooted, it is impossible to separate media from that ageism. From that standpoint, we cannot point to such images as causal, as if they somehow stand apart from the culture from which they stem. But they certainly reflect that ageism.

Stereotypes draw attention to the instances in which the stereotypes fit "while screening out or cordoning off the ones that don't" (M. Walker 1998b, 193, citing Code 1991). One reason for this is that individuals want to believe that the "social structures to which they belong are just and fair"; thus, people whose actions or behaviors confirm stereotypes about them may be "particularly welcome, as such confirmation makes the world a fair and predictable place" (Cuddy, Norton, and Fiske 2005, 276). It is as if the identity that stereotypes bestow "naturally befitted the people" (M. Walker 1998b, 178), making it particularly difficult for the individual older person to alter expectations. This difficulty is one reason that women like Hillary Rodham Clinton or Nancy Pelosi or Madeleine Albright, for example, or hurdle-jumping or marathoner grandmothers persist as anomalies without changing the more familiar stereotypes. They have not led to more generalized incorporation of "stereotype-incongruent information" (Cuddy and Fiske 2002, 15). I wonder if the Facebook generation of old people will result in disconfirming stereotypes since we may "know" them through their postings before we know their age.

In general, these understandings may explain why presenting the "facts of aging" in contrast to the "myths of aging" have not succeeded in overcoming ageism. Facts of aging are another way of trying to dissolve difference. But difference is stubborn, and myths serve the important function of making us "not them" for as long as possible. Nor can "facts" overturn the loss in status that accompanies the withdrawal from socially valued roles. In general, as older people lose status, that loss precipitates an altered view of their competence, as Sandra Bartky (1999) so clearly describes. As Cuddy and Fiske (2002) observe, "Older people have suffered the loss of status as a result of displacement from the workforce, loss of income, transience of extended family members, and the obsolescence of the spoken word" (13). None of these trends is apt to be reversed, but they point to the deep and complex structure of ageism.

In the concluding chapter, I will explore the possible options we may have to resist this demeaning and inaccurate assessment of old age. At a minimum, we must name it whenever and wherever we can. It is also one more reason to be wary of the "ageless" language. If we can be held accountable for our failures to resist becoming old, we reinforce that scapegoating agenda.

CONCLUSION

The forms of resistance that are so prominent today will not alter societal ageism. Individual acts of defiance and agency will not alone, in the long run, change the system (Furman 1999). Resistance, to be comprehensive, needs to systematically involve many people in some organized way. It will probably start at the middle level and work its way outward (Blaikie 1999). I'll touch upon this theme here in brief and then pick it up in more detail in the book's last chapter. In advance, I suggest that we start not with the complexities that originate in age relations and in the intersections of multiple inequalities but with women taking responsibility for proudly owning the "inevitability of aging" and poking fun at our society's unrealistic idea that youthful beauty and sexuality are obtainable and desirable for all (Furman 1999, 17). We need what Hilde Lindemann Nelson (1999) calls a counterstory that allows us to "sustain or reclaim a practical identity that is threatened by something or someone she can't control" (85). How much better it would be if we tell these stories to and with others.

Thus, I believe that one important way to approach negative valuations of age is not to deny differences but to embrace them and then tell the stories that will change, over time and with good fortune, the meanings associated with those differences and, perhaps one day, the power also associated with them. When we critique age relations as often and as publicly as we can, we can help others see that marginalization doesn't have to happen. It is the result of the "intersections of multiple hierarchies" and thus helps to explain the problem with, for example, successful aging (Calasanti, Slevin, and King 2006, 15). That paradigm fails to notice that it leaves out people with low incomes, with little leisure time, and with a history of poor access to health care, yet those very people will then be the victims of ageism. In so many ways, old women collaborate with those who would demean us as we resist being old. If we avoid it, why should anyone who is younger than we are reward it?

I don't, however, want to ignore the political and the institutional. We may need to be angry in order for change to occur. I want to show anger without being labeled a grouch, which is often how displays of anger by old women are taken. As Kathleen Woodward (2002) observed, "Anger can be a sign of moral outrage at social injustice, at being denied the right to partici- pate fully in society" (206). Avoidance of "outlaw emotions" (Jaggar 1989) gives tacit permission for injustices to continue. Anger is an indictment of a society that permits the old to be patronized, that limits us in the social roles we can play and the identities we can enact and sets us up as the "other," on the wrong side of the binary. Anger will call out Jon Stewart when he mocks the old, and anger will challenge the privileged decision makers who have adopted a narrative about old age that omits far too many people but uses that narrative as a justification for budget cutting.

Reluctantly, I reiterate questions that Kevin McHugh (2003) posed a decade ago: Is ageism so ingrained in our society and culture, including the enterprise of gerontology, that no resistance will work? Or can we learn from movements to mitigate sexism and racism and make some changes, if not eliminate it completely? Is it so embedded in relationships of power that it can be ameliorated only in small ways until those systems are fundamentally altered? What we see and hear about most commonly are efforts to negate old age. As described in chapter 3, when I asked a group of women gerontol- ogists, all over sixty-five, what they meant when they promoted "positive" aging, I felt a little hopeful. These women spoke tellingly in language that did not rely on being "not old." They recognized that age was more than a number and that we are not only as old as we feel. I would plead, however, that the term "successful" " aging be abandoned and replaced with embracing old age. Why introduce yet another binary that assumes an unequal relation- ship? Or we might turn to Margaret Cruikshank's (2009) suggestion—that if we are to learn to be old, we must try to imagine ourselves free from at least many negative beliefs about old age and imagine a society in which policy supported healthy aging. We learn to be old by shedding the norms and values that others impose on us.

To reverse age denial and be old proudly means redefining "old" in our own terms. Yet I believe that we must do so not by valorizing the excep- tion—the head-standing great-grandmother—but by defining "old" so that it narrates the complex identities, the many pleasures but also the pains, and the ways of life that constitute old age. Not only does the anomaly—the head-standing great–grandmother—not translate into greater acceptance, but it upholds standards that are alien to most of us. In brief, we need to work to create and engage in paths of resistance so that no one will think those ageist birthday cards or jokes are just fun. We will hold Jon Stewart accountable for his ageist words and try to recruit him as a spokesperson. We will need to name unequal power relationships when we see them so that they become part of the political debate in this country. To age consciously and tell our stories about what it is like for us is one way for us to be in charge of our identity as we become and are old. As we learn to be old, we also can teach others (Cruikshank 2009). As we refuse to cede power to younger people to define what is good and desirable, we claim our ability to define our identity on our own terms. As Ray (2006) further reminds us, "We must allow women's bodies, minds, and spirits to grow into old age" (42). These tasks will not be easy, but they are necessary if we are to have the chance to age well both now and even when we begin to experience limitations (see chapter 5).

I return to Simone de Beauvoir (1973), who says, "If we do not know what we are going to be, we cannot know what we are: let us recognize ourselves in this old man or in that old woman. That task must be done if we are to take upon ourselves the entirety of our human state" (14). The old woman we brush past or fail to notice is our future self (ix). It is really up to us. If we cannot own our own aging and respect what we are at sixty or seventy or eighty or ninety, how can we expect others to respect us? As a feminist and critical gerontologist, I see all that I write and speak about as a way to transform the inequalities that continue to define life for old women. My friends and colleagues may grow weary of my insistence that we embrace our old age and seek ways to make the personal the political, but if we cannot do it, who will?

Chapter Three

The "New" Old Age

From Productive Aging to Anti-Aging and
Everything in Between

In the late 1980s, Scott Bass invited me to a meeting at the Boston campus of the University of Massachusetts to discuss productive aging with the intent of producing an edited volume (see Bass, Caro, and Chen 1993). Then, in my late forties, my immediate response was to ask, "Why would we want to valorize productivity as a new norm for late life?" It seemed to me then, as it does now, that its market and monetized orientation would inadvertently disadvantage women as the norms of market productivity did throughout their earlier lives. It made little sense to advocate for the continuation of a system that was fundamentally inequitable and exclusive. This issue was just one of many that I wondered about before, during, and after that meeting and that I will discuss more fully later in the chapter. At the same time, while I have been a critic from these early days, I have appreciated then and continue to appreciate the commitments to end ageism, expand opportunities, and reject negative portrayals, captured in the greedy geezer imagery (see chapter 6) that I heard at that meeting. My disagreements, however, reach deeply into the approaches adopted to reach these ends and with the conclusions reached.

Whether this new and dominant discourse about late life is called successful aging or the third age or productive aging or the new aging (my preference), it reflects a particular model of what old age is and ought to be that centers on agelessness, independence, activity, productivity, and the self as an independently constructed project (Biggs et al. 2006; Lamb 2014). These

91

ends are disconnected from one's gender or race or class or other significant shapers of one's life. Based on assumptions about individual health and relative affluence, the new aging praises and rewards certain behaviors, universalizes their value, and assumes equal potential and responsibility to enact these behaviors, which are deemed good for individuals and good for society. By linking these two ends—individual and society—the new aging transformed the "good" old person, that is, the person who best realized these aims, into the "good" citizen. This paradigmatic person represented the neoliberal view that the individual and not the collectivity or the public sector was responsible for individual well-being.

These attitudes and cultural values stimulated scholarship and infused popular culture. In the transition, however, scholarly responsibility dissipated. It is important to bear in mind, however, that even responsible scholarship, which lacks a specifically critical element, tends to reinforce rather than interrogate dominant values. It is more apt to analyze how those values can be achieved rather than questioning the values themselves. Thus, in what has become broadly inclusive and widely accepted as a public, cultural discourse has become a yardstick for self-evaluation, a base for policy deliberations and decisions and the grounding for a new ageism, although its intent was the opposite.

Because the new aging reflects and reinforces culture as deeply as it does academic research, in what follows I turn first to the broad sociocultural context in which it was birthed and now flourishes. While I do not attribute causality, researchers and their chosen research questions are not immune from broader social and political values. Thus, when I tried to separate the new aging from its contemporary context, I couldn't do it. It would not have happened, for example, in the 1930s or the 1960s. Take just one of its aspects—individual responsibility—and try to place it in a speech that might have been given by President Roosevelt in 1936 when he assumed it was the responsibility of the public sector to assure than no one should be ill housed, ill fed, or without medical care. Compare these views to those that dominated in 2008 or 2009, when the United States faced its worst economic crisis since the Depression, and the power of cultural and political norms becomes clear.

From the context, I will briefly describe the new aging's scholarly and popular components, which together define what may be described as a new stage in life—the third age—that comes between retirement and the onset of life-limiting disabilities (Laslett 1991) that transcend age. I will thus be considering "a new public discourse about what it means to be old" (Martinson and Minkler 2006, 321). My main concern, however, is to consider why its power to inspire cannot override its limits, an argument that I have already foreshadowed. In my conclusion, I will consider how we might develop alternative strategies to reach worthy goals of the new aging, which I will look at more fully in the last chapter.

THE BIRTH OF THE NEW AGING:
ITS SOCIAL, CULTURAL, AND POLITICAL CONTEXT

While perhaps obvious, the movement to research and promote the new aging did not occur in a vacuum. It fits with the political, cultural, and social context that took shape in the late 1970s and persists today. While I will not try to trace its origins, the late 1970s witnessed an upheaval in ideas that birthed the individualism that we see exemplified in the new aging, in neoliberal politics, and in much of social life today. Intellectual historian Daniel Rodgers (2011) points out that in the late 1970s, this country began, not by chance, to move from one "thick with context, social circumstances, institutions, and history" to one that stressed "choice, agency, performance, and desire. Strong measures of society were supplanted by weaker ones. . . . One heard less about society, history, and power and more about individuals, contingency, and choice. . . . Identities became fluid and elective" (3).

Similarly, journalist and Brookings scholar E. J. Dionne (2012) comments that "our country has witnessed the rise of a radical form of individualism that simultaneously denigrates the role of government and the importance most Americans attach to community" (5). The concept of society itself seemed to disappear. In this same individualistic vein, women in the 1970s were told they could "have it all" solely by their own hard work (Rosen 2000), and many men and women embraced the narcissism of therapeutic culture (Lasch 1979; Rieff 1966). These shifts in ideas and their practical consequences in many areas of thought and practice as well as the basic fact that many of us were indeed living longer and in better health are the foundation on which scholars, popularizers, and many old people developed and promoted the new aging.

These broader changes in society also fit with changes in thinking about the life course as traditional age categories shifted and blurred (Settersten 2007). Experimentation with new lifestyles made possible in part by greater affluence fostered acceptance of even further changes. While grandmothers continued to babysit for grandchildren and some also assumed responsibility for raising them, they also went back to school or took up new hobbies or continued working into their seventies. The postmodern commitment to self-invention touched the old as well, although perhaps in more limited ways than its advocates had hoped (Gergen and Gergen 2000). Yet certain "life-style" retirement communities are built upon the values that define the new aging in all its varieties (McHugh 2000).

The new aging also had its prominent leaders, geriatricians like Drs. Robert Butler and Jack Rowe, which contributed to its favorable reception (Dillaway and Byrnes 2009), and for many in the gerontological community, successful and productive aging opened new areas of research that quickly generated a relatively vast scholarship. The new aging also gave women a platform, supported by AARP's and other popular publications, from which they could distance themselves from negative stereotyping and decline im-agery. That appeal extended to commercial interests that invented "senior living industries" and created a booming market in anti-aging products. Ready to offer support were also the more affluent among the "baby boom-ers" who saw themselves as harbingers of change who would not allow themselves to conform to traditional negative stereotypes about old age (Ja-coby 2011). Thus, while arguably each generation has looked back and as-sumed that it differed from past generations (Jönson 2013), in the last quarter of the twentieth century, this view "took" and lent popular support to the new aging. Often forgotten, however, in the enthusiasm for the baby boomers as change agents is the fact that the "boomers" were and are a pretty heteroge-neous group; one in six, for example, emigrated from Asia or Latin America (Mutchler and Burr 2009). Thus, while it may be that some boomers will participate in redefining late life, for many others late life will be a time of increasing vulnerability.

Even attitudes toward voluntarism changed. While it has always been an important part of American life, during the period that E. J. Dionne (2012) calls the long consensus that followed World War II, it was a supplement to and not a replacement for public responsibility. Today, to some of its advo-cates, voluntarism is often characterized as both an obligation and a necessity to replace the erosion of public-sector commitments (Morrow-Howell 2000; Reilly 2006). Lost, however, was the fact that the need for such actions emerged from systematic injustice and economic inequality. Yet all this made sense as the devolution of the state emerged as a matter of policy.

This background, I hope, suggests why the new aging caught on among serious scholars, the media, biomedicine, businesses, and also old people themselves. The way we think about late life is not outside history, culture, or politics. Its fit with contemporary culture and politics is what makes it seem so natural and normal. As Rodgers (2011) notes, ideas have practical power. The ideas that have been so seminal in the past thirty or forty years confirm Rodgers's observations that what is important today is individual choice and agency and not context and society. If we look closely, we can see how these underlying ways of understanding society and our place in it play out in everyday life. Think of something as seemingly simple as one's individual right to recline airline seats without taking into account the person in whose lap we land, an example of how individual rights trump the social good.

THE DISCOVERY AND FLOURISHING OF THE "NEW" AGING

Universalizing to all the evidence that some Americans were living longer and in better health, the new aging sought to further optimize health and well-being and to remedy ageism by challenging the "greedy geezer" image and other negative stereotypes that had become associated with late life (see chapters 2 and 6). These ends would be achieved by addressing health optimization activities, by opening opportunities for and demonstrating the continued productive activities and social contributions of old women and men, and by presenting positive representations of old age. These aims fit well with a scientific methodology. Thus, research, for example, provided evidence-based prescriptions about health behaviors. It also offered professionally designed programs and services tools to make such health-inducing behaviors known and more widely available. It led to what Jason Karlawish, a medical school professor, observes in a September 21, 2014, *New York Times* op-ed, that "aging in the 21st century is all about risk and its reduction. . . . We are becoming a nation of planners living quantified lives" (Karlawish 2014, SR5). Research also generated proof of productivity and of the often remarkable achievements of people in late life. What is harder to capture, but I attest to it, is the sense of excitement and discovery that accompanied this research in the 1980s and 1990s.

In their very influential work on successful aging, for example, Jack Rowe and Robert Kahn (1987, 1998) maintain that to age successfully is to avoid disease and disability, maintain cognitive and physical function, and remain actively engaged with life. Their 1998 book, *Successful Aging*, gained wide recognition and attention partly because of the publicity generated by the MacArthur Foundation that funded the research and partly because it fit so well with the social, political, and cultural context of the times that I described above. A particularly resonant theme was that "individuals should be able to overcome personal barriers and work toward successful aging at all times; indeed this is their responsibility" (Dillaway and Byrnes 2009, 705). While Rowe and Kahn (1998) recognized that some people would be more apt than others to meet the rigid test of successful aging, they gave little attention to the role of lifelong health and other disparities that put some in a wheelchair and others on the ski slopes (Holstein and Minkler 2003). As a geriatrician and a psychologist, they focused on individual action and responsibility, and that focus became the norm.

Although the term "successful aging" was not new (Havighurst 1961; Baltes and Baltes 1990), its rapid incorporation into research and popular conversation was. As Jon Hendricks describes it, successful aging was "greeted as a lodestar for moving the field of aging toward a new understanding of what permits effective functioning in old age" (cited in Holstein and Minkler 2003, 787), and to Stephen Katz and Toni Calasanti (2014) it is "one of gerontology's most successful ideas" (1). As a "guiding theme in gerontological research" and as a family of like-minded themes, it has appeared under labels that include "active aging," "positive aging," and "productive aging" (Lamb 2014, 44).

Productive aging, with which I opened this chapter, was always a centerpiece; it was soon joined to a new movement labeled "civic engagement." These components added specificity to Rowe and Kahn's concept of active engagement with life. I note that the 1980s meeting that I described above took place almost simultaneously with the introduction of both the "greedy geezer" imagery and the intergenerational equity debate that are products of the new conservatism. Thus, the immediate agenda of productive aging proponents was to "prove" that the old were contributing members of society and therefore neither social burdens nor selfish consumers of public resources. Both descriptive and normative, combining the "is" and the "ought," this argument for productivity and its further popularization, as I shall consider below, was politically and personally consequential. In this view, the situation of reduced public spending will "demand increased volunteerism . . . thus society may require the productive engagement of older adults" (Morrow-Howell 2000, 1). Worth was thus linked to contributing, generally in the public sphere and preferably in the monetized economy (Bass, Caro, and Chen 1993), that is, it accrued not by caring for one's grandchildren or one's ailing spouse but rather by starting a day-care center or having a job.

Not surprisingly, as the specific linkage of the new aging to work took root among policymakers, the new aging became linked even more strongly to economic usefulness (Biggs et al. 2006; Estes, Biggs, and Phillipson 2003). In this new narrative, the aging citizens avoided the stigma associated with dependency by fitting themselves into the market economy (Katz 2000). In the United Kingdom, these views were captured in policy documents, which imply that one can, without losing anything important, group in a single vision the seventy-five-year-old and the fifty-year-old, especially through "inclusion by work" (243). While not specifically enshrined in American policy documents, the tacit assumption in policy discussions about "entitlement reform" (see chapter 6) relies on a similar assumption. Work and voluntarism captured this country's self-image—individual initiative, private action as opposed to government intervention, neighbors helping neighbors, transforming into a national priority what we have seen happen in times of disaster. Productivity was still primarily linked to monetized activity, fitting in well with market norms that operate under norms of justice as reciprocity—deservingness based on the extent of one's contribution (Martinson and Halperin 2011). These norms, as I shall argue below, were ill suited to women's lives.

While for some, productivity was broadened to include a variety of volunteer activities, engagement with people, physical activity, lifelong learning, and, for some, such tasks as housework and caregiving (Bass and Caro 2001; Herd and Harrington Meyer 2002), the dominant understanding was still linked to public activities that could be measured and counted. Whether specifically defined as an obligation, a regulative ideal for later life, or important for aging successfully, the notion that such activity is both good for us and good for society has become conventional wisdom (Johnson and Mutchler 2013). Stephen Katz (2000) astutely observes that to reject the importance of activity as a vital component of successful aging would seem perverse, even "heretical" (136).

As it expanded in scope and faced critical reactions (e.g., Katz 2000; Holstein and Minkler 2003; Minkler and Fadem 2002; Martinson and Minkler 2006; Martinson and Halpern 2011), the new aging began to migrate from academic and biomedical discourse to popular and consumer culture, where its key features adopt the norms of successful aging but extend them further, particularly in terms of wide-ranging consumerist interventions to retard or prevent aging and to preserve one's youthful appearance. Attention also turned specifically to sexuality as essential to aging successfully and to the creation of lifestyle communities that exemplified the busy, active lifestyle that the new aging valued. Individual effort and control continued to be hallmarks of consumer culture.

In popular culture, one could age "successfully" whether that term was self-defined or based on external criteria, whether it was meant as a dichotomous term (in opposition to failure) or not, and the view was that our success or failure in achieving this status was up to us. It created a new binary— between those who fulfilled the new norms and those who did not. Its greatest attraction was its positive portrayal of aging and the belief that it was possible to assess aging in terms of success rather than in terms of a relentlessly downward spiral that saw old age as primarily about individual losses to which elders and societies needed to adapt (Phillipson 1998). These values resonated with a culture that venerated youth, devalued old age, and cultivated fears of an aging apocalypse (Robertson 1999). By avoiding dependency and contributing to society, successful agers made life better for everyone else. They were "satisfied, active, independent, self-sufficient, and above all, defiant of traditional narratives of decline" (Katz and Calasanti 2014, 2). To question this picture of the successful ager or the assumptions on which it rested or its unintended consequences became the task of the critics. Committed to these norms, its proponents sought to demonstrate how they could be achieved and what such achievement might mean in terms of health, life satisfaction, and even societal well-being.

EXPANDING SUCCESSFUL AGING: SEX, HEALTH OPTIMIZATION, AND ANTI-AGING

A flourishing anti-aging industry directed at keeping aging in any form at bay and a pointed inclusion of sexuality as an essential component of successful aging were hallmarks of the new aging's expansiveness. In the popular media, age lost its meaning, except as the "before" images in ads or in the sad conditions of people who did not act to optimize their health. While only slightly exaggerated, public images suggested that sixty- and seventy-year-olds were living in a romantic dreamworld of love, sex, busyness, spa sessions to keep up our youthful appearance, and indeed floating along in the "golden years" rather than the tarnished ones so many experience (Schulz and Binstock 2006) while the less beautiful, less slim, less sexy were further isolated. The successful aging paradigm has thus traveled widely, with evidence suggesting that it has created an "ideal vision of aging" that many people in their forties, fifties, and sixties hold (Flatt et al. 2013). Among its primary attributes is a kind of agelessness that led geriatrician Muriel Gillick (2006) to wryly comment that the best way to avoid anxiety about the perils of old age was to "eradicate it completely" (195).

The popularizers of successful aging used academic research, sometimes selectively, to construct the public face of the new aging. I turn first to discussions about sexuality, which partake in both. Two books bookend this movement and the changes in one generation about how to think about sexuality and old age. In the forefront of defining the "new" old age, Dr. Robert Butler and his wife, Myrna Lewis (1976), wrote *Sex after Sixty: A Guide for Men and Women in Their Later Years*. Butler and Lewis appropriately assumed that sexuality was an ongoing part of human life. Thus, they addressed the practical questions that women and men might have about their sexuality. Contrast this book to Gail Sheehy's book, *Sex and the Seasoned Woman* (2006). In it, she addresses the transition to old age with a paean to aging sexuality, offering anecdotes about women who are living fully and passionately.

Much research draws the unsurprising conclusion that sexual interest continues even as sexual activity declines (Gott and Hinchliff 2003). Women, because of the death of a spouse and the absence of an intimate relationship, are less likely to be sexually active then men (Lindau et al. 2007), confirming a conclusion that Merryn Gott and Sharron Hinchliff (2003) reached from their ethnographic study of the importance of sex in later life. They conclude that "sex is seen as an important component of a close emotional relationship . . . although no interest was expressed in sex outside this context" (1626). In their study, many older people reprioritized sexuality as their life situation changed or health factors impeded sexual activity, even as they saw sex and intimacy as important components of a good relationship (Syme 2014). In concluding an extensive national study of sexuality in late life, John DeLamater (2011) concludes that sexual activity continues into the seventies and eighties, that aging-related physical changes need not lead to a decline in sexual functioning, that good attitudes and access to a healthy partner are key, and that regular sexual expression is good for one's health.

Given these basic findings about sex in late life, I want to direct attention to how it fits with the new aging in several ways. First, and most directly, attention has focused on the many health benefits associated with continued sexual activity (Syme 2014); it has become to many an essential element in aging successfully (Katz and Marshall 2003). The popular trend is thus to assert old age sexuality "as a natural and even as a fundamental component of healthy aging" (Scherrer 2009, 7).

Second, it has elevated heteronormative sex that speaks in the language of men, youth, and performance, relying on biomedical and consumer products to assure that sexual functionality and bodily appearance meet standards of sexual desirability (Calasanti and Slevin 2001; Calasanti 2007). Third, like much else in the new aging, sexual health is tied to a narrow range of activities that Barbara Marshall (2012) describes as "overly essentialist" and measured in terms of youthful standards of sexual function and attractiveness (341). Thus, as language has moved from sexual decline to sexual dysfunction, achieving sexual functionality becomes another element in the antidecline narrative, and "sexiness" becomes a way to define oneself as "not old" (Katz and Marshall 2003; B. Marshall 2011, 394). The availability of products like Viagra or Cialis helps to create a situation where opting out of sex is not acceptable (Gott 2006).

As features of the new aging, popular representations of sexuality and old age communicate messages about the subjects of the new sexuality. The fit body is a central image. In TV ads for products like Cialis, a treatment for erectile dysfunction, which can help men be ready anytime the "time is right," both men and women are beautiful. These ads suggest that men who would be interested in this product and the women for whom they want to be "ready" are slim and attractive and either dining by candlelight or playing a vigorous game of tennis. While there is no comparable product to enhance a woman's libido, she can try out natural hormonal replacement therapy to improve her sexual functionality. "Female sexual dysfunction" joined male sexual dysfunction as a disease category that implied "everyone can be perfect—should be perfect—and is to blame if they don't do everything (i.e., buy everything) to make themselves perfect" (Teifer 2002). Women are thus recast in an image that rests on "idealized gender relations that prevail among younger men and women (Calasanti 2007, 345). Popular ads inform us of how we should be sexual (B. Marshall 2012) while a youthful iconography represents what it means to be a sexually attractive woman (Segal 2013). This desirable body—fit for sex—reinforces the notion that keeping the body fit and sexy is yet another lifelong project that also defines the boundary between the third and the fourth ages for those interested in establishing such boundaries (B. Marshall 2011). There seems to be no place for the hardscrabble couple sitting at Burger King in jeans and sweatshirts or the austere couple in Grant Woods's *American Gothic.* In contrast, Lillian Rubin (2007) observes that contemporary sexual imagery, instruction manuals, and the all-or-nothing language is just another fantasy that we are supposed to want. She asks, "How come the researchers don't talk to the people I do?" (74).

In other ways, as the new aging moves further away from the work of scholars into popular culture, "market jargon such as *boomers* and *empty-nesters*" becomes part of a "popular sociogerontological vocabulary aimed at disguising the negative realities of poverty and inequality in old age" (Katz 2001–2002, 28; italics in the original). In the popular press and in other media, the new narrative about late life is thus less cautious, more fulsome than is fitting for scholarship. Instead of the sexless, sedentary, and incompetent seventy-year-old, the old are rich and not poor, making their mark as consumers in the well-developed gray market. Since selective images are meant to transform how we see and think about old age (Laws 1995), open any popular magazine, especially ones directed at women, and it seems as if nearly every page has an ad for some "anti-aging" product, most often for skin care or makeup but often far wider ranging. In publications directed at people fifty and over, ads for active retirement communities contend with those for exotic vacations.

The apogee of consumer culture and its foundation in successful aging is reflected in the ads for Sunbelt retirement communities. While these ads have marketing goals, they also are "mold and mirror of ageist attitudes and cultural values." This kind of retirement, idealized and romanticized, idyllic and timeless, captures how ageless people might see themselves (McHugh 2003, 166, 169). In these communities, the retiree can fill every moment with activities; new friends are in the offing and self-indulgence the creed. Fitting best with the postmodern idea of old age as a time of fluidity, self-invention, and youthfulness, media images of retirees reinforce the idea that this kind of life is possible (if not probable) for all of us.

This is the new aging among its popularizers. Both reflecting and provoking a certain way to think about late life, it wholeheartedly endorses consumerism in pursuit of youthfulness. While defying age and, with it, avoiding dependency are recurring themes in history (Hayflick 1994; Haber 2001–2002), now the tools to do so have advanced, and the political environment is ripe for them. Since age avoidance responds to fears about the new demographic profile that the aging of the population defines, according to this framing, we are obliged to take advantage of whatever consumer culture offers us—to avoid burdening society.

Anti-aging interventions serve two primary ends. For individuals, they offer a "therapeutic opportunity" to enact our responsibilities to not age (Mykytyn 2008, 313). And less overtly, they promote a "widespread anti-aging culture" that serves commercial capitalism (Katz 2001–2002, 27). By cultivating personal dissatisfactions, especially women's (see chapter 1), consumer culture has created a billion-dollar industry, a barrier to any efforts to disrupt anti-aging campaigns (Gullette 2011). If we do not take advantage of these opportunities, we may be held individually responsible for our failures as moral blame is attached to forms of aging that are deviant, that is, not positive (Katz 2001–2002; Calasanti 2007). Anti-aging interventions are thus "powerful forces shaping the exclusion of old people" (Calasanti 2007, 339). The "consumer body" is a powerful contributor to how we define our identity (Katz 2001–2002), especially if one belongs to a privileged sector of society where going to the gym or coloring one's hair is virtually obligatory (Ephron 2011). The ads that feature "heavily retouched models imply that we can all look like that"—and should (Gullette 2011, 33).

In his book *Better Than Well*, bioethicist Carl Elliott (2003) argues that Americans often go to great lengths not to heal but to improve themselves, to achieve the body, the appearance, and the psyche that they've always wanted to have. Although, as he suggests, we are not sure what we are looking for, we are sure that others have what we want. As consumer culture suggests the possibility for us to liberate ourselves from all limits, it offers us the tools to pursue a life of endless self-realization and personal choice (Kaye 2009). Demanding constant monitoring, the obligation to optimize health, that is, not to be healthy relative to one's age but having a body that is like that of a twenty-five- to thirty-year-old is made manifest (Mykytyn 2008). Biomedicine, in a comfortable relationship with successful aging, has fostered the idea that "health is a personal, social-ethical imperative," an agenda that is revealed through official materials on health promotion, popular attention to diet and exercise, and also corporate wellness programs and discounts on insurance premiums for health-enhancing behaviors (Lamb 2014, 43). The goal is a somewhat vague notion of improving an overall feeling of health. Self-responsibility is the keyword. Similar to other cultural norms that are now so prevalent, the belief that one can, indeed should, enhance one's health has become a dominant cultural belief enshrined in the idea of holistic health (Mykytyn 2008). It shares with other aspects of the new aging an emphasis on individual responsibility in a rather open-ended process of self-improvement.

FROM DESCRIPTION TO CRITIQUE

Getting Specific: Claims and Counterclaims

As I assess the new aging, I will be looking at it as a conceptual whole, as a new way to think about aging and old age, as an answer to the question of what old age ought to be about. This approach, however, means that some subtleties may become lost, some adjustments made in response to criticism not addressed. Thus, I note in advance that not all versions of the new aging deny age-related changes. They instead speak to the value of coping with and adapting to them (Baltes and Baltes 1990; Moody 2009). Nor do all authors maintain that continuation of midlife norms takes priority over norms that may fit best with late life. Further, when research turns to the voices of older people, the definitions of successful aging are more varied and often more able to integrate changes in health and other changes as well (Hung, Kempen, and deVries 2010; Lamb 2014), but these are not the voices that achieve public visibility. It is to that dominant discourse about the new aging and its stress on productivity, vitality, health, and, to a large extent, agelessness (Lamb 2014; Katz and Calasanti 2014) that I will respond.

As noted above, my disagreement has two parts. The first is basic. Positivist biomedical and social science research are not apt vehicles with which to address questions about how to live in old age. Yet that is what they have become. While it is unlikely that there will be full agreement about its original intention, the various components of the new aging have become, whether intentionally or not, an instruction manual defining a good old age or, more to the point, how to live our later years without becoming old. Thus, to live a good old age is being just like we were ten or twenty or thirty years ago. Aging itself thus has no meaning or purpose.

But what constitutes a good life is an age-old philosophical and religious question; it cannot be solved by science, although science offers needed and important information (Cole 1992). Instead it calls for explicit deliberation about values. Such deliberation involves dialogue, narrative, and analysis that will be suggestive but not definitive. Like old age itself, there won't be one answer that is the predicate for a sentence starting with, "Old age is . . ." While reasons are important for the answers given, they are rarely definitive or universalizable (see Holstein, Parks, and Waymack 2011 for an extended discussion of these issues). In contrast, science not only does not engage with values, but it maintains that its research is value neutral. Yet scientists, like all of us, "absorb prevailing images and ideas from their life world" (Cole

1995, S342). Earlier in the chapter, I offered my understanding of what that life world is like and how the new aging is at home in it. In a way, Robert Kahn (2002) acknowledged that the reason he and Jack Rowe focused on individual control was that they could address that while they could not expect policy changes. While proponents of the new aging may have different ideas about the normativity of their views, much writing implies that one can be evaluated on the basis of one's conformity to the new aging's values with no attention to context.

Thus, I open this section of critique with my sense that there is a largely unbridgeable gap between proponents and critics of what is now a larger "public cultural discourse" (Lamb 2014) about late life. I see two primary reasons for this gap. The first is that the new aging, as I just discussed, moves unself-consciously from the "is" (e.g., scientific data about what contributes to good health) to the "ought" (e.g., how we should live in late life). Thus, for some critics, the assurance with which proponents offer their views about how we ought to live in late life gives to science a competency that it cannot claim. A good life, says Aristotle, is not a scientific problem but a problem calling for practical wisdom, the mean between extremes that we find through experience. The second source of this gap is discomfort with how a narrow, partial view of the good life is universalized. The new aging is a master narrative that privileges some while excluding far too many others. Can these norms speak equally well to the House minority leader, Nancy Pelosi, and also to the coal miner's wife in a small town in West Virginia? Unrealizable expectations cannot be ethically defended. We cannot be held accountable for what we cannot do (Flanagan 1991) or, I add, what does not meet our considered understanding of what is a good life. Thus, the second kind of critique focuses on those answers. To frame my reactions, I turn again to Aristotelian practical wisdom (Aristotle 1962). The new aging, whether so intended or not, is a normative enterprise, and so it must be assessed as such and must be understood as possible and desirable by women who occupy all social locations.

Since one reason women resist being labeled old is the negative associations that accompany it, the new aging seeks to overcome those associations by showing that to be old was not necessarily to be dowdy, poorly dressed, and asexual. Nor was it necessary to observe behavioral norms that limited one's choice of activities. But it was not practically wise to try to rupture the assumptions that produce and reproduce negative stereotypes by offering equally exclusive but almost relentlessly positive representations that fail to resemble most of us. Our environments provide us with the materials that help us negotiate what to value, thus unrepresentative cultural figurations, tropes, and narratives can lead to the internalization of values and expectations that may conflict with important elements of our biographical selves, elements that include our socioeconomic status, gender, and race as well as our important self-conceptions. These representations make it more difficult to find our own voice among the clamor of dominant images (Meyers 2002).

Similarly, it was good to offer information about health-promoting activities and to design health promotion and wellness programs to help us stay well. It is not wise, however, to impose an obligation to enact those behaviors, assume we all have equal opportunity to do so, and thus judge us if we "fail" and develop health problems. Balance between health-related goals and everything else in life is needed. It is not wise to ask us to live by a checklist. Further, to suggest that we can achieve a healthy old age primarily through our own efforts is to assume far too much when, for example, many people do without the dental care they need that may then affect their health because they can't afford it. Recall the public health adage that it is not one's blood pressure or cholesterol measures that determine our health status; it is our zip code as that is the source of many health disparities that plague us throughout our lives. It was also good to weaken conventional attitudes about proper roles, actions, and even dress for women at sixty, seventy, eighty, and beyond but not to expect us to look and act as if we were forty or fifty again.

Most importantly, however, I see two primary difficulties with the new aging that lack practical wisdom. It conceptualizes the good and worthy life in narrow, exclusive, and backward-looking terms and thus fails to give full attention to what I see as the unique developmental possibilities of late life. The new aging's ideal person is, in philosopher Margaret Urban Walker's (1999a) terms, one who sees "life as a career," planned and well executed. That person is a fit and energetic person who conforms to society's rules and institutions and has already found favor with that society. That person fits well with market-oriented values that have rewarded him or her with the rewards of cumulative achievement. This description is not in synch with how most women live. It models a life of individuals not involved in caregiving, domestic chores, or more general nurturing activities that occur in the private sphere. Walker (1999a) thus asks if these "prominent conceptions of valuable lives and admirable character . . . embody assumptions and invoke exemplars" inhospitable to the lives of older women, among others (100). Marty Martinson and Meredith Minkler (2006) thus argue that the new aging was best suited for white middle- and upper-class and healthy people who had done well in a market economy.

It is about volunteering or working and not taking care of one's grandchildren or writing a poem or struggling to make ends meet by whatever job is available. Many old women are already busy, very busy. They do not retire from anything except perhaps paid employment. Yet what they are busy with counts for little. The new aging cannot speak to women who have spent most of their lives unrecognized and poor. For them, the rules were always unfair. How can the new aging speak to such women? Thus, the new aging is not practically wise because it upholds values and norms that are relatively exclusive, relevant for some women some of the time and for many women none of the time.

It does not speak to me. After forty-plus years of "to-do" lists and responsibilities, my purposeful life, to use the expression of Civic Ventures founder Marc Freedman, is not voluntarism but quietness, freedom to make each day my own, a gift that the women of Mayslake speak of so lovingly, the freedom to be themselves and to not conform to anyone else's idea of what they should be. I believe it was Carolyn Heilbrun who said that above all, we don't want younger people telling us how to live, and I add, especially younger people from a different social location.

By being so specific in its assessment of what constituted the good life, it truncated the various ways to be old and left little space for the ambiguities, uncertainties, and existential needs that inevitably are a part of becoming and being old (Gillick 2006; Scannell 2006; Biggs et al. 2006). One paradigm replaces another—health and vigor rather than decline and loss—and with that replacement, the potential for strength and personal growth, even when and if one is frail and dependent, is neither noticed nor valued. Tom Cole (1992) reminds us that "hope and triumph were linked dialectically to tragedy and death" in early American history, an "existential integrity" that is now lost (231). Imposing midlife norms of health and productivity means losing an opportunity to acknowledge differences that come with getting older and building from there. This loss of possibility is one reason that I find boundary setting between the third and the fourth age so troublesome (see chapter 4). From her eighty-plus perspective, Rubin (2007) contrasts the real old age for those who live it with the old age of those who write about it. She argues that they "grasp at half-truths and offer them up as if they were the whole story" (7–8). In the whole story, we are all vulnerable to injury, disease, economic risk, and societal and/or workplace marginalization. Linking human value to independence further marginalizes people who are impaired and need help. Yet the new aging's dualism in dividing the "good" third age from the "bad" fourth age hinders our ability to work with and through the paradoxes that will contribute to a new understanding of what it can mean to be old in contemporary culture. If you can't beat them (i.e., the young), join them is an endeavor that means we inevitably fail since it is their reality in which we are seeking to participate.

The content of the new aging is thus one key problem, but so too is the route by which it is to be achieved—individual effort and control. These commitments absolve both the public sector and private employees from their responsibilities toward workers and residents of this country. Individual control is built on a faulty assumption that there is an equal starting place in terms of health, financial security, and leisure, the very attributes that women are less likely to have than their male counterparts. Individual volition and lifestyle choices do not overcome the lifetime disadvantages, for example, created by poverty or inadequate health care (Katz and Calasanti 2014). To be born with the proverbial silver spoon in one's mouth leads to quite a different range of opportunities in old age than being born in a low-income housing project or even into a working-class family that is marginally making ends meet. Both advantages and disadvantages accumulate (Dannefer 2003), but the new aging's blindness to the interlocking system of inequalities marginalizes those who cannot, or will not, meet expectations. Yet the reality of such differences does not free one from blame, including self-blame when things don't work out, when we "fail" to age successfully. A lifetime of "women's work," like caring for family members or being an aide in a nursing home or flipping burgers at McDonald's, will most likely make a woman a failure rather than a successful aged person.

A further problem that results from this failure to see that some can live into old age "unburdened by actual signs of ageing" (Segal 2013, 18) while others cannot is political—reduced political support to meet their needs. If old people can age successfully on their own, they have no need for government support. Thus, Lillian Rubin (2007) sardonically observes that what is needed is not social programs but more individual responsibility. Reinforcing that comment, Richard Settersten (2007) notes that "amidst all this agelessness . . .we do ourselves and old people a great disservice. . . . These emphases threaten to obscure . . . the real underbellies of aging and old age that must be acknowledged if they are to be dealt with effectively" (25).

It is not practically wise to translate new opportunities into new obligations as some advocates do (Reilly 2006) or to assume it was possible to
widen roles without addressing the inequalities that disadvantage so many
women and often men as well. Compartmentalizing old age into successful/
ordinary, productive/nonproductive, and defined by external standards displaces rather than eliminates ageism, which remains for those bodies (gendered, raced, sexed, and classed) who are the least likely to meet the new
standards and, perhaps by virtue of self-understanding, reject them as valued
goals. Thus, while rejecting the "greedy geezer" imagery of the 1980s was
important, doing it by upholding the contributions that the old made to society (Bass, Caro, and Chen 1993; Morrow-Howell, Hinterlong, and Sherraden
2001) suggests that worth is attached only to those who contributed in certain
rather specific ways and that to need help is to be less than worthy. It links
human value to independence and thus further marginalizes people who are
impaired and need help. Recall the words of the women of Mayslake, who
thought others saw them as burdens, and their plea for understanding that
they have worked all their lives, done what other people wanted them to do,
and so enjoying their freedom was one of the pleasures of late life. I thus
return to the Aristotelian concept of the mean, the place between extremes.
We have many ways of contributing as these women do in their own communities, but most are not measurable and so they gain no recognition.

In my discussion of sexuality I noted the elevation of a certain form of
desirable sexuality and the kind of body that would partake in such sexuality,
which was then linked to aging successfully (Marshall 2012). These ideals
add one more disciplinary practice to what it means to maintain one's "not
old" status. While it is good to affirm that sexual interest if not sexual activity
does not disappear when one reaches seventy or eighty, it is not good to
attach that affirmation to yet another particularistic concept of how it ought
to be enjoyed. As Barbara Marshall (2012) observes, "The contemporary
rendering of 'sexual health' in later life seems particularly impoverished,
equating it with a particular form of sexual functionality and underpinned by
an overly essentialist conception of sexual drives and sexual bodies" (341). It
is not practically wise to set up a dichotomy between the asexual old and the
sexy old. Such dichotomies do not reflect what the voices of experience
suggest (Gott and Hinchliff 2003), nor do they honor a wide range of intimate behavior. Nor is it wise to associate sex in old age with certain kinds of
bodies represented in the popular media. Public attention to sexuality and old
age can thus easily exacerbate the already tenuous connections between most

women and the ideal of womanhood, now extended to old age. Like so much else in the norms related to successful aging, research on sexuality is blind to the influence of social location, personal context, and personal history on attitudes toward sexuality.

The anti-aging industry carries all these concerns to their outer limits. It encodes a tacit ageism —why would anyone try to rid society of something that was valued? Thus, if we don't have to get old, how foolish we would be not to seize the opportunity to be a perpetual forty-year-old. As increasingly negative cultural meanings are assigned to physical decline, women will also feel pressured to keep their physical appearance in line with youthful norms, given the importance of women's bodies to how they are perceived in the world (see chapter 1). It thus raises this question: "Is it desirable to face even more years of disciplined (and costly) efforts to keep one's body in line or to feel condemned for not doing so?" (Holstein 2001–2002, 41). Indirectly, the anti-aging movement gains revenues, sales, and research funds only to the extent that it exacerbates the harmful stereotyping that contributes to this devaluation (Holstein, Parks, and Waymack 2011). My concern, then, is that old women, especially "unimproved" ones, will be further devalued and blamed for needing help that they could (theoretically) have avoided by their own actions. After all, if we can still be vigorous at ninety-two, it must be our fault if we are not.

Thus, the anti-aging message is problematic in many ways. It will exacerbate inequalities since consumer products will be costly. It will make the acceptance of limits, which must come, even more difficult than it already is. Anti-aging interventions are one more way to devalue old age and thus contribute to "the cultural attitudes that compound everyday efforts to stay whole in an ageist society" (Holstein 2001–2002, 42).

In so many ways, then, the new aging, especially as it is integrated into popular culture, adopted extreme positions. Instead of introducing limited aims, it sought to redefine old age itself, often assuming that an ageless future was at hand. It forgot that old age is "more than a state of mind"; it is also a state of the body and of the psyche (Scannell 2006; Gillick 2006; Biggs et al. 2006; Holstein and Minkler 2003). "Nobody, it seems—in the sense of dependency, withdrawal from society, plus a limited ability to both produce and consume—is old anymore." Differences based on age are thus "a result of wrong attitudes" (Biggs et al. 2006, 242). Yet for every eighty-year-old woman who runs the Chicago Marathon, untold numbers are worried about making it up the short hill to their apartment for reasons that are largely beyond their individual control. While we may all have the capacity to stay as fit as the marathoner, hard physical labor or other life priorities close that as a possibility for most women.

From her eighty-plus perspective, Rubin (2007) maintains that many people who write about aging "grasp at half-truths and offer them up as it they were the whole story" (7–8). In the whole story, we are all vulnerable to injury, disease, economic risk, and societal and/or workplace marginalization. Linking human value to independence further marginalizes people who are impaired and need help. Yet the new aging's dualism in dividing the "good" third age from the "bad" fourth age hinders our ability to work with and through the paradoxes that will contribute to a new understanding of what it can mean to be old in contemporary culture. If you can't beat them (i.e., the young), join them is an endeavor that means we inevitably fail since it is their reality in which we are seeking to participate.

While I have touched upon the link between the new aging and neoliberalism throughout this chapter, I'd like to bring these ideas together as a form of summary. Perhaps most worrisome is that the normative values the new aging represents undermine the reasons for the social and economic supports that so many women (and men) need to live decently. Thus, if we "fail" in our efforts to age successfully, to avoid dependencies, we have decreasing hopes for support, for someone to catch us if we fall (Ruddick 1999). Without wishing to return to the "compassionate ageism" that Robert Binstock (1983) described, it is worrisome that "aggressive improvements in elder well-being and codification of "successful aging" set the stage for the "greedy geezer" and allied epithets directed toward an allegedly "coddled older population" (Hudson and Gonyea 2012, 278). One sees a coddled older population if one does not look very closely at the data, perhaps a form of willful blindness or the common tendency to see what one wants to see in that data. Neoliberalism thus turned on its head political philosopher John Rawls's (1972) notion that any deviation from equal treatment can only be justified if it benefitted the least advantaged. The reverse becomes the new norm. Deservingness is grounded in reciprocity. The person who contributes to society as a matter of obligation thus receives public rewards and recognition (Martinson and Halperin 2011).

While I am sympathetic to the motivations, I find the new cultural norms about late life deeply disturbing. I often shudder with dismay as I see the enthusiasm with which the new aging seeks to obliterate "old" in favor of an endless middle age, that is, until evidence of decline sets in and we are shunted aside as a "burden" on society that we could have prevented if only we had taken charge of our lives more effectively. The uncritical avowal of positive and active aging suggests that by our own efforts we can avoid becoming a burden to the state, as if needing help makes us unworthy and as if we could wipe out all that happened to us across our life course that disadvantaged us then and continues to do so now. The new aging elides the complexities and ambiguities that mark late life as we try to live as well as we can in a cultural and political context that places market values and individual achievement over more social and communal values, that holds us accountable for how our lives turn out by disregarding important but inconvenient facts. It fails to see that advantages and disadvantages accumulate across the life course, largely as a result of vast societal inequalities and the retrenchment of the state and not because we didn't eat right or we disregarded our health. It does not see that many of us will need to learn to live with dependency without the support we need to do that in ways that preserve our integrity and identity. This blindness to the interlocking system of inequalities marginalizes those who cannot, or will not, meet expectations. The new aging thus penalizes women and lower-income men who have generally been at the fringes of the new economy while it elevates those for whom the new economy worked. Its blindness to these inequalities led a friend and colleague to ask, "What about the people in Appalachia?" And it contributes to a painful irony: the very people—low-income or poor women—who are most apt to experience the effects of ageism, for example, the women of Mayslake, are the ones who are further penalized by the images and ideals of the new aging that have infiltrated their thinking but reflect neither how they are living nor how they want to live. The new aging reinforces the outsider status that they already feel, an unsurprising occurrence when norms are defined by people more privileged than they are.

In her discussion of the perils of what she calls positive active aging, feminist scholar Lynne Segal (2013) observes that "this scenario is itself partially complicit with the disparagement of old age, refusing to accept much that ageing entails, including facing greater dependence, fragility and loss, as well as the sadness, resentment or anger that accrue along with life itself" (18). The relentless struggle against deterioration reinforces ageism. The goal, it seems to me, is to accept that these occurrences are likely possibilities in old age at the same time that neither are they what old age is all about nor that there are not strengths along with losses. We ought not to trade one paradigm for another as if they don't share essential qualities.

IF NOT THE "NEW" AGING, THEN WHAT?

To return to that meeting on productive aging, I wondered what a group of women would say if given a chance to discuss what it would mean to honor old age in all its complexities. What would they uphold as values that accounted for what is unique about late life rather than look backward to a time that was past for all of us? What would an inclusive rather than an exclusive take on late life look like? How would it include the woman who wanted to spend her days studying poetry or practicing meditation or the woman who had continued responsibilities for a disabled child or an ailing spouse? So I wondered what norms, if any, working-class or poor women would develop if they were the ones who controlled the story. As noted, the view from the corner office is very different from that of the mop closet in a downtown office building. I anticipate that many women would talk about having the greatest freedom possible to flourish in whatever ways that make sense for us. Science can help us understand what may be health giving without telling us how to live. It must, however, be a freedom based on a secure foundation.

A few years ago, in an informal discussion about the meaning of positive aging with a group of friends, who are also women gerontologists, I, who oppose the term, asked what they meant by it. They cited a chance for personal growth and an opportunity to know oneself and a wish to stay healthy, embrace transitions, and have time for reflection and introspection. In terms of virtues, they identified generosity of spirit and forgiveness of oneself and others. They worried about how to create an environment that nurtures these possibilities since ageism, health disparities, caregiving responsibilities, and media images of aging work against these "being" parts of the self and instead sanctify the active, "doing" self. The women of Mayslake wanted recognition for their competence, their maturity, their complexity, and their involvement in helping others in their community. Old women want what most people want—to have others see them as they see themselves, to be recognized as individuals, and to live in a safe and comfortable environment.

These goals are practically wise, as I see them, but to attach the label "positive" to them seems inappropriate and apt to link to the paradigm of successful aging that I have been critiquing. Perhaps they are best described as aging with awareness or reflectively, but that assumes that one has the conditions that make choice possible. A "bottom-up" development of stories about "my old age" is one way to get us there, a theme to which I will return in the last chapter.

I suggest that we work toward cultural norms, images, tropes, and schema that find worth in a far richer array of identities than we see today. Perhaps it starts with something very basic—what kind of people we are and what virtues are particularly suited for late life, a theme that the late Sarah Ruddick (1999), a feminist philosopher, introduced. She suggests modest goals, ones that do not become "burdensome to the people who are meant to be governed by them" (46). As Ruddick deftly reminds us, "Displays of independence mingle with other, albeit often quieter requests: 'help me,' catch me if I fall" (59). She suggests that in order to create mutually helpful and respectful relationships in which we can fall and be caught with dignity, "we have at least as much to learn from elderly people who fall as from the vigorously healthy" (59). Ruddick wrote these words when she was in her sixties and suffering from Parkinson's disease.

I suggest that certain virtues she proposes, which are relevant for all our lives but have particular salience in late life, be open to conversations among women. Because virtues are about our character, they are not achievements that we can accomplish as we might achieve "success" in how we age. Instead they are what we would work toward in relationship with others. These virtues may include gratitude, curiosity, generosity, appreciation, the capacity to forgive, affection, and concern for others, especially those who care for us, and wisdom. They require, as Ruddick adds, social policies that give us the chance to "enjoy the sunset" or to "buy a new sweater" or to "control some of the conditions of [our] death" (54), underlying conditions that we all need at whatever age we are to live decently. To honor these virtues does not mean, however, to be passively accepting of unjust conditions; thus, anger is also appropriate (Woodward 2002: Meyers 1997a). How else to identify and protest against the injustices one faces? Ruddick perceptively notes that representations of "positive" aging that appear in ads or in AARP magazines or in other media may intimidate women, who may feel "exhausted, sad and fearful" (46). Ruddick's identification of virtues that reflect ongoing efforts to live well and comfortably when the years past are far greater in number than the years to come is an evocative philosophical approach to a "good" old age that facilitates reflection about how to actively enact these virtues.

As I argued in the introduction, I think the answer needs to start with the acceptance that old is something real that cannot be set aside as if it had no relevance. While age is not the primary source of identity for most women, it counts. It counts because we generally feel deep commonalities that bind us to our age peers (Rubin 2007). It also counts because we are simultaneously all the ages we have ever been, and that includes "old," although, as described in chapter 1, the mask of aging selects "young" as what we really are. In rejecting the label "old," women often say, "But I don't feel old," a comment that assumes feeling old categorically means something apart from the social constructions that assign meanings to it.

CONCLUSION

The normativity of these ideas communicates the message that "this"—however that is defined—is what one does to have a good old age. I once thought that older people could be moral leaders; at last freed from the day-to-day needs of earning a living and caring for their family, they could assume leadership roles in society (Fahey and Holstein 1993). I am now many years older than when we wrote that, and now I fear that role would be a burden that I would not want to impose on anyone. Today, I have no conclusive answers. In fact, I don't believe that there is one single answer.

We need first, however, to commit to creating the conditions that make it possible for disadvantaged groups to reach seventy or eighty with lowered levels of disability so that longevity is truly democratized. This aim means more public health and related responses that try to mitigate the factors that correlate income status to life expectancy (Minkler, Fuller-Thompson, and Guralnick 2006). Throughout this chapter and indeed this book, I have highlighted the critical importance of context in making later life a place of reasonable contentment and acceptance. I have also stressed the need for a political agenda since, in its absence, too many women will lack the leisure to do anything with their lives but work and fear falling off the edge. If later life is to be truly a time of freedom for women, they need the resources to make it possible, and they need to liberated from new rules that instruct them about how to live or that do not give them the opportunity to experience the freedom they might otherwise enjoy.

Thus, in sum, I am anti-anti-aging. I am pro-aging as a time for exploration and the development of personal meanings that look forward as well as backward and take advantage of what we have learned in the years we have lived. I am for integrating our understanding of late life so that there is room for both its pleasures and its pains, its strengths and its weaknesses. As hard as it may be to accept, we all will die, and most of us will experience a time of ill or declining health before that time. That period also needs to be meaningful, not a throw-away time, a signal of failure (see chapter 4). Thus, a reconsideration of older meanings of successful aging that focus on adaptability to and coping with change (Baltes and Baltes 1990) would see late life more realistically while perhaps less romantically.

I encourage dispersed "bottom-up" talk about what it means to live a good life when we are old. Top-down thinking elides the importance of both social location and the realities of change, decline, and even mortality; it reflects a privileged perspective; it tacitly accepts the neoliberal political agendas that "require people to adopt risk-aversive, active, self-reliant lifestyles" (Katz and Marshall 2003). It fosters popular images of aging that we see, for example, in the ads for retirement communities in the Sunbelt and opens the way for the industries that "make gray gold" (Minkler 1991) to create new myths of the new old (or rather the "not old"). What I would like to see is the chance for women and interested men to come together to claim their own voices, to wrest power from the young, the healthier, and the more affluent. In small groups, whether in living rooms or public places, conferences or virtual communities, much like the consciousness-raising groups of the 1970s, older people can discuss and generate ideas of different ways to live well when we are in our sixties, seventies, and later. From there, ideas may travel "upward" so that they can begin to transform cultural attitudes and reflect the facts of aging and the multiple voices of people from the margins as well as from the center. The starting place for a denser, more democratic sense of the potential for both the third and the fourth ages is "the embodied, socially situated, and divided self" who is able to develop a "rich understanding of what one is like" and is also able to make adjustments as one's capacities change (Meyers 2002, 22). What is seen as a valued life in old age must be open to more than the relatively few. It must also recognize that intragenerational diversity needs more than acknowledgment. It must be taken seriously as calling for multiple paths to a meaningful old age, a theme to which I will return in the last chapter. This diversity must include sexuality as described by the women who are interested in its multiple forms, not simply performance and a youthful body.

As a feminist, I take from social ethicist and theologian Karen Lebacqz (1995) that practices acceptable to women must be life living and justice inducing and they must address the needs of the poor and the oppressed. As noted throughout this book, women are more disadvantaged than men socially and economically. The possibility for a very long life does not ameliorate this situation. Thus, "anti-aging" interventions can further deepen women's marginalization if they do not or cannot take advantage of them. Hence, we need counterimages and counternarratives, for example, that elicit richer and more nuanced ways to think about sexuality while making broadly available interventions that some may need for its full expression. In this way, we can celebrate our lifelong human need for physical and emotional connectedness without imposing new standards and expectations or narrowly categorizing its form.

While gerontologists might have limited social power, the media and other cultural vehicles that pick up the new discourses have far more power. But we who work in the field of aging need to be extra aware of how our fears and prejudices influence what we say. Our claims get adopted and translated in ways far beyond our control. I thus suggest that challenges to these norms must also occur in the professional circles in which they have taken hold. The excitement that these new norms generate is palpable. Acts of resistance are difficult, in part because these "third age" ideals are so attractive, but they are necessary lest these emergent norms become even further entrenched (Holstein, Parks, and Waymack 2011). The critical perspective continues to provoke questions about the unexamined commitment to norms that are potentially damaging to so many. We must take advantage of every opportunity (and create opportunities) to offer more emancipatory imagery.

Chapter Four

Disruptions and Repair

Identity and Chronic Illness

How much can they take from us and still be us? (Mayslake, Feb. 11, 2014)

As I get older, I am acutely aware that my currently "abled" body can change in an instant. My friends and I talk about the unknown future—perhaps a stroke or dementia—and what that would do to our lives. Despite our improved health (at least for the more affluent), serious physical and mental impairments are still an everyday reality. And women, who live longer than men, are also more likely to experience these illnesses. While change can happen at any age—a car accident or a life-threatening illness—that risk increases greatly as we age and as our bodies become more vulnerable. It may take us longer to recover if we become ill or make it harder to handle aggressive treatments for illnesses. A slip on the ice, a broken hip, surgery, and weeks of rehab may or may not restore our capacity to where it was before the accident, but in any case the sidewalk may seem threatening in a way that it hadn't before. It could be osteoporosis that limits our movements, or heart failure, or multiple chronic impairments that change our relationship with our body, with our family and friends, with how we are in the world, and with our ability to manage our day-to-day lives. It disrupts the relationship of body and self and causes us to rethink our identity and those features of our lives that give it meaning.

I have been lucky so far in that the chronic conditions I have and take medications for do not limit me in ways that threaten my identity, although, as discussed in chapter 2, societal ageism has already begun to shake the habitual links between body and self that I have maintained for much of my adult life. While I thus anticipate losses and wonder how I will react, I also believe that chronic illness may permit me, without recrimination, to choose a slower but equally satisfying way of life. Whether beneficial or detrimental or a combination of the two, reestablishing my identity will be essential if I am to learn to live as well as possible should I develop life-limiting conditions. These acknowledgments and fears tell me that such changes will call for the most significant rethinking of my identity since my teen years or the first years of being a parent. Already, turning seventy has provoked such a rethinking.

Hence, chronic illness signifies a major transition that will alter our lives but not eliminate our need for meaning and an identity that is simultaneously continuous with our past but different because of our changed condition. I wrote in chapter 1 about the fluidity of identity as our changing bodies and appearance provoke societal devaluation and, for many women, a commensurate challenge to their sense of self. Chronic illness exacerbates the problem of identity since it pushes us further to the margins of the valued self and often gives others power, even when most benign, over our lives. And with the contemporary emphasis on individual responsibility, we are often also blamed for developing the condition that limits us. We are now relegated to what is now often labeled the "fourth" age, where social goals are limited, where others have power to define our condition, and where the regnant vales of independence and individualism are simultaneously hard to maintain and hard to relinquish (Hurd Clarke and Bennett 2013).

Thus, I write this chapter for several reasons. Most simply, I believe it must be done. If we value the whole of life and how we experience each part of it as women, then evading the more painful subjects of physical and/or mental decline is not an option. To shunt decline aside, to box it into the abject "fourth" age, reinforces already powerful cultural fears about bodily suffering and old age, fears that further marginalize the people who live with debilitating conditions (Morell 2003) while blinding us to their hopes, dreams, and struggles. While the popular image of lifelong vigor and productivity may be appealing, it makes it so much harder for us to see how we can learn from the "realities and spectrum of life as it is lived" (Lamb 2014, 49). To understand how we try to live as well as possible with chronic impairments in a cultural and policy environment that is more apt to blame us for our disabilities than richly support us offers a window to changes that can make a difference.

To resist reductionist views about chronic impairments promoted by biomedicine and the service sector calls for a counterstory that tells us how women try to integrate their limitations into their identities and the complications they face in doing so. The decades-long effort to reverse "decline and loss" as the central paradigm of old age has succeeded almost too well, thereby placing the added burden of failing to age in vigorous good health on those for whom loss is an important feature of their lives. Often labeled with the categorical term, "fourth age," which I will discuss more fully below, they are cast as the "other" in words that "masquerade as truths" and demonstrate the power of one group to define another that reinforces already existing inequalities (Thorne, McCormick, and Carty 1997). Instead of allying with the struggle for meaning and identity, the dominant discourse and its definers make it all the harder to manage the "odyssey of self" that is a major task adapting to chronic impairment (Charmaz 1995). As we have learned from disability rights advocates, we may not be able to change the body, but we can change an inhospitable environment.

Women's voices as heard through ethnographies and in autobiographies, fiction, and personal stories help us to understand how women make sense (and most do) (Whitbourne and Sneed 2002a) of the chronic impairments that challenge their taken-for-granted lifeworlds. These illustrative narratives say much about how we develop and transmit meanings about the self, how we form, reform, and repair our identities as we face change, and how we contextualize our stories in culturally specific ways (Rozario and Derienzis 2009; Becker and Newsome 2005; Chivers 2003; Lindemann Nelson 2001; Becker 1997; Bruner 1990). My goal in this chapter is to consider how efforts to incorporate major physical and/or mental changes into one's identity take place and how culture, biomedicine, policy, and ethics can impede rather than facilitate the process.

CORE IDEAS

I start from several core ideas, which I will explore more fully in the remainder of the chapter. The first is the abiding importance of meaning to all human life. I am not concerned with meaning in a cosmic sense like the "meaning of life" but rather how we think about it in the practical, everyday world where, in philosopher Charles Taylor's (1994) terms, we find "horizons of meaning" that give certain ways of being "inestimable" value; absent such meaning we risk anomie. Second, we find the meanings on which we establish our identities in a particular social, cultural, and political context. Our identities are developed in and through our relationships with others that give us the "tool kits" (Bruner 1990) with which we come to choose our horizons of meaning. Third, our ability to act autonomously, to be moral agents, does not demand that we separate ourselves from our connections to others but instead that we recognize that autonomy is developed because of these relationships, a point made by feminist scholars so that the concept of autonomy speaks to women's lives (Walker 1998a; Mackenzie and Stoljar 2000; Meyers 2001; Fiore and Lindemann Nelson 2003). This view challenges the standard individualistic approach to ethics in practice settings that narrows its meaning and so narrows its associated obligations. This modified view of autonomy links to the fourth core idea—that we are not only who we think we are but who others take us to be. Recognition is critical. This cryptic-sounding comment means that our identities often require the involvement of others for their realization (Lindemann Nelson 2001; Strauss 2003). We cannot define ourselves as a good neighbor without affirmation from our neighbors, nor can we think of ourselves as wise old women if no one listens to us. And even for patients with advanced Alzheimer's disease, we have learned that the quality and types of relationships they have with others directly affect their behavior (Kitwood and Bredin 1992). The last core idea is that narrative provides the connective tissue that forms our identity (Mackenzie and Stoljar 2000, Lindemann Nelson 2001) and also reveals openings where change becomes possible.

CHRONIC IMPAIRMENTS

One way to think about chronic illness is to look at how it differs from acute illness. The main distinction is the "temporal duration and the prospect of recovery or cure" (Agich 1995). It may range from the invisible to the intermittently painful to the constantly troubling. It will not go away, and it may—indeed it probably will—get worse. It can cause physical or mental limitations or both combined. It may cause intermittent flare-ups that then require reformulating what one can and cannot do. It often requires long periods of supervision and care. It can make the familiar strange; perhaps the bathtub becomes an enemy to be conquered, or the flight of stairs once handled with ease becomes a barrier to reaching one's bedroom. These changes will interrupt our lives, often dramatically, and so will call upon us to reformulate our identities with the knowledge that this process will be ongoing. In 2002, the World Health Organization suggested that "disability is a process by which a person's health, environment, and personal factors influence his or her body structures, activities, and participation"(cited in Schoeni, Freedman, and Martin 2008, 49). Most simply, it refers to limitations in our ability to manage personal care and other daily activities.

In 2005, 133 million Americans—almost one out of every two adults—had at least one chronic disease (Centers for Disease Control 2012), although these conditions did not generally limit their ability to manage day-to-day life. I would be included among that number. Women, individuals on both Medicare and Medicaid, and non-Hispanic blacks and Hispanics had the highest prevalence of six or more chronic conditions (Centers for Medicare and Medicaid Services 2012), which often translates into activity limitations. The people most likely to have such activity limitations were people over seventy-five, women, and those with very low incomes (Ralph et al. 2013). Thus, we see how intersecting inequalities reveal themselves.

The important message is that gender, race, and class matter in the development of chronic conditions, in our ability to get the care we need, and in our efforts to find wholeness. As Andrew Blaikie (1999) cogently observed—we may make our own histories, in terms of agency, but we cannot choose the circumstances in which we exercise that agency. Our choices are not open ended. Black Americans, for example, live fewer years than whites and more years with chronic health problems for reasons that are linked to social determinants of health, including income, education, access to medical care, and racism. Analyzing trends in disability, Schoeni, Freedman, and Martin (2008) observed that "socioeconomic factors appear to have played a substantial role" in the decline of disability, but the reasons for that decline are less clear (80). It will be interesting to note whether the growing inequality in this country will affect trends in disability in the years to come.

CULTURE, MEANING, AND IMPAIRMENT

Women's efforts to render life meaningful develop dialectically through social interactions and, in particular cultural and policy contexts. The woman's specific context also matters—her income, her family, her race, ethnicity, and gender—and the more elusive but important ambient notion of what it means to be a "normal, valued and successful human being" (Lamb 2014, 51) in a particular time and place.

Today, culture offers impoverished and meager representations of older women with multiple impairments whose lives do not meet the expectations of the new "third" age. We do not often see representations of women like eighty-year-old Florida Scott Maxwell (1968) who acknowledges both her frailty and her fierce energy, albeit often unrealizable because of the frailty. Far more than just a body, she shields her bodily woes from younger people because they don't want to hear about them. And thus the young lose the opportunity to see how pain and zealousness for life coexist. This lacuna further deprives women who are struggling for wholeness with culturally valid models to help in that effort.

While I do not want to romanticize the difficulties of living with a disordered body (Toombs 1995), especially for women who live alone on modest incomes, I have come to appreciate what it takes to come to terms with physical or mental decrements and then to integrate the illness into a continuous and meaningful life story. I see how it is possible to say, as the French writer Colette did, that "near-immobility is a gift" (Ladimer 1993, 254). These women, with their experiences, deserve the visibility—and the respect—now lavished on the seventy-five-year-old mountain-climbing grandmother.

EXPERIENCING CHRONIC ILLNESS

Philosopher Kay Toombs (1992), who has multiple sclerosis, tells us that chronic illness means the "body loses its silence." No longer able to take our body for granted, it swamps "other factors in determining matters like morale and well-being" (Twigg 2004, 64). A few months after a slight stroke and recurring fibrillations, at age seventy-three, respected and prolific poet, novelist, and journal writer May Sarton (1989) wrote, "Youth . . . has to do with not being aware of one's body whereas old age is often a matter of overcoming some misery or other inside the body. One is acutely aware of it" (35). She observed that the "stroke has made me take a leap into old age instead of approaching it gradually" (35). In the worst days of her illness, she would remind herself that "the body is part of our identity, and its afflictions and discontents, its donkey-like refusal to do what 'ought' to be done, destroys self-respect" unless we can "ascend *inside* to what is happening *inside*" (125). This ascension may mean giving up all that can be given up "because other things become more important" (125). It may also mean accepting what cannot be changed and accommodating to what one can no longer do. Illness changes us, but we also remain the same. Continuity of self does not exlcude change (Andrews 1999).

Bodies that are impaired challenge cultural ideas about normalcy, about aging "successfully," and about value and so provoke conflicts for individuals between the "desire for normalcy and the acknowledgment of difference being enacted over and over again" (Becker 1997, 16). Given the social construction of "normalcy" for a person of a certain age, an understanding that women commonly internalize, the struggle as one moves further from that norm, now so frequently defined in terms of "successful" aging, is necessarily an ongoing process (Gooberman-Hill, Ayis, and Ebrahim 2003, chapter 1). "As a concept, *disability* assumes a self-evident departure from the abilities of *normal* individuals." Yet, what is taken to be natural or normal for a person of sixty, seventy, or eighty has changed significantly in the past thirty or so years suggesting that definitions are culturally and politically, rather than objectively, determined (Thorne, McCormick, and Carty 1997, 2). As such, the prevailing understandings start from the assumption that we each have an equal opportunity to achieve that "normal" status. They do so by ignoring life histories and prominent patterns of inequality. For most of us who live in this culture with these definitions, we stray from "normal" as our bodies change, as they become in Kay Toombs's (1995) language "disordered." Yet, she further observes, even then we do not want to see ourselves as "abnormal." While a full discussion of the issue of the "normal" and the dilemma of difference (Minow 1990; Douard 1996) is beyond the scope of this chapter, I raise it because people with serious impairments bring it into their understanding of themselves (Becker 1997), which can create yet another source of judgment about our inability to live up to social expectations and another hurdle to clear in the search for meaning.

As I think about potentially life-altering effects of stroke, for example, I am reminded of a guest at a recent Thanksgiving dinner. He is a foundation executive in his seventies who must now use a wheelchair. As I observed him, I saw how the wheelchair altered his perception of the world and of himself. He had to look up to almost everyone, making it difficult to integrate himself into conversations, especially in a crowded room, even though his mental capacity was intact. As we were preparing to leave, he sat alone by the elevator, excluded from the rituals of goodbye. Familiar to many people with activity-limiting conditions, he was able to choose what he wanted to do, but he lacked the ability to execute his wishes, a problem that Bart Collopy (1988) describes as the gap between decisional and executional autonomy. Kay Toombs (1995), also in a wheelchair, observes that the "frustration of intentionality" and being treated as a dependent—people begin to refer to you in the third person—reinforces the shame that often accompanies having a "disordered body style." In the situation of chronic impairment, power is often visibly demonstrated. A person in a wheelchair sits while others often stand and look down. It also happens when we are naked and the more powerful person is clothed. Lives are "regulated, ordered, known, and disciplined" (Twigg 2004, 65).

CHRONIC ILLNESS AND MEANING

In his magisterial *Sources of the Self,* Charles Taylor (1994) employs the concept of frameworks to explicate our commitments and motivate our actions. A framework generates our answers to a succession of key questions, starting with "Who am I?" But it continues with other questions. Can I make sense of my life and my place within it when my physical or mental self no longer supports my activities in the world? What values and belief systems give me the cognitive maps of my life so that my experiences are more than a string of unrelated events and the anticipation of my death without meaning? What happens when I cannot make sense of what is happening to me? What would it be like to live without a "cognizance of order, coherence, and purpose," absent worthwhile goals and the accompanying sense of fulfillment" (Reker and Wong 1988, 221)? This need is what makes serious chronic illness an existential as well as a physical or mental problem. I return to Kay Toombs (1992), who observes that illness is about the physical but is fundamentally about the self and the threats to identity.

Throughout our lives, we adapt and change as circumstances, including our bodies, change. Think of the transition to puberty or to parenthood or perhaps the death of a spouse or another loved person. Each time our biographies—the way our lives had been going—shift, it takes renegotiation to remake our personal worlds (Becker 1997). As I have suggested in chapter 1, we go through that process of negotiation as age changes our appearance, or our physical strength, or our confidence in our ability to negotiate our environment. In that discussion, I wrote about the need we have for congruence between how we see ourselves and what we present to the world. This end cannot be individually achieved; it requires social recognition. In chapter 2, I noted how ageist assumptions narrowed our world. Imagine how much more difficult to gain social recognition when our bodies deviate in very substantial ways from the normatively valued. Many questions will confound our search, but an important one is this—shall I protect myself by withdrawal, or shall I eagerly participate in the world of the unimpaired (Bernard 1996)? In her consideration of the virtues of age, feminist philosopher Sara Ruddick (1999) describes what she calls "wise independence," that is, in part, "the ability to acknowledge one's limitations and accept help in ways that are gratifying to the helper" (50). Wise independence, she observes, happens not to us alone but between and among people; it is not something we can do alone. It may mean adjusting our aspirations to our remaining capacities or accepting uncertainty and being "sensible." It may mean holding on and letting go. It may mean many different things, but it rarely means relinquishing the "exercise of will and self-determination" (Lloyd et al. 2014). Thus, how we manage change, how able we are to integrate it into our lives in meaningful ways, matters deeply to how we experience chronic illness.

In a study of patient empowerment, Aujoulat and others (2008) found that while individuals wanted to understand their illness, they also wanted to assign meaning to the illness experience to meet the larger goals of seeing their lives as "meaningful, coherent and worth living" (1237). Hilde Lindemann Nelson (2001) simply states that "we are what we care about," which is not so easily established after our habitual ways of life are disrupted. She argues that we build our identity around the "significant things I've done and experienced, my more important characteristics, the roles and responsibilities I care most about, the values that matter the most to me." But she further observes that our individual identities are also "constituted by the stories other people construct around me" (72). These interactional and relational elements of identity making, when joined to the concept of the "normal" and other features of our social and cultural environment, suggest how hard the task of biographical reintegration may be as our conditions change. Each element supporting our identity is important and needs to be rethought.

CHRONIC ILLNESS IN CONTEXT

This urgent need to have a meaningful life and a secure identity happens in a context. If one defends the view, as I do, that our identities are socially and historically constructed, it matters greatly that the contemporary context leaves little space for those who are less than well. This context is broad. It includes dominant discourses about "successful aging," the subcultures of biomedicine and social services, and the prevailing concepts about autonomy and independence. I will also touch upon the particular concerns related to gender in the particular context of contemporary socierty while turning later to narrative accounts of gender and its relationship to our experiences of chronic illness.

Cultural Norms

We do not create order and reestablish a knowable world outside of culture; hence, our narratives are personal but also reflect wide social, cultural, and historical forces (Gooberman-Hill, Ayis, and Ebrahim 2003). More than two decades ago, Jerome Bruner (1990) argued:

> The symbolic systems that individuals used in constructing meaning were systems already in place, already "there" deeply entrenched in culture and language. They constituted a very special kind of communal tool kit whose tools, once used, make the user a reflection of the community. (11)

We see these influences even in the language we use to talk about illnesses and our responses to those illnesses (Charmaz 1995; Werner, Isaksen, and Malterud 2004; Roberto, Gigliotti, and Husser 2004; Hurd Clarke, Griffin, and PACC Research Team 2008).

The obvious downside of being so culturally embedded is that it limits the stories we can comfortably tell (Radley 1989). Simultaneously, however, it offers an opening for the creation of transgressive stories. Thus it is important to see how contemporary culture, with its consistent portrayal of the most well-off and often the healthiest older people as the visible face of aging, offers fewer resources than richer and more diverse representations of old age might do. Even the emphasis on transgression ("aging disgracefully" by disrupting the social order) reflects a representation of old age that, I suspect, few can or wish to adopt as their lifestyle. Instead, what we most commonly see is that the experience of chronic illness exposes most sharply the dissonance between extant cultural ideals and the resources needed to remake a self when former certainties and ways of being in the world become displaced (Cole 1995). When we may be anything but plucky and energetic, these norms may intimidate us when we feel tired or sad or fearful while still wanting to see ourselves as a good person (Ruddick 1999).

As our physical capacities move us further from normative ideals based on productivity or activity, these dominant norms continue to be elements in one's life story even when they are hard to fit in. Contemporary social categories and the iconography that accompanies them are thus one more difficulty to overcome when women face the compounded difficulties of being women and chronically impaired in a society that devalues both their gender and their health status. Recalling that societies are organized on the basis of age, gender, race, and class relations (see chapter 2), we can see how being a woman who has a serious chronic condition falls on the wrong side of the power balance, a problem that deepens if she is also poor.

Autonomy and Independence

Compounding the problems created by a stroke or another serious chronic illness are popular understandings of individual autonomy, control, and will. These contrast sharply with how we experience (Kaufman 1988). The prevailing autonomy paradigm, conceived in terms of self-direction, becomes increasingly problematic as we face limits. Not only may it fail to describe how most of us actually live, but it downgrades interdependency and leaves no room for dependency, a feature that is part of all our lives, at least on occasion, but normative for people with chronic illnesses. For many women, autonomy, as traditionally understood, is not a singular goal; instead, women commonly value interdependency—identity in the context of interpersonal relationship. Our society's failure to acknowledge the fact of dependence for all of us by virtue of our embodiment and its persistent state for people who have serious chronic illnesses devalues both the persons who experience illness and those who assist them (Dodds 2007). The cultural elevation of both independence and autonomy, defined as uncoerced choice, can blind us to the vulnerability we all experience. Especially when we are seriously limited, the standard autonomy paradigm and its individualistic focus can deprive women of what may be most needed—not uncoerced choice but a loving touch and recognition (Hoffmaster 2006). The ethos of individual responsibility and independence further limits the cultural resources available to women as they grapple with making sense of their lives.

The Professional Cultures of Biomedicine and Social Services

Subcultures, like biomedicine and social services, especially long-term care, create further difficulties for those making the "odyssey of self" that I referred to above (Charmaz 1995), in large part because they focus entirely on the body and its functions rather than on the person who is facing these functional limitations. Comprehensive assessments ask certain questions that only address issues that they have the capacity to address. These do not include the broader goals that are assumed for younger people with disabilities, such as integration into the community. While substantial sums are directed at high-cost curative medicine, far less goes to intervening in ways that promote reintegration for old people with chronic impairments or interventions that will make their living arrangements health inducing rather than health destroying. I recall one case when an old woman kept reappearing at the emergency department at a Philadelphia hospital with breathing difficulties. When Arthur Caplan, the director of the ethics program at the University of Pennsylvania, suggested getting her an air-conditioner, her visits to the ER ended. Examples of this sort are commonplace and reinforce the power over options that professionals have.

Biomedicine makes it harder to create a meaningful integration of one's physical or mental impairments with one's life story. While the expanding corpus of illness narratives may partially fill this void, the problem will remain as long as our culture prizes individual health above all else and remains intractably hostile to decline and decay (Cole 1992). Defining disease predominantly in materialistic terms, biomedicine offers meager resources to address suffering or to help patients narratively reconfigure their lives. Meaning itself is not a central focus or task of medicine. Because it eschews teleology, the very idea of moral purpose to the illness experience is a biomedical impossibility (Kleinman 1993). Instead, the biomedical approach focuses on single causal chains that specify the specific pathogenesis of structural flaws and mechanical mechanisms. Because it is so centered on what can be seen, it tends to relegate the psychological, social, and moral to the realm of epiphenomena in the experience of illness (Kleinman 1993).

Biomedicine cannot overcome the fact that the individual who becomes sick does so in the eyes of his or her society, in relation to it, and in keeping with the modalities fixed by it (Herzlich and Pierret 1987). "Medical knowledge, authority, and responsibility both respond to and influence [the experience of chronic illness]" (Kaufman 1988b, 340). The very norms and language of biomedicine have moral implications. They uphold a "duty to be healthy" so that one can age "successfully." If one becomes ill, it imposes the obligation to seek medical treatment because everyone has the "duty" to get well (Herzlich and Pierret 1987). In this way, health may become a coercive moral standard as health is equated with goodness and ill health with a failure of control (Calasanti 2005).

By focusing on the body of the individual sick person, the biomedical model also strips away the social context of illness; hence, it renders invisible the ways in which that context affects the course of illness and recovery and, alternatively, the way illness matters in how we experience social relations (Kleinman 1993). Frequently, biomedicine also silences the voice in which the patient tries to explain her illness. The "voice of medicine" often drowns out the "voice of the life-world" (Mishler 1984). It tells us how to talk about our illness, and so women fit their stories into acceptable biomedical scripts, particularly emphasizing strengths (Werner, Isaksen, and Malterud 2004), which makes asking for help when needed all the harder. This absence of recognition and a woman's own voice accelerate her suffering (Charmaz 1983). Yet, and often to her detriment, she may share the values of biomedicine and notions about the use of medical practice. Thus, when biomedicine fails her (when it cannot restore functioning), she often blames not it but herself. Biomedicine names the illness, prescribes for its care, but does not participate in the story making that will find a place for the illness in the individual's autobiography. It often cannot answer because it doesn't hear the deeper question: "How the hell have I come to be like this? . . . because it isn't me" (Williams 1984, 175).

The standard quasi-contractual relationship between physician and patient, where the central focus is on decision making and the expulsion of the alien presence of disease, is inappropriate for long-term impairments. Listening to the voice of the patient, the voice that explains what the illness means, is generally the role of a social worker or chaplain, and if they are not available, that voice is often unheard. Further, as discussed in chapter 2, ageism manifests itself in this encounter when older patients, especially women, are discounted and their symptoms attributed to age. It is not unusual for the world of biomedicine to demonstrate esteem-robbing, unacceptable treatment (Lloyd et al. 2014).

Gender

Deep old age is predominantly a woman's experience; hence women experience simultaneously disadvantages that accrue because of their gender, their age, and their lack of conformity to health norms. Women are likely to face multiple chronic impairments in part because we live longer than men; we are also apt to face them alone (Thorne, McCormick, and Carty 1997; Administration on Aging 2012). If we need assistance, we may need to rely on the public sector, where we must give up a great deal of privacy, which, as noted above, defines us in limited functional terms and where the rationing of services means that our desires and self-defined needs most often cannot be met. The result is that women stop asking for what they want and need and accept what is given (Aronson 2002). To protest is to be ungrateful. Women are thus put in a difficult position if they want to resist the definitions that the public sector uses to define them, such as frailty. If they comply, which they must to get services, they also face "the implications of such classification and compliance" (Grenier and Hanley 2007, 218). Their task then is to find ways to resist the marginalization that accompanies the definition of frailty, a problem compounded by relative isolation and/or physical losses. If not the public sector, we must often turn to family and most often to the women in our family (see chapter 5) for care, creating tensions with the unwillingness to be a burden. Health-care spending further reveals how gender neutrality penalizes women. Spending on high-technology—and high-cost—medicine continues to expand, while neoliberalism has undercut spending for the social care that so many women need (Thorne, McCormick, and Carty 1997) (see the introduction and chapter 5). The primary interest is on what medical interventions can accomplish and not on making living with serious chronic illness easier.

So women who are chronically impaired simultaneously face several problems—we are more likely than men to have such activity-limiting conditions; we are apt to be facing these problems as single women; we have fewer resources than men to get the help that we need and so are reliant on the public programs that neoliberalism and the narratives of the new aging are undercutting; or we rely only on our families, primarily women family members, for help. And, as discussed above, we often internalize the normative values of American culture and one of its key institutions, biomedicine, which initially validates the medical condition but also serves to set boundaries to the reestablishment of a new identity.

ILLNESS AND NARRATIVE

These constraints on redefining what is so critical when living with a chronic illness—a sense of order and coherence—suggest that what is needed are new stories about the self that can unite the positive and negative poles of aging, that honor strength in frailty, and respect the difficult task that is meaning making when we are so far from the normatively desirable, as discussed in chapters 1–3. To be labeled and categorized as "disabled" when only a very specific type of the abled body is valued is to experience a very specific kind of exclusion. Yet, as with younger women maintaining that they will never be like "that" when it comes to appearance or bodily function, separating people into the abled (good) and disabled (bad) is inculcating prejudice against our likely future selves (Wendell 1992). Thus, absent a story about how women and men can find meaning despite their disabled selves and the visual representations that can accompany that story, the task of making sense of chronic impairments and the new form of life we are living is made more problematic than it already is.

Thus, in crafting our identities and recovering and often discovering meanings, narrative has a critical function. Stories offer a means to "offset the powerful constructs imposed on older women's bodies" while giving them the freedom to describe their sense of self (Grenier and Hanley 2007, 212). "The analysis of narrative is a primary means for uncovering how disruption is experienced and how continuity is created, and for examining disparities between cultural ideals and people's experiences" (Becker 1997, 18). Stories tell us about a life and how illness has altered that life. They reveal how people address their life situations and the problem of identity that serious illness creates (Werner, Isaksen, and Malterud 2004). While our narratives may be multiple—we talk about our bodies; we talk about what we value; we talk about our relationships; we see ourselves in the context of "normalcy" and extant cultural frameworks—together they help us to answer the question "Who am I?" Stories demonstrate the linkages between personal and collective identities (Jacobs 2002) and reveal the ways in which yearning for continuity seems to be a core construct in American life (Becker 1997). As we tell our stories to others, they may deepen our explorations and also help us to overcome the power of master narratives, such as those built around race or gender or age (Lindemann Nelson 2001). Narrative is also a "conduit for emotion and a means through which embodied distress is expressed" (Becker 1997, 14). If they gain public recognition, narratives also have a wider social role. Stories about old women, especially old women with debilitating conditions, can contribute to altering social attitudes about women who do not have normatively valued bodies (Woodward 1999a). We need to *see* old women with bodily limitations through their words because as they talk about their disrupted lives against cultural discourses about aging and old age, they represent efforts to explain how they are trying to live up to expectations but also how they may fail to do so despite their efforts (Becker 1997). Narrative renders visible their complexities and continued person-hood.

NARRATIVE THEMES

Narrative sources—ethnography, autobiography, fiction, the conversations at Mayslake and with our friends and colleagues and any other place where stories are told—are no more likely to yield grand narratives about the experience of chronic illness than about the experiences with our aging bodies more generally, but they do reveal some common themes. These themes will help us to understand women's fears, what matters to them as they live with chronic illness, and the different coping strategies they adopt to make living with chronic illness understandable to themselves (Becker 1997). Their stories will reveal the importance of context and social location in experiences of decline and disability (Grenier 2005; Silverman et al. 2009) and also demonstrate the importance of class, race, and gender in shaping their responses (Becker and Newsome 2005; Hopp et al. 2012). That specificity is often lost since samples are small and often do not or cannot obtain the diversity sought. Their stories will often demonstrate forms of resistance, often nearly invisible, against professional categorizations used to sort those who are or are not eligible for services (Grenier 2005).

Narrative and Gender

While I will turn below to approaches women have adopted to integrate chronic illness into their lives, I note here that studies tend to be gender neutral and context free (Thorne, McCormick, and Carty 1997). Yet the limited studies that specifically compare the experiences of men and women demonstrate that these experiences are loosely tied to the gender roles they have historically played (Solimeo 2008; Hurd Clarke and Bennett 2013). In a study of Parkinson's disease, for example, Samantha Solimeo (2008) found that similarity of somatic symptoms between men and women did not translate into similar experiences of impairment. Because women and men generally have played different gender roles, they interpreted the somatic symptoms as they related to their ability to continue those roles. Thus, women emphasized symptoms that impaired their ability to engage in, maintain, and strengthen social relationships while men focused on appearance and strength. Thus, challenges to their ability to perform physically most threatened the continuity of their gendered roles. Thus, Solimeo observes, "gender is a salient site where the meaning of somatic experience is produced" (S47). Should it ever be possible to design more responsive social-service interventions, knowledge about gender differences would be critical in assuring the system could appropriately respond to these differences.

Other research suggested, for example, how gender-appropriate roles shaped the stories that men and women told when they faced chronic illness (Hurd Clarke and Bennett 2013). Women, for example, often express concern about how their illnesses negatively affect the lives of others or might do so in the future. "You become dependent on other people instead of helping other people and it's an awful hard blow to take. It's really hard" (Hurd Clarke and Bennett 2013, 352). The women of Mayslake expressed similar fears about who would take care of them while they fiercely resisted asking for help, especially from children.

More broadly, in his powerful account of being with chronically ill patients, Arthur Kleinman (1988) noted that studying "the experience of illness has something fundamental to teach us about the human condition, with its universal suffering and death" (xiii). Narratives of illness, including fiction, help us to understand what it feels like from the inside to be felled by a stroke, or be bent over from osteoarthritis, or slowed down by COPD or heart disease, and they permit us to see the person as a whole and not as a bundle of stereotypes—stroke victim, Alzheimer's sufferer. They allow us to see what an aging body might feel like and thus aid in our ability to develop our sympathies (Mackenzie and Scully 2007). We learn what a person's actions mean in their own terms against the backdrop of their lives, making sense of what otherwise might seem strange (Holstein 1994). Literature can reveal the pain and humiliation and also the triumphs of people not like us while symbolically enacting the "various existential possibilities available to human beings" (Said 1982, 11). Perhaps above all, they provide a source of knowing that is an alternative to the more distant, power-laden professional narratives about "them." While I don't mean to suggest that social workers, geriatricians, and others lack concern or even empathy for the people with whom they work, they are constrained by time but also by differential access to control and power.

Learning from Texts

Ethnographic studies provide us with multiple examples of how women (and men, too) find ways to incorporate chronic illness as part of their identity, although, as discussed above, studies rarely consider different experiences based on gender and/or class. One theme was that adaptation of people's sense of self to having a chronic illness depended on how well they could do what they wanted to do and their understanding of what caused their illness. It mattered, for example, if they assumed responsibility for their illness (Charmaz 2006). Studies generally involving only women also suggest how individuals construct culturally embedded "possible selves" that reveal how ideas about aging, ageism, and their own beliefs influence how they negotiated their identities and evaluated their health (Roberto and McCann 2011, citing Henchoz, Cavalli, and Girardin 2008). Even when we are most vulnerable, our language reflects the "key values and beliefs that define a particular culture" (Becker 1997). African Americans, for example, emphasize resiliency and independence, traits developed in the context of racism (Becker and Newsome 2005).

Narratives of chronic illness are complex and frequently contradictory. Women often continued to describe the incongruence between their perceived and actual age, presenting themselves "as not old even in the face of their experience of chronic conditions" (Rozario and Derienzis 2009, 549), but they also described how chronic illness exacerbated "feelings of oldness . . . and the perception that they were no longer attractive to others" (Hurd Clarke, Griffin, and PACC Research Team 2008, 1088). Women described how negative readings of their bodies and lives, the need to rely on others, and the inability to engage in favored activities contributed to a sense of worthlessness and of being trapped in their own bodies. The inability to "meet cultural norms of health and attractiveness led to expressed feelings of "low self-esteem resulting from the realities of their current appearance and functional inabilities" (Hurd Clarke, Griffin, and PACC Research Team 2008, 1092). Yet others pointed to efforts to transgress, to defuse the way aging and chronic illness became the singular definition of who they were (Rozario and Derienzis 2009).

As important, however, as the experience of disruption and the resulting challenges to self-esteem, women's stories also revealed how displacement led "to efforts to restore life to normal" (Becker 1997, 27; Aujoulat et al. 2008). It is quite a juggling act—to be recognizable to oneself and to simultaneously be the same yet a different person, a reconciliation that came about once they could accept the material realities of bodily aging while also affirming what they can still do (Lloyd et al. 2014). By accepting the loss of control as part of a "personal transformational process," it became possible to redefine empowerment so that it included accepting and integrating "the illness into their social and personal identities" (Aujoulat et al. 2008, 1236). Cultural recognition and appreciation of this struggle would be a gift to those so engaged.

Fiction can take us deeply into the inner lives of women who are living with chronic illness in what may be radically different circumstances from our own, providing an opening to develop sympathies for their experience (Mackenzie and Scully 2007). Alice Bell, the central character in the last part of Pat Barker's (1983) novel *Union Street*, is a very old, very poor, very impaired old woman who has suffered a devastating stroke. We see throughout, as she becomes increasingly frail, her struggle to maintain control over her own life despite what both her son and the authorities want for her. She resists their plans for her and also resists their definition of her in purely functional terms. She defines herself as a good friend, a good neighbor who helps others as much as they help her. Those who want what is "best" for her cannot hear her voice.

The limited view of autonomy and assessment based in what she could not do that prevails in community care has no place for exploring her goals, values, and treasured identity. Her strengths and her self-knowledge, not based on activity or other socially valued traits, were invisible. They are not part of how culture represents old women. Like the African American men and women whom Gay Becker and Edwina Newsome (2005) interviewed, Alice resisted imposed definitions of what would be good for her. As these African Americans, she saw herself as an equal participant in a mutual aid system (Holstein 1994). For many poor women, the insistence on strength even when one doesn't feel strong seems to be characteristic. They rely on the strategies that they have used all their lives to negotiate in a context where their poverty and often their race made life particularly difficult (Grenier 2005).

Class and all the features of one's life that class affects are vividly displayed in Alice's struggle for identity and self-esteem. Biannual visits from the social security people humiliated her—"the posh voices, the questions, the eyes everywhere"—and only strengthened her commitment to preserving her independence (Barker 1983, 216). More affluent people would have been able to hire help without accepting the public understanding of frailty (or, in

professional language, inability to perform "activities of daily living") necessary for entry into the publicly funded social service system. Alice's story
reveals how the self as protagonist often needs assistance from the external
world in order to undertake its tasks. She ultimately wandered out on a very
cold night and froze to death. Intentionality was unclear, but what was clear
is that in the absence of a meaningful choice, the idea of choice itself has no
meaning.

An account like Barker's is echoed in different ways in other fictional
accounts of women with serious chronic illnesses. Jill McCorkle's *Life after
Life* (2013) takes us inside an assisted living residence in North Carolina,
where the residents, while physically and sometimes mentally disabled, are
actively engaged in life-affirming pursuits. Fiction can reveal the "complex
and equivocal manifestations of physical and mental disability even in one
person" and hence urge us to be open to ambiguity more widely (Holstein
1994, 826). We can preserve a continuous sense of self, moral and spiritual
development, and growth and reciprocity even when the body is no longer
agile and forgiving. As Thomas Cole (1992) noted, earlier images of aging
demonstrated how "spiritual growth coexisted with physical decline" to offer
a nuanced, nonoppositional view of the "good" and the "bad" in old age.

Consider the reflective notebook of Jungian analyst Florida Scott Maxwell (1968), writing in her eighties. Scott Maxwell anticipates Sara Ruddick's (1999) work on the virtues of age as she notes her duty to all those
who care for her, a duty to not be a burden. She instructs herself that each day
she must be "all right," but that duty does not extend to friends her own age
with whom she "cheerfully exchange[d] the worst symptoms, and our black
dreads as well" (31). She comments that "disabilities crowd in on the old;
real pain is there, and if we have to be falsely cheerful, it is part of our
isolation" (32). Unlike the interviewees who insist that the best attitude is
acceptance, Scott-Maxwell objects to pretending, out of some sense of no-
blesse oblige, that aging is nothing. Our bodies don't work well; little things
have become big things.

THE NEW BINARY: THE THIRD AND THE FOURTH AGES

As the "third age" was birthed, so too was the "fourth age," a dichotomy that
isolates health status, primarily the condition of the body, as demarcating the
good and the valuable and its opposite. No matter how the "fourth age" is
defined, and disagreements are common, its use represents no one well, for

example, it also casts people so defined, women like Florida Scott Maxwell, out of full membership in the moral and social community. It is yet another binary that devalues disability and loss.

Among scholars the definition of the "fourth age" is contested. It seems unclear whether it is used to mark the onset of serious chronic illnesses in general or whether it is reserved for those people so limited that they can display no agency (Gilleard and Higgs 2010; Lloyd et al. 2014). I rely on what I see as its everyday use, that is, to refer to people who no longer meet the norms of "successful" aging as that term is commonly understood. Recalling that British social historian Peter Laslett introduced the "third age" as a catch-all phrase to represent the movement for positive aging that emerged in the mid- to late 1980s, the "fourth age" becomes the time when losses become significant enough that the fit between the normatively desired features of the "third" age become harder and harder to use descriptively.

Given this understanding of the "fourth" age, it is reductionist, a generalization that further marginalizes and isolates people, and especially women, who no longer measure up to the culturally valued norms of the "third age" despite their often painful efforts to "fit" those norms. Entry into the "fourth age" devalues their ability to act, their intimate relationships with others, and their ongoing efforts to sustain a meaningful life despite their losses. Activity-limiting disabilities do not, as I hope the narrative accounts made clear, reflect giving up but rather a profound struggle to reconstitute a meaningful identity. While Alzheimer's disease, especially in its later stages, may be the trump for the "fourth age" concept, I will try to show that such labeling can negatively affect the person even then.

As I think the glimpses that ethnography, fiction, and autobiography gave into women's experiences, to speak of what is going on as "decline and loss" inadequately represents the work that takes place. It focuses entirely on the disabled body as if that were the single value of a person. Certainly there are many fears and uncertainties that are familiar to people with serious, chronic conditions, but, for the most part, they actively seek continuity with their past lives, integrate the illness into their present lives, and continue to have relationships with family and friends as well as medical and social-care personnel. There are, of course, losses, but there are also, for many, gains.

The experience of chronic illness can be experienced as enabling, sharpening the person's appreciation of remaining powers and abilities, quickening sensibilities and talents that had been dormant, and bringing out a depth and strength of character previously untapped and unrealized (Jennings, Callahan, and Caplan 1988, S7). The women of Mayslake noted the pleasures of slowing down and so noticing what previously had been invisible.

Both abjection and dependency are cultural products that we need to counter by rendering visible people with activity-limiting chronic impairments. Such visibility will simultaneously decrease their marginality while facilitating sympathetic understanding by people not so impaired. In its absence we will misjudge their quality of life and see people who are differently embodied as a category—"fourth agers"—and not as they see themselves or wish to be seen. The tiny and bent old woman in a nursing home unable to get around without a wheelchair whom I once knew and often talked to was as full of yearnings for friendship and connection as someone twenty or thirty or forty years her junior. A childless widow, she told me wistfully that her best friend had recently died and so she no longer had anyone to talk to. That loss of a primary relationship deepened the threat to her selfhood that her chronic impairments and residency in the nursing home had done.

Without diminishing the precariousness and uncertainties that are part of what it means to live with serious chronic illnesses, I see categorization and labeling—the third age and the fourth age—as a disservice to the whole of life. In an ageist society, the motivations for doing so are understandable, yet by dividing late life into third and fourth ages, ageism is simply displaced. The very people who most need the support and affirmation of others as they move even further from normatively favored bodies and minds become its "victims." If we relegate a time of progressive disablement and loss of valued roles and possibilities to the fourth age—in order to preserve the positive features of the third age—we risk further isolating and "othering" the person who can no longer meet those norms. It permits the stigma associated with disability to continue and disallows accepting disability and death as "acceptable and respectable human experiences" (Morell 2003, 83). By so doing, we further damage women's ability to see themselves as anything but a burden on society.

In rejecting the fourth age conceptually and linguistically, I do not wish to suggest that there are not profound difficulties associated with chronic illness, both existential and structural, elements that are often intertwined. As discussed above, people with chronic illness are often isolated and shamed; many, especially women, are beholden to the state and to their families, especially their daughters, for care. Since what happens to the body also happens to the self (Toombs 1996), chronic illness imposes the difficult task of integrating the loss of physical or mental capacity and identity. It is made even harder when others impose an illness identity on us (MacRae 2010) or categorically situate us in the devalued fourth age.

In critiquing the fourth age, I want to comment upon Alzheimer's disease and other dementias. Dementia clearly poses a very grave threat to self. I recall a woman greeting me as I got off the elevator at a nursing home with these words: "Do you know who I am?" as she flung her thin dress above her head and then posed a second question, "Do you know who you are?" Is Alzheimer's disease the time when the dialectic between strength and frailty, dependency and independence, finally collapses, when others must define us since our ability to do so ourselves seems to be gone? Perhaps, though, that is the key—how do others see and define us? Because I accept the argument that the late Tom Kitwood (1993) made some years ago that neuropathology is not the sole determinant of behavior but that social relationships are also key, it seems possible that even with the identity problems that dementia causes, a social identity remains possible, but that identity is contingent on our relationship with others. The fear is that malignant positioning deprives the person with Alzheimer's of the opportunity to construct a valued social identity (Sabat, Napolitano, and Fath 2004). The individual may not experience the loss as severely as those who see only what once was.

While my intent is not to draw an overly rosy picture of what it is like to have Alzheimer's disease, a condition I fear deeply, I use this example of social identity and its potential to enhance the lives of people who are too often seen through a filter of their disease and the final redoubt of the fourth age. The result is that all behaviors are viewed through that filter and so often reinforce the person's difficulties with identity and self-worth. The first-person writings now available demonstrate both the potential of affirming social interactions and the harms brought about by malignant ones. The novel and the play *Still Alice*, by Lisa Genova (2007), demonstrate this well while supporting Stephen Post's (1995) argument that in the West the focus is too fully on a person's cognitive capacities to the relative exclusion of her affective and emotional elements. The language of the fourth age, even for people with Alzheimer's, can detract from the moral and practical tasks of paying attention and being with the person so that she can maintain a social identity for as long as possible. To depersonalize it by focusing on the medical—its neuropathology—thus means to place half of the people over eighty-five who have it into a category of outcasts.

ETHICAL DIMENSIONS OF CHRONIC ILLNESS

I turn now to the last "lesson" that I take from this consideration of serious chronic illness—the need for an adequate moral foundation to address issues that chronic illness raises. Having touched upon this limitation elsewhere in the chapter, I want here to refocus on definitions of autonomy and the absence of a "critical" approach to ethics that permits a richer view of its scope and obligations. This means rethinking the nature of the self, challenging the conception of independence as the normal human condition, and considering how our day-to-day actions are morally significant. Thus, how we give a person a bath, the respect we show (or don't show) for the old body, the dignity enhancing (or eroding) ways in which we talk and listen to the older person are all ethical in nature. These topics are complex; thus, my treatment here will be abbreviated (for a more extensive treatment, see Holstein, Parks, and Waymack 2011).

George Agich (1995) noted that chronic illness, where abilities are compromised and its main features cannot be altered, is "strikingly discordant with the conception of the robustly autonomous person" (133). This model valorizes self-reliance, personal preferences, and self-assertion—the very antithesis of what a person with chronic illness may want and need. As a social self, dependence is a nonaccidental feature of the human condition (Parks 2003; Kittay 1999; Tronto 1993). This societal and relational view of autonomy understands individuals in concrete ways and sees autonomy as a meaningful reflection of their identity (Holstein 2010). Given this broadened understanding of actual autonomy, to respect individuals means that "we attend to their concrete individuality, to their affective and personal experiences" while also learning "how to acknowledge their habits and identifications" (Agich 1990, 14). It means, to start with, that we offer not merely choice to people, but meaningful choice, a redefinition that will expand the obligations of the social service sector.

Further, the prevailing autonomy paradigm cannot embrace and appreciate both abilities and disabilities (Morell 2003, 80), and so it elides an essential element of our character. This cultural accent, labeled the "enlightened view of old age" (Cole 1986, 7), can leave the frail, the "non-productive," and the "non-autonomous" in an existential abyss. As George Agich (1990) argues, "giving" a "frail" elder a range of choices or "letting" the elder choose may be "ethically less compelling than helping the elder to live in the face of frailty, loss, and ultimately death" (17). Individualistic definitions of autonomy thus make it difficult to see that we have collective needs if we are to live well, a need that living with limiting disabilities exacerbates (Morell 2003)

Hence, a critical ethics establishes claims upon society that allow us to meet our responsibilities to ourselves and to others and establishes the moral grounds for such claims. It insists that one cannot be a responsible social or health professional in the absence of resources to meet our obligations well (Lloyd 2006; Tronto 1993). It criticizes our current insistence on discussing public life from a vision of autonomous, equal, rational actors each pursuing separate ends. This is a faulty vision of the self and serves older people poorly (Holstein 2010). This problem often imposes a limited view of independence and the demand to live up to some standard while limiting the conditions to help realize that possibility.

A REFLECTION ON "LESSONS LEARNED"

Carefully I set down the words "lessons learned." Perhaps the most important lesson is that while chronic illness dislocates our taken-for-granted world, women, as reflected in narrative accounts of their lives, seek and generally find ways to reestablish continuity with their past selves so that life continues to have meaning and purpose. They often do this against significant odds. For culture to be more enabling, a richer assemblage of norms, virtues, and representations can enlarge the scope of valued lives. It can also deepen the moral sympathies of those who care for us when we need assistance and even the strangers who judge us as "other." Such sympathies can expand understanding by deepening the connections between people (Mackenzie and Scully 2000).

Biomedicine, itself a subculture, puts further obstacles in the way of women learning to live with and make sense of their physical and mental changes. A central need, then, is to restore the voice of the patient not primarily in terms of consent but rather as a conversation partner as she constructs the story of life with her chronic illness, not all chronic illnesses.

In addition to the cultural invisibility of women's late-life efforts to lead meaningful lives and biomedicine's limitations are the effects of lifetime inequalities, the retrenchment of the social safety net (see the introduction and chapter 5), and the inflexible, unresponsive social service system (Aronson 2002; Grenier 2005; see chapter 5). Rendering visible their lived experiences can (I cannot say will) lead to more sensitive policies that confront the barriers many women face and so facilitate their drive for continuity and meaning. This task lies ahead. These include a richer tool kit that shows women the many ways other women have made sense of their experiences of chronic impairment. Many more and varied representations of women are both possible and desirable. I would include this need in arguing that we need a richer ethical framework for thinking about chronic illness.

CONCLUSION

The goal in this chapter was to pursue understanding of the multiple sources of meaning for women with chronic impairments and the impediments to finding such meanings. To that end, I argued that we need rich representations of women to rupture the binary between the third and fourth ages that inevitably devalues the last part of life. Each lesson just addressed can be deepened by probing for an understanding of the complexities, ambiguities, opportunities, and constraints that those who are differently embodied may experience. Addressing each of these lessons can aid in creating a hospitable social, political, and cultural environment that will see us through serious health problems and impairments. Familiar themes like productivity, individual responsibility for health, and ideas about normal aging dominated people's stories as they tried to fit themselves into these persistent norms. They can be altered. The illness experience influences an individual's capacity to engage the social world while the social world, including "societal attitudes, social practices, public policy, influences the subjective experience of illness" (Toombs, Bernard, and Carson 1996, x). The embedded, embodied individual cannot alone create a satisfying "fit" with an environment that is not supportive.

We can see from older women's stories how their experiences with chronic illness clash with the "dominant organizational and professional understandings of disability and decline as corporeal and functional risk" (Grenier 2005, 139). Functionality counted far less than the ability to negotiate the contexts of their lives, an arena that can be modified as the ADA has assured kneeling buses and curb cuts. To respond to these stories and understandings means adopting a far broader and richer view of what social obligations to older people with chronic illness ought to be. Our medical care system will transplant kidneys to an eighty-year-old but will not assure that she has a place to live that won't require her to climb three flights of steps. Or it will pay for costly ER visits rather than provide an air-conditioner or it will manage activities of daily living and not provide her with easy-grip utensils, home modifications, and maybe one day, robotic arms to allow her to cook.

Part II

Aging Women in Contemporary Society

Chapter Five

A Looming Dystopia

Feminism, Aging, and Community-Based
Long-Term Care

Any real society is a caregiving and a care receiving society, and we must therefore discover ways of coping with these facts of human neediness and dependency that are compatible with the self-respect of the recipients and do not exploit the caregivers. (Nussbaum 2002, 188)

Remember the old Beatles refrain—"Will you still need me, will you still feed me when I'm sixty-four?" But what if I need you when I'm eighty-four? What if I have congestive heart failure and arthritis and can no longer bathe or cook or dress myself? What if I have Alzheimer's disease and need basic support with almost all activities? Medicare will not pay for what is commonly called "custodial care." Thus, I ask, "Will anyone be there?" How will I pay for it? How will I simultaneously ask for the help I need while maintaining my self-respect? Since I am a woman, the chances are that I will be unmarried: a widow, divorced, or ever single. Thus, unlike most men, I will have no spouse to care for me and, if I do, he'll probably be ninety and not in such great shape himself. If I'm lucky enough to be comfortably off, perhaps even affluent, I can hire someone to assist me with the daily activities that I can no longer do for myself. If I am among the 7–10 percent of Americans who have long-term care insurance, it will cover some but not all of my care needs. If I have very little money and almost no assets, I might receive some services from my state's home- and community-based Medicaid waiver program. It will assess me, focusing primarily on my functional limitations, develop a care plan, and, unless I live in a state that permits consumer-directed care, it will ask me to choose a home-care agency that will send poorly paid but often very dedicated home-care aides to help me dress and bathe and eat. Even with such help, I will probably need supplementary care from my family or some unknown others. If I am too poor to hire anyone and too "rich" to qualify for Medicaid-funded services, a common expectation is that my daughters will do the caring work. They may earn public praise, accolades even, though these may be scarce since they are only doing what is expected of them; however, they will not have a real choice, an issue that I turn to below, about whether or not they assume responsibilities for hands-on care. Having grown old and anticipating growing even older in this culture that elevates independence and scorns dependency, I will resist the need for care, often display hostility toward my helpers, and may even blame others like me for their weaknesses despite my own losses (Agich 1990). My resistance to care might lead me into that uncertain condition of "self-neglect," but if I seem to have the capacity to make decisions, it is unlikely that a "hotline" call to my state's community care program will lead to an intervention. The assumption will be that I am choosing a way of life even though it may harm me (for a fuller treatment of this question, see Holstein, Parks, and Waymack 2011).

Individuals, families, and the public sector are parties to a historical, cultural, ideological, and policy context in which assumptions about families, obligations, gender, and the role of the public sector lead to a "shared understanding of what seems 'natural' and what is considered possible" (Aronson 1990, 67). Added to this almost impenetrable belief system is the unfounded assumption that public support will lead to the "woodwork" effect as women caregivers abandon their older family members and turn care over to paid home-care aides (Hudson 2010a). No matter how lovingly and willingly families provide care, the inequalities that divide caregivers from noncaregivers promise to deepen as the population ages and public budgets are tightened. These problems, already difficult, will worsen over time for reasons already known to us. The overarching reason is neoliberal policymaking that has led to the shrinking of the social safety net since the 1980s, the delegation of risk to individuals and families, and the increasing marketization and privatization of care. Further contributing to the deepening responsibility of "informal" caregivers are worthy and important policies targeted at expanding community care for people with long-term care needs. Yet absent attention to the unintended consequences of these policies, family responsibilities are apt to climb. Often implicit but nonetheless pervasive is the long-standing assumption that care by the family is natural and the way it ought to be (Buhler-Wilkerson 2007). This assumption is also a major contributor to the resiliency of gender inequality (Ridgeway 2011).

In brief, as an old—and not affluent—woman in contemporary society who lives in the community but needs assistance to make it through the day (or, more specifically, needs help with the "activities of daily living" and is not in a nursing home), my choices for care will be limited. Hence, my reliance on the "informal" sector, from which I will get most of my care, will expand as I get older and perhaps frailer. As noted above, for me as a woman living alone, my primary caregivers will be my adult daughters rather than a spouse since women generally outlive their spouses. Only 42 percent of women over sixty-five were married, compared to 72 percent of men; this ratio worsens as women get even older (Administration on Aging 2012). Women are thus more easily defined as a "burden" on the state than are men.

In the neoliberal state, with its fractured bonds of community and shrinking safety net, it is unlikely that this situation will change. Family members will have primary responsibility for care—typically, daughters and daughters-in-law will be responsible for hands-on care and sons for more instrumental activities like bill paying, home maintenance, or driving a parent to doctor appointments. Respite, training, and other help for caregivers will continue to be vitally needed, but the aims will be limited to making it easier for caregiving to continue. It will not address the more difficult structural and cultural roots that create the near-inevitability that families will assume responsibilities for care (Holstein 1999). It will be difficult to challenge these naturalized perspectives, although advocates will wage intense efforts to mitigate its problematic consequences (*BetterJobsBetterCare* 2005; Feinberg et al. 2011). The "care crises" will not only persist (Stone 2000) but will worsen—the "dystopia" of my chapter title. As the population of the very old grows, the dollars available for human services shrink, the workplace becomes less rather than more hospitable to employees with caregiving responsibilities, and women's economic insecurity deepens.

CHAPTER GOALS

I pose this question: Why has this country not taken steps to assure that all who need care are cared for without exploiting others? Care given out of love is still an exploitation when the price paid by the caregiver is high, as I shall discuss below, and when she has few options to be loving without being on call twenty-four hours a day. Yet in this country today, that responsibility for care provision is essential (Glenn 2000). As the sketch laid out above suggests, care is heavily dependent on the contribution of family members, primarily women. In what follows, I will consider more deeply why the system looks the way it does. Why is intimate, hands-on caregiving primarily the responsibility of women family members despite the often devastating personal and economic costs they experience? If the care that families provide were monetized, their total contribution would be four times the combined public expenditures primarily from the means-tested Medicaid program (Feinberg et al. 2011). A corollary question is why so many old women are often reluctant to ask for the help that they need from adult children while welcoming the intimacy and connection that families can bring.

The answers to these questions are embedded in this country's values and assumptions about old age, women, the family, dependency, and the role of the public sector in addressing risk. They also rest on commitments to individual responsibility that define care recipients as "failures" and hence social problems while devaluing and marginalizing caregivers at the same time that they are upheld as "saints." Especially saintlike are the women who dedicate their entire lives to caregiving (Blustein 2004).

I will argue that the system deepens already existing gender and class inequities. The relatively affluent can be loving sons and daughters while knowing that someone else will change the sheets in the middle of the night if mom has an accident. The affluent have actual choices that others do not have. I will further suggest that in this system, neither caregivers nor care recipients, no matter their income, are immune from judging their own actions against dominant cultural assumptions about being a "good daughter" or a "good wife." Yet both wives and daughters, the most common dyad in home care, seek to "set limits on their caregiving and receiving" as a way to protect their own integrity (Aronson 1990, 69), indicative of the continued need to recognize oneself and to maintain one's identity. While it is not easy to separate gender norms from the pride and satisfaction that many women derive from caring, major shifts in women's social and economic roles over the past forty years have transformed the social conditions that once grounded women's caregiving responsibilities, but the centrality of family support has not changed. In fact, "adult children, and that increasingly involves sons, providing personal care and/or financial assistance to a parent has more than tripled in the past 15 years" (Feinberg et al. 2011, 2) despite the substantial contribution of Medicaid, the major public source of funding for long-term care services. It covers 40 percent of long-term care expenses, the "formal" care as opposed to the "informal" family care, much of which is directed at formerly middle-class older people who have either spent down or transferred assets in order to qualify for Medicaid (Grogan and Andrews 2010). Hence, as Medicaid's overall role in the health-care sector expands as a result of the Affordable Care Act, it will be stretched between obligations to older people, primarily women, and the health needs of poor and near-poor families (Galston 2012). Since old people are already faulted for their consumption of public resources (see chapter 6), we can anticipate that such blame will contribute to additional efforts to cut age-related entitlement programs.

In drawing this chapter to a close, I will undertake an imaginary excursion to the "dystopia" of my chapter title to envision the changes that I imagine as likely if the current trajectory continues. I will conclude the chapter by arguing for a different and more just system of care that respects the relational bonds between old women and their families without diminishing self-respect or the generous impulses of the women—and often the husbands and sons—who give care. I will recommend some intermediate steps that might mitigate the exploitation of women caregivers while protecting the critically important reciprocity and intimacy that care by family members implies. And, finally, I will look further into the future to see what possibilities deserve attention and how we might move in that direction.

GETTING CLOSE TO THE GROUND: THE IMPOVERISHED COMMITMENT TO CARE

The way care takes place in the United States today is unsurprising given our historical patterns, widely shared cultural norms and assumptions, ideological commitments, and structural constraints that place care on the periphery of public obligations. This limited public obligation holds true despite Medicaid's investment in nursing home and home- and community-based care. As noted above, Medicaid is a means-tested program that serves low-income women and less often men but also supports long-term care costs for middle-class people who have transferred assets or spent down. Ironically, these payments to formerly middle-class individuals are a mainstay of support for the program (Grogan 2010). Thus, while "family values" or not "killing granny" (as expressed in the summer of 2009, when "Obamacare" was a key issue at legislators' district meetings) are embedded in this nation's political rhetoric, we do far less than other industrialized countries in our support of either families or "grannies."

The one move in this direction was the passage of the Family and Medical Leave Act (FMLA) in 1993 with much opposition from conservatives and a decade of delay. It allows for twelve weeks of unpaid leave in a twelve-month period for a variety of caregiving activities, but it has had little impact on either the gender or the class of caregivers since only those women who can afford to be without pay can take advantage of the benefits. Business interests rather than gender dominated the policymaking around the FMLA (Prohaska and Zipp 2011, 1441). The primary beneficiaries have thus been married, often more affluent, white women, while African American women and women with lower incomes who expressed the most need (Gerstel and McGonagle 1999) can rarely take advantage of it.

Thus, in the United States, the tacit agreement appears to be that "in some way [care for the chronically ill] ought to be socially sanctioned and partially subsidized" only for the very poor; for the rest of us, individual responsibility and family assistance is the expectation" (Buhler-Wilkerson 2007, 632). This stance permits erosion by a thousand cuts to the social safety net in the name of personal responsibility, preferences for market solutions, and deficit re-duction. Today, advocacy organizations like AARP (Feinberg et al. 2011), feminist scholars, and liberal policy analysts (Tronto 1993; Harrington 2000; Kittay 1999; Holstein 2007; Kittay and Feder 2002; Fine 2007; Engster 2007; Glenn 2000, 2010; Galston 2012) continue to identify and propose ways to remedy gender injustices and for making long-term care more af-fordable without major new public outlays. These ideas, however, do not lead to wide public or legislative discussion, nor do they directly challenge the assumptions and cultural norms, to which I now turn, that both justify and enforce the existing system.

INDEPENDENCE AND CONTINGENCY

The contemporary long-term care system reflects three strongly held cultural beliefs: that as individuals we are independent, autonomous, and personally responsible for how our lives turn out; that the need for care is contingent rather than universal; and that families, primarily their women members, have primary responsibility for the care of both old and young and, as such, the public role should remain residual. Older people, who have been acculturated into this society, translate these beliefs into a message that tells them not only that they ought to be independent but that independence is individually achieved. Hence, they struggle to deny those features of their lives that cause them to need care and thus often try to forgo the help that they need (Agich 2003; see chapter 4). Because refusing help is thus a "morally virtuous position" (Breheny and Stephens 2012, 441), a means to preserve their sense of worth and integrity, they seek to "conform to the cultural injunction" not to "impose burdens on their children," a subject position that allows them to "behave in accordance with the norms of self-reliance and individualism" (Aronson 1990, 71). Thus, they interpret anything other than independence as failure, a condition that should not exist beyond infancy and childhood.

This position is publicly useful. The myth of independence conveniently supports the interpretation that those who need care are "costly social problems," the root of what Ann Robertson (1999) described as "apocalyptic demography." "The discourse of 'costly social problem' evinces resistance and resentment to paying a cost that really 'should' not be a public 'burden'" (M. Walker 2006, 157), thus justifying reduced public spending. Reinforced by the neoliberal agenda to privatize and marketize human services, care can be marginalized and reduced it to its most elemental form, what Jan Baars (2006) has called a "pit-stop" model of services.

By assuming that care is contingent rather than universal, decision makers and other people of privilege do not have to notice the rich array of personal services that make it possible for them to do the visible work for which they receive recognition, credit, and, not incidentally, a wage. That wage allows them to perpetuate the myth of their independence. Moreover, unlike caregivers, whose work is not seen as such, this wage marks them as full and equal citizens deserving of earned rights such as unemployment insurance or Social Security benefits. The fact that they can "command care from others" allows them to see themselves as different from "dependent" old people; they get the assistance they need without "burdening" others or being blamed for their needs (Glenn 2010, 187). As recipients of the caring work of others, they "presume an entitlement to such care" and so have little inclination to examine or even notice the needs that they count on others to fulfill (White and Tronto 2004, 442). While this "privileged irresponsibility," in White and Tronto's language, is not a sought-after trait, it permits the myth of independence to flourish, an end not achievable for those who cannot purchase the care they need. As Evelyn Nakano Glenn (2010) argues, "The fiction of liberal philosophy that independent and autonomous actors exist also obscures the actual interdependence among people and the need for care that even 'independent' people have" (85). In contrast, the visible needs that old women (and men) display signal the much-maligned attribution of dependency.

CAREGIVING: A PRIVATE, NOT A PUBLIC, RESPONSIBILITY

This "social-problem" discourse reinforces the already dominant view that caring for older family members is a private, not a public, responsibility. A Heartland Alliance study described this policy as "tough love"—it's up to individuals and families to provide care except in cases of real poverty, when the state will provide modest assistance. As such, public and private are assumed to be "discrete areas that serve different purposes, perform different functions, and operate according to different principles" (Glenn 2010, 184). That, of course, is not so. Families take care of ventilator-dependent children; they suction the lungs of a patient with COPD and care for a person with Alzheimer's disease. Sadly, this functional overlap and the major demands it places on care providers makes it particularly difficult for families to do what they actually can do best—practice the identity-preserving and relationship-sustaining values that make many older people and their families prefer care at home. It seems as if policy has taken the part for the whole—provide care for people in the least restricted environment without also assuring that such care exploits no one and helps the person receiving care to have her goals and values met. These extend far beyond the site of care.

The major upheavals in gender relations and the role of women in society more generally, the aging of the population, and with it the increasing likelihood of chronic disease have not substantially altered the societal norm that "as a mark of genuine affection and concern, family members (and especially female family members) set aside whatever competing projects and commitments they may have and devote themselves entirely to the care of their needy loved ones" (Blustein 2004, 130). Women take care of their impaired parents "because that is what one does, because they feel that it's their responsibility, and because the mother brought the child into the world and this is what the child must do" (Levitsky 2006, cited in Hudson 2010a, 17). In essence, these internalized cultural norms transform what is most often a necessity into a choice, albeit not always a comfortable one—pride in doing what one should do contends with the loss of opportunities, the costs, and the conflicting demands they face (Aronson 1990). Unlike men, women cannot easily plead work or other obligations since these "excuses" rarely count (Holstein 1999). As a result, for men domestic labor is a choice; for women it is an obligation (Clement 1996; Calasanti and Slevin 2001). Moreover, the gendered labor market reinforces this social expectation—since women earn less than men, leaving the workforce or reducing their working hours to engage in caregiving makes economic sense. Given the multiple tasks involved in caregiving, the time required, often measured in years, and the very real consequences that result from caregiving, the question without an answer—at least at this time—is whether or not these obligations can be bounded.

The consequences women face are serious and raise problems of justice. Their interrupted work histories and part-time work affect their immediate and future financial well-being and their lifetime earnings (see chapter 6). Estimates from fifteen years ago—a situation that has likely worsened as budget cuts have continued and women's wages have not changed substantially—show that such women forgo nearly $660,000 over a lifetime in lost wages, Social Security, and pension benefits (MetLife 1999). Out-of-pocket costs further erode their income. Thus, the persistence of gender-based inequalities in caregiving creates a powerful barrier to equalizing economic and other opportunities between women and men and is a predictor of women's economic disadvantages and risks for poverty in old age. As Glenn (2010) shows, women are 2.5 times more likely to be poor in old age if they provided care when younger. These inequalities accumulate over time and "intensify with changes in marital, health, and employment status" (Wakabayashi and Donato 2006). The working poor bear the greatest costs because they have the fewest options and because they lack the workplace flexibility that many professional women have. They are forced to leave work or reduce their working hours when they have little income to spare (Parks 2003).

Thus, what occurs in the private realm has a powerful public side. While once in American history caregiving was often a communal activity where women sustained one another (Abel 1991), today it is far more isolated, a fact that takes an emotional toll on both the caregiver and the care recipient. This isolation, as well as the intensity of the tasks involved, also excludes a woman from primary liberal commitments to individual freedom and equality. She has neither community nor freedom. Both she and the person receiving care are "othered" because they no longer meet the market criteria for moral and social worthiness. These views about the private nature of care make it problematic for women to be fully participatory members of society;

the attitude also serves as the unwarranted justification for limiting public benefits.

Despite these baleful consequences, which give lie to the frequently heard argument—why can one mother take care of four children but one child be unable to take care of one mother—that argument persists. This argument provides a convenient and, on the surface, a logical justification for the continued privatization of care. Looked at more closely, the analogy to a mother caring for children cannot be sustained because it ignores the complexity of the tasks performed, the caregiver's age, and her loss of social mobility and personal autonomy. It falters even further when one compares the escalating needs over the approximately eighteen years spent caring for an older person and the seventeen years of caring for a child who becomes increasingly independent and less in need of hands-on care (Glenn 2010). The tasks may, at times, seem endless and a changed future too far distant to imagine. Further, in contrast to elder care, the normal activities associated with child rearing and family maintenance do not demand that one person sacrifice or put on hold their own financial and emotional security. Yet symbolically, elder care completes the cycle of generations—as we were cared for, so we care.[1]

By successfully drawing a sharp line between what is and what is not in government's purview, what is public and what is private, and by tacitly condoning rampant and accelerating inequality throughout society, decision makers have no reason to assess the damages that result from caregiving. It is one more example of an unnoticed inequality for which remedy is not in sight. Rather than perceive it as a problem of justice, it is easier to call women caregivers "saints" than to give them assistance that will address the long- and short-term difficulties they face. Ironically, the women who pay the heaviest price rarely call for action since they accept what they do as the way it must be, what the loving child must do. Today's neoliberal agenda is foundational to this stubborn insistence on the private nature of care. As discussed in the introduction, this neoliberal "turn" has meant that responsibilities for care have shifted even more fully to individuals and families as collective responsibility to meet human needs has attenuated. It is up to us to make it or not with minimalist assistance from government. Moral perception is key here—do we perceive this as a moral wrong that demands remedy, or do we accept it as just the way things are? Is it so normalized and naturalized

---

1.   I thank my friend Madelyn Iris for this observation.

that efforts to displace it get little traction? Yet, recall the words of Richard Bernstein (1992) in the introductory chapter—it is the task of the critic to identify fractures in society with a view to remedying them.

ESSENTIALIST IDEAS ABOUT WOMEN AND THE MATTER OF CHOICE

The continued evocation of essentialist ideas about gender and the assumption that caregiving is freely chosen buttress the private nature of care. Women are naturally more adept at giving care than men, or so go the claims, and, moreover, they freely choose to play this role. "A good woman," observes feminist sociologist Cecilia Ridgeway (2011), "should be, as a deep moral obligation, intensively committed to her family and this commitment should take precedence over all others" (129). All the "informal" caregiving in this country—now estimated to be worth $450 billion each year (Feinberg et al. 2011) and still primarily done by women—seems to support both claims. In a country where choice is central to our understandings of autonomy and where obligations are all putatively chosen ones, it is not a stretch to assume that the act of caregiving itself becomes proof of choice. To observers, the sheer number of hours family members devote to caregiving (Feinberg et al. 2011; MetLife 2011) serves as evidence that they have voluntarily adopted this role. In one sense, they have chosen the role, but how real is the choice when desirable alternatives are absent?

This assumption negates the fact that many of our obligations are unchosen. "Choice" may also reflect one's class position, the persistence of gender expectations, and the fact that there really are no choices for many women except abandonment, which is hardly a choice. Women become caregivers for multiple reasons, especially love, but to suggest that they actively chose the role is to assume that they have good alternatives from which to choose, a fundamental requirement for autonomous action. Those alternatives do not exist. Often the task is thrust upon them by circumstances they do not control. Think of this situation: Jane and her mother, Grace, have a warm and loving relationship. Grace, who is eighty-two, has emphysema and osteoarthritis. She has trouble getting around, bathing, dressing, and preparing meals. She lives on her $1,500 monthly Social Security check and the modest assets that she and her late husband saved; she lives in her own home and wants to stay there. Jane lives twenty miles away and supports her mother's wish to stay at home, but she also has a job, which does not give her any flexibility in her working hours, which she needs to help support her family that includes two teenage sons. Grace does not qualify for public assistance and can pay for only occasional assistance from a paid home care aide. Jane honors all that her mother has done for her over the years and wants to do what she can to make Grace's life easier. Given the family's financial constraints, the only option she sees is for her to do whatever her mother needs to have done. She steps into the breach because she loves Grace, because she knows it is expected of her, and because there is no other way for Grace to get the daily help that she needs. Yet the prevailing assumption, generally unexamined, is that Jane has chosen her path from available options as if there really were options. Instead, she acted according to "cultural scripts, consistent with prevailing ideology and institutional arrangements," made easier by her love for her mother but not governed by that love. By constructing the notion that actions like Jane's are individual choices and using the cultural framing of women as the communal caregivers, policymakers "can avoid general responsibility for the inequities [that result from caregiving] and justify the maintenance of the status quo" (Fineman 1999, 21). Stated ironically, women are doing just what they want to do and what they are naturally best suited to do.

Thus, women who give care partake in deeply ingrained, gendered cultural scripts. They are simultaneously proud of what they do, view it as an obligation, and are expected to do it by others. Worth noting as well is that women who care for older parents are often older themselves (it is no longer surprising that a sixty-five-year-old woman is caring for her ninety-year-old mother) or are the mothers of children who still live at home, the proverbial "sandwich generation."

These assumptions—that women are naturally better at it than men and actively opt for the caregiving role—make it unnecessary to engage with the ethical question of how to allocate caregiving responsibilities among individuals, families, and the state. For all the changes that second-wave feminism wrought, including the notion that modernization has freed people from their historically predetermined roles, women's status roles have not been significantly altered (Beck 2002). Because staying at home to care for families, whether eighty-two-year-old mothers or two-year-old children, has negative value in our society, even as it is extolled by social conservatives as the desired option, at least for middle-class women, women's role as the primary providers of care impedes the likelihood that the gender relations that reinforce men's hierarchical advantages over women will soon be ruptured. "The gender organization of the home . . . is a wellspring for the system of cultural beliefs and material arrangements that sustain gender inequality" (Ridgeway 2011, 128).

Thus, we need to ask these questions: How can women speak in their own voice without being encumbered by persistent and often oppressive cultural norms? How do social structures and political institutions maintain the status quo in ways that often silence their voice and perpetuate gender inequality (Lugones and Spelman 1983; Meyers 2002)? At this time, a choice not to give care would be socially disruptive, unacceptable, and potentially devastating to the person who needs the care. But it can also damage the caregiver's sense of self—her gender identity—since she knows the cultural expectations well and also cannot risk harm to her mother or other close family members. She cannot manage these multiple demands on her own—she needs the collaboration of policy to give her the choices that allow her to speak in her own voice as well as the dissolution of the cultural norms that reinforce institutional arrangements that seem to suit everyone but the caregiver and often the care recipient, who is also enmeshed in the cultural norms that she not be a burden.

The notion of choice also extends to the recipient of care. By emphasizing the continued good health, independence, and productivity of older people, recent efforts to focus on "positive" aging mean that it is a short step to blame people who need care as responsible for their own plight (Holstein and Minkler 2003; see chapter 3). The focus translates into individual responsibility for managing later life, and that includes both financial planning and adhering to the lifestyle choices that allow one to age successfully—as if that, too, is fully an individual choice. Unsurprisingly, its individualistic focus elides the context that promotes or limits such health-promoting activities. The gospel of personal responsibility, deeply embedded in this country's response to human need, means that if I, for example, have to rely on Medicaid because of persistent chronic illnesses and Mrs. Jones can still climb steep hills and hire whomever she wants to simplify her life, I clearly made poor choices over my lifetime. "These conditions of privilege that are most often ignored, unexamined, and undervalued" (Holstein 1999) facilitate a culture of blame. Decision makers, but even others like me, can hold me accountable for these failures (Tronto 2006). Thus, women manage their sense of marginalization by limiting what they ask for (Aronson 1990).

FINANCIAL AND STRUCTURAL CONTRIBUTIONS

Further reasons for the impoverished commitment to care in the United States are embedded in the piecemeal way that health-care policy and, more specifically, long-term care policy developed. The gospel of individual responsibility, decision makers' blindness to their own reliance on others, and the unfounded fear that families would abuse public benefits reinforced the commitment to locate long-term care in the limited welfare sector. The slow, often random accretion of responses to human needs left little room for a thoughtful planning process that involved both givers and receivers of care. Like health policy more generally, Medicare and Medicaid grew out of a political struggle. To expect it to cover "custodial" care for people who are not poor would represent a sharp break with both the past and dominant ideas about family. Once these policies were in place, especially as the private, for-profit nursing-home sector grew in power and wealth, change came in slow, disjointed steps. Thus, in 2012, despite a sustained effort to reverse the dominance of nursing homes, the bulk of Medicaid dollars was still going to institutional care.

In recent years there has been some resistance to that dominance, expressed through a policy commitment to reallocate Medicaid dollars from the nursing home to the community. This policy choice lacks a larger vision about the ends of such care. What does it mean to assure that people have a good quality of life once they are in their home or in the community (Kane 2001)? This important policy shift makes no serious effort to address either the quality-of-life question or the consequences of community care. The policy of deinstitutionalization is a fragmentary remedy for a much larger problem—creating a fair and balanced system of long-term care inclusive of older people, family caregivers, and paid caregivers. "Caregiver burden" assumed a dominant place in the gerontological literature and in community care programs, but in that literature and that setting, questions were rarely, if ever, raised about the moral imperative that this "burden" communicated and the moral responses that ought to become the subject of public discourse. Not only did this focus minimize the moral importance of the relationships that are central to care provision, but it also left in place the piecemeal structure and financing of long-term care (Holstein and Cole 1995).

IN SUM

In this system, many old women are torn between two powerful cultural scripts. One script upholds independence, continued activity, personal responsibility, and not burdening their children. As such, it devalues the need for help, especially from family members. It reflects the older person's ambiguous position both in families and in the wider world. If one can buy help, the illusion of independence can be maintained. Yet an alternative script upholds the virtue of family connectedness and reciprocity, a "special time of intimacy" and an expected part of intimate relationships. How to reconcile these two subject positions is both problematic and without an obvious solution in the absence of policy changes (Breheny and Stephens 2012, 443).

These elements—that independence in old age will be normative and achievable by personal actions and the obvious participation of families in providing care—serve to justify limited public responsibility for care, a position that history and ideology reinforce. Thus, despite the emancipatory movements of the past thirty years, both givers and recipients of care are enacting cultural prescriptions of what it means to be a good daughter and a good mother. These prescriptions mean that the "broad pattern of care of old people goes unchallenged—rather it is sustained and reproduced" (Aronson 1990, 76).

Situated in the same cultural context and ideological framework, it is not surprising that the moral framework underpinning current practices reinforces conventional understandings of autonomy, rights, and responsibilities. While public concern for the caregiver is very real, in practice consumer autonomy trumps justice as the yardstick for these programs. Current caregiver support programs and policy efforts now under way primarily seek to ensure that family members are supported as they continue to provide care. A recent recommendation by AARP, however, to "recognize and assess family caregivers' own needs as part of a person *and* family-centered care plan" (Feinberg et al. 2011, 15) is worth noting. Yet the commitments to care at home and to client autonomy are so powerful that even the possibility of "negotiated consent" (Moody 1988), where families and the older person together determine what ought to be done, is a reach. Further reductions in public spending reinforce the tensions that both caregivers and recipients experience as they try to control the situations in which they find themselves.

This picture is discouraging. It seems as if everyone involved in the human necessity of giving and receiving care partakes in a cruel cycle where caring is "devalued, underpaid, and penalized" and "relegated to those who lack economic, political, and social power and status" (Glenn 2000, 84). As such, it reinforces the class, gender, and racial characteristics of care provision and the inequalities that result (Marks and Lambert 1997; Estes and Associates 2001; Duffy 2005). But it does even more damage to the people involved since it creates difficult, if not unresolvable, tensions as prescriptive cultural norms further constrain choices already limited by the minimalist public response.

THE DYSTOPIAN FUTURE: 2034

This futuristic vision rests on these main components: no change in the assumptions about who gives care to whom and the more pervasive social and ideological positions that drive policy. Committed to "transferring more and more of the risks associated with aging—the threat of poverty, the need for long-term care, and the likelihood of severe illness—to individuals and families" (Putney, Bengtson, and Wakeman 2007, 123), this ideological position offers no opening for change. The individualistic focus of today's dominant ideology, described in the introduction and throughout the book, permits its adherents to shroud the difficulties faced at any age for people ill served by the market. These ideas are so ingrained that they make counterarguments seem both irresponsible and unrealistic despite evidence that nothing has quite worked out as predicted by the neoliberal agenda. Free markets and free individuals, minimalist government, and personal responsibility with no language for social cohesion and collective responsibility bode poorly for the moral and political goals I will defend below. My dystopian vision rests on the policies that these ideologies embrace.

While there is no single way that policy issues and their related ethical values gain attention, I will base my predictions on this understanding of policy formation: policy originates with policy elites; then those policies give rise to politics that motivate the formation and the actions of organizations and individuals (Hudson 2010a). In practice, this means that any shifts in the policies and value commitments described above will rely on a dramatic change in policy elites (e.g., high-level bureaucrats, elected officials, major think tanks). Instead, shaped by what is and influenced by the ideological commitments I have described, advocacy and other related organizations work within a relatively narrow arena that can lead either to expansion (with minor improvements to what is) or further retrenchment. I base my predictions on this view.

In brief, then, the current political agenda is dominated by retrenchment in the resources devoted to human services. A recent story from the Center on Budget and Policy Priorities (Park and Broadus 2013) predicted that the Ryan plan to cut Medicaid by nearly a third would mean that more than twenty million people would lose coverage. With the proposal to block grant Medicaid, states can restrict eligibility, increase cost sharing, enact family responsibility laws, and decrease services. As a result, the degree and type of unmet needs will expand and the exploitation of all who give care will deepen. These moves, however, will be hyped as liberty-enhancing, fiscally responsible measures. With fewer people eligible for Medicaid-funded services, family responsibilities for posthospital and long-term care will increase along with their out-of-pocket expenses. As in the 1980s, canes versus butter (or bicycles or scooters) will typify the competition for resources. Older people will be blamed for their resource consumption and even for the chronic conditions that make them dependent.

Retrenchment in the budget for low-income housing, an essential for continued community living, will result in "at least 250,000 voucher holders across the nation . . . [facing] eviction" following the 2013 sequestration (Carson 2013). Even before the threatened cuts, vouchers served fewer than 25 percent of the people eligible. The results of these cuts, which will leave the housing budget at its lowest levels in a decade, will be more and more substandard housing and an increase in homelessness (Rice 2011). As federal and state policy accelerates deinstitutionalization in favor of "aging in place" (a desirable goal if the appropriate supports are in place), more rather than fewer low-income rental units will be needed. They will not be there. To avoid homelessness, we might see an increase in intergenerational living exacerbating the tensions that living in close quarters can generate. For many people, especially widows, the foreclosure crises of the first decade of the twenty-first century led to losses of homes they thought would be theirs through late life if not to their deaths.

Continued high rates of unemployment may mean that households will expand to include three and four generations, thereby increasing women's caregiving responsibilities even as they need to continue working. These caregivers will themselves be older and will have almost no support from the public sector. They will, however, be free to hire workers from minimally regulated agencies that have developed with the introduction of the rule, in the name of choice, that any willing provider, after meeting some basic requirements, can be licensed to provide home care. As the need for paid home-care aides expands, the already existing shortage of paid care workers will worsen (Feinberg et al. 2011). While higher pay and better working conditions offer possible ways to increase supply, the track record so far in achieving those ends is poor. Therefore, I imagine that to meet that need, a new guest-worker program will be introduced in which women from poorer countries will be given temporary visas to work in caregiving roles. If they cannot speak English, they will be unable to communicate with the care recipient. This barrier will further erode the relational aspects of caregiving. Care will thus become increasingly routinized with technology (which can be very beneficial *if used properly*), replacing human hands in ways that may be problematic. Unions, especially ones like the SEIU, which organizes care workers, will be further weakened, especially with the recent Supreme Court decision that workers do not have to pay union dues even if they benefit from union negotiations. As a result, workers, including home-care aides, will have even less power than they now have to improve their working conditions.

Reduced spending on entitlement programs like Social Security and Medicare (proposed for FY 2014) will exaggerate the financial problems of both caregiver and care recipients (see chapter 6). Other social service and income-support programs, such as Supplemental Security Income, will also be negatively affected if proposed changes in the calculation of cost-of-living adjustments are implemented. If Medicare is "saved" by being transformed into a voucher program, as House Republicans have been proposing, beneficiary costs will increase, ultimately leading to higher incidence of chronic impairments because of delays in seeking care. Since our bodies encode all our life experiences, we can also anticipate that life-expectancy discrepancies between the comfortably well insured and everyone else will widen.

The ethical norms in 2034 will continue their individualistic focus, while old and young women will still be bound by the cultural prescriptions of what it means to be a good daughter and a good mother. These expectations are likely to deepen as incomes of the middle class and the poor decline (Stiglitz 2012), making it virtually impossible to hire outside help. At the same time, Medicaid waiver programs will serve fewer and fewer people. Tensions will intensify as incomes decline and families are pressured into accomplishing more with less. The shifting picture of old people that effaces dependency (Holstein and Minkler 2003; see chapter 3) will suggest that being "old" is an avoidable condition (Biggs et al. 2006, 242).

Three factors—the neoliberal ideology, the role of policy elites in generating policy directions, and the policy directions that are already visible as I write these words in late 2013—provide the foundation for the predictions that I have made about the dystopian future. This dystopian future also rests on cultural norms about women, the narrow scope of ethical thinking in the practice realm, the emphasis on personal responsibility for all that happens to us in old age, and the well-intentioned but problematic effort to promote positive images of aging. I hope that my dystopian picture is an exaggeration of what the future will be like.

RETHINKING LONG-TERM CARE POLICY, PRACTICE, AND ETHICS

In a recent book that I wrote with two colleagues, we noted that "policy and ethics share a central commitment—to make evaluative judgments about what is good and right in human conduct" (Holstein, Parks, and Waymack 2011, 103). Both are about the values we ought to embrace (Churchill 2002). That said, the bridge between the two is often difficult to make since the styles of policymaking and the styles of ethical analysis are very different. Moreover, there is a clear reluctance in the policy arena to use the language of ethics other than in morally apodictic ways (e.g., abortion is wrong). Yet because policy tells a story about what is important and what we value (Lakoff 1996), we can, in Hilde Lindemann Nelson's (2001) terms, offer a counterstory about long-term care. In the following pages, I will tell a story that offers an ethical foundation for a long-term care system that rests on a relational ontology that affirms "commitments to personal and social interdependence and solidarity, dignity and social justice" (Holstein, Parks, and Waymack 2011, 104). Afterward, I will touch upon elements of that system and venture some guesses about how it might come about.

WHERE TO FROM HERE?

Given today's limited and technocratic approach to "reforming" long-term care, a new story will be, in Seyla Benhabib's (1992) account, utopian. It will seek to imagine something quite different from what we have now. To move in this direction, I start with the empirical observation that despite advances in biomedicine and efforts to live healthfully, the universal need for care, including the hands-on care needed by many older people, will not disappear. It is even possible that these conditions will worsen as poverty accelerates and medical care costs rise, leading to delays in seeking treatment. In a society where care is inadequate and the givers and receivers of care are disparaged, except when sainthood is ironically bestowed, that is, so glad that you're doing it because I can't see myself doing that work, to achieve an end where people get the help they need, when they need it, in the way that they would like to receive it, without exploiting family members or imperiling their dignity or self-respect, feels at this moment like an impossible dream. The tensions that caregivers and care recipients face and the multiple consequences that result cannot be resolved within the current system of long-term care and the moral, cultural, and policy assumptions that support it. All need to be changed.

One place to begin thinking about change is to reimagine the moral foundations for long-term care. We might start by arguing that a justifiable moral foundation for long-term care policy starts from the position that our need for others is neither pathological, nor avoidable, nor the result of human failings but is a universal and inevitable part of human development (Fineman 1999). Thus, accepting that risk is universal and that it is the many and not the few who need assistance from others is the appropriate way to understand the need for long-term care services (Tronto and White 2006; Hudson 2010a). This view differs from the neoliberal worldview, shaped by a privileged perspective, that I have addressed throughout this book. To be "independent" does not mean to go it alone. Accepting these premises means that we can defend a system in which "individuals and their societies [are] responsible for attending to, assessing, and weighing responsibilities for human needs and for acknowledging our needs for each other" (M. Walker 2006, 148–49). It opens the way to think of independence as a collaborative effort "based on mutual and collective support, learning and action" (Croft 1986). A relational understanding of care (Tronto 1993; Hooyman and Gonyea 1995; Kittay 1999; Holstein 1999; Calasanti and Slevin 2001; Fine and Glendinning 2005) captures this necessary concern for mutual welfare and grounds broad risk sharing as foundational to achieving both justice and care. It seems that what we also need is a guaranteed right to care, supported by a collective responsibility to provide that care (Engster 2007). Care is, after all, a human necessity that does not end when we outgrow the hands-on care of infancy. Accepting that care is a collective and not an individual responsibility would also dissolve the cultural assumptions of what it means to be a "good" mother and a "good" daughter," which keep the "major portion of responsibility outside the public realm" (Aronson 1990, 79).

Yet in today's society there is no right to care; no one is explicitly required to provide care. Instead, it is tacitly assumed that needs will be met (passive voice intentional) without holding anyone, including the government, accountable. As noted, the duties that government assumes are for the very poor and they are quite modest. As a result, people who need care are put in a difficult position—without an enforceable right to care, they are often forced to choose between resisting asking for help or accepting it while fearing that they are a burden. To address this problem of burden frequently requires a subtle and often troublesome and tacit negotiation of boundaries about the extent of the care that caregivers will provide so that they can meet other important goals (Aronson 1990; Breheny and Stephens 2012). To create an alternative way to provide the assistance that so many people need but do not necessarily want and to do so in a way that respects that reluctance while honoring family norms of mutual care but does not exploit caregivers is the next step.

MOVING TOWARD REMEDIES

To incorporate a justice-based foundation for long-term care requires challenging its taken-for-granted foundations, including the cultural proscriptions that make today's system seem inevitable. In terms of policy, it requires recognition that continued good and loving care cannot be achieved only by will and modest support services. Policy makers must do more than extol the sacrifices of a few by adopting a shared sense of obligation that includes the person who needs care and offering a wider array of actual choices and goals for care. It means recognizing that Medicare, designed to address acute conditions, a "male pattern of health care usage" (Hudson 2010a, 7), is inadequate for the chronic needs that are now so prominent (see chapter 4). Ironically, high-cost medical interventions that often offer minimum benefit generally go unchallenged and indeed have become normalized (Kaufman, Shim, and Russ 2004).

Several changes are essential. First, caregivers at all income levels must have viable options that allow them to choose not to provide hands-on care without sacrificing their self-respect or betraying their self-expectations. These requirements will call for both practical and cultural shifts. Second, women or other family members who choose to become caregivers require support beyond the interventions that are available today. This change means making decisions about both Medicare and Medicaid and providing a revamped Family and Medical Leave Act that is designed specifically to address gender inequalities and pay issues (Prohaska and Zipp 2011). And, third, a new moral and cultural framework must be introduced into community-based programs that moves beyond individual autonomy and independence as the twin goals.

Rethinking Autonomy

Community care programs generally define autonomy as simple choice—between A and B or maybe C. The choices are limited by what the programs can offer. Thus, the commitment to autonomy does not impose the obligation to consider the individual person's values and goals if these fall outside the services available. As such, they may address her functional limitations and the quality of her care but not her quality of her life, a gap that Rosalie Kane (2001) argues should be our focus. Nor does its narrow definition encompass helping her to reorient herself as she tries to remake her world (Agich 1995, 124). A richer view of autonomy means more than removing barriers to and honoring choice. With an understanding of autonomy that emphasizes the chance to live in both habitual and meaningful ways, autonomy becomes concrete. It commits us to foster the development of the self and the expression of individuality (Agich 1990) as a positive duty. What we would seek, then, is to create ways for people to live in habitual ways—and for most people that means taking into account those with whom they have significant relationships. The right to choose means little when it simply suggests the absence of coercion. It gains meaning when the older person is given the space and the conditions to help him or her answer the question of "who am I?" As discussed in chapter 4, that we live our lives coherently and purposefully matters at any age. Autonomy also needs to be expanded so that it is seen relationally—it cannot focus only on the choices made by the recipient of care without taking into account the person or persons who will be providing that care (Parks 2003).

BARRIERS

Achieving these ends, which occasionally enters public discussions, will be difficult since resistance, driven by ideology, culture, and history, will be strong, but there are also counterweights appearing suggestive of change (Feinberg et al. 2011). The growing needs of families caused by downward economic trends will make a different approach to long-term care imperative, but the needed changes will clash with the commitment to limited government that endorses the private nature of care. Also serving that agenda is the belief that women actively choose to assume caregiving responsibilities among other alternatives as they would choose where to vacation or what car to buy.

MAKING REAL CHOICES POSSIBLE

Thus, it is essential to tackle the underlying assumptions that keep the system intact while making efforts to take modest incremental steps, I want to focus first on making real choice a possibility for caregivers and care recipients. I start by questioning the common assumption—and the policy direction that today dominates community-based long-term care—that care at home is always best. I ask this, in part, because the worthy aim to help sustain people in the community creates the problematic corollary—the probable need for family or other "informal" support. It also makes any publicly supported care more costly because of its geographic spread; it often isolates the individual, and at times it increases the risk of abuse, neglect, and self-neglect. While not suggesting that staying at home is not a good choice, I suggest that well-designed alternative living arrangements can fill important needs.

These alternatives can range from small-scale independent living, with help available on an as-needed basis, to affordable assisted living, to small- and modest-sized group homes. Home-care providers can be on-site at larger residences so that individuals can get help in short spurts when they need it. Well-designed and well-staffed congregate living, familiar in Scandinavia but also in parts of the United States, can simultaneously meet several goals. It can facilitate mutual support and provide an extra measure of safety without resembling an institution; to achieve that end is a design and an organizational task. Such residences would free family members to do what they do best—be available for loving attention without getting up in the middle of the night to calm a frightened parent—while facilitating the older person's dual subject positions—as living independently without burdening the family while remaining part of that intimate relationship. It should reduce the costs of care since efficiencies of scale would be put in place. When people live in a shared residence, support can develop among them, as I have seen over and over again at Mayslake Village. These connections are important; they deepen dignity and alleviate the isolation that many old women feel living alone in their homes or apartments. Knowing that such residences are available to people at all income levels and that they are places to which they can move when they do not yet need care, old women can have the security of knowing that they will get care they require when they need it, at an affordable cost.

Since I am committed to the notion of real and meaningful choice in the framework of collective responsibility, I believe that women who genuinely want to assume the responsibilities of providing hands-on care deserve certain core supports. If a society wants to facilitate family caregiving, then we need to support workplace policies that make this possible (Harrington 2000). These supports include the following: paid leave from their jobs, flextime if they continue working, guaranteed positions when they return to the workforce if they need to take leave, and sustained respite. Caregivers also need training, mentoring, and a "hotline" to assist them with the more complex tasks that caregiving frequently involves. More practically, a public ethic of care means valuing what caregivers do as contributing to the nation's productivity and assuring that, as workers, caregivers receive credit toward Social Security, that they are given generous sick leave and vacation time, and that they have an opportunity to participate in a supplemental public pension program akin to a 401(k) but with the government assuming the employer role. We need to remind ourselves that this country is "a nation of private striving and public engagement, of rights *and* responsibilities" (Dionne 2012, 251). This message will not be easy to communicate at the shrine of individualism, but it is a necessary one.

There are other steps to be taken if we hope to reverse the practical and ideological trends toward increased individualization, privatization, and marketization of so many human services. One step is to make increasingly public the actual situation of long-term care in this country. Through work in the community, I and others have discovered that many, if not most, people assume that Medicare will cover the services that they need. For this reason, we need to get out facts about who pays for long-term care and at what cost in any way that we can. We need also to move caregiver stories more broadly into the public conversation, not to praise their saintliness but to demonstrate what it means to assume these tasks. With so many social media sites available, stories can be circulated in ways that were never before possible. Whenever feasible, care recipients also need to talk so that we learn how they feel when they see how their needs affect their daughters and other close family members. As caregiver and care-recipient stories become increasingly public, a process that is already under way (see the *New York Times* "New Old Age" blog; Reinhard, Levine, and Samis 2012), public responsiveness may also increase. The next task will be to broaden the reach of these stories so that the universality of care, the complex tasks associated with it, and the loss of the caregiver's own independence become more visible. Caregivers and care recipients are the best definers of what they need, but as a result of their relative isolation, their anomalous state, and the vagaries of the political process, they rarely participate in public life. But defining needs is a political rather than an objective or neutral act (Fraser 1989). Who better to define the needs of the cared for and caregiver than people in those roles? But as long as caregiving is on the periphery of public life, "those involved in caring relationships will be perceived as 'other' and their rights as citizens will be attenuated" (Lloyd 2004, 248). To try to avoid a grim dystopian future, we must seek as many public vehicles as possible to forcefully make the argument that the trajectory we are now on will devastate the gains that women have made in the past fifty years. Our task is to aim for a system of long-term care that give women the same opportunities to make choices about their lives that men (at least white, well-employed men) can make. As long as women's role in the home is viewed as a moral and practical necessity, the inequalities that I have raised throughout this book will not be remedied. Care must be a shared responsibility, as morally obligatory on men as it is on women, and the public sector needs to be an active partner in making that happen. This goal means recalling the civic side of this nation's public values and recapturing the ties that bind us to one another (Dionne, 2012).

But we need advocacy as well. Some years ago, Deborah Stone (2000) proposed a caregiver movement as exists in Canada and the United Kingdom; that idea needs to be revived and developed. The aging organizations need to venture beyond well-honed recommendations that are important but will not alter the status quo. They have the ability to do videos and other representations of the caring relationship in their publications. They can sponsor "speak-outs" that encourage women who are giving and receiving care to tell it "like it is" and to offer counterstories of how it might be done differently. They can welcome the totally other and embrace the skills that women need to speak in their own voice (Meyers 2002). I recall the power of just such a speak-out at the founding meeting of the Older Women's League in Des Moines, Iowa, in 1981.

One hope is that as more women enter public life, especially legislative life, these messages can be translated into a governmental agenda that responds to the legislator who in 1965 opposed Medicaid coverage of home care with the observation that anyone would want to have their beds made and their meals prepared (Weinberg 1999). One might wonder when he last made his own bed or prepared his own meals. Privilege permits one to not notice the help that one gets to make the day go smoothly. When women speak from their own experiences, they can raise objections to these voices of privilege. Supreme Court Justice Sonia Sotomayor's recent dissent in the court's 2014 affirmative action case is a powerful indictment of the privileged view that blinds people to the actual experiences of others unlike them. Women can call attention to the consequences of giving care in a society that does not value it other than rhetorically since it does not restructure work so that care becomes possible at all stages of a person's life, does not protect women from the economic effects of caregiving, and simply takes for granted that she can and will assume such responsibilities. As feminist philosopher Eva Feder Kittay (1999) argues, to give care we must be cared for.

These tasks require active engagement in the public sphere: electoral politics, blogs, letters to the editor, op-eds. Pundits want to cut entitlement spending; advocates for a more just long-term care system need to assume responsibility for regularly responding with an analysis of the consequences of what seems like a practically necessary idea. One can begin making the case that Medicare be expanded to cover long-term care provision at some level through an earmarked tax paid on a sliding scale, such as Medicare Part B. Coverage might introduce certain requirements about care, much like the introduction of a Medicare hospice benefit did. While such an entitlement is unlikely at this time, without getting the idea out and discussed, change can't happen. Perhaps one day it will be possible.

We might start building alliances with younger generations. E. J. Dionne (2012) turns to the millennial generation (born after 1981) because surveys have indicated that "helping others in need is a high personal priority for members of this generation" (253). Heather McGhee, now the president of Demos, similarly argues that millennials are likely to believe in government and collective action because of the problems they see in contemporary politics (McGhee 2012). While we cannot assume homogeneity among the millennials, there is something appealing about asking younger generations to join with older ones since it is they who will have added responsibilities for their elders if the economy doesn't improve or if cuts to essential programs are made. To open a discussion about collective action is an important move beyond the neoliberal focus on individual responsibility and private charity, a view that may be almost unknown to younger generations. An alternative agenda that includes such responsibility, broad risk sharing, the recognition of human vulnerability, and a commitment to some sense of the commons might take root. Recall how different issues, such as domestic abuse or gay rights, moved from the private realm to the public one. In these early years of the twenty-first century, college campuses and other places where younger people gather are places to start a democratic discussion about human needs and mutual responsibilities for meeting them. That segment of society can become a strong force for resisting changes in Medicare and Social Security that will be so punitive to the less affluent among us. However, they must first believe that these programs will be there for them. It is in the interest of the right to insist that if radical changes are not made, these programs will not be there. In that way, millennials and others can undercut the political support for budgetary austerity (see chapter 6). We need to rebuild that support by demonstrating that there are reasonable and doable solutions (see, for example, the websites of the National Academy of Social Insurance, the Medicare Rights Center, and chapter 6).

CONCLUSION

With great respect for the individuals and organizations who now work against great odds to provide the best services they can to older residents of their communities, I think it is essential that if and when we have the opportunity, we challenge the narrow visions of autonomy, independence, and moving long-term care to the home without also addressing the consequences that are so dominant. It is not that these ideas are wrong, but they are misleading and inadequate for the work that is needed. They do not take into account the phenomenological world of older people with multiple chronic impairments; they do not see how devaluing any form of life other than independence marginalizes individuals who cannot meet those norms and that often keeps them from asking for the help that they need. While I know that community providers of care and researchers are deeply concerned about the "burden" of caregiving, the prevailing ideas need to push further to ask us to imagine what the likely effects will be on each person involved in home care as more and more care is transferred to the home. Care is fundamentally relational, and that relational element deserves a place in the conversation. While, as noted above, I am not advocating for a return to nursing homes or other such institutions, I want us to, at least, consider the varied ways we might provide congregate but not institutional living to facilitate care and mutual support while alleviating the burden on family members. Perhaps the continued expansion of the Villages' volunteer arm (see chapter 8) will offer yet another way to care for the caregivers while supporting the care recipient. My concern, however, is that voluntary activities, however wonderful, cannot replace rights founded on notions of justice.

While change will not be easy in this age of deficit frenzy neoliberal devotion to the market and elite decisionmaking, there are openings to communicate alternative messages, and so we must do so. There are large numbers of newsletters, websites, training sessions, other educational opportunities, and public forums where new ideas, some of which are outlined above, can be introduced. Academia must join with the community to help enlarge the vision so that newer and deeper concepts of autonomy can gain a foothold and values other than independence can be discussed and honored. Academics can help challenge assumptions about women's roles and the so-called naturalness of caregiving. We must find ways to parse the issue of choice to help women see that they can do much for their older family members without thinking that almost singular devotion to caregiving is the way to handle the situation. As the Tea Party gained prominence, so, too, can an alternative agenda that reawakens the almost hidden value of commonality and connection. We have vehicles available to us that did not exist before. As noted above, social media can make a caregiver movement a reality; it can give voice to care recipients. It can formulate ideas about the universality of care needs and can point out the ways in which we all rely on it. It can remove the onus that defines old women who need care as social problems by pointing out that a good society does not neglect the least able among us and that so much of what happens to us when we are old is not under our control. We can talk together in print, online, at meetings, in classrooms, and in the popular and academic press to develop strategies for change. If we don't want to see the dystopia that I imagined, we need to act now.

Chapter Six

Retirement

In Pursuit of Women's Economic Security

The economic security of Americans is under siege. (Hacker 2007)

We may stop working for pay, that is, retire, by choice or by necessity, but will we be able to do so and still live decently? For many of us, the answer is uncertain. Unless we are fortunate enough to have inherited a substantial amount of money, are in a long marriage to a partner who has done well financially, have been lucky enough to have a career or job that came with pension benefits and a generous enough salary to permit us to save, or choose bank robbing as our encore career, our economic future is tenuous. This problem is serious and promises to worsen as the three legs—Social Security, pensions, and savings—of the proverbial stool supporting retirement security are all threatened.

The coming struggle about the future of retirement is particularly critical for women, people of color, and all low-wage workers. Without basic resources we have few opportunities to make actual and meaningful choices about our lives. In a society that overwhelmingly favors freedom, economic insecurity limits that freedom. It denies us the most basic of all human needs—to be safe and secure. And it leaves open a basic question—will the choice to retire be an option for anyone but the most affluent?

Why now? Why is something as fundamental as basic economic security so threatened today? How did this country arrive at this juncture where Social Security has become part of an ideological struggle that pits dramati-

cally different social and economic values against one another—the free
market and individual initiative as the best route to such security with
government at best serving a residual function versus the social contract that
binds generations to one another and sees government as an essential part of
that contract (Svihula and Estes 2007)? Often framed as generational equity
versus generational interdependence or solidarity, this debate "emerged between the late 1970s and the mid-1980s as part of an ideological swing to the
right in American society" (Williamson and Watts-Roy 2009, 154), a theme
to be addressed more fully later in the chapter. The predicted shortfall in
Social Security's ability to meet its full obligations by 2035 provided the
immediate opportunity to transform a campaign to undermine the program
that had begun almost forty years ago into a political program. To those who
opposed a strong public role as the foundation for economic security in
retirement, what was to most analysts a manageable problem became a crisis
constructed around dire predictions about the deficit, the retirement of the
baby boom generation, and the future of the economy (Quadagno 1996). In
this way a crisis mentality entered public discourse often based on erroneous
assumptions about Social Security and the deficit, which magnified the crisis
mode.

This seemingly abstract ideological struggle has very practical consequences. Not only does it lead to specific policy proposals, but it binds
people to taken-for-granted ways of looking at the world (e.g., the free market and low taxes are universally beneficial) that limit systematic internal
critique or compromise (Estes, Biggs, and Phillipson 2003). Challenges to
Social Security fit into a larger agenda that included radically reducing the
size of the state; privatizing services, including Social Security and the military; expanding the role of the free market; diminishing the power of labor;
elevating individual responsibility; and effectuating deregulation. Social Security, the most prominent of the New Deal's programs, has become a battle-
ground in large measure because it is the antithesis of these values. It is a
large and prominent government program that is built on commitments to
generational solidarity and shared risk. In play, as Larry Polivka and Carroll
Estes (2009) observe, are "intense conflicts between 'big capital' . . . , the
state (government), and the sociocultural forces of sex and gender, race/
ethnicity, age and generation" (57). A subtext is the legitimization of great
inequality as demonstrated by accusations of "class warfare" any time inequality is challenged.

In defining and describing the predicted shortfalls in Social Security's future funding and making recommendations for addressing them, these differences become politically visible. In brief, for the market-oriented neoliberal right, the preferred solution is privatization or at least partial privatization achieved by creating individual retirement accounts, familiar to most Americans as the result of an earlier policy choice—the introduction of 401(k)s during the Reagan presidency. Privatization became President Bush's second-term priority. While it gained few adherents at the time, it has by no means disappeared as the favored strategy among political conservatives. It has also made other proposals, like raising the retirement age for full eligibility, seem modest (Kingson and Quadagno 1995) although, as I will argue, deeply problematic.

Advocates of generational solidarity offer alternative strategies to address the immediate funding problem including new revenue derived from lifting the cap on contributions to the program and modestly raising the payroll tax, proposals that have strong public support (Pew 2011; NASI 2013). This support perseveres despite fears that Social Security won't be around when they need it, a nonaccidental element in the decades-long effort to undermine confidence in the program. Sowing doubt about Social Security's future along with actual confusion about technical issues such as the "integrity of the trust fund" is not accidental (Quadagno 1996, 391).

Today, the generational equity framing has caught on among many elite decision makers (Quadagno 1996; Svihula and Estes 2007; Williamson and Watts-Roy 2009). The frequently heard observation, for example, that more children live in poverty than older people, if not examined with attention to why children are poor (e.g., wage stagnation, high unemployment) or why older people are less poor (e.g., Social Security) is rhetorically powerful. Yet with few notable exceptions, legislators like Senators Sherrod Brown (D-OH), Elizabeth Warren (D-MA), and Bernie Sanders (I-VT), columnists like Paul Krugman and Eduardo Porter of the *New York Times*, and target-specific organizations like the National Academy for Social Insurance (NASI), there are few voices challenging this framing.

It will be interesting to observe how aging interest groups like AARP respond when legislative proposals are formulated and put on the table. Will it rebut what has become almost conventional wisdom among those who are considered serious, responsible decision makers, pundits, journalists, and others, that "entitlement reform," which generally translates into benefit cuts, is necessary? The irony is by now familiar—powerful people, predominantly men and generally affluent, casually accept the rightness of benefit reductions that will have little or no effect on them or promote an extended work life for people whose jobs are not anything like theirs. It is easy to preach responsibility if those with less power in society pay the price. Journalist Thomas Edsall (2013) notes that the Washington cognoscenti rarely mention "subjecting earned income over $113,700 to the Social Security payroll tax"; nor do they have any real connection to the risks that the median voter knows so well, a comment he takes from Brookings Institution economist Gary Burtless. I will return to this privileged perspective, which means you don't have to notice those who are not like you, later in the chapter.

My concerns in the remainder of this chapter are how all these unsettling proposals about changing Social Security benefits affect women and others who face the gravest threat of economic insecurity in late life. That concern extends to my deepest fears about the future well-being of what was once a solid middle class and the future of individuals and families who have always lived close to the edge. In what follows, I will consider the assumptions on which Social Security rests and the long-term consequences for women, low-wage workers, and communities of color that resulted. I will then situate today's proposals more fully in their historical context, primarily focusing on the 1980s, when free-market conservatives initiated their case against Social Security with the long-range goal of replacing it with a privatized system. This backdrop will inform our understanding of today's reform agenda. I will argue that the immediate problem—the need to shore up the program's financing to prevent an approximate 25 percent reduction in benefits in the next quarter-century—could be addressed relatively easily if it were not situated in the larger ideological struggle that we see evidenced almost daily in Congress and in competing news channels. I will challenge the remedies proposed as morally and practically indefensible. Because all policy choices ultimately rest on values, I will suggest alternative values that can be used to assess policies and policy recommendations. I will then turn to recommendations that will sustain Social Security into the future and make life more economically secure for women and others whom the current system does not serve well.

While I maintain that all people, not only elders, deserve to live absent the humiliating impact of economic insecurity, my central concern in this chapter is with people who rely on a strong Social Security program. It strikes me as particularly cynical that arguments about the putatively "rich" old should become the justification for cutting the very program that has lifted so many out of poverty. Greater societal equality might mean providing everyone with a guaranteed livable income, which would help to remedy the poverty of children and create a society that is better for all. Instead, we are facing proposals that will reinforce inequality. Poverty, as economist Joseph Stiglitz (2012) observes, is a condition that is directly influenced by policy decisions and not by blaming the poor for their poverty. Social Security is "our most effective anti-poverty program" (Hartmann, Hayes, and Drago 2011, 1), but policy choices can erode its successes.

BACKGROUND

In 1935, in the depths of the Great Depression, with the passage of legislation creating the Social Security program, this nation made an important commitment—that later life should not be a time of economic peril. Some key choices accompanied this commitment. It was tied to waged labor, that is, one was rewarded for the work one did in the moneyed economy, which meant that much of (white) women's productive labor—caring for children and elders, home maintenance, kin keeping—did not count. The social norms that determined what labor one undertook and what labor was rewarded meant that men's careers led to greater retirement security than women's life situations. Benefits were thus calculated and awarded based on a man's paradigmatic career path, a model that did not change as women entered the workforce in large numbers. In 1939, when Congress added wives and widows as beneficiaries, their benefit rested on their marital status, reinforcing their status as dependent on their husbands and devaluing their reproductive labor in calculating benefit levels (Herd 2009).

Over the next few decades, Congress expanded Social Security to new groups while also improving coverage, benefits, and programmatic elements. Amendments passed between 1968 and 1974 "substantially increased benefits, raised the wage base, and implemented automatic adjustments" and so guaranteed older workers "a true retirement wage" (Quadagno 1999, 153). Today, Social Security covers 95 percent of all retirees, scores of spouses and children of deceased workers, and people with serious disabilities who are unable to work. This fact alone, often ignored in claims about the putative "greed" of old people, speaks to the program's intergenerational features.

As a result, Social Security is now one of the most popular and protected of American public policies. In polling done in 2011, 87 percent of those polled rejected any cuts in Social Security (Pew 2011). In a recent report, the

National Academy of Social Insurance (NASI) reported that "large majorities of Americans, both Republicans and Democrats, agree on ways to strengthen Social Security—without cutting benefits" (2014, 1). The only evidence of a slight decline in support between 2000 and 2010 was among the young and those who believe in less government, but in general most citizens still believe that the government is spending too little or just about the right amount (Quadagno and Pederson 2012). Even participants in antigovernment Tea Party rallies supported Social Security, often without recognizing that it was the very apotheosis of what they fought against, that is, government programs. They see it as an earned benefit and not a government handout (personal communication, June 2011).

A TURNING POINT: THE 1980s

While rooted in the economic changes of the 1970s, the early 1980s marked a turning point in the program's steady improvement and expansion. Along with growth in well-funded conservative think tanks and foundations, Ronald Reagan's election in 1980 capped and symbolized the resurgence and legitimation of the new conservatism in America. The stage was then set—a visible and empowered aging lobby and the conservative agenda that Ronald Reagan represented—for confrontation (Hudson 2010b). This period also saw the beginnings of a newly constructed image of the "advantaged" old (see chapter 3), which lent tacit support to Social Security's critics, who used it to buttress the generational equity argument. The brewing conflict made its dramatic debut at the 1981 White House Conference on Aging, described as beset with "chaos and controversy" (Johnson 1982, 125) when the Republican National Committee sought to "pack" the conference with delegates who would support recommendations designed to undercut much of the social safety net, including Social Security (Anderson 1983; Clayman and Seidman 1981). In a staged walkout, led by Arthur Fleming, a Republican, the former secretary of Health, Education, and Welfare (HEW) under President Eisenhower and the recently displaced chair of the US Civil Rights Commission, in which I participated, elected delegates succeeded in turning aside the administration's efforts to rig and politicize the conference. This sustained advocacy, however, became part of another reconstructed image of the old—as a potent political force who voted in their own self-interest, despite evidence that they did not vote as a bloc (Binstock 1983).

Social Security no longer fit the era's redefined and revitalized conservative agenda grounded in neoliberalism's retreat from the state. The conservative opposition to Social Security as a public rather than a private system that continues to this day took its paradigmatic form in 1983, when an article by Stuart Butler and Peter Germanis (1983) appeared in the *Cato Journal*. Arguing for Social Security privatization, they recommended a strategy to neutralize elderly voters' support for the program by undermining younger people's confidence in it. They introduced catchy and now familiar arguments: Social Security is going broke and Social Security is a Ponzi scheme. By downplaying the program's social insurance and safety net characteristics, they were able to focus on one key feature—its return on investment compared to the earnings that are possible in the equity markets (Campbell and King 2010). The introduction of 401(k) plans under the Reagan administration was one way to acclimate people to "private accounts that would be layered on the on top of the core public program of Social Security" (Hacker 2004, 256). Thus, as certain segments of the population amassed substantial savings through these accounts, a competing policy path for retirement income would be in place, modeling what privatization could do and thus introducing the language of the market—rate of return—as an element in the reframing of Social Security from a social to a private good.

Americans for Generational Equity (AGE), founded in 1985, was the first organizational effort to advance the notion that this country was squandering its wealth on "entitlements for the elderly while children remain impoverished" (Quadagno 1990). While the poverty of children is a serious problem, albeit not caused by Social Security, for AGE it served primarily as a rhetorical tool. As Robert Hudson (2007) trenchantly observed, "The young have nothing to gain by our cutting benefits to the old under the current political regime" (280). While AGE quickly faded and did not achieve its policy goal of transforming Social Security into a means-tested program, it succeeded in introducing the now commonly used generational equity framework while also defining the problem of Social Security in "crisis" terms (Williamson and Watts-Roy 2009). For free-market conservatives, this agenda was unproblematic.

Henry Fairlie's (1988) cover story in the *New Republic* titled "Talkin' 'bout My Generation" succinctly captured this new line of attack. The old, redefined as well-off, politically potent, and self-interested consumers of an ever larger share of the federal budget, were scapegoated for their privileged position in terms of public and other programs (Binstock 1983). This shift threatened the social compact that socialized risk by spreading it among citizens of different circumstances while undermining late life as a time for an earned retirement protected by social welfare policies (Phillipson 1998).

To address financing issues in anticipation of the retirement of the baby boom generation, in 1983, President Reagan appointed a National Commission on Social Security Reform, chaired by Alan Greenspan. Working in a highly politicized and charged environment, the commission's report proposed significant concessions on benefits (gradual delay in the age of eligibility for claiming full retirement benefits, delaying the cost-of-living adjustment [COLA], and taxing the benefits of higher-income individuals). The commission succeeded in shoring up the system for years to come while rejecting privatization and means testing and preserving the program's universal, contributory features. It also maintained the program's commitment to both equity and adequacy without fully defining what those terms required (Achenbaum 1986). Unintentionally, however, it created a problem that Social Security's critics, including President Bush, used to suggest that insolvency was inevitable. The confusion was about the trust fund, where surplus taxes were held (and invested in T-bills) until such time as they were needed to pay benefits (Hacker 2004). While adjustments will need to be made when the Social Security Administration needs to cash in the T-bills to pay benefits, that problem is different from insisting they are worthless IOUs. Finally, the commission's work marked the effective end to Social Security expansion and led to a 19–25 percent reduction in lifetime benefits that current retirees now face.

The prosperous 1990s slowed these attacks, but they did not disappear. For one, the definition of Social Security—both implicitly and explicitly—became linked to the "entitlement crisis," a view that flourishes in the presence of stereotypic images of the old as "greedy geezers" (Kingson and Quadagno 1995). This link has persisted despite the major differences between, for example, Social Security and Medicare. Second, in May 1996, the *Atlantic Monthly* featured a lengthy article by Peter Peterson, who warned of "an all-engulfing economic crisis" that would come when the baby boomers started retiring unless immediate action was taken to "balance the budget, rein in senior entitlements, and boost individual and pension savings" (1). The script of greedy old people whose benefits portended economic catastrophe made for a good story, yet it ignored the fact that few of the old were truly affluent (earning over $1 million a year), or that benefits they received accounted for "less than one-fifth of 1% of all the benefits paid" (Kuttner

2012, 2), or that entitlements differed significantly from one another and so could not be lumped together. In the 1990s, the Concord Coalition, taking many of the same positions as AGE, worked to spread the word through meetings with editorial boards, faxes, op-eds, and issue briefs that Social Security was on the ropes (Lieberman 2013).

THE PRIVILEGED PERSPECTIVE

Groups such as the Business Roundtable have, for example, recently asserted, apparently without irony, that the best route to retirement security is individual savings. They made this claim while the policies the member companies have put in place made workers less rather than more able to support their own retirement. They have eliminated or reduced defined benefit plans and have run up "shortfalls in their employee pension funds of between $4.9 and $22.6 billion" (Carpenter 2013). They, however, personally have average retirement savings of over $14.5 billion. Even when President Obama established a commission to address deficit reduction in February 2010, he appointed two very wealthy men as the cochairs, including former senator Alan Simpson of Wyoming, recipient of a generous public pension, who in 2010 commented that Social Security was a "milk cow with 310 million teats" (cited by Jacoby 2011, 156). It is not as if credible women were unavailable to serve as chairs of the commission. There would at least have been a chance that the commission would have taken into account that longer lives and better health were not equally distributed among the older population, the justification for recommending an extended work life, or that older workers, especially women, do not find work easily and do not have jobs quite as comfortable as do commission members. Work has very different meanings at the margins than at the center of power (Gonyea and Hooyman 2005).

Privileged people, on the winning side of the inequality ledger, do not need to note the effects of deep and deepening inequality (Stiglitz 2012; Reich 2010) or how quickly and far people fall when they "lose their financial footing" (Hacker 2007, 3). Nor do they have to note that recovery from the 2008 economic collapse has left salaries and wages stagnant and unemployment high, especially for women who have lost jobs at older ages— indeed, all older workers. The business community, whose values they represent, has effectively withdrawn from its role in the social contract forged in the more stable economy of the past (Hacker 2007; Reich 2010), and no one is holding it accountable for its retreat. Rarely do we hear calls for businesses to share their growing productivity with the workers through improved salaries and benefits as once was the case (Smith 2012). Hence wages have been stagnant, making saving even more difficult. The transfer of responsibilities for "risk protections against the so-called vicissitudes of life from the public to the private sector and from institutions in both the public and private sector for individuals and families" is the most salient policy development of the past quarter-century (Hudson 2007, 2). Employers, who are likely to be on the market side of the ideological divide, can thus matter greatly in accelerating or decelerating the risks associated with retirement. I shall return later in the chapter to the issue of tax-subsidized retirement accounts. The notion that hard work, good choices, and doing right by one's family will assure middle-class status has been shattered (Hacker 2007).

As Social Security loses its place as the "third rail" of American politics and as old people are repeatedly defined by others, often with their own concurrence—as a means to escape the seemingly inexhaustible negative stereotyping—other programs can also be affected. We have already seen repeated efforts to change Medicare into a premium support, that is, a voucher system, while other safety-net programs have already experienced reduced appropriations, a strategy of those politicians whose primary agenda is cutting the deficit through spending cuts.

THREE DOMINANT POSITIONS ABOUT
SOCIAL SECURITY TODAY

There are three main positions about Social Security today, each backed by a narrative about the obligations of government, the status of the "elderly," and attitudes toward inequality and the social responsibility of business (Kingson and Altman 2011). The moderate or rational position accepts that the long-term sustainability of Social Security means that some changes are necessary. It accepts that older people are in general healthier and living longer, and so many can work longer. Rationalists accept modest reductions in lifetime benefits through raising the retirement age and changing how the COLA is calculated; they add some protection for the oldest and neediest among recipients. Neither new revenue not broader concerns about retirement security are on the agenda. For the neoliberal right, privatization is preferred, which they will not get, at least at this time, so they are willing to accept any proposals that will weaken Social Security while continuing to undermine faith in its future by repeating the rhetoric that it is going broke. Most problematically, they have made changing Social Security an acceptable, indeed a necessary, political cause. Finally, the progressive position advocates more, not less, spending on Social Security; the emphasis is on inequality and the predicament of the less advantaged. Progressives argue that Social Security expansion is essential to avoid "an unprecedented crisis of millions of baby boomers in poverty" (Rosenfeld 2013, 1). The progressive agenda builds on strong intergenerational support for Social Security and for mitigating the consequences of the vast and growing inequality in this country.

SOCIAL SECURITY "REFORM" TODAY

The issue directly related to Social Security that needs attention today is the anticipated shortfall in program resources by 2035 (Blahous and Reischauer 2013), when the Old Age Survivors Insurance (OASI) trust fund will be exhausted. That claim, however, does not translate into "Social Security is going broke." Absent the unlikely possibility that no changes will be made, the system will still be able to cover 75 percent of retirement benefits based on incoming payroll taxes. In their 2012 annual report, the trustees expressed continued faith in Social Security and concluded that legislators should act "in a timely way in order to phase in necessary changes and give workers and beneficiaries time to adjust to them" (Board of the Treasury 2012, 4). The dominant narrative is the moderate position that calls for tweaking the program to assure that "it remains solvent perhaps through manageable benefit reductions and revenue increases" (Kingson and Altman 2011, 5). As noted above, polling data demonstrates that this position is not shared by the American people (Quadagno and Pederson 2012; NASI 2013). They suuport raising the payroll tax rather than reducing benefits. They hold this position even though the payroll tax is highly regressive, taking a much larger bite from the earnings of lower than higher wage earners since it is capped at $113,700 and only includes salaries and wages, not dividend income.

The Prevailing Agenda: Entitlement Reform

The most popular proposals today call for a gradual increase in the retirement age for full eligibility and altering the calculation of the COLA. Taken together, these proposals would result in a 7 percent reduction in lifetime benefits. The arguments for these changes are familiar—they're necessary for Social Security's future sustainability; they are essential to reduce the deficit, which is necessary to give businesses the confidence to hire, expand, and prod investment that will, in some unidentified way, protect our children and grandchildren from bad outcomes. The challenges to these claims get little attention in the popular press or among most legislators. Many politicians, for example, whose central concern is deficit reduction and a balanced budget, generally include Social Security as one of the "entitlements" that must be cut. In a recent fact sheet, Strengthen Social Security (2013) notes that deficits can only be reduced by cuts in programs that are financed though the general fund and not through the earmarked taxes that go toward paying Social Security benefits. Admittedly, the relationship of Social Security to the deficit cannot be easily parsed. While Social Security is part of the unified federal budget, it can only pay out what it takes in from payroll taxes and, if needed, from the trust fund that is invested in T-bills. It cannot go into deficit. Thus, lumping Social Security with all other public expenditures is a political and not an economic position (Krugman 2011). When the government needs to cash in the T-bills to pay current benefits in the years to come, there will be some costs involved, costs that should be manageable if the economy doesn't go into freefall. Yet, repeatedly, pundits, journalists and others present "entitlement spending," which includes Social Security, Medicare, and Medicaid, as catastrophic drains on the federal budget. It is beyond the scope of this chapter to compare these programs in any detail so I simply note that their differences foreclose such casual joining under one rubric of entitlements.

In the face of these arguments, progressives face a tough choice—between a belief that cuts in Social Security, Medicare, and Medicaid should not be made and recognition of what contemporary political realities might demand. As Brookings scholar Henry Aaron (2013) observed, progressives may have to give some on benefits but with the caveat that if benefits are reduced, these cuts should fall primarily on those with the most education and earnings since these are also the people who have seen increases in longevity and so may have the chance to extend their work lives. More about these possible changes below.

RETIREMENT (IN)SECURITY AND WOMEN TODAY

I have the relative freedom to write these words today because I have Social Security, which represents almost half of my income (the remainder comes from earnings and savings). This simple fact means that I often lie awake at night doing calculations in my head, wondering how much I need to earn from work and how much I can take out of my savings each year so that my resources will hold out until I die. According to an article in the *New York Times* about a decade ago, I have about half the assets I need to continue living as I am living now, not extravagantly but with the ability to do many things that I value. But I am lucky. I've been able to save because I have had good jobs and no serious illnesses or caregiving responsibilities that forced me out of the workforce. I can do the kind of physically undemanding work that allows me to continue earning a modest income. But perhaps most importantly, I have a fairly decent Social Security benefit. In contrast, a news article in the *Washington Post* (Marte, *Wonkblog*, Aug. 7, 2014) reports that almost 20 percent of people nearing retirement age have no savings. Overall, 31 percent of people have no money saved. For many people, particularly part-time workers, the primary reason was lack of access to a retirement plan and low wages that limited opportunities to save.

For all the gains that women have made in the past few decades, many women cannot expect to have an income that will allow them to live decently in retirement. It is unlikely that women who are young today will be better prepared for retirement than older women today (Herd 2005). The reasons are not hard to find. "On average, women earn 19% less than men throughout their lifetimes and live longer but have more chronic health conditions. As a result, women 65 and older have a higher poverty rate than men—12.0% of women versus 6.6% of men" (Hartmann and English 2009, 110). Women's median retirement income is 58 percent of men's retirement income (Rappaport 2008). "In 2011, Social Security kept almost 38% of women out of poverty, compared to only 32% of older men" (Shelton 2013).

Not surprisingly, a lower income means that accumulating assets is particularly difficult. By doing socially essential but not socially rewarded work—reproduction and care provision—women juggle the competing needs of care and family that result in "frequent periods of unemployment, part-time employment, and absence from the labor market." For a system design based on the traditional male model of work, "over a lifetime, these disparities aggregate and become glaring in retirement, especially for those from communities of color and those who live to an advanced age" (Estes, O'Neill, and Hartmann 2012). Hence, a woman's average benefit from Social Security is only about $1,200 a month, about 61 percent of what she needs to meet her basic needs if she is a renter (Wider Opportunities for Women 2013).

Social Security represents 90–100 percent of retirement income for almost 59 percent of women and 29 percent of men (Gonyea and Hooyman 2005). The situation is worse for unmarried older women, who make up more than half the older population; nearly 28 percent of unmarried women are poor—their income is lower than the federal poverty level—or they are near poor, with an income lower than 125 percent of the federal poverty level. Thus, women are at a much greater risk of falling into poverty in late life than men (Gonyea and Hooyman 2005). The worst off are unmarried women of color. They relied on Social Security for 90 percent of their income (Estes, O'Neill, and Hartmann 2012). As Alicia Munnell (2004) observes, "of all the factors associated with poverty in old age, the most critical is to be a woman without a husband" (1).

Women have several ways of accessing Social Security benefits. They can earn them as the result of their own work history. They can obtain them as the spouse or the widow of a covered worker, or they can get them as a combination of the two. Regardless of the specific mix, when a married woman's husband dies, "the total amount of Social Security benefits paid to the household are reduced by as much as 33 to 50%," a reduction that is even larger if both spouses had nearly equal earnings (Estes, O'Neill, and Hartmann 2012).

A campaign for real retirement security would hold employers responsible for fuller participation in pensions and improved wages and salaries to facilitate savings. Even more boldly, it would address the broad social and economic inequities in our society that directly influence our ability to save for retirement. Some changes are quite direct, for example, improving Social Security's minimum benefit (see below), but others are more complex because they are rooted in gender ideology and in the social, economic, and cultural contexts that differentially affect how we age, a topic to which I will return later in the chapter. Most simply, advantages and disadvantages accumulate over one's lifetime, are amplified in later life, and hence influence our retirement income (Crystal and Shea 1990; Gonyea 1994).

Further, even if it is financially necessary, many women may have little ability to continue working longer because they lack the physical capacity to do certain low-wage jobs or they are not hired for whatever jobs are available. The result is that many must apply for a reduced benefit at the earliest age permissible, which translates into a lifetime of reduced benefits. The view from privilege can blind its holders from seeing that continued work as a matter of choice is quite different from taking whatever job is available as a matter of necessity.

The fact that the occupational pension environment has shifted from defined benefit to defined contribution plans has a particular effect on women who have greater risks associated with lower workplace earnings and family position. Individuals who work for larger companies are more apt to have access to a pension plan than those who work for smaller companies, while part-time workers are least likely to have access to pension income. For the 32 percent of women (compared to 55 percent of men) who receive employer-sponsored pensions, their average benefit is less than half that of men (Munnell 2004), largely because they worked fewer hours than men as a result of their unpaid work responsibilities.

In a *Washington Post* op-ed, Charles Lane (Dec. 14, 2013) asserted that 70 percent of the older population will replace 75 percent of their income in retirement. He did not provide the commensurate statistic—75 percent of what income? The more scholarship exposes the important differences among older people—the intragenerational inequities—that rest on the accumulation of differences across the life span, the less justification there will be for policymakers to generalize from the experience of some—generally those defining the agenda—and assume that they have reached a meaningful set of understandings.

Explaining Women's Disadvantaged Status

While there are conflicting ways to explain the broad inequalities that divide this nation into "two Americas" (Smith 2012), gender inequality is more easily understood. It rests, in large measure, on the unequal distribution of domestic responsibilities, primarily reproduction and caregiving, and the gendered labor market. Gender is a primary means of organizing social relationships, and to it are attached ideas about competencies and cultural expectations that do not easily change (Ridgeway 2011). Women, whose lives have changed dramatically since the passage of Social Security in 1935, still have not achieved pay equity or equal power and shared responsibilities at home. Women's caregiving, for example, is estimated to be worth $450 billion annually (Feinberg et al. 2011) but does not count as deserving of "just desserts" in terms of Social Security. We are a "breadwinner" state (Herd 2005). As sociologists Toni Calasanti and Kathleen Slevin (2001) observe, it would require a "reduction of inequalities" that can only come "from policies that disrupt the gendered (as well as racialized and classed) nature of social institutions themselves; they must address the inequities that begin earlier in life and accumulate over time in addition to policies that target age-related issues" (119).

Sociologist Madonna Harrington Meyer (2010) sums up women's disadvantage thus: women are more vulnerable than men in old age because we are disproportionally responsible for unwaged domestic work, particularly caring for children and the frail or disabled; because of persistent gender inequalities in the labor force; because of higher morbidity coupled with longer life expectancy; and last, because there are so few policies aimed at "buttressing older women's social and economic positions" (834). These connections between the economic insecurity of women and life course issues appear to be unnoticed by elite opinion. I often wonder how those with privileged status would save for retirement if they had a family with two children and earned the median income of $51,700. Would they advocate continued work if they had to move out of spacious offices and reduce their generous salaries and give up the luxury of someone making their bed and preparing their meals?

DECONSTRUCTING THE CRISES AND THE PROPOSED SOLUTIONS

It has become common to hear from media, legislators, and other establishment figures that "the country can no longer afford to give seniors so much" (Lieberman 2013, 1). This position buttresses the other mainstay of the argument—that the federal deficit must be reduced and Social Security must contribute to such deficit reduction. Although financed through an earmarked tax and by law not allowed to go into deficit, it is grouped with all other "entitlement programs." With such slippage between shoring up Social Security financing and "saving" it and using cuts in it to reduce the deficit, confusions abound. In a sharp critique of the media's response to discussions about "entitlement reform," Trudy Lieberman (2013) argues that too often the arguments of Social Security's critics were accepted at face value. And since old people are so affluent, indeed are "greedy geezers" who are self-indulgent, living too long at too high a cost and being unconcerned about younger generations, no harm will result from benefit reductions. This convenient but erroneous framing cites the statistic that people over sixty-five own 75 percent of America's assets. What they fail to note is that only a tiny percentage of old people are affluent, and of those who do have investments, most see a very small return, if any, from them. Indeed, almost "half receive no income at all from assets," and among those who do, "half receive less than $2,000" (Jacoby 2011, 161, citing Purcell 2009, 12).

What's wrong with this crisis mentality? The declaration of a crisis undermines the possibility of reforming Social Security for its own sake "rather than as part of an austerity plan designed to shrink the size of government" (Estes, O'Neill, and Hartmann 2012). It paints an unusually optimistic picture of the financial and health status of older people that fails to account for the intragenerational differences among them, one that is clearly demarcated in terms of gender, race, and class. Claims based on aggregates can be skewed by a small group at the extremes and can obscure significant differences in income, health status, and life expectancy. Lower-income earners and less-educated individuals, for example, are not living longer; the richer and whiter you are, the greater the gains in life expectancy (Minkler, Fuller-Thompson, and Guralnick 2006; Long et al. 2002). So "raising the retirement age inflicts a double-blow on lower-income Americans: They already work more physically demanding jobs and die younger than the rich, but now they're being told to work those jobs longer because people who aren't them have seen large gains in life expectancy" (Klein 2011, 1). Echoing this, in his column in the *New York Times,* Paul Krugman (2010) asked: "Why should janitors work longer because lawyers are living longer?" Raising the retirement age falls the most heavily not on the legislators who tend to work into advanced ages but on those with the worst jobs who will be forced to continue working, if they can, because Social Security benefits are the mainstay of their retirement income.

In brief, the proposed increase in retirement age and the changed calculation of the COLA means little if one has other sources of income, but its effects are rather substantial if one does not. Nor does the proposal protect workers who cannot continue working for lack of suitable jobs or because of poor health, a problem that women and people of color are more apt to experience than are white men (Quadagno 1999). In particularly tight job markets, women, especially minority women, might encounter the historic patterns of race, gender, and other forms of job discrimination as well as skill obsolescence.

In addition to delaying the age of eligibility for full benefits, the other cost-saving proposal is to use the chained Consumer Price Index (CPI). The concept behind the chained CPI is that as costs of certain goods climb, the consumer can replace them with less costly goods. While it may be true that if one's "market basket" includes discretionary items like a new smartphone, or the choice between organic apples or conventional ones, or hamburger rather than steak in response to price fluctuations, the logic fails when the costs are nondiscretionary and nonsubstitutable, like health care and drugs, which are the costs that most affect an old woman's budget and are generally beyond her direct control. Since medical care costs are rising more rapidly than the general CPI, I can expect to pay more each year, a trend that has slowed in 2013, but there is no guarantee that it will not climb once again. Am I supposed to simply switch to cheaper care or not get my teeth cleaned regularly or not replace my glasses when needed (all out-of-pocket expenses)? I already take generic medications. While the chained CPI may work for younger, urban workers who can trade off consumer goods depending on price, it is not a sound measure for the Social Security retirement program (McIntyre 2012).

Like delaying the retirement age, the long-term effects of the chained CPI would reduce Social Security benefits for all recipients by approximately 0.3 percent per year (Gross 2011); and since it would compound annually, the people who live the longest—women—would be most harmed. By the time she reached eighty-five, a woman would have about $1,139 less per year to live on (Lieberman 2013)—approximately ninety dollars a month. This may be pocket change to the Koch brothers but not for the older woman whose basic benefit is approximately $1,200 a month. And such estimates do not take into account inflation. Let me be clear: these proposed changes are designed to prevent the shortfall in the Social Security program that is anticipated by 2037. This does not preclude politicians and other decision makers from believing that "measures to lower projected Trust Fund gaps could help close future budget deficits" (Aaron 2011, 386). As noted above, over two hundred other economists wrote a letter to the president in which they clearly stated that Social Security does not contribute to the federal government's deficit. Since it cannot pay out what it doesn't collect from payroll taxes, it cannot go into deficit (April 12, 2011). They follow that by affirming that the anticipated shortfall be eliminated without cutting benefits, including without raising the retirement age.

In sum, advocates for making changes in benefits through delaying the age of retirement and through changes in the COLA rely on several faulty and/or unproved assumptions. More importantly, however, they do not consider the ramifications of changes for almost half of older people in this country who are within 200 percent of the poverty line. Today's lower middle class, defined as those people with an income between 100 and 250 percent of the poverty line (that is, an annual income between $15,000 and $60,000) are already finding it harder and harder to make ends meet and so to save. Almost half of the families in the United States are in this situation (Harris and Kearney 2013) at a time when government tax and transfer programs are being phased out. These proposed changes come on top of the changes written into the 1983 reforms that were designed to anticipate the retirement of the baby boomers. Reducing lifetime benefits by 19–25 percent (Reno, Bethell, and Walker 2011) may appear to be modest; however, such changes matter greatly when Social Security is the dominant source of retirement income.

It's Not Over until It's Over: The Wolf in the Chicken Coop

After the failure of President Bush in 2005 to achieve his second-term priority—privatizing at least a portion of Social Security—that goal is dormant. Dormancy does not, however, mean gone. In such a system, the beneficiaries would assume all risk and, for all but the most affluent, expect little gain, especially if they retire during a bear market. Women, who live longer than men and have fewer material resources to begin with, would be more likely to outlive their private investments, a situation that cannot happen with Social Security. Further, privatization would have huge start-up costs if money were diverted from FICA to private plans. It would thus jeopardize the financial stability of Social Security itself, harming those people who choose to stay with the traditional program. Privatization would damage the provisions for risk sharing and the allowances for adequacy in the current program. These provisions are especially important for women and other lower-earning individuals. Further, the COLAs would disappear. Privatization, which would move Social Security into the "risk embracing 401k world will introduce the intrinsic bias of DC [defined contribution] plans that currently prevail in the labor market, biases related to earnings inequality, gender-related marital and childbearing risks, as well as market uncertainty" (O'Rand and Shuey 2007, 301). What would also disappear is one of the last surviving remnants of intergenerational solidarity, a value that polling data affirms since young as well as old people support a strong Social Security program. In sum, it would be bad for women and for all but those earning over $100,000 a year who generally have many more opportunities to prepare for retirement than lower-wage workers.

The other possibility that is periodically raised is to convert Social Security to a means-tested program, in which benefits would be awarded only to the people who demonstrate need. Partial means testing can also be done by making the program less generous for moderate- and higher-income people (Estes, O'Neill, and Hartmann 2012). The real risk even for this approach is determining where the line will be drawn; a less-than-generous Congress can draw it at relatively low levels of income. While it is easy to understand the impulse to do so, means testing would be a very troubling choice. It would do away with broad risk sharing since it would be difficult to justify taxing people who might not collect benefits. It would mean that older people would be forced to prove their deservingness and that Congress could similarly modify the income that would qualify as deserving annually. That would make one's retirement security contingent on the state of the nation's financial health and the party in power. Converting what most see as an earned benefit to a welfare benefit would undermine the dignity of getting an assured benefit based on one's contribution.

My extreme wariness about any changes to the program that give Congress power to decide who does and does not qualify for benefits has yet another cause. Pithily stated, Social Security is where the money is. Deficit hawks know that, and they give no indication of disappearing. How, then, can a seventy-five-year-old woman trust that her representatives in Congress will not reduce her benefits, arguably as a budgetary measure? While Congress was unwilling to raise taxes on incomes over $250,000, it was clearly willing to cut food stamps or not reauthorize extended benefits for the long-term unemployed. Yes, of course, new Congresses will be in place, but for anything as important as the primary source of income in retirement, a polity so influenced by neoliberalism and the retreat of the state cannot be trusted not to do the same with Social Security as it did with other safety net programs. Can we expect those members in Congress who have steadily reduced social spending and already believe that government is "pandering to old people" to think generously if benefit levels are put into their hands?

Contrary to current proposals, a guaranteed income from Social Security does not place older people, people with disabilities, and surviving widows and children in a position of subordination to legislators and bureaucrats. As noted above, within the present system, claiming their rights is not demeaning because it does not require such subordination to power. It is also administratively simple. These commitments to assuring a modicum of decency in old age have reduced poverty among older people, one of the great achievements of the past half-century. In apt phrasing, James Schultz and Robert Binstock (2006) warn us that without such strong commitments, the "Golden Years" can easily become "the Tarnished Years."

THE REAL CRISIS

While Social Security is not in crisis, there is a real one that gets little or no attention in the current austerity environment. That crisis is the future of retirement itself for many older people. Recall the image of the three-legged stool and picture it with two of the three legs collapsing. Specifically, lower wages or no wages at all have led to reduced or nonexistent savings. The shift from defined benefit to defined contribution pensions or no pensions at all has further marginalized the less affluent, especially the growing number of part-time workers, who have limited resources to contribute and less ability to withstand bad times. Moreover, participation in these plans is largely determined by income, educational levels, and race. Approximately 80 percent of these retirement-savings benefits go to households with incomes above $100,000 (Lowrey 2012).

People with an intermittent work history, like many women and lower-income men, cannot comfortably set aside money for retirement, and even if they do, limited savings result in limited accumulation of assets. It is hard to save for retirement when current needs trump future ones, a problem that also leads to early withdrawal of such savings for other emergency uses (Smith 2012). Thus, the growing inequality in income derived from assets like 401(k) plans mirrors the other inequalities that pervade society. The lingering recession has worsened these problems significantly. In fact, "between 1996 and 2004, participation rates for those without a high school degree fell from 3.8% to 2.7%" (Herd 2009). In contrast, if one has a graduate degree, participation increases; for example, rates for those so educated rose from 38 percent to 43 percent during the same period (Lowrey 2012). Low-wage workers do not do well with individual accounts since it is more difficult to manage risk with limited resources. Further, risk aversion is also associated with gender, so along with lower earnings and hence lower contributions and more conservative investments, women wind up with "cumulatively unequal pension balances" (O'Rand and Shuey 2007, 292). Hence inequality in pension wealth conforms to other forms of gender inequality.

As in tax policy more generally, the more affluent can accumulate more wealth for retirement than can lower-wage workers. Tax credits that are given for retirement savings are taken most often by the affluent. Known as tax expenditures, they cost the federal treasury over $114 billion a year (Ghilarducci 2007), thus reducing general revenue without generating new savings (Lowrey 2012). They also lower an individual's tax rate. Given that both pensions and savings are contingent on the strength of the market, one's investment choices, one's financial literacy, and the amount that one can actually put into such retirement savings, it is no surprise that these conditions favor the more affluent. Tax expenditures of this sort do little to help lower earners, including women.

The recent economic recession offered a telling lesson about the risks associated with private forms of retirement savings. The losses meant that individuals with modest savings, if not wiped out completely, could no longer anticipate the moderately comfortable retirement they had expected. Cash assets dropped by as much as 40 percent. Reich (2011) reported, "In 2009, some 50 million workers lost a total of at least $1 trillion in 401(k) plans." Assets in terms of housing, where many middle-income families had most of their wealth, plummeted by $2.7 trillion (Herd 2005). These changes exacerbated already-existing inequalities. It is easier to weather a 40 percent loss and wait for a rebound when one's assets are a million dollars or more than it is when one's assets are under $100,000, which actually far exceeds the assets (outside their homes) that most Americans have. These basic facts reflect a fundamental problem in intragenerational equity, an unsurprising continuity of what was true in retirees' working years.

While the above is not an argument against the importance of individualized retirement plans in general, it is a warning that what works for better-educated and higher-income individuals is unlikely to work as well for women and lower earners. Like so much else of the rhetoric related to retirement, the privileged perspective maintains that if others would just do what I do, they could do so much better than with Social Security. Described as an empathy gap, growing out of the increasing stratification of society, it means that "readily dismissing inconvenient people can easily extend to dismissing inconvenient truths about them" (Goleman 2013, 2). The ever-expanding inequality gap makes it more difficult to see oneself in a "less advantaged position" (Goleman 2013, 3). It would be an interesting thought experiment to see what positions people would adopt if they were in the "original position," a concept introduced by justice theorist John Rawls (1972) to see the choices people would make if they had no information about themselves— age, gender, race, and so on.

A fundamental question is this: Is retirement and the opportunity for leisure, perhaps freedom, something that a good society should promote? As Hudson (2007) reminds us, an extended work life, part of the mantra of the "new" aging, described in chapter 3, "may ring truer for those for whom it is an option than for those now coming along for whom it will be an obligation" (178). Is the United States prepared to abandon its commitment made in 1935 that in old age, people ought to be able to sustain a standard of living that at least approximates what they had before and that all Western democracies support? It was not, however, to be done by Social Security alone: recall that Social Security was to be only one leg of a three-legged stool, "designed to complement private pensions" (Quadagno 1988, 185).

Some core questions seem ripe for revisiting. What obligations should society assume for its aging population? Will public policy "re-residualize" the aged so that it is only the frail and dependent who are granted benefits (Hudson 1999)? As a society, will we opt for individuals and/or their families to be responsible for economic security in late life, or will we continue to support at least some collective responsibility? Will we see a revitalization of the collective identity once known as the common good?

For now, it is unlikely that such discussions will take place in the public sector; that does not mean, however, that it cannot be the subject of discussions elsewhere. At this time, as noted throughout this book, the strong focus on individual responsibility and the narrative about the affluent and "greedy" old mean that retirement security is also reduced primarily to an individual achievement. Social Security is thus a critical and essential rebuttal to that view.

RETIREMENT SECURITY IS A MORAL NECESSITY

In a quick recap: it was a great breakthrough in 1935 when this country joined other Western democracies in affirming that retirement is an earned right that is at least in part a public responsibility. It recognized the diversity of market rewards. At that time, and even more so today, it is clear that individuals reap different rewards from work in a market economy (Mashaw 2005). Social Security's design took these differences into account and sought to balance individual effort and collective responsibility. Social insurance was a shared responsibility against the social disharmony that inequality provokes, whereas pensions and savings, the other "legs" of the stool, focused on individual effort.

Equality is not promised by any American social welfare program that focuses instead on the alleviation of poverty (Quadagno 1988), but a recurrent question is how much difference is morally defensible. In this country, the issue of inequality across the life span has been a concern of progressive economists like Joseph Stiglitz (2012) and Robert Reich (2011), to name just two. But politically it has received little attention until President Obama (2014) spoke out about the vast and growing inequality that is dividing this nation at its heart. He made it clear that there are policy remedies for this inequality, starting with education, strengthening the unions, and raising the minimum wage.

Today, even more than in 1935, we recognize that social, economic, and political factors, generally outside of an individual's control, directly shape our retirement experience. As described above, a woman's life history will give us a strong indication of the kind of retirement she can anticipate or even whether she can afford to retire at all. Equal opportunity is a dream, yet we take pride in it as if it were a reality. Equal outcomes are not even a dream.

It is thus important to ask, if we continue to believe, as I do, that retirement is a valued time in human life, how to address retirement security fairly in a society that is confronting major demographic shifts and fiscal constraints. Since these changes are largely beyond individual control, it is even more important for us to ask: *What does fairness require?* It starts, I believe, with the commitment to giving each individual an equal opportunity to make his or her way in the world and to live one's own version of the good life. We cannot do this without a secure economic foundation. Autonomy does not exist in the abstract. Today, the conflict we must address is the justifiable balance between individual and collective effort to permit retirement without impoverishment. One answer is the one offered in 1935 by the passage of the Social Security Act—that achieving a basic standard of living that lessens the risk of poverty is a shared individual and collective responsibility. It also suggests that a good society owes this basic security to all people and not only to those who are old. Yet it seems particularly perverse to argue, as the rhetoric about protecting our children's future does, that the way to make children more secure is to make the old less secure by reducing benefits.

Given a basic concern for women who rely most heavily on the public or collective side of the ledger, what will help women and others now marginalized by the economic lottery to grow old with dignity and with a sense that someone will "catch them if they fall" (Ruddick 1999)? My belief is that we must challenge the hyperindividualism and the elitism that has dominated society and has contributed to the nation's deepening inequality and, arguably, the moral failings that helped to create this inequality (Dionne 2012). In an era that focuses almost exclusively on protecting individual autonomy, retirement security calls for a very different perspective—interdependency across generations. It is virtually impossible for all but the wealthiest individuals to retire without a strong Social Security program based on broad risk sharing. Thus, those of us who are collecting Social Security benefits today rely on those younger than we are to pay into the system. In the future, they, too, will rely on the commitments of future, unknown strangers. In this way, we acknowledge that all people live in an interdependent world where we neither succeed nor fail entirely on our own. As a general proposition, all people owe a debt to past generations and a responsibility toward future ones. While these ideas do not provide instructions about translating social solidarity into specific policy choices, they do call for an intergenerational approach that sees all people moving through different roles during the course of their lives and so demands that each person be sensitive to each of those roles.

FROM ENTITLEMENT REFORM TO RETIREMENT SECURITY

I have been arguing that social insurance cannot fall victim to the excuse that this country cannot afford entitlements or that Social Security must be means tested (to save money) or privatized (to increase return on investment for some and, indirectly, to benefit Wall Street). Why should Social Security recipients, most of whom are not affluent, and the oldest among whom are women, be expected to sacrifice what is at best a modest source of income, especially when other sources of retirement income are minimal? Why should benefit cuts be the primary route to "saving" Social Security while the government provides more affluent people with up to $100 billion in tax savings toward their private retirement accounts? From this standpoint, any modifications to Social Security should be largely in the form of increased revenues. In order for a Social Security reform to be ethically defensible, it must not harm the least advantaged while assuring that the more affluent are unable to exit the system. Without resources from across the income spectrum, the program will not take in enough revenue to support an adequate benefit structure. Thus, a good beginning is an increase in the percentage of taxable wages gradually to 90 percent of payroll, where it has been in the past, if not lifting the ceiling on taxable income completely. The proposal would still not tax for purposes of Social Security unearned investment income. This modification in revenue has many benefits: (1) it would generate revenue immediately; (2) it would improve the long-term financial solvency of the trust fund; and (3) it would close almost one-third of the funding gap over the next seventy-five years (NASI 2013).

Second, and a much bolder step, would be to broaden the payroll tax base to include new sources of income such as income from investments. This expansion would bring substantial new revenues into the system. This change can be made gradually and phased in over a long period of time. It would close the trust fund gap by almost half over the next seventy-five years and almost one-quarter in the seventy-fifth year (Aaron 2011), and it would recognize that the more affluent, who obtain so much of their income from dividends or carried interest, carry a far smaller burden of the FICA taxes supporting Social Security than do lower-wage workers.

For women, additional safeguards are necessary given the unlikelihood that the gender, race, and class inequities that help to determine their retirement income will be modified anytime soon. Recalling feminist activist Tish Sommers's long-ago comment that women are one man away from poverty, a good place to begin is to assure that a spouse's death does not result in benefit reductions. This problem is particularly acute (a 50 percent loss) when both worked and received comparable benefits in retirement. That problem can be eased if a "widow, widower or surviving divorced spouse were provided with 75 percent of the couple's combined benefits" (Estes, O'Neill, and Hartmann 2012). A further recommendation aims at remedying the economic effects of caregiving. Dropping out of the workforce to provide care lowers women's lifetime earnings and limits their ability to save. Thus, women should receive credit for up to five years for family service according to a formula to be determined. Additionally, a more effective determination of the special minimum primary insurance would help to remedy both the effects of historically low-wage work and caregiving. Further, rather than adopting the chained consumer price index, which results in reduced lifetime benefits, the Social Security the COLA should be based on the consumer price index-elder (CPI-E) that is pegged to the actual spending habits of older people and is a far more accurate measure than either the current one, which underestimates the actual costs old women (and many men) face and the losses that the recent recession brought about. Further, given the multiple ways that families are formed, at the time of this writing, same-sex couples, whether married or not, deserve the same benefits as traditionally married couples (Estes, O'Neill, and Hartmann 2012). These recommendations—a more accurate COLA, a more responsive minimum benefit, improved treatment of widows, recognition of nonwaged work, like caregiving, for calculating benefits, increasing revenue by expanding the earmarked revenue stream—demonstrate that Social Security can be sustained over a long period of time without harming women and low-wage workers. These changes can strengthen the program and make it fairer.

If this country cannot maintain our commitments to provide basic economic security for the older generation, such financial wherewithal will have to be borne by the next-younger generation. While people may have romantic notions about intergenerational family living in the past, historians have demonstrated that family economies are damaging to both the older and younger generations (Haber and Gratton 1994). Instead, it is essential to be reminded that Social Security is one of the few public expressions of social solidarity and interdependence that bind generations to one another so that they can support one another without imposing undue burdens on any one generation, a view that is strongly held by both young and old individuals (Pew 2011).

A LONGER-RANGE ISSUE: SOCIAL JUSTICE

The socially constructed focus on intergenerational conflict has detracted attention from the intragenerational problem that is rooted both in the deepening inequalities that mark our society and the long-term effect of gender and race inequities. While I have focused on Social Security, fairness requires addressing the mixed system of public and private sources of retirement income in the United States as a whole. Given that occupational plans and personal retirement accounts benefit from favorable tax policies, they, too, should have social responsibilities. Since they do not now have any such responsibilities, the disproportionate benefits that the more affluent derive from individualized pension plans like 401(k)s and IRAs raise problems of justice. Is it fair that pensions and savings, generally understood as private as opposed to public goods but considered by Social Security's founders as each necessary for retirement security, exacerbate inequality in retirement while resulting in a $100 billion savings for private investors? The public sector has responsibilities to level the playing field between lower-income earners and higher-income earners so that all continue to have ways to restore the missing legs of the proverbial Social Security "stool." As the Elder

Economic Security Index (Wider Opportunities for Women 2013) demonstrates, women cannot make ends meet on their average Social Security benefit. If a woman is single and owns her home without a mortgage, for example, Social Security would cover only 65 percent of her total living expenses. It would cover less if she were a renter or still faced mortgage payments. Why not redirect some of the $100 billion in tax expenditures to substantially improve the benefits that are now available to women and other low-wage workers? In this way, Social Security can reclaim its original goal to alleviate poverty at a time when its ability to do so is reduced as a result of broad societal forces like wage stagnation, unemployment and underemployment, women's responsibilities at home, and the rise in the numbers of unmarried women, who fare the worst under current arrangements.

CONCLUSION

The promise of retirement that supported the passage of Social Security in 1935 was intended to do more than keep retirees out of poverty; it was to give them the chance to maintain the basic living standards that they had during their working years (Quadagno 1996). To be clear, however, it was not to replace their pre-retirement income dollar for dollar, but in combination with the other legs of the stool, it was intended to allow them to continue their current lifestyles. Given the racial and economic disparities in the United States today, that goal is even more important than it was in 1935. Yet there seems to be so little political will to mitigate the accumulation of lifetime disadvantages that contribute to this inequality.

The politics of Social Security and retirement security more generally pose a greater threat to this essential program's survival than its immediate financial condition. Yet, as I hope the above has demonstrated, ideology, inaccurate information, and faulty generalizations make the problem primarily political. This country's public agenda has moved far to the right in a process that journalist George Packer (2013) describes as "the unwinding," in which systematic corner cutting, rule bending, and self-dealing at the top infiltrate all of American society. It has resulted in a transformed economy— "from an all-in-the-same-boat world of shared risk toward a go-it-alone world of personal responsibility" (Hacker 2007, 4). Programs like Social Security that were put in place during the New Deal are the antithesis of the antigovernment ideological perspective. Yet, as described above, it is not only successful as a mitigator of poverty, but it is also consistently popular among people of all age groups. While younger people might not think of it in this way, it is collective rather than individualistic. It represents a tacit compact between generations; and it is mildly redistributive in that lower-income individuals get a higher replacement income than higher-income individuals. If not a strong and responsive Social Security system, then who but the younger generations will bear individual responsibility for the older generations? How might organizations, advocacy groups, and individuals build on this support and the dangers of an even less sufficient benefit structure?

Pensions in the form of 401(k)s and IRAs, with their substantial tax advantages and their individualistic foundation, meet the neoliberal agenda but not the social agenda. They respond to the market since they are less costly for business than the former defined-benefit plans. And because they do not create additional savings and primarily benefit the already advantaged, they do not meet the demands of fairness (Rawls 1972). With high unemployment, business has fewer motivations to do what benefits workers than it would if the situation were reversed, as it was during World War II, when expanded benefits was a way to attract scarce workers. Given the assumptions on the right that people are unemployed as the result of their own inactions, it is hard to see how this problem will be remedied.

Despite political and media attempts to depict the Social Security retirement program as being in "crisis," the reforms described above and the work of organizations such as the National Academy of Social Insurance have demonstrated that modest modifications will make the system sustainable for many years to come. The program's social insurance structure is sound and must be maintained. Its future funding gap is moderate and can be ameliorated primarily through increased revenue that I highlighted above. There is no reason, except for Social Security's critics who favor a more privatized system, for provoking a crisis over future funding.

Increasing payroll taxes should be manageable by younger workers, especially if they are made more progressive, an observation confirmed by polling data (NASI 2013). Similarly, expanding the tax base to include high earners and investment and other unearned income will be borne with minimum, if any, difficulty by this group of earners. A reduction or even closing of the tax expenditures related to privatized retirement savings can also be used to support the program. Such changes would primarily affect individuals who would save with or without tax breaks since they have ample disposable income. It is also critical to reawaken the responsibilities of business to the role the creators of Social Security envisioned for them and that their predecessors supported (Quadagno 1988). Further, the myth of the greedy geezer must finally be put to rest. Not only is the phrase offensive, but it also distorts the actual situation of the vast majority of old people, particularly old women.

The current system addresses many needs at once. It supports dignity and relative financial independence, thus protecting both younger and older generations. This universal system, as we have seen, pools resources from people at different income levels and by so doing protects most of the old from financial hardship in old age. In the years leading up to the bill's passage, it was upheld as a choice between its passage and the poorhouse (Haber 1983). While there may be no more poorhouses, the need to be protected from the risk of impoverishment is still with us. While individuals can do much on their own, everyone benefits from a recognition of and support for the "ties that bind" us together (Kingson, Hirshown, and Cornman 1986). With all the changes and varied threats that lie ahead, it is time to revitalize the submerged communal values that motivated this country in the past. Hyperindividualism and meritocracy sliding into elitism have served a few very well, but for most, they have failed. It is time to switch.

Chapter Seven

Beyond Rational Control

Reflections on End-of-Life Care

Even though in the West there is broad agreement about what constitutes a "good death"—symptom relief, holistic care, being accompanied and comforted, able to discuss freely what is happening, choice and control over site of care and treatments, and family and friends comforted and cared for (Lloyd 2010)—we are still reaching for it. As dying has become increasingly privatized, medicalized, and seemingly infinitely postponable, our choices expand at the same time that we may have a harder and harder time assessing them and saying no to them as more complex interventions become commonplace (Kaufman 2010). And because death has become increasingly isolated from social life, we have few chances to learn from others about the questions to ask or the meanings of unintentionally coded messages (Butler 2014); yet it is on such knowledge that our ability to be fully autonomous rests (Meyers 1987).

Like so much else this book addresses, these goals are both more complex and less individually realizable than they seem at first look. How we die is situated in intersecting factors beyond our control; these factors include the culture of medicine (see chapter 4 and below), gender and racial inequalities, insurance status, fears of litigation, geographical location, and cultural resistance to addressing death and dying. How we die is also influenced by this country's elevation of rationality and individuality, enacted in autonomy as uncoerced choice. Extending that understanding to end-of-life care, it assumes that one of the essentials of good end-of-life care is documenting our wishes, often when we are healthy, about our treatment wishes and then appointing a surrogate to carry them out if we are no longer able to do so. This rational and individualistic approach means that our surrogate is stripped of his or her role as spouse, daughter, or best friend. They become ciphers whose role is to expressly carry out our wishes (High 1991). But they often find this difficult, especially since what they face is usually new to them and communication is often less than clear (Kaufman 2002; Butler 2014). It is hard also when they think about their responsibilities in relational and not contractual terms, a challenge to the rational model often demanded by hospital risk managers and the concept of advance directives. As a feminist, I find it difficult to accept the individualized conception of autonomy that is the "gold standard" for treatment choices—it elevates a view of autonomy that detaches us from our relationships, broader values, and the particular features of our immediate situation. Making decisions is also hard because certain choices are simply not open to us, the result of resource and other constraints. I may want to die with hospice care in my own home, but if I don't have a full-time caregiver, that will probably not happen. The "taking charge" model requires no structural, cultural, or policy changes except legalizing surrogate decision making. To implement this model only asks that hospitals or doctors encourage their patients to complete a directive and asks about them when needed. It assumes that people will willingly talk about their own deaths and that others will listen to them, an assumption that is contestable (Drought and Koenig 2002). To function as expected, it makes many more assumptions, which I will turn to below, that are equally contestable.

I am interested in reflecting on what we might do to help people draw their lives to a close in ways that preserve their integrity, that honor the lives they have lived and the relationships of which they have been a part. My goal in this chapter is to look critcally—albeit sympathetically—at the reasons why current approaches to care at the end of life often fall short. To foreshadow the argument, I note that the emphasis on rationality and control rest uneasily with the emotional vulnerability, uncertainty, and fears that I think are inevitable parts of our dying. While if we are lucky we can preserve our integrity for as long as possible, we are different in important ways when we are near death from when we are thinking about it while we are healthy. We are vulnerable in ways we've probably not experienced since we were infants. My argument continues several themes that recur in this book, in particular the ways in which the focus on advance care planning overemphasizes individual autonomy without attending to the underlying conditions that either hinder or expand one's options. Further, my interest extends to how gender influences what our care at the end of life may be like. Research is limited, but I will note the times when I think it does matter. In conclusion, I will offer recommendations about what we might do to make death with dignity a reality for more women (and men).

I open with a story about what I learned accompanying my friend Susan in the thirty-one months from her diagnosis of metastatic breast cancer to her death. By then imagining my own ideal death—in brief—and juxtaposing it to what I think is the probable reality of what will happen to me, I hope to further isolate elements that might matter in caring at the end of life.

WITH SUSAN

My friend Susan died on October 22, 2001, of metastatic breast cancer. She was fifty-eight years old, an independent scholar, a linguist, and a recommitted Jew who celebrated her bat mitzvah on June 5, 2001. Barely able to walk, she climbed to the *bima*, resplendent in a blue and white *tallith* and *kippa*, read her Torah portion, and gave her *D'Var Torah* (sermon). Quite a party followed. Outside, on her wet patio, and later in her living room, she held court among her friends and family. She did not touch a morsel of food.

The bat mitzvah and that chilly June party were her last hurrahs. Her condition worsened rapidly—her back pain slowed her movements to a crawl, including crawling up the steps to her apartment when her legs were too weak to support her; her bowels rarely worked; she ate almost nothing; and she experienced breathing problems that she attributed to asthma. Every physical change that she faced had a cause—but not the cancer that was rampaging through her body. She accepted enthusiastically every test and treatment, although I doubt that they had many practical benefits since her pain was seemingly unrelenting. I don't think she ever said, "Do everything; I don't want to die," but each dose of Taxol and Herceptin—and later radiation to her brain—raised her hopes while she obsessed about a new apartment, without stairs, near a café, in a neighborhood she liked. It was no surprise that a nurse's mention of hospice or DNR (do not resuscitate) threw her into a rage. She had work to do, a class to teach, a book to finish, yet all she could do was watch the *telenovelas* on Spanish television (her doctorate was in Spanish and Portuguese) and talk—about her body's stubborn refusal to perform or about a time in Colombia, South America, when she was

acclaimed as a scholar with her son proudly looking on. Only once, before
the very end, did I hear her rage—on a rainy, gray Saturday morning in May,
she called me. A brain scan, for which I had taken her the night before, had
revealed some grainy "spots," causing her to exclaim, "Now I have brain
cancer, too!" By this morning in May, the pain had become acute—every
movement, even reaching into the refrigerator for food, hurt. Defeated, she
was at her wits' end. But that mood passed when her oncologist discounted
those grainy spots. Radiologists, her doctor said, look for things when they
know a patient has cancer. Her oncologist, an older woman at an academic
medical center, urged her to "work through the pain." When the pain got very
bad, Susan blamed herelf for not making a "big deal" of it so that it would be
addressed. For whatever reason, I think Susan's oncologist condoned excess
pain. The cancer, which seemed like an abstract concept, seemed manageable
in contrast to the unremitting and essentially ignored back pain that no one
explicitly linked to the cancer. Her orthopedist gave her one round of corti-
sone for her back pain but was reluctant to do more because of the cancer. He
advised physical therapy. When Susan suggested that he call the oncologist,
he said, "Why don't you do it?" Her internist was similarly reluctant to make
the call. Since I, of course, heard about these conversations from Susan, I
can't attest to their accuracy, but if that was the truth as she saw it, I would
imagine that her doctors were taking cues from her—don't confront the
cancer; they let her go along interpreting symptoms and even pain in her own
way, and so the pain was undertreated.

Her last months in a nursing home and in the hospital brought complaints
about nurses who didn't care (she "fired" one) and her sister who wasn't
looking hard enough for that new apartment. She fretted about her unfinished
book and her legacy. I wondered if she could still access those good memories that once filled our conversations, kept her company when she could do
little else, leaving her radiant and calm. A former colleague's visit elicited
the "old" Susan, albeit much weakened, but speech eluded her. Her son
rarely left her side. We listened to music of sixteenth-century Sephardim, but
contact was difficult. Her face remained clear, starkly beautiful. She went
home a few days before she died. One hospice visit saw her through to the
end.

I think Susan died as fully herself until the last few months, when she
could barely lift her head off the pillow. She rejected hospice. She neither
implicitly nor explicitly accepted death. She died as she wished—full code
and treated to the end. Her unspoken goal was to be fully alive in ways that

confirmed her identity (Halberg 2004) and until the very end, when her mind failed her, I think she realized this goal. Despite all the changes, I think, if asked, she could have said, "I recognize myself as 'me,' and others whom I respect acknowledge this identity." She coped in her own way largely by not naming her disease and its role in her terrible pain. The only time I heard her utter the word "death" was during a frustrated outburst directed at her oldest friend: "Did you come to watch me die?" For as long as possible, she did not feel isolated from life around her.

She asked for and got most of what she wanted without worrying about being a burden. She took a trip to Spain, foraged in the archives, bought a new car, demonstrated against a new neighborhood Starbucks, and fretted over her unfinished research. She enjoyed almost to the end human contact, sharing memories, hand and foot massages, *telenovelas*, the Friday evening liturgy (she tuned in via the telephone until the very end), study, her sister, her friends, and, most importantly, her son. Except for study, and until her brain shut down, she enjoyed all of this almost to the end. She accommodated each change in her condition without comment. When she could no longer walk up the stairs to her apartment, she turned to paratransit. Her financial resources were thus an adjunct to her coping. If it had been offered to her, I think she would have accepted even being tethered to machines if her brain still functioned.

In many ways, Susan was able to die her way because she had the support of her sister, Ruth, who came from California to Chicago to be her full-time caregiver. She had adequate resources; she had her friends as her audience and her helpers and she had excellent insurance that allowed her to opt for every treatment and medical care from a oncologist who recognized Susan's priorities, for example, by accommodating her treatment regime so that Susan could give a paper at Princeton. But very little of this would have been possible without Susan's willingness to ask for what she wanted and Ruth's ability to give it to her. Ruth and Susan's friends did what needed to be done—but mostly it was Ruth, who was on the verge of collapsing from exhaustion by the time Susan died. Ruth gave Susan the social support she needed to die as she wished but at a tremendous price to herself.

I learned much from Susan about dying. Take care of the pain. Susan suffered because her doctors, perhaps taking a cue from her, seemed to avoid confronting the dreadful pain and its cause. The omnipresence of pain was a constant distraction, but alleviation of it might have kept her from the intensity of her wish to live fully. Find ways to be present as that person wants your presence. For Susan, that meant making time so that she could tell the stories that narrated her life.

Bringing her friends together immediately after the diagnosis for a tea party, Susan instructed us to exchange information and phone numbers. She gave us assignments and started the storytelling that marked these months. I and others became collaborators in preserving her identity by listening and asking questions. No one insisted that she find meaning in her suffering, talk about dying, or let go. Hence, no one questioned her belief that she could return to her favorite café or finish her book. Medicine, while probably vital in giving her thirty-one months from diagnosis to death, was peripheral to what was important to her—it was the background that enabled her to do what she cared about. No one seemed to struggle over treatment choices because it was assumed that whatever could be done, she'd want. If there were to be an instructive headline to her life while dying, it would be listen to me, help me be the person I have always been. Let me have the context in which I can live as best I can.

Ruth's presence underlined the importance of social support for the person who is dying but also demonstrated the costs of relying almost entirely on one person for such support. While friends helped, Ruth was the person on call for twenty-four hours each day. Thus, Susan's ability to die as she wished was intimately connected to the social circumstances of her life. How much better it would have been had Ruth been able to count on public-sector support for caregiving (Holstein 1999; see chapter 5). As it was, Ruth almost became the patient herself after months of sleeping on a mattress on the floor and not getting an uninterrupted night's sleep. Imagine if she were an eighty-year-old spouse instead of a fifty-something sister. Everyone had a role, and that role was to support Susan in practical and psychological ways. Oddly, I think Susan's death was a "good one" if one can set aside the idea that she was only fifty-eight and that her pain was nearly relentless. She did it her way; she asked for what she wanted and generally got it and was able to pay for services that helped her do what she wanted.

DYING—AS I IMAGINE IT

Susan spent her last few days at home, where most people want to die but few do, in a clean, safe environment rather than at the long-term care facility where she had gone intermittently. Ruth's utter devotion, Susan's good health insurance, and her financial resources helped, too. As I imagine my own death, I think first of context. I am at home and have available to me the care of a palliative care team and a full-time caregiver so that my daughters can be with me as often as they can without being responsible for hands-on care. I will be certain that I am ready to die, having addressed regrets, atoned for harms done, and said my goodbyes. I will continue to live in habitual ways, although I will need others to make that possible. My daughters will not become so uneasy or frightened by my condition that they transfer me to the hospital, but if they must, it will be a hospital wing that has been redesigned to be as homelike as possible. My doctor will not have forgotten me once I am beyond cure. Maybe I'll even be like my old friend Laurie Shields, the cofounder of the Older Women's League, who declared shortly before she died, "I only hope that I live long enough to vote against Ronald Reagan." I note, however, that in one way my view is atypical—when asked, most people wish for a quick and easy death (Aries 1981; Howarth 1998).

What seems rather certain to me, however, is that I probably won't die according to my romantically imagined description, so inflected with images of death watches in paintings and literature. Instead, I suspect that rather than being in a room with warm, filtered sunlight, I will be in a room lit by fluorescent lights, which I dislike in almost all circumstances, in a hospital or a nursing home. I will be wearing a skimpy gown, perhaps tethered to a heart monitor and other equipment that will give regular readings of my vital signs when a close look at me might tell the tale. Instead of silence, soft music, or the voices of those I love, there will be nurses and doctors and the cacophony of noises that makes hospitals distinctly unlike home. Strangers will hover around my bed, quietly talking about me—but only occasionally to me, and then to cheerfully ask "How are you?" an irrelevant question at best. A hospitalist, whom I do not know, will be in charge of my care. I will face interventions I might not want but which become difficult to refuse as medicine gets better at repairing my individual body parts even as my body as a totality is falling apart. At hastily arranged meetings with my family, my doctors will ask my daughters about trying one more treatment that might benefit me. My daughters, with whom I have discussed what I want as I near death, will feel uncertain about what to do even though they have heard my rants about not wanting to hold on, about not wanting to consume resources to no good end—but that was all said when I wasn't imminently dying. I think I have sketched an illusion, a wish for how I might be but not as I will probably be.

As Julie Rothstein Rosenbaum (2010), a physician but also a daughter and a sister, observed as her mother lay dying, "There is only so much advance deliberations you can engage in, and . . . nothing can quite prepare you for the actual decisions when the time comes" (8). Instead, the moment of decision can be clouded with doubt and uncertainty. And if I am competent, who knows what I will feel about one more day, one more month, one more year. My friend Kathleen, an attorney who died in 1996 at the age of forty-eight, had vigorously spoken out against expensive treatments that had minimum long-term benefits in her role as a health-care advocate. She changed her mind when she was the patient, and acknowledging the irony, she accepted these expensive treatments that might delay her death by even a month or two. Will I feel the way that Kathleen did?

I thought about the dying experiences that I have just described as I watched a *Frontline* documentary, "Facing Death" (PBS 2010), which poignantly revealed just how hard it can be for a terminally ill person to die, even with loving families and engaged physicians. As one physician observed, medicine can support "almost every body system for years," leaving people in a state of "suspended animation." Another physician described her patients in intensive care as "broken survivors." Wasting away, breathing through tubes, mouths agape, and families hovering, unsure of what to do but wanting to do what was best, patients were often bit players in the drama of the ICU. Contemporary medicine, Jeanne Guillemin (1995) observes, effaces the patient, the primary actor, from the dying process. The dominant assumption is that every cause of death can be "resisted, postponed, or averted in the struggle to maintain vital functions"—a triumph of the medicalization of death (Clark 2002, 905) but also its potential for depersonalization in hospital settings. "Physicians, other health care professionals, families, patients, and the extended community know how to *provide* care and even improve the quality of life when cure is unlikely; the harder task is to *respect* such care as profoundly as we honor curing. The exigencies of the new medicine, where time is a budgetable commodity, make caring well for dying patients difficult, but do not eliminate their need for the best care we can give them" (Holstein 1997, 849).

LESSONS LEARNED

As I wrote these words about Susan, thought about my own dying, and reflected on both Kathleen's experience and that of the patients and families in the *Frontline* documentary, I came away feeling increasingly certain that the most important element in good end-of-life care is a supportive context that is mostly available at home and does not require regular assessments of treatment options or rely on worn-out family caregivers like Ruth. As I shall discuss below, once we have a good understanding of the patient's goals and values, making decisions can often be diversionary, a shield that protects us from the emotional complexity of dying. Rationality and control—knowing what we want, preparing for it, and then getting it—fits well with notions of individual responsibility and narrow concepts of autonomy that I have often questioned but also accept as a part of the moral universe. But I also believe that along with reason, attention to and respect for emotion and embodiment, which are central features of our lives at all times but especially when we are dying, are also essential. "Vulnerability," in the words of philosopher Barry Hoffmaster (2006), "marks the limits of individualism" (43).

ADVANCE CARE PLANNING

I told Susan's story and reflected on how I think I want to die and how I probably will die in part to interrogate a popularly and professionally held consensus about the meaning of a "good death" and "death with dignity." While there is considerable uncertainty about the effectiveness and the extent of their use, advance directives and the role they play in meeting our wishes and easing the responsibility of surrogates are taken as a commonsense way for us to die as we wish. I heard this belief expressed regularly—that directives would control what happened to them and that their families knew and understood their wishes. "I am all prepared," said one woman during a discussion on care at the end of life. We have such confidence in the workability of advance care planning. Yet research casts doubts about many of these certainties, both in the narrow sense of treatment choices and in the broader sense of the quality of care for individuals and their families (Kaufman 2000; Fegerlin and Schneider 2004) or improving end-of-life care. In a national study of advance directives and end-of-life care, a team of researchers concluded that "singly focused public health interventions, such as the PSDA and its reliance on AD completion, will not improve end of life care. Rather, multifaceted and sustainable interventions are needed to truly improve the care of the dying and those around them" (Teno et al. 2007, 194).

There are many reasons why advance care planning often does not work as intended. I offer a few reasons that I think are particularly important. My first concern is the contestable assumptions on which they rest. It may not be as easy as the logic once suggested for us to anticipate a time in the future when we are dying and, in advance, decide what quality of life is not worth living. In fact, it may be that as death comes closer we may opt for quantity over quality, as feminist essayist and novelist Susan Sontag did (as reported by Rubin 2007). It assumes that death is essentially subject to rational control, that people would "routinely, comfortably, and meaningfully confront and consider not just their own mortality but also the process of their physical decline and dying in an engaged and rational manner" (Drought and Koenig 2002, 115). It assumes that we can tell our designated proxy what we will want in unknown circumstances and that they will be able to act decisively in what may be conditions of uncertainty, fear, and pressure. It assumes that our proxy or others will willingly engage in conversations about our death with us even though there is great resistance to having these conversations (Hurd Clarke, Korotchenko, and Bundon 2012). It further assumes that it is about "us" only and not about us in the context of our relationships, which often have primacy over what we may want for ourselves. If we are in the hospital, it assumes that the familiar impulse to treat will be tamped down and that physicians will explain our options or perhaps not even offer options when there are no real choices that will sustain us in recognizable ways, even as it delays death. It assumes that our physicians and others will help us to negotiate what are often gray zones between life and death (Kaufman 2005). And, it assumes that our choices are unrelated to matters such as our insurance status or resources (see Holstein, Parks, and Waymack 2011 for an extended discussion of these issues). Thus, the question that governs advance care planning is how medicine can return to patients (and/or their proxies) control over treatment choices, a simple goal in a far-from-simple biomedical context.

Another interesting irony is that choices about individual treatments may be less important than the campaign around directives suggests. A national study ranked fifth out of nine the wish to make individual treatment choices (J. Hofmann et al. 1997, cited in Winzelberg et al. 2009). For many patients, defining broad goals of treatment was more important than making specific treatment choices. But perhaps even more significantly, people wanted surrogates to do what they thought best, and they wanted surrogates to take their own interests into account (Hickman et al. 2005; Hawkins et al. 2005). When near death, people, perhaps particularly women, do not want to be isolated from the people who care for them and about whom they care. Their obligations to others continue to shape their lives, even when they can no longer actively engage in decision making.

While the Patient Self-Determination Act (1994) has made advance care planning possible, large groups of people simply do not do it. Cultural differences, bad experiences with the medical care system, and religious views about dying are often impediments and can lead to unwarranted paternalism (Dula 1994; Blackhall et al. 1995; Krakauer, Crenner, and Fox 2002; Murray and Jennings 2005). People may be more worried about accessing care than limiting it (Dubler 2005). Several years ago, I was doing ethics training in Indianapolis for one hundred maintenance men who worked in senior housing. When one of the men brought up the subject of death, the reluctance, even refusal to talk about it led to some angry outbursts. The offer to meet with the administrator of the housing complex to talk about signing an advance directive had no takers. Some insisted that it was God's decision, not theirs, about when they would die.

There are other impediments that include the "wars" against disease that make death a defeat and so to be resisted in any way possible, the ability to intervene in more and more complex ways to stave off death, the normalization of increasingly sophisticated treatments for people at ever more advanced ages, the medical profession's commitment to cure, its uncertainties about prognosis, its limited training in being with the dying patient, and the quixotic cultural attitudes toward the increasingly privatized experience of dying and death. Lillian Rubin (2007), writing in her eighties, astutely points out that "even when people make the decision to forgo treatment, it's almost never without mixed feelings—conflict that's fed by the medical establishment for whom any death is a failure and by a family that wants to hold on for just a little longer" (152). But even if there was no pressure, we live in a culture that is as committed to denying death as it is to denying old age. "Hope," she says, often "triumphs over reality" (153).

Rubin's view seems about right to me. Especially for the educated middle class, insisting that they want such control and certainty that they know under what circumstances they will not want to be kept alive makes sense. Like old age itself, it is hard to imagine ourselves wanting to continue living with a body that no longer works. From a distance, we assume we can manage fears about the unknown that may come near the end of our lives. Nor do we know how we or our surrogates will respond to the increasing availability of more and more medicalized interventions, many of which are taken as normal and natural by physicians (Kaufman 2010). This comfort with advanced medical interventions that may have only the smallest likelihood of success should not be surprising in a society that often thinks it can defeat death (see chapter 3). Or interventions may be minimal and so hard to refuse, even though they cascade into subsequent ones that are less minor.

There are also subtle dangers. Barry Hoffmaster (2006) notes that "a familiar strategy for fleeing from fear and discomfort is to become task-oriented." The preoccupation with decision making often means focusing on the task rather than on the person for whom the task is being performed (42). Hand-wringing replaces hand-holding (Holstein 1997). No one wants to make a mistake, to give up too soon. And, even more practically, in our litigious society, hospitals may be unwilling to terminate treatment in the absence of a named surrogate (even though most states have surrogacy laws) and identified preferences, especially if there is disagreement among family members. While hopefully the Terri Schiavo case is an anomaly, given how she became a cause of the "right to life" movement, it is an example of how badly things can go when families disagree, when different medical opinions are offered, and when religious views of family members may trump those of the patient who is no longer able to speak for herself, all of which happened in Terri Schiavo's case.

These cautionary notes do not mean that for some people, in some circumstances, these assumptions and goals make sense. Taking charge of our lives is what much of the modern women's movement was about. Advance care planning works best for people who are comfortable with legal documents, who trust the medical care system, and who habitually exercised control over their lives. Hence, it bears noting that this approach may be another graphic example of how some people translate their wishes about end-of-life care into a universal assumption that does not hold for all people. The lens of privilege can assume universality when what it sees is rather particularistic.

While patient control doesn't quite capture a rich conception of a "good death," it is easy to put in place albeit harder to practice well. It doesn't require significant structural changes in medical practice or policies that determine what is reimbursable or not. But perhaps most importantly, it only touches on one of the many values that make for a "good death."

Hospice and Palliative Care

The first hospice in this country opened in Connecticut in 1975. In 1982, Congress passed legislation that provided Medicare funding for hospice care for those individuals who had six months or less to live; many private insurance companies followed suit. Hospice sought to do what the medicalization of death could not do—facilitate dying at home with assistance for families as well as patients. Some hospice units now exist in nursing homes and in step-down units in hospitals, although the lack of a resident caregiver like Ruth remains a barrier to hospice care at home, especially for women who are more apt than men to live alone. So I see this shortcoming as an important barrier to women who need and may want hospice care. Few women can afford full-time caregivers, a necessity to benefit from the professional and volunteer services that hospice makes available.

Hospice tends to work best for patients with cancer when prognosis is relatively reliable, but even then, the decision to recommend and accept hospice care requires an acknowledgment by the physician, patient, and family that death is inevitable and relatively imminent. Yet, as research (Drought and Koenig 2002) has suggested, negotiating that gray zone between life and death and confronting the fact that the death process has begun is an expectation that often is more difficult than our best hopes and common assumptions anticipated. For patients like Susan, even the mention of hospice is anathema.

Eleanor Clift (2008), an American journalist, describes how hospice care worked for her husband, Tom. It did exactly what its founder, Cicely Saunders, envisioned. Tom was not in pain, and Eleanor had just enough freedom to continue her professional life while feeling supported during her husband's dying. Tom's case was an "ideal" one for hospice care. Suffering from kidney cancer, Tom chose hospice when medicine had exhausted every known therapy that might have bought him more time. Both Tom and Eleanor knew—and accepted—that death was the only outcome available to him.

Palliative care carries many of the same commitments as hospice to providing comfort care to patients and assisting families throughout the illness continuum. It does not eschew treatments; it is not limited to the last six months of life; it focuses on treating and preventing suffering and offers care in hospitals and nursing homes, where more than 55 percent of Americans die (Foley 2005). Palliative care is particularly important because it can offer services to patients and families as illnesses progress and change. It is not reserved for the very end when, in some ways, the decisions may be simpler. Palliative care specialists "help people make tough decisions that are less about dying than about how they want to live at the end of their lives" (Brink 2009, 2). The problem, however, is the absence of specific reimbursement for such services, which has limited its expansion. In the time since I initially wrote those words, palliative care services are expanding, at least in most major hospitals, and under the Affordable Care Act, rules about hospice and curative interventions may also be changing, but it is too soon to know how they will be implemented and what effects they will have.

Aid in Dying

Physician-assisted suicide (PAS) or physician aid in dying (http://www. compassionandchoices.org), with which I am sympathetic, is the last redoubt in the effort to tame death. Legal in just Oregon, Washington, Montana, and Vermont legislation requires that patients be competent, request aid in dying at least twice, and have a prognosis of six months or less to live. They must be able to take the prescribed medications by themselves to prevent charges of homicide. PAS is distinct from "mercy killing" or active euthanasia, in which someone else is the cause of one's death. That is not legal anywhere in the United States. One more definitional clarification: while there may be religious or other reasons to make a distinction, there is no moral or legal distinction between never starting treatment, for example, ventilator support, and stopping it once started. This is important because it is sometimes useful to do a trial run of a treatment knowing that it can be withdrawn if it appears not to be working.

PAS clearly elicits strong arguments on both sides, including a fundamental disagreement about how women will fare if it is legalized in more states. Will women's wishes to end their lives not be respected (Parks 2000), or will women feel pressured into requesting aid in dying so as not to be a burden or to be self-sacrificing (Wolf 1996)? Will the availability of PAS become one more way in which women's lives are devalued? Almost twenty years since this discussion was launched, the evidence for either option is slim since so few people have opted to take advantage of the possibility to terminate their own lives, and of those, white men predominated (US News 2013). It has been a lightly traveled path, so fears that it would slide to involuntary euthanasia, for example, are so far unfounded, as are those that women would feel pressured into making that choice.

In brief, then, I offer a few comments about the arguments for and against it. For some, it signifies a rejection of the "technicalization of medicine and death and the misery rather than the promise that technology is currently felt to offer" (Christakis 1991, 27). Such fears apply particularly to deaths that occur in hospitals. For others, it is the last act of a person asserting the ultimate in control—choosing the time and place of his/her dying but doing so with knowledge and without violence (compared, for example, to a shotgun blast). Yet control, while accurate, may not capture what for many people makes PAS desirable: easing existential and physical suffering, mitigating fears of being a burden, and protecting their dignity. For physician and former editor of the *New England Journal of Medicine* Marcia Angell, the objections initially raised have not been borne out. It has been mostly relatively advantaged and well-insured white men who have taken advantage of the laws that exist, and it has not diverted attention from palliative care, and quite simply it has been modestly used (Angell 2012). Yet counterarguments (Foley 2005) that rely, for example, on a commitment to pain relief, efforts to relieve suffering, and the ethical obligations of physicians are offered in response. Professional discomfort with helping a patient to die since it seems to directly violate the mandate to cure might be compared to the patient's voice as reflected by Dr. Timothy Quill (1991), a Rochester, New York, physician. His patient Diane was suffering from leukemia. She had been his patient for a long time, and so he had seen her through difficult periods in her life. Aware of the side effects of treatment, she decided not to go through it again following a recurrence. Her disease was terminal. Dr. Quill told her what she needed to do to end her own life and gave her the prescriptions for the medications she needed to do so. He was public about what he did but was not indicted by a grand jury, even though physician-assisted suicide is not legal in New York State. For supporters of physician aid in dying, Dr. Quill is a model of how such assistance ought to be provided.

Other Problems: The Culture of Medicine

Ironically, cultural norms in the United States may romanticize the "good death" while seeing death itself as a failure, almost an obscenity. The culture of medicine reinforces this irony. Pauline Chen (2007), a liver transplant surgeon, reflects on mortality as follows: "Our professional fear and aversion to dying is the most difficult—and the most fundamentally human—obstacle to changing end-of-life care" (217). Family members often feel abandoned by physicians who are both rushed and do not take the time to explain the patient's status and anticipated outcomes in a language that is free of jargon (Braun et al. 2007). Chen (2007) echoes this concern and calls upon physicians to accept the "the honor of worrying—of caring, of easing suffering, of being present" as "our most important task" (218). This task, however, may be the most difficult for the curative culture of medicine to realize. Medical students are now exposed to more training in end-of-life care than in the past, but that training is limited, and the discomforts that result—reinforced by cultural resistance to talking about death—carry over into practice. Training does not prepare physicians to discuss with patients the limits of life-sustaining interventions, and they are not observed or supervised if and when they do hold such conversations (Lo 1995). The chief of geriatrics at an academic medical center once unhesitatingly affirmed, "Talk to my patients about dying? No way that I can do that" (personal communication). While this view may not be dominant, it reflects a common resistance to acknowledging that death is near while reminding us that physicians are not immune from fears about dying.

As noted above, medicine's success in curing successive diseases and thereby transforming acute conditions into chronic ones further complicates the dying process. Each "disease" can be treated separately and often successfully (Gillick 2006; Kaufman 2000). This ideology of treatment marginalizes the cumulative effects of embodied frailty. It is especially hard to let a person die—or even to face the reality of the dying trajectory—when the intervention is by no means "extraordinary." Medical intervention or the concept of choice "seems to present a choice that does not exist—the choice not to die of a terminal illness" (Drought and Koenig 2002, 115) as patients and families translate a statistical possibility of benefit into a choice not to give up and die.

Ironically, the alienation and privatization of death, especially given medicine's "boundless frontier," often seems to eliminate the patient from the ritual of dying (Guillemin 1995). Patients are also absented from society at large, and "if the process of dying is lengthy and requires long-term hospital treatment," even families may be less present (Howarth 1998, 675). All these factors—the wars against disease, the ability to intervene in more and more complex ways to stave off death, the medical profession's commitment to cure and limited training in being with the dying patient, the problematic assumption that dying is a rational process that can be anticipated and planned for, and the privatization of death—all contribute to the difficulties we face in improving end-of-life care.

WHAT ELSE? PRESERVING IDENTITY

What ends might we seek? And how might we attain them? While not replacing the need to make decisions, we can do more leading up to that time so that the actual decision becomes less significant. I am thinking about life as a story, and all stories need to be drawn to a close. The chance to tell stories is not always an obvious need, but these stories reveal what matters as they did with Susan; they illuminate the "self we live by" (Holstein and Gubrium 2000). Susan's stories recalled for her listeners that she was more than the dying self. People who listen to our stories grant us the social recognition that is essential for our identity, which we achieve in social relationships. Listeners tell us that we still matter in their eyes. Susan continued to be a social being, a person who was formed and transformed through her "intimate and non-intimate relationships with other people" (Mackenzie 2000, 139). Our attentiveness facilitated her ability to protect and preserve valued elements of her identity in the face of overwhelming losses. We also support our identities by permitting others to help us continue doing what we value, writing our words if we can no longer do it on our own, supporting us if we decide not to eat, as social worker Bonnie Genevay (2011) reported as she neared the very end of her life.

I think that Susan and Bonnie continued to feel like agents and authors of their own lives, capable of effective action to sustain their sense of worthiness (Mackenzie 2000). Both were willing to involve others in helping them get what they wanted and needed. Consider this understanding of autonomy juxtaposed to the individualistic view represented by advance care planning. One does not replace the other, but without support for identity-maintaining activities, facilitating treatment choices honors only a narrow notion of personhood. For these reasons, I think time granted freely to the ill and the dying by people who matter is critical. It might be the greatest gift we can give them. Even at the very end, if we are conscious, as thoughts drift in and out, to have a listener confirms our identity.

It is possible that stories—told and retold—can help patients formulate new meanings, perhaps even about dying. Although undoubtedly told in bits and pieces, disconnected or narratively ordered, it is the story of our lives, the last chance that we will get to tell it, and a gift we can give to others. As I discussed in earlier chapters, it is important that others see us as we see ourselves. At the end, we can be fully revealing. While not everyone will be able to do this or want to do it, having conversations that start with "tell me about your life" rather than questions about what treatments you do not want—or want—might be a welcome recognition of your continued moral agency.

One of the loveliest images in the film version of Tillie Olsen's (1995) *Tell Me a Riddle* is when the dying Eva vividly recalls her revolutionary youth in Russia, an image that is closely matched in intensity when, in her wheelchair, she dances to the music of her childhood. Sharing pictures was another way she brought herself to life for her granddaughter. Eva finds her joy in relationship with others, especially this granddaughter who was willing to share what Eva wanted to remember (Holstein 1997, 854).

Dying at Home

Dying at home may be a clearly demonstrable benefit of advance care planning. Patients with directives were more likely to stay out of the hospital at the end and die at home or in a nursing home (Degenholtz, Rhee, and Arnold 2004). Hospitals are not good places to die, yet more of us die there than anywhere else. Yet staying at home is contingent on having a caregiver and the ability to get medical care when we need it. Given the policy context in which we live and the fact that women are more likely than men to live alone mean that these essentials may not be available. As Susan's story revealed, she could not have died at home without her sister Ruth and Ruth's willingness and ability to put everything else in her life on hold. To stay at home also means that medical care will be brought to the home to manage pain but also to protect the patient from bed sores, other skin breakdowns, or any other situation that causes discomfort.

All this is possible if it becomes a societal priority. But, as I have argued throughout, a commitment to the social is regularly undermined by the neoliberal emphasis on individuals and families. There are undoubtedly costs involved in helping people stay at home, but there is also the potential for cost savings by delaying or avoiding hospitalization. Since so many women are like me—we live alone and our children are neither geographically close enough to be with us and, perhaps as importantly they have busy lives—we need more than an advance directive to die as we might want to die. Family and friends can help, but we need the assistance of paid caregivers. Unfortunately, I do not have the resources to hire anyone for more than a limited number of hours, and I probably will not qualify for publicly funded care until I use up all my resources (see chapter 5). The problem that I face is both class and gender based. While home hospice has the capacity to give me what I need to stay at home, it can do so only if I have a full-time caregiver. That caregiver would need special training in order to support people who are near the end of their lives. She would need minimal equipment: a comfortable bedside chair, body lotions, training in administering pain medications and in recognizing when she needs additional help, which is then available from trained nurses or home care physicians. In the long run, paying for such specially trained caregivers will cost the public sector less than transferring me to the hospital.

Hence, by expanding public support for home care aides—or creating more residential hospices—we can facilitate death at home or at least in a homelike setting. If I and other single women are fortunate enough to have attentive caregivers, the aides can handle the more instrumental tasks like bathing and cleaning that can exhaust family members so that they have little time or energy for remembering, touching, atoning, and all the other intimate activities that only loved ones can do. Sharing responsibilities for care also eases the marginalization and loneliness that so many people who are dying, or caring for people who are dying, experience. Yet, as noted in chapter 5, to assure such care, this country would need to reenvision its values so that care and those who give care are accorded both respect and support (Kittay 1999; Dodds 2007).

These goals fit well with a palliative care model of care if there are commitments to providing it at home rather than primarily in hospitals and in nursing homes. It would also mean developing more and better-supported training and fellowships in palliative care so that physicians and other health-care professionals would choose it. Right now there are very limited slots for training in palliative care. If widely available, it can then be offered to the patient whose dying trajectory exceeds six months but for whom little or no good will come from one more diagnostic test or one more round of chemo (Martensen 2011). Ironically, cost seems to be no object when it covers one more day or week in the ICU, but when it means care at home, the money is less likely to be there. It strikes me as peculiarly American that we have the "right" to say no to complex and costly interventions but not the positive rights to get the home care that we need where we want to receive it. To commit to providing the supportive services that we need to die in the place of our choosing supports a link between medical care and public health—imagine the public health nurses of years ago and what it would be like to have them back on call for people nearing the end of their lives.

None of these seemingly simple steps will be easy to accomplish. Though far less expensive than complex interventions, Medicaid-funded home care is limited, and to pay privately is beyond the budgets of most older women (see chapter 5). As noted above, if the almost universally available Medicare system would support care at home more fully, it would likely save money if it prevents or delays the far more costly hospitalization. That cost saving, however, is unacceptable if the burden of care at home is shifted to unpaid caregivers. Perhaps we need to imagine a very different kind of setting that will be as homelike as possible but without the rules that make so many people avoid talk of hospice. It would make care available to people who are nearing the end of their lives but who lack the resources to pay privately for care at home and do not have adequate support in the community. A Medicare benefit that focuses on holistic care for the person nearing his or her end might help to overcome the resistance of physicians to provide, and patients and family members to accept, care.

Yet in these days of hyper-antigovernment rhetoric and budget slashing, the very idea of an entitlement to good care at home at the end of life seems at best a pipe dream. But as I argued in chapter 5, until we imagine what we want, name it, and bring it into the public dialogue, it will always be beyond our reach. I make this plea for women—and men, too—who are often like me—living alone with children thousands of miles away. Should the circumstances of my life that are beyond my control keep me from the kind of death I imagine as "good?" In my imagination, I often think of people who live in very substandard housing where there is little light and comfort, and then I imagine what it might be like to die in such an environment. I see this an another argument for affordable housing so that the dream of safety and security extends to the environment in which we are to die.

If the resources to assure that people can remain at home are too steep to even imagine, then we must ask what can be done to make residential care settings more comfortable places to be at the end of life since Medicaid covers these more costly places to live for many people. To their credit, many nursing homes are no longer hiding the death of residents and are finding ways to celebrate their lives. While delving deeply into how residential care settings can be hospitable places to die goes beyond my purposes in this chapter, I am convinced that this transformation can happen if we learn from the many models now evolving through the culture-change movements in nursing home care. Small-scale residential homes, such as adult foster care, can also become comfortable places for people to die if they have the staffing and oversight that is required to fulfill what I think is an essential commitment—to not let a person die alone.

Reversing Normalization of Complex Interventions

Clearly we can't reverse medical progress. Nor, I suspect, do we want to. And some people will be hospitalized no matter how good care at home may be. Hence, I want to propose several approaches that recognize the powerful technological imperatives that now dominate in the hospital setting but find ways to work around them. What if, through some collaborative process of determining best practices for patients who are dying of different conditions, the decision points would be decided in advance? Joanne Lynn (2005), a physician-ethicist, challenged us to look at the illness trajectories of the three most common pathways to death. We start a period of slow, progressive decline from some condition like Alzheimer's disease, or we have cancer, where we might plateau and then decline slowly until we face a precipitous decline, or we have conditions like COPD or CHF, where we have episodic exacerbations and then plateau until we have another exacerbation. Caring at the end of life becomes an issue of systems design, which would give people what they need automatically in the absence of strongly expressed alternative wishes, rather than focusing on forgoing life-sustaining treatment or decision-by-decision choices. Different from the age-based rationing that philosopher Daniel Callahan (1987) has been defending since the 1980s, it would depend not on age but on the person's medical condition. This strategy would undoubtedly mean that many life-prolonging treatments might not be offered—perhaps no organ transplants for people on the long, slow pathway to death. It would also ease the terrible tension that family members often feel when yet another decision faces them which seems to suggest that there is a real choice to be made that has life and death implications but instead might marginally delay the inevitable without great gain (Drought and Koenig 2002). What I particularly like about this albeit unlikely approach is that it removes micromanaging decisions from individuals and surrogates so that attention can be focused on critically important human and embodied needs that are not about decisions or treatments.

If patients or proxies objected, they could appeal to the ethics committee, but the issue of reimbursement would then have to be faced. If an override is not granted, the care may not be paid for but it will be provided if a physician and hospital are willing to provide it. Perhaps the more affluent will pay privately for such care, but that doesn't strike me as being unjust in ways that I find the reliance on women as caregivers as unjust. The ethical distinction between the two, as I see it, is that the more affluent paying for care that is not advised or within the range of practice protocols is a luxury; relieving a daughter who would otherwise have to set aside many of her important values and goals to take care of her mother is a right owed to all people. I see that there is no right to medically nonbeneficial care. What is also unjust is the inability of many people with limited incomes to get the specialty care that they might need after a diagnosis, a recurring problem for people who are uninsured or even on Medicaid. These treatments are seemingly beneficial by all accounts. Using practice parameters (in Lynn's words, "mass customization"), doctors and patients would be giving up some individual autonomy, but it may also be that families are relieved that the heavy burden of choosing is lifted since many interventions would no longer be routinely offered. To preserve trust, it would be essential for this policy to be established and monitored at a systems level to avoid bedside rationing. This approach might have a side benefit for older women, who are most likely to live alone. For one, they don't have a living spouse who knows them intimately enough to decide what ought to be done or might have a difficult time letting go, and second, women's wishes tend to be less honored than men's wishes when end-of-life decisions need to be made (Parks 2000) and, as a result, they may get more treatment than they want.

Such a system would challenge at the most profound levels the American commitment to individual choice, even if those choices are unavoidably inflected by broad cultural norms and the narrower norms of medicine. Physicians might need to forgo a diagnostic workup, for example, for a patient with a new symptom but with serious existing comorbidities and on an identifiable trajectory toward dying. I learned this about twenty years ago from Dr. Vinson, a family medicine physician. Mrs. Smathers was a patient in a nursing home, in her mideighties. A stroke restricted her movements, and macular degeneration left her with very limited vision. She had also seen her two adult children die over a period of two years. She was quite clear about her readiness—indeed her wish—to die. She developed major abdominal discomforts. Dr. Vinson tried treatments to ease her discomfort but did not attempt to find the underlying cause. Mrs. Smathers was hospitalized and made comfortable, and she died a few days later. Dr. Vinson was clear about her decision—why do a diagnostic workup if we are not going to offer any treatments other than keeping her as comfortable as possible?

I didn't see any moral or clinical uncertainty as Dr. Vinson cared for this patient. As the ethics consultant, I was comfortable because I knew from my many discussions with Mrs. Smathers that the narrative of her life was over; she was just biding time until she died. We couldn't give her what she wanted—to have her daughter and son still be alive, to return to her own home (it had been sold), to help her to see again or to significantly improve her mobility. She could do nothing that mattered to her. Yes, she was depressed, and for very good reasons, but none of these reasons was fixable. Letting go by choosing to keep her comfortable rather than treating her for the actual but unidentified medical condition seemed to be the kindest—and most moral—act.

Advance Care Planning Revisited

My goals, when near the end of my life, as I look at them now when still healthy, are captured not in whether or not we control my bladder infection, or my "failure to thrive," or my sepsis but rather what kind of life I will have if these conditions can be cured. But as I say that, I do not want to forget Lillian Rubin's (2007) admonition that we can't know in advance how the fear of death, "the terror that the very idea inspires, is a near-natural consequence of a society so committed to its denial that the alternatives that might allow for a different choice don't get much serious consideration" (152). Similarly, we know from the work of disability scholars that a condition that once seemed intolerable may not seem so when we have learned to live with it.

The rational planning or consumer choice model, encapsulated in the phrase "advance care planning," as I hope I've demonstrated, is incomplete as a pathway to death with dignity. It addresses, in a fairly narrow way, one aspect of what is important to many people at the end of their lives. And it does so in a way that makes it possible to neglect the social context of our choices and our values. Its individualistic perspective can negate the social nature of the self, thereby rendering invisible a lifetime of shared decision making and the possibility that serious harms may accrue to others from our getting what we want. Moreover, focusing on choices can be diversionary, a distraction from the attentiveness and love that may be what people need the most when they are so vulnerable (Holstein 1997; Hoffmaster 2006). Philosopher Barry Hoffmaster, in writing about vulnerability, recounts a moment when his father, who was near death and very vulnerable (that is, had essentially lost power over most of his life and had not spoken an articulate sentence in a long while) simply said, "I like your shirt," and then commented about an arrangement of colorful glass fish, saying, "That's very nice" (44). Hoffmaster interprets these words as meaning his father was saying, "You matter to me and I can see that I matter to you."

FROM CONTRACT TO COVENANT

It would seem that care at the end of life fits poorly with a contractual or legalistic model, for example, disposing of one's estate. "Clear and convincing" evidence, as some states demand, of my wishes before my daughters can act is not suitable to the shifting circumstances at the end of life. With that as the standard, they would be little more than conveyors of my wishes, if I even had any about the specific circumstances I was in at that moment. A relative stranger reading a statement about my wishes could do that. For most other treatments, I favor flexibility and collaborative decision making where my daughters and their lives count as much as or more than mine, which is now winding down. As I touched upon in the opening section, we might think of the relationship between patient and proxy in covenantal terms in which the surrogate considers the person's life and values, his or her relationships, and the medical information at hand. Decisions can then be made "with interpretive discretion" (Fins et al. 2005, 56). When making decisions for me, my proxy has moral obligations to be true to me but also to reflect on the relationship that has led to her designation as my proxy. How can that relationship be honored as I lie dying? How can my integrity, that is, fit with the whole of my life, but also let hers be honored? That kind of statement allows for flexibility with or without guidelines, for example, ventilator support is acceptable for a trial period if there is some hope that I can be weaned from it and returned to a life that I value.

This view simply reminds us that as we die, we are not radically different from when we were younger and healthier—we confirm our commitments to the people we love and who love us. "Dying may not be the last bastion of control and choice—a somewhat disembodied view of who we are more generally but particularly as our lives are ending—but rather a time to affirm the lifelong relationships that are essential to our identity" (Holstein, Parks, and Waymack 2011). When executing a directive it is, of course, possible to say that my proxy knows me well, understands my values, and has my interests at heart. I thus leave it up to him or her to work with my doctor and others to whom I am close to do what they think is best for me at the time.

A NOTE ON POLST

Today, in an effort to improve compliance and to address the situation immediately at hand, a number of states have implemented programs based on the

POLST (physician [or practitioner] orders for life-sustaining treatment) instrument. Developed in response to identified limitations with traditional advance directives (not available when needed; not transferred with the patient; not specific enough and capable of being overridden by the treating physician), POLST was "to help ensure that patient wishes to have or limit specific medical treatments are respected near the end of life" (Hickman et al. 2004, cited in Dunn et al. 2007, 330).

Cultural Conversation about Death and Dying

While I am not sure what it would be, I think we need a new language to talk about death and dying. So often, the "war" metaphor leads to the belief that resistance, victory over death, is the primary goal. I am not sure how to seek ways to make dying less a medical event and more a human one, how to restore the human elements, as Brian Morton (1998) describes in his novel *Starting Out in the Evening* when one old man, when visiting his dying friend, simply asked—"Is there anything I can do for you?" and the response was, "Please rub lotion on my feet, they are so dry." We all want to die with dignity. To do so, I suggest, calls for the awareness, to the extent that patients are aware, that intimates, caregivers, and even strangers see them as I see myself, as my friend Susan struggled to assure until the very end. What can we learn from the old "death watch" scenes so present in art and poetry? While nostalgia for the past is hopelessly risky, I wonder whether it is possible to recapture some elements of how death was once integrated into life (Aries 1981).

CONCLUSION

I am frightened of dying abruptly, to be here one moment and gone the next. Yet, as Sarah Bakewell (2010) tells us, the French philosopher Montaigne advised us to stop fearing death because, after all, we wouldn't know about it once it happened, so why be frightened? But I also don't want to linger in a liminal state between living and dying. I want to be alive as long as I can have some connection to life and people around me. I don't want to be an object of fear or veneration. I don't want my children, as my proxies (one is appointed, but I have requested that they decide together), to be anguished about whether or not they are doing the "right" thing. It is unlikely that there will be one right thing to do. I had no wish to sign a durable power of attorney but did so for fear that my daughters would have a hard time limiting my treatment in a risk-aversive hospital environment. I'd like them to have a clear idea of my prognosis and a treatment plan to which they assented based on the likely course of whatever trajectory I was on and then no further decisions to make so that the time they had with me was uncluttered with decisions that probably no longer mattered. I'd like my doctor to be actively involved not only as a purveyor of information but as a moral agent who uses her experiences and knowledge to guide my daughters as they sought to make decisions. I would like her to free them from the burden of choice by letting them know that possible "benefit" doesn't mean that the old mom will return. If I decide that I want to hasten my death with physician assistance, at the moment not legal in my state of Illinois, I will talk to my daughters first so that they understand I am not abandoning them but saying goodbye like at the end of a lovely weekend. I would like future laws to permit me or anyone else choosing assistance in dying to not be left alone. I'll have to gauge their responses carefully since I don't want them to feel they have to try to talk me out of my plans, but if it really troubles them, I might need to reconsider my decision.

In brief, I think several important changes are necessary: facilitate dying at home; or, if hospitalization is necessary, provide the supports necessary to make choice actual rather than abstract; challenge the acceptance and normalization of complex interventions for terminally ill patients; concentrate further on modifying the culture of hospitals and other health-care facilities to make them more responsive to the complex and often shifting values of patients and families and to create a more homelike environment; focus less on rationality and control and more on vulnerability and the values that draw us to those we love; and, perhaps the most difficult, reopen the cultural conversation about death and dying so that we find new language to describe the different ways we might wish to move from life to death. My hope is the end result will be comfort and support for dying people and those close to them, a continued sense of membership in the moral community, and care that is coordinated across settings and open to shared and evolving decision making.

With so many national panels and working groups considering what might be done to make end-of-life care better, I know that my concerns are shared. I sense that a certain calmness comes when we know the end is near—like my mother having no other wish but that she see me one more time before she died, which, sadly, did not happen since I was three thousand miles away and no one told me how close to death she was. We should be able to die without a set of rules telling us how to do it, as I recall a theologian-ethicist did more than twenty years ago when he said that we must live up to the occasion of our own death. Already I try to imagine a world without me. It's hard but necessary, since I don't want to hold on. This then, is perhaps the only ending I can offer. Many years ago, when my long-term partner died quite suddenly, the marvelous physician who cared for him in the ER counseled me, as one Jew to another, that we must live every day as if it were our last. While I assume that my children and grandchildren will miss me, especially on special occasions, I am also assuming that they will walk around the block at the end of the *shiva* and close the circle and continue living as if any day might be the last, that is, living as fully as possible each day that they have.

Part III

I'm an Old Lady and Damn Proud of It (Maggie Kuhn)

Chapter Eight

Resistance and Change

Where to from Here?

I come to this last chapter with some trepidation. It is hard to wrap up what has been part of my life for so long, in thought and then in execution. In the process, I have learned much as I reflected on my own aging, read the work of others, and continued to rethink what I once thought I had resolved for myself. Whenever I talk to other women, sometimes even a passing remark adds something to what it means to be an old woman in today's society. Recently, an acquaintance in her sixties whom I hadn't seen in about a year commented that she liked my hair a little longer. I said, "It's an experiment," to which she responded, "Isn't it all?" suggesting the adventuresome element about growing and being old. In other conversations, I was regularly re-minded about the great gap between women who are fortunate enough to be financially comfortable and those who rely entirely on a monthly Social Security check of $1,200. Since their worlds do not cross, opportunities for mutual understanding are also lost. It makes me feel that women with limited income are doubly invisible—as women and as poor or near-poor. I also heard what I can only consider manifestations of internalized ageism, for why else would a woman in her seventies insist that she wasn't old, only older, because she didn't feel old, as if feeling old, however she understood it, was both identifiable and bad?

I add to these casual thoughts my reflections about being an old woman. I try to use the phrase as often as I can both to practice owning "old" that I write about but also in the hope that I will stimulate conversation and begin to broaden perceptions of what that label can mean. I neither fit the increasingly familiar positive representations of women as slim, elegant, tanned, and off to play a game of tennis, nor do I fit the negative representations seen in the "before" ads. Yet I have a visceral awareness about my age. Perhaps it is because I have spent so much time with undergraduates or because I know that I can't do the physical things I once was able to do, whether on the hiking trail or in the yoga studio, or that I tire more easily. But I think most of all it is about the time I have left. Consciousness about time makes each day uniquely important. Not that long ago, I told my daughter that if I were lucky I could hope for ten more "good" years. While I didn't define good at the time, I think I meant that I would be able to continue living much as I do now even if I moved a little more slowly and was no longer able to get down on the floor to do puzzles or play games with my grandchildren. Living in habitual ways, a wish that I suspect most of us have, is how philosopher George Agich (1990) defines actual autonomy. Good years also mean that I will continue to honor both human interdependence and community (M. Walker 1999a). My social commitments are not contingent. Thus, each day it will be important to check in and ask how I'm doing. I respond to the virtues that Sara Ruddick (1999) proposed and that I discussed in chapter 3. If this were my last day, I'd want to be able to say that I am satisfied with how I have been living my old age. That's both a burden and a responsibility that has been with me for much of my life but has escalated in importance as I have gotten to seventy-three.

I also know that what is possible for me is not open-ended. Andrew Blaikie's (1999) observation that we may choose the kind of life we want to lead but not in a context of our own making makes good sense to me. I am lucky right now to have the health and the modest resources, education, and experience that allow me to make many meaningful choices. I don't, for example, see a splendid Marigold Hotel in my future, nor do I see a walking trip in Patagonia. Yet, I consider myself fortunate. Many women are not so fortunate. There are too many stories of women, and men, too, living in dismal apartments or basement rooms, as chapter 6 described. Even when the issue is end-of-life care, as discussed in chapter 7, advance directives offer us the chance to make some treatment choices in the face of death, but we often do not have access to the assistance we may need to choose what may be our most important wish as a moral agent—to die at home without overburdening or frightening our families.

I am repeatedly struck by the ironies that result when the specific features of women's lives are neglected. On the one hand, the ways in which we differ from one another become a reason to reject "old" as a category but then that rejection is promptly forgotten when the new aging is universalized as both possible and desirable, indeed an expectation, for all. Efforts to redefine the old in part to counteract the portrait of us as selfish consumers of our shared national wealth become "evidence" that reducing entitlements is unproblematic. We are very different when we are old, more than at other times in our lives for reasons that are not hard to identify, but there is also much we share.

As women, the gendered life course and the ways in which it manifested itself in unequal power relations affected our experiences at home and at work. When we become old, these earlier inequalities are further made manifest in basic features of our lives like income inadequacy. As old women, we are at the nexus of subordinating positions—gender and age and often class—that result in intersecting inequalities that contribute to multiple disadvantages, as discussed throughout this book. And yet we are held—and often hold ourselves—to the same universal standards that derive from a privileged perspective and thus, not surprisingly, suit the more privileged among us. Moreover, this same privileged perspective buttresses the political ideology that vests primary responsibility in us as individuals for how our life goes without attention to the roles played in our lives by social structures and institutions, cultural norms, and the now familiar subordinating "isms." By eliding these constraints on our life opportunities, the regnant stories of what it means to be a "good" old person and a "good" citizen, stories that we do not write, matter profoundly in what our old age will be like.

I raise these points to reemphasize the close ties among culture, politics, and the individual experience of old age and how changes in one will affect all the others. I also raise them to stress why it matters so much that old women do not partake in narratives that can harm us. Resistance can serve a dual purpose—it helps us to speak in our own voice about the many things it means to be old and a woman while it also undermines politically expedient narratives that will make old age so much harder than it need be for many women but also for many men. Thus, I reaffirm that while our feelings and reactions to being of a certain age matter greatly in our experience of that age, many of us also face regular threats to our ability to live safely, securely, and with self-respect no matter our age, race, gender, ethnicity, sexual preference, or physical and mental status. We seem to be trapped in a chain of thinking that more and more often gives society a pass—a reason for doing as little as possible. The times in which we live, as I have argued throughout the book, cannot make us sanguine that these threats will be noticed and addressed.

In several other chapters I focused on policy. Here I want to ask how we might intercept or deconstruct the cultural messages that narrow acceptable ways of thinking about aging and hinder our ability to redeem old age as a valued and important time in human life. It seems critically important for women to claim their own voices so that they have the chance to narrate the multiple stories of old age. Our individual voices can lead to different but collective counterstories that spill over into the public arena so that the meaning of being old is a story told by women rather than deduced from scientific data or narrated by the privileged among us. Such stories become a way for old people, both women and men, to find a comfortable place, one in which they don't have to work at being "not old," one in which the expression "I don't feel old" is not the only way to reject the negative stereotypes associated with the term "old." While self-acceptance is critically important, the next steps are even harder—gaining social recognition for stories of our old age and convincing decision makers to let our stories guide policy and practice. There is a role, as well, for academic and other research to provide empirical information that supports a more inclusive understanding of late life. The end of all this work will contribute to repairing the social marginalization of older women and their devaluation as moral subjects and to severing the power of particularistic perspectives about late life that are assumed to be available and suitable for all.

These tasks are hard, but I think about my rabbi's words in his Rosh Hashanah sermon on September 25, 2014. He told us that we had a duty to be engaged even when the task was hard and we were uncertain about what course to take. Having an outraged and aroused moral sense may be necessary to claim a more just society. I know that critique is easier than remedy, especially in an environment that is increasingly unpredictable, risky, and dominated by elite perspectives, but that is only the beginning of what must be done. We need to look for openings where feminist and critical scholarship and activism can move us toward a society where age and gender no longer are sources of inequality. Even as I suggest some ways to do so, I know that rupturing the conditions that perpetuate age and gender inequality will be an even more complex project than the one I am taking on.

POSSIBLE PATHS TO CHANGE

It will take multiple pathways to make such changes happen. I start with the simple observation that there are more women in important positions in government, in academia, in think tanks, and even edging into the upper echelons of business. While we cannot assume that they all speak with one voice, I am hopeful. I use as an example Supreme Court Justice Sonia Soto-mayor's dissent in a recent affirmative action case, in which she drew from her own experiences as a young Puerto Rican woman who was a beneficiary of affirmative action. Her words gave voice to the marginalized and demonstrated that where you stand shapes what you see (Harding 2003). Women in such positions are a source of potential power; they can speak from the particularistic experiences of women rather than from experiences of elite men, which policymakers and others who are instrumental in setting the public agenda often adopt as universal.

We also have a model bequeathed to us by second-wave feminism. It gave us the popular adage that "the personal is the political." As women gathered to meet and talk, they found that what they may have seen as only their story was shared by many other women and, perhaps even more importantly, that it had political causes and consequences and so could be changed politically and socially (Ray 2007; Collins 2009). As these stories entered into more public domains, other women also realized that they could tell different stories about their lives. While today's political and cultural contexts are far less receptive to hearing counterstories than in the late 1960s and early 1970s, the model of women coming together to talk to one another and create transformative narratives can still be a powerful tool for change. Second-wave feminism demonstrated that when ideas radiate outward, political change can occur. While progress has been less complete than we might have wished, spousal abuse or date rape are no longer just private problems, while other important issues like universal child care and elder care remain essentially private and so continue to limit women's choices. Women still find it hard to find jobs that allow them to work and to meet the responsibilities at home that are still primarily left to them (Hochschild 1989; Ridgeway 2011). But the most important lessons might not be the specific accomplishments but rather the strategies for moving issues into the public sphere.

To that end, I offer the beginnings of an agenda that, like a pebble spun into the water, radiates out from the personal and intimate to the academy, to the political, and beyond. Feminist activism has historically incorporated overlapping strategies, a reason why the analogy with "waves" has worked. A wave captures the ways in which feminism developed in nonlinear ways, often starting with one issue in a particular place and then spreading more widely "to affect social relations in other locations" (Walby 2011, 53). As feminist activism matured, grassroots mobilization joined with more formal structures that engaged with the state and policy.

LESSONS FROM OUR FOREMOTHERS
(AND SOME FOREFATHERS, TOO)

In thinking about how to effect change, in addition to the history of second-wave feminism I look to the work of other advocates and scholars who have begun and continue this work. I start with the Older Women's League, now OWL. Founded by Tish Sommers and Laurie Shields as a prelude to the 1981 White House Conference on Aging, OWL linked gender and age in a dual strategy that joined research and advocacy with grassroots organizing. Organizing efforts focused on the strength of engaged women who were able to speak directly and passionately about the issues that affected their lives. This organizing strategy placed women where they belonged: as the individuals best able to define their needs and develop strategies to meet them. And that was only the beginning. Working with media professionals, Sommers honed the messages that OWL would use to make its goals clear. On occasion, metaphor and even bumper-sticker language are essential means of communicating.

More recently, organizations such as Wider Opportunities for Women (WOW) and the Institute for Women's Policy Research (IWPR) continue to teach us much about old women's economic status as disadvantages accumulate over their lifetimes. The following is only a sampling of the work being done by these and other scholars. Age-studies scholars such as Margaret Morganroth Gullette (1997, 2004, 2011), who introduced the term, and literary scholar Kathleen Woodward (1999), who uses it as a frame for her own psychoanalytically inclined work, remind us about the importance of age as a defining feature of who we are across our lives and the ways in which culture shapes these experiences. Feminist philosophers and social ethicists like Margaret Urban Walker (1999a), Frida Furman (1997), Diana Meyers (1989, 2002), Eva Feder Kittay (1999), Jennifer Parks (2003, 2011), and Hilde Lindemann Nelson (2001) have called attention to how patriarchal society constrained women's skills as moral agents, fostered dismay with their appearance, and sidelined ethical problems like caregiving. They have also offered a way to think about repairing gender-based harms. Feminist gerontologists working both separately and with one another—like Toni Calasanti and Kathleen Slevin (2001, 2006), Pamela Herd and Madonna Harrington Meyer (2002), Nancy Hooyman and Judith Gonyea (2004), Margaret Cruikshank (2009), Meredith Minkler and Carroll Estes (1991, 1999), Ruth Ray (1999, 2004, 2007), and, in the United Kingdom, Molly Andrews (1999, 2000), Liz Lloyd (2004), Julia Twigg (2004), and Miriam Bernard and her colleagues (2000)—all have sought to understand gender and aging through a single intersectional lens, thereby enriching our understanding of both women and age while also exposing the economic and related difficulties that women face as a result of public policies that fail to account for the specific features of their lives. All this work—and that of others whom I have not specifically identified—suggests that a new feminist agenda, perhaps a new wave, is in order.

We need this work to continue so that scholars and activists can honor what I see as a major commitment of reform work—to reveal the hidden, explore the ignored—and to work toward remedying the marginalization of older women so that we can participate as fully as we want to in society and be respected not for how "youthful" or "ageless" we are but for how we use our experiences. By revealing the harms that result from not carefully disaggregating the old—not all are healthier than ever before or living longer or have adequate incomes to retire comfortably by saving enough to do so—we can pursue the critical commitment to challenge the taken for granted in our personal and professional lives, to work toward changing what is unacceptable to women, and to respond regularly to popular and professional distortions of what "is." With such a commitment, we have the beginning of an agenda.

THE FIRST WAVE: STORIES OF OUR LIVES

Claiming Our Voices

As noted above and often in this book, cultural imagery is a critical component in how we understand and shape our subjective experiences. It is about how we see ourselves, how we think others see us, and how we make sense of our changing bodies and capacities. Thus, part of our task as women, especially as old women, is to find and claim our own voices—and thus our moral agency—amidst the ready-made cultural frames through which we view our experiences (Meyers 2002). Thus, we need to look at our own bodies and try to see them detached from the images that are regularly presented to us. Sometimes it is hard to keep my commitment to my gray hair when I know that color might make me more acceptable. I have quoted Maggie Kuhn, who proclaimed that "I am an old lady and damn proud if it"; I'd like to hear many women making such a proclamation. The women of Mayslake want a big button with those words on it as well as a T-shirt that says, "I don't do cultural scripts." But to wear that button or that T-shirt means first facing our own internalized ageism, which makes it so hard to value being old. We can ask ourselves: Why do I resist? What is it about being old that I don't accept? How can I instead define old in my own terms, not in the ready-made terms that are so ubiquitous in our culture?

To write our own story in ways that liberate us from the conventional story that now infuses our culture is best done in small groups so that we can identify elements that we share and that can be remedied by social action. The consciousness-raising groups of the 1970s are a good model. As feminist philosopher Diana Meyers (2002) reminds us, "Accessing one's voice is a skilled, ongoing and relational undertaking." We cannot simply discard the realities of "enculturation and unconscious desire" (22). To recognize that we are embodied, socially situated, and evolving is thus the beginning of finding the voice that best represents what is important to us.

A few questions might start our discussions. How can we separate ourselves from the "default templates" that define what is good and valuable (Meyers 2002, 27)? How can we embrace age and invent, if need be, a new language to give us power instead strip us of it? To speak in our own voice can be hard; it calls upon us to separate our "desires, values, and goals from the clamor of subordinating discourses and overwhelming social demands" (Meyers 2002, 20). It means that we resist imposed definitions of what it means to be a good old person and that we create "new meanings and visions for old age" (Furman 1997, 175). This work calls for imaginative skills that allow us to see viable options, images, and plot lines to pursue; it requires volitional skills that allow us to resist pressure to capitulate to convention and interpersonal skills that enable us to join with others to challenge and change cultural norms and institutional arrangements that denigrate, if not pathologize, our priorities and goals (Meyers 2002). As we do this work, we can move to a deeper understanding of what we are like, what we want to become, and what desires, values, emotions, and relationships will help us reach that goal. By so doing, we can test our identities and develop strategies to gain social recognition for our definition of valued selves that honors the multiplicities that mark our aging selves. We can demonstrate our strengths of connectedness, attentiveness, and concern that are demoted in the public sphere.

These stories can make visible our pride in and attention to our bodies without ignoring the pain, suffering, and loss that can accompany embodiment. To reject the expectations of others that we so often share and come to like, if not love, what we see when we look in the mirror is an important act of resistance. I recall the words of an old friend, nearly seventy, by no means tall (about five feet and four inches), who told me that she feels tall and so acts like a tall person, reflecting her pride in her appearance. It won't happen all at once, but in our groups, then, we can parse the messages in anti-aging ads that tell us that we are not okay the way that we are and work toward resisting what they try to impose on us and what we all too often accept.

In the video *Let's Face It* (a selection is available on YouTube), a group of women fifty and over come together to talk about their faces and seem to come away more comfortable than when they started out. Thus women can create communities in which dominant cultural expectations, including those about our bodies, are "examined, debunked and, if necessary, actively resisted" (Furman 1997, 175). At Julie's International Salon, the site of Frida Furman's ethnography, women exposed their fears and troubles. In this safe space, they were able to speak openly because the mutually supportive relationships they experienced there freed them from the "prohibitions of the public square" (Furman 1997, 5). Furman describes Julie's as a community of resistance where the women demonstrated their resistance not in theory or through ideology but in how they treat one another. The problem is how to move these forms of resistance out of their safe space so that women with double chins and wispy hair can achieve social recognition for the strengths that they have gained by living for so many years.

The women of Mayslake reflected the value of being and meeting together in a small group. In the course of us talking together they have been able to clarify that what was important to them was not to be "young at heart" or insist that they are "not old," where they started out, but rather that they wanted others to see them as they see themselves, which is different than how they think others see them. The gap is startling. When I asked, after meeting regularly for twenty-eight months, what was the most important insight they gained from the group, they said, "I learned to embrace my age," and "I can now comfortably ask for help and offer assistance to others." It is important to note, however, that living in an age-segregated environment means that in their day-to-day lives they are in a safe place. Such an environment can foster confidence and encourage sharing with age peers. For them to become communities of resistance will take leadership that they are now discussing.

Stories can tell others what it meant to face trials and what they learned from them and so can help others who are on a similar journey. We can come to understand how different women have learned to (or not) live with the many contradictions that make old age both exciting and troubling without resorting to the socially prescriptive story of what it is good to be in old age. Heterogeneity of the category "old" is worth celebrating, and thus stories told from the "bottom up" can be an exciting venture.

THE POWER OF COLLECTIVE COUNTERSTORIES

For many old women, the story of their lives is about oppression, about being locked into gendered identities that silenced them. Hilde Lindemann Nelson (2001) tells us:

> Because oppressive identities are constructed by other people telling our stories in ways that diminish us, and because we all tend to believe what other people tell us, it is helpful to have a community of sympathetic others who can conform the dissonance between the way we see ourselves and the way our oppressors identify us. (86)

As described earlier, Carol, a Mayslake group regular, described herself in her earlier years as being a cipher, taking on the identities that others imposed on her. Now sixty-nine, she regularly affirms that "I am free to be me." From what we learn and uncover in our individual stories, we can create what Hilde Lindemann Nelson (2001) calls counterstories. Women can both reject the stories they had lived by until now while also creating a collective counterstory to provide an alternative to the story that the new aging tells about a positive life of ongoing achievement and the aim of agelessness. This homogenizing account, which we did not write, can be as oppressive as the earlier, less positive scripts. Our counterstories can be flexible and adaptable to changes we experience. They do not demand a universal theme or a master story, especially one that demands we be "healthy, sexually active, engaged, productive, and self-reliant" (Cole 1992). Nor do they demand that we be slim, graceful, and energetic. What if one is fearful and not so spry?

Sandra Bartky (1999) both skewers American culture's "disciplinary practices" vis-à-vis women and contrasts those practices with older women's ability to affirm one another and effusively praise one another's clothing and appearances. She describes her aunt's group, "The Wednesday Girls," who meet regularly, dress up to attend plays or concerts, and treat each other to regular praise for how they look. They affirm each other in ways that the broader society rarely does. Perhaps another group would focus on other features of their lives that would be equally affirming, like books or music, although I don't want to debunk the importance of clothing and appearance for many women. They become a statement of how they see themselves, a chance to "be voluble, grandiose, experimental, wild. Be imperfect" (Weiss 2014, 16).

Stories that affirm our diverse experiences in alternative communities of meaning can also remind us that we cannot evade the dark side of aging but that we can also live with it. Stories can offer models of resistance that demonstrate how other old women integrate change. Stories can make viscerally clear that the "third age" is "lived against a background of realization of what comes next. The meaning of any activity . . . is colored by awareness of a powerfully ambiguous future" (Rubenstein 2002, 39).

By exploring and narrating how they experienced gender and other inequalities in their lives and how they arrived at where they are now, their stories can demonstrate how one's earlier life experiences in the public and private spheres and in the interactions between the two shaped their possibilities when old. In our individualistic society, the message needs to be expressed repeatedly that gender relations operate as a fundamental "cultural and cognitive tool" (Ridgeway and Correll 2000, 111). Our collective stories can demonstrate how problematic it is across our lives to live in a subordinate position, thus serving as a counterstory to the tales of individual control and achievement that might make sense to the CEO of a hedge fund who doesn't need to see how his dominant position has aided his climb to the place of privilege he now occupies.

Our stories can tell an alternative tale to the optimistic and often celebratory views of the proponents of new aging by demonstrating how that message misses much about our lives. I am thinking of Betty Friedan's (1963) manifesto, *The Feminine Mystique*, that helped to launch second-wave feminism. Her message was really for bored, white, middle-class women who had the luxury of staying at home, not for the many women for whom work was an economic necessity. We can speak out and say that the new aging is also centered on the more affluent and well-educated who are living longer and healthier lives and who thus may have the time and energy to engage in multiple pursuits. I have spent many words in this book critiquing that view in large part because its elements of accuracy—many of us are living longer and healthier lives—masks its inattention to diversity and social justice. The chances to reach those laudatory states of well-being are not equally distributed. We can, at least, offer a different account of what is possible for many of us.

By our stories that address the impact of life course issues on our present circumstances, we can develop strategies that resist the rampant individualism that results in blame for "burdening" society with our needs but also leads us to turn against ourselves. Audrey at Mayslake recently told us that she should have taken better care of herself when she was younger so that she would not have developed the health problems that forced her to retire early from a job that she loved. She internalized the neoliberal message that she alone is responsible for what happened to her. While I am not suggesting that we have *no* responsibility for what happens to us, Audrey, like the rest of us, has grown up in a certain context that reinforced certain behaviors over others. Yet individualism sets aside that context. It absolves anyone else of responsibility. We can expose the faulty logic that turns our longer lives into a problem and uses our good health as reasons to impose new expectations. We can insist that many of the difficulties we face are social in origin so that the primary task is to fix those rather than encouraging the beauty industry and consumer culture to "fix" us. Neither cosmetics, nor surgery, nor Botox can repair what a lifetime of inequities helped to create.

The stories we narrate in our groups can travel "upward" so that the challenge to conventional but dominant attitudes becomes a public good. What would happen if we read stories told by women at the margins who are not sipping wine on the patio of a beautiful inn? These stories can serve as demonstrable rebuttals to privileged perspectives that suggest we can die in the arms of our lover at ninety-two. What is seen as a valued life in old age must be open to more than the relatively few.

We can confront and name the mixed messages that we hear. The expectation that we will continue working or be productive, for example, is upheld at the same time that neoliberalism provokes generational resentment about the reduced opportunities for young people as a result of commitments to elders. On our side is the fact that generational warfare has been a media message more than it has ever been a reality. As noted in chapter 6, the young are just as committed to protecting Social Security as are the old, even when they fear it won't be there for them. We need to join with other progressives in recalling that Americans have traditionally valued both individualism and community. Individualism inevitably exacerbates inequalities in old age since the erosion of a commitment to mutual care (Phillipson 1998; Dionne 2011) creates harms not easily rectified.

In communities, we can also practice a new assertiveness that demonstrates that anger and "outlaw emotions" (Jaggar 1989; Meyers 1997a; Woodward 2002) are essential if we are to right wrongs. In safe spaces we can both "empower and strengthen ourselves to struggle against those who wish to maintain the status quo outside this space" (Ferguson 1995, 372). How, then, to move these stories that are both collective and personal into other settings where we are either invisible or hypervisible in the least desirable ways?

In our groups, we can make a strong and vocal commitment to social justice. By justice, I have in mind the following: that we equalize the chances of individuals to reach old age in good health and that we assure the basic resources for them to live decently no matter their age. I endorse working to improve one's communities, but that commitment cannot replace the moral commitment to a more just society. I also endorse what seems to be an almost hidden fact—that private foundations that support voluntarism and the not-for-profit sector rarely spend more than the required minimum 5 percent distribution of their assets (Madoff 2014). Thus, they have not even begun to compensate for reductions in federal spending.

Moving Our Stories Outward

From small groups we need to extend outward so that what we discover becomes part of the public dialogue. Fortunately, there are far more sources to do so than there were in 1981, for example, when OWL introduced messaging about older women. Why not a public interest campaign to show, along with our words, visual representations of old women to which many women can respond? While some seventy-two-year-olds can still wear a Speedo or a bikini, most can't and probably have no wish to.

Social media offers a place for more representative images that can be accompanied by narratives. We can boldly display the nonnormative parts of our bodies, like our loose upper arms, juxtaposed with pictures of us doing familiar things like taking a walk, or doing a yoga asana, or out on a hiking trail, or reading to a grandchild, or giving a talk, or reading, or having coffee with friends. While it seems that younger people are aware of how we differ from them and judge us as a result, they have little idea of the ways that there is also continuity with our past and much overlap with what they do. I did yoga at thirty and I do yoga now. I was more agile and stronger then than I am now, but I still do it. Margaret Cruikshank (2009) advocates displaying the culturally unattractive parts of our bodies when we teach younger people so that they can sever the link between what we look like and the associations of that appearance with negative stereotypes. These images need not be of us doing headstands or climbing mountains since most of us don't do such things, but rather they can be everyday sorts of things that people twenty or thirty years younger than we are also do. I simply selected a few potential representations from my range of familiar activities. The goal is to create recognition not that we are just like the younger person but that my crinkly upper arms or my graying hair doesn't mean that I am different in every way from my thirty-year-old neighbor. While age will probably always remain a central part of how others relate to me and to other old women, I want them to also relate to the parts of me that are continuous with my past. Those images are intended to be unifying ones and to suggest that our appearance is not the best definer of who we "really" are.

Some women carry image-altering to far greater lengths. Whether they are members of the Red Hat Society or Raging Grannies, they present counterimages to the competent, kindly, whiny, and angry images that now prevail. Maggie Kuhn would stage guerrilla street protests or have an audience of two thousand growling like panthers. The fine line here is to rupture stereotypes but to do so in such a way that does not earn us the label of "cute." That fear is one of the reasons that I don't think groups like the Red Hat Society will be a vehicle for social change rather than a subject for paternalistic responses.

Ceremonies marking transitions and honoring what we are can bring visibility to old women. Frida Furman (1997) looks to religious institutions to create ceremonial occasions when one moves from one status into another. She points out that institutions creating new rituals can serve as "communities of resistance," and because rituals can "maintain power relations as well as call them into question . . . institutions that try out new women's rituals make a political as well as a ceremonial statement" (170–71). Rituals, she further observes, "can destabilize established power relations, calling for change in the directions of gender equality and inclusion" (170, 171). Institutions can honor women's transitions that dominant cultural norms tend to efface. Ruth Ray (2007) focuses on croning ceremonies as rituals that challenge our society's preference for youth over age by celebrating women's maturity. To become a crone is to become a wise old woman, according to theologian Rosemary Reuther (1986); I supplement that with the need for wise anger when it is necessary.

Because we are social beings and the problems we face are complex, we also need to act collectively; we need to organize returning us to the grassroots strategy that Tish Sommers and Laurie Shields sought to put in place in the 1980s. While that effort did not continue for many reasons, it is possible to join grassroots organizing to a larger collective strategy if there is some support for it. While proponents of the new aging in foundations invest in civic engagement, they do not invest in organizing efforts that are designed not to replace reductions in federal spending but to create a new social justice agenda for women.

INTERGENERATIONAL AND ORGANIZATIONAL APPROACHES

Because negative images of older people begin early in life, another way to disrupt the old-bad nexus is through facilitating intergenerational contacts. While I think that educational programs or having old people in schools are one way to begin to alter the perceptions of the young, I think that the more powerful way of doing so is to bring people, in this case women and girls, together in groups so that they can discuss, for example, how each experiences the effects of stereotypes or negative self-assessments. I imagine the possibility of adopting the approach used in "peace circles," where people can come together across differences in order to try to address mutual harms proactively. My vision is that we get the old and the young together to share stories about how negative stereotyping affects them. I feel quite certain that the sixteen-year-old no more wants to be accused of self-interest or other undesirable behaviors than old women want to be seen as incompetent. Regular efforts to ask basic questions, like "How do I think others see me?" "How do I see myself?" and "How do I want others to see me?" can awaken conversations that would not otherwise occur. They can then be converted into action agendas as the feminist wave analogy suggests. We can turn to schools, religious congregations, service clubs, and any other location to sponsor such events. We are hoping to begin them at my synagogue in the fall after six months of conversation about exploring our aging selves.

But I also imagine the continued development of national and local organizations dedicated to forwarding the issues that have been this book's theme. These organizations conduct research and do policy analysis and, on occasion, advocacy. It will be important for existing aging organizations such as AARP to take some responsibility for teaching not only about the new and positive views of aging but the ways in which it excludes and marginalizes many women. Their communication vehicles reach large numbers of people who need introductions to the differences among their age peers and the early sources of many such differences. It is a missed opportunity to not broaden their reach. I see the development of new organizations or new perspectives for already existing organizations that recall a different kind of society, one that took shape in the years after World War II and lasted until the late 1970s when the new conservatism took shape (Dionne 2011). We need to find a way to gain legitimacy for a society in which we hope for the safety, security, and respect we all want and that is so necessary for our well-being.

Universals need to be disassembled so that the role of gender across the life span is clearly etched. By focusing on gender as a framing device that permits inequalities to persist, organizations that are primarily about gender can widen their focus to tell the relevant story of how what happens to us at thirty-five matters when we are sixty-five. Clearly, gender inequities start when an old woman is a young woman, and so we cannot wait to address them until she is sixty-seven. The Family and Medical Leave Act (FMLA) was an important nod in the direction of supporting caregiving activities, but it mattered most to women, not men, and to women who could afford to take time out without pay. Organizations interested in women and gender can launch campaigns that teach that gender inequalities will not be remedied until men do the jobs at home and in the workplace that have traditionally been relegated to women (Ridgeway 2011). This is one approach to turn attention to the persistent gaps that leave so many women in serious difficulties when old.

Organizations can build a case demonstrating how structural changes in work, supported by public policies, can begin this process of deconstructing gender norms that disadvantage women. They can develop and promote policies that guarantee equal pay for equal work, policies that encourage family care as a shared obligation of women and men (Sweden is a good example of this) and flexible work policies that permit the integration of family and work for both men and women, are one way to begin to disrupt the beliefs that permit male superiority and leave women in late life seriously disadvantaged. This observation gets almost no attention in the aging press, although it is well documented in feminist and critical research.

RECOVERY OF THE COMMON GOOD AND COMMUNITY

A few years ago, I had a conversation with a neighbor named Erin about Social Security. She's a smart, self-confident, politically savvy young woman who recently completed her master's degree at Northwestern. I opened this conversation because I feared that she, like many others, would have the now-familiar attitude—it won't be there when I need it—that may erode political support for this essential program (see chapter 6). So I described the program and observed that its future is primarily a political and not a financial problem. To solve the financial problems is relatively easy; to address the political problem is not. The problem started when I argued that Social Security represented a visible example of a tacit compact between generations, reflecting the important but often submerged American value that there is something that we may call the common good. Her response startled me. The very idea that there may be something called the "common good" was anathema to her. Essentially, her disdain rested on what she saw as the virtual abandonment of her generation—no good jobs, no loyalties between employees and employers, and a seemingly unsure future. This response is consistent with news reports about the plight of young people today. They have not experienced a society in which, for example, productivity gains benefitted both employer and employee at the same time that they are saddled with student debt. Today, productivity gains have not been shared, and so wages and salaries are stagnant. Businesses are not held responsible. Today, with the possible exception of sporting events and our local responses to catastrophes like earthquakes or hurricanes, we seem to have lost this connection to what unites us. Even civil society has undergone a transition. Rather than having a deep connection to their respective communities, community organizations are now dominated by moneyed interests that are global in scope. They seek not government action but government inaction, not social good but private benefit.

I reiterate that the human condition is more about vulnerability, dependency, and human connectedness than it is about independence and strength. We all rely on others and are all shaped by our "socio-historical and biographical contexts" (Dodds 2007, 501), thereby challenging the illusory notion that we are individually responsible for how our lives turn out. If only we could begin to see how much we all rely on others for our lives to go well, then it may not be so hard to accept help at eighty-four. Further, to accept the view of the human condition as essentially vulnerable and dependent can alter perceptions about what we need from others, what we need to give to others, and what we need from government. Appreciating the common good and the intergenerational solidarity that it reflects and the strong government that is needed to enact these values are fundamental to making our society a more hospitable place in general, as well as one in which to grow old. We can tackle these likely occurrences in old age alone or with the help of family and friends, but how much easier, kinder, and more dignified to know that we are not marginalized by our communities when we might need the assistance that makes life go more smoothly.

The contemporary context makes it difficult to think in terms of the common good and human dependency in other ways. In chapter 3, I discussed the dominant images of aging that are actually possible for only a small percentage of the American population but expected of all of us. We no longer have "leisure" communities; rather, we have beehive communities of people who can only slow down to sip wine as the sun goes down over the ocean. It seems that all romantic trysts occur facing west. This comment is not a rejection of age-segregated retirement communities but rather a rejection of the specific images that are used to advertise the communities. The residents of Mayslake do not look or act like the people seen in these ads, but they do remind us of the importance of communities like Mayslake. While it is important that we don't think of old age only in terms of losses, these golden images threaten our emotional security at a time when our physical and economic well-being is also shaky.

Our local communities can help. The blossoming Villages across the country, local efforts to create communities that are friendly to the old people who live there, are enacting the adage that it takes a village to age well. The Villages reflect the need to grow old in caring communities where neighbors help neighbors and where old people themselves play leadership roles in organizing and in determining actions to take. In this way, members of the Village are a positive force in the community. They are a community resource at the same time that they rely on the community to notice and care about them (personal communication, Mitzen,[1] 2014). That this can happen in communities scattered all over the United States is a good example of what the common good can mean in practice. While I don't think that volunteer efforts can replace justice-based interventions since they tend to be highly localized and thus separate people based on geography, they represent what Tocqueville saw as uniquely American. The more we facilitate such community action, particularly action that is intergenerational, the more likely it is we can recover the lost value of the common good. The Villages can also include intergenerational projects. Working together toward a common end can help people come to know one another while making communities more hospitable to both old and young. While these efforts might not move outside the circle of familiarity, it seems to me that we need to begin somewhere.

From the Academy to the Public Realm

A rich literature from feminism, critical gerontology, cultural studies, and elsewhere has challenged conventional understandings of a well-lived life, recognizing that our lives are shaped by many factors beyond our control, including unchosen and relational commitments. These commitments mark our lives in important ways but receive little public recognition or social sanction (Walker 1999a; Mackenzie and Stoljar 2000). These messages need to move outside the academy.

Moving outward from the academy can mean developing strategies to gain social recognition for women's strengths, such as their mutual support and their responsibilities toward others. But it means doing so without presuming that these were natural features of women's lives. Instead, these traits would be redefined as worthy and so to be nurtured in all people, just as masculine traits have been used to assess women. How interesting it would be to judge men by traits that have been viewed as natural to women, such as caretaking. I repeat that caregiving is a very useful example of how and why gender inequalities persist and is one reason that feminists have observed that it is as important for men to partake in caregiving roles as it is for women to do so-called men's jobs in the public sphere (Hooyman 1999; Ridgeway 2011). Recent studies (e.g., Calasanti 2006, 2007; Russell 2004) have begun the process of analyzing men's participation in such care work.

1. Phyllis Mitzen is president of Skylake Village in Chicago.

In reaching beyond the academy, feminist efforts can focus on the self and the unity of the internal and external selves. It will help women to understand that despite postmodern claims about a fragmented identity, most of us experience ourselves as continuous (Atchley 1999), even as our hair turns gray or shorts get tossed from our wardrobes. As we have adapted and changed over the course of our lives, we will continue to integrate these changes into our self-understanding. It is for this reason that eighty-year-old women may say they feel like eighteen. We are eighteen when we are quietly reading and eighty when we go into a crouch and can't get up without help. Accepting our age will mean not splitting the internal eighteen-year-old from the external eighty-year-old but seeing them as "inextricably bound together, part of an integrated whole which comprises our being" (Andrews 1999). Building on the stories that emerge in small groups, feminist and other scholars will introduce ways to think and talk about old age so that its "intractable vicissitudes" (Cole 1992, 233) are revealed, thus eliminating the dualism between the desirable and valued third age and its opposite, the fourth age. The messages will be about owning age in all its complexities as a work in progress as we build from many pieces, some of which are already there and others waiting to be discovered.

The movement from the academy to the public sphere will be most difficult when it confronts consumer culture and ageism. Old bodies are undesirable bodies, especially if they are unimproved. The result is that consumerist beauty norms infiltrate women's awareness. This threat compounds the problems caused by negative stereotyping and the ageism that such stereotyping spawns. It is hard for me to imagine large-scale protests that refuse hair dye or expensive anti-aging products, although I have vivid images of what such a protest might look like. It will take some work to determine how such an effort might be undertaken.

Ageism, I think, is a most difficult to address since its causes are so recalcitrant to interventions. As addressed in chapter 2, ageism harms us in multiple ways. It harms because it often leads us to narrow our worlds so that we avoid the threat of negative stereotyping. It harms because it can demean and patronize us. At seventy, we are not "young ladies." It harms every time older people are called geezers. It harms when we lose our jobs or are not hired despite the Age Discrimination in Employment Act (ADEA). It harms when we are not referred to mental health specialists or when we are blamed for the dependencies that we may have because of activity-limiting conditions. It harms when we are seen as "kind and incompetent" or angry, whiny, and troublesome. It harms, and I quote Iva Brown once more, when "they" think we don't know anything. These many harms can be the beginning of a campaign to get people to pay attention to their own attitudes and behaviors. It is also possible for women to teach ourselves how we can use an "oppositional stance" that "anticipates ageist bias" and contests it preemptively (Furman 1997, 178).

This movement outward from the academy will also document and communicate the ways in which gender inequality stalks us throughout our lives. Without a very specific gender lens it may be difficult to see how the balance of risks and benefits in old age will be played out. Critical gerontologist Chris Phillipson (1998) observes that "old age does threaten disaster—poverty, severe illness, the loss of a loved one. But it also can bring the opposite: freedom from restrictive work and domestic duties; new relationships; and a greater feeling of security" (125). Without a gender lens one may fail to see that these dualisms are not equally distributed. We must assist the privileged (usually white, middle-class, heterosexual) male decision maker see that the income or the health status of the seventy-five-year-old woman is the end product of the circumstances that disadvantaged her at many points in her life. As my daughter once said to me, for good reason, "Has it ever entered your mind that I am not you?" That's what privileged decision makers need to hear repeatedly. There is a reason why so few Fortune 500 CEOs are women or why, given identical resumes, the one with a male name is chosen for an interview (Kristof 2014). Thus, inequality in old age, a theme that recurs regularly in this book, is nagging, pervasive, and a worsening problem that is directly tied to gender and age (Ridgeway 2011, 3). As long as masculine norms remain dominant, it will be hard to alter the ways in which social relationships at work and in the home play out. This is the "bedrock problem around which the achievement of gender equality turns" (Ridgeway 2011, 197).

POLICY, IDEOLOGY, AND THE STATE

In the introduction and in chapter 6, I looked to the late 1970s and the 1980s as an important turning point in how the new conservatism redefined old age. Neoliberal politics took shape in those decades, and its antigovernment politics of retrenchment, steady attacks on the public sector, and the power of the privileged to set the public agenda solidified. Fragmentation over community prevailed. Deficit reduction became the mantra that did not shift even as deficits declined significantly because, as Paul Krugman (2014) observed, deficits justify "big cuts in spending" (A23). This privileged perspective, that is, not "having to notice or think about people who aren't like you" (Lindemann 2006, 41) is not good for old women.

It is no surprise, then, that neoliberal politics and elite policymaking also seize on whatever narrative of aging fits their agenda. As addressed in chapters 3 and 6, for the past forty years or so, conservatives have been trying to frame the discussion about population aging in three ways—the old as burden; the old as selfishly concerned only about their own interests; and the inevitability of generational conflict. As noted above, the new aging is an unintentional ally of the new politics. The "silver tsunami," the "burden" of an aging population, and "our children's future" further justify reductions in social spending. Some advocacy organizations, like the National Academy of Social Insurance or Social Security Works, are countering these claims and have succeeded in keeping radical change, like privatizing Social Security, off the table, at least for now. We cannot ease up on the message.

We can learn from the new conservatism that took shape in the 1970s and 1980s about developing a political strategy that enlists public figures as allies, that develops easy-to-understand manifestos and facilitates broad grassroots participation. We have those allies in the Senate, the House, and the media. Just as I was dwelling on my pessimism about broad social change, I read a story about Senator Sherrod Brown, a Democrat from Ohio, who was calling on progressives to fight to strengthen Social Security rather than to permit further chipping away at its benefits. We also have organizations that have not bowed to the middle ground. Perhaps it is time to strengthen organizations like OWL and return it to its earliest approach—combining grassroots organizing with research and political advocacy. While I do not have the expertise to devise an organizing strategy, I will suggest what I think ought to be the main themes of the political agenda.

Continued Inequality: On Not Being Safe and Secure

While a central theme throughout this book, in drawing it to a close I want to reiterate the importance of persistent inequality that translates into economic insecurity and its ramifications in all aspects of women's lives but also the lives of many men, especially men of color and historically low-wage workers. As sociologist Richard Settersten (2007) pointedly observes, "The chasm between those who do and do not have resources creates experiences in old age that are worlds apart and this chasm is likely to grow" (22). Thus, for baby boomers, social and economic uncertainty is as likely as is the brave new world of a liberated old age. We need much more than individual responsibility and one more targeted activity to live healthily and happily into our nineties. The cheerful images of independent old people living life to the hilt desensitizes both the public and politicians, who are given cover, to the problems of those who are not sunning themselves in Aruba but worrying about finding an apartment they can afford and still eat (Rubin 2007; Jacoby 2011). It thus behooves us all to respond regularly to the ways in which proponents of the new aging and many decision makers renarrate the aging experience so that it appears to be one of affluence and well-being. I am not proposing a retreat to the doom-and-gloom scenarios of the past, but I am maintaining that we have a responsibility to challenge overly rosy scenarios that do not respect the many ways in which we grow old. I am uneasy when I read about new directions for research into successful aging that aims at identifying the specific activities that relate to good health outcomes (Johnson and Mutchler 2013). It's like proposing a grape cluster to a hungry person when she hasn't had a solid meal in two days.

MOVING FORWARD: POLICY

All that said, I return to the critic's role as explored in the introduction. This task is to seek openings, to reveal the fractures in society (Bernstein 1992) so that we can locate places to intervene. In previous chapters, I have made suggestions for policy changes that would address income inadequacy, care provision, and the problems associated with end-of-life care. In chapter 6, for example, I argued for lifting the income cap for Social Security taxes, modifying the payroll tax to bring more resources into the system, and improving benefits to low-income individuals. While nonstarters at the moment because of congressional refusal to consider a tax increase of any kind, keeping it alive as an idea is within our control. I also considered changes that would address its specific inadequacies related to women, including credits for drop-out years, a minimum benefit that lifted women above the poverty line, and a recalculation of the widow's benefit. These modifications would be aided greatly by an add-on pension system that would provide older women another source of income in retirement that is available to more affluent people through private pensions and savings. Retirement, which I see as endangered, is a vitally important time in life; thus, it should be possible for all people, not just the privileged.

In chapter 5, where my focus was on caregiving and the provision of care to people with chronic impairments, I argued that who cares for whom reveals the relations of power in society (Tronto 1993) and that it is women who primarily do the caring work for both the young and the old in this country today. There is a close link between women's work in the home and their role in the workforce that demands remedy if women are to have an improved economic status in old age (Hooyman 1999). Further, it is, in my view, a moral and practical imperative that care should be available for all who need it without exploiting others, especially women, who are the likely care providers. Care should not be a responsibility borne primarily by women. Care must be redefined as a citizen right and not an individual responsibility, and whatever care families provide must be a shared responsibility. As noted above, by relegating caregiving and other home responsibilities to women, the task of overcoming gender inequalities will be nearly impossible to achieve (Ridgeway 2011).

I also defend the view, as I did in chapters 5 and 6, that business has obligations in both these areas—to help to make retirement possible and to facilitate the ability of both women and men to be caregivers. In chapter 7, I argued for a more expansive approach to end-of-life care that responds to what many people, especially women, identified as important to them—to die at home without burdening their families and to have their broad goals met. Once again, our ability to have these preferences met is contingent upon context—will there be sufficient support, both medical and social, to grant these wishes? Right now we can choose treatments and we can even choose to stay at home, but we cannot choose to have the underlying conditions that make it possible, that is, adequate assistance with nonmedical services. That calls for a strong version of citizen rights—to get the care we need when we need it—that is not currently part of the American way of death or long-term care.

None of these changes will be easy or quick. The ideological strength of neoliberalism continues to be reflected in the politics of austerity, deficit reduction, and steady attacks on the public sector. It is also class driven; those best endowed with lifelong opportunities to accumulate both health and wealth are most likely to find neoliberalism a comfortable ideology. My tools of resistance are basic—letters to the *New York Times*, supporting progressive legislators, posts on social media, letters to recalcitrant legislators, bringing these issues into the classroom, and writing about them in as many places as I can. I talk to anyone who will discuss these issues with me, including the generations after me—my children, their spouses, and my grandchildren when they get a little older—and lend support to organizations that see social justice as an essential concern of a good society. Yet the people I know and talk to basically share my views. The challenge is how to reach out to others.

Throughout the book I have tried to offer counterarguments to the conservative framing of the aging experience. I hope that those of us who are committed to a more just society will respond whenever we hear these arguments used. I am not, however, an organizer and so look for this conversation to continue among individuals and organizations who have the skills to advance the conversation.

ONE DAY . . .

Who, then, but us—old women—can assume the responsibility for our future? But we cannot do it alone. We can shape the stories that can become the materials from which a new agenda is born at the same time that these stories help us to claim our voices. Like people of all ages, we want to be seen in ways that transcend appearance, to be known as the multidimensional people we are. Thus, we can take advantage of the new media to reveal ourselves as we see ourselves. It is also up to us to insist on the chance to be free, free from expectations and stereotypes that narrow our worlds just when we are looking to broaden them. It is up to us to tell the stories that reveal a counter-imagery that gives us an inner sense of continuity. We need to join with women of all ages who want/need to be free from restricting images, images that often cause them to judge themselves negatively. We also need to join with other generations in shattering the root causes of gender inequality. We—old, young, and in between—are in this struggle together. Thus, our advocacy is for those of us who are already old but also for our daughters, granddaughters, sisters, and others who must continue the work we have started. It also means that our younger sisters need to see themselves in us. As we were once young, so they, too, will be old even though they now believe that "I will never be like that," however they define "that."

My hope, not surprisingly, is that accumulating scholarship and activism will lead women to reclaim the meaning of "old," defining it in their own voices and wearing it proudly. An immediate example of how hard this will be: recently, I was on the phone with a representative of the company that manages my savings, trying to set up my online account. In the course of the discussion, she needed my birthdate, which I gave her. As we were completing our call, she referred to me as "young lady." I thought that here was a teachable moment. I said, "No, I'm an old lady." Sounding both shocked and offended, she insisted that I was not old and was only willing to say that I was "seasoned." My efforts at persuasion failed. I should have asked her why she thought it was so offensive to see me as an "old lady." Exchanges such as this one and the one I mentioned in the opening paragraph suggest that the new aging has not rooted out the negative connotations attached to "old" and so has not made it acceptable to be a woman of a certain age. Rather than changing the images of aging, it has remade late life into an extended midlife, thus perpetuating an internalized ageism. We can be "seasoned" or "older" but not "old."

Since efforts to demonize "old" seem to be working, the special meanings associated with late life hardly have time to blossom and flourish. As Lynne Segal (2013) observes, "To argue that age is irrelevant thus runs the risk of turning our attention once more away from the varied distinctiveness of old age, with its gains and losses, its demanding challenges and fluctuating temporalities" (66). I am not just like I was at fifty, nor, I add, are my friends. One important distinction, besides physical changes, is that we are free in ways we haven't been free in decades. What we will do with our freedom (and we are fortunate enough not to need to work full-time to make ends meet) is the adventure of late life, of old age. The new aging advocates, who are telling us how to live, risk forgetting that if women are to become truly emancipated, we must be trusted with our freedom. The effort to limit that freedom in the name of productivity or civic engagement, for example, is one reason that I resist them so strongly. Joining with organizations and government, we can continue to work toward opening opportunities without transforming opportunities into normative expectations. We need not continue to pay rent for the space that we occupy, especially since for many women their traditional roles do not disappear when they "retire" from paid work.

When, in terms of the weary cliché, do we get to smell the roses? I add the words of Lillian Rubin (2007) offered as both a researcher and an eighty-plus-year-old woman:

> We can erase the lines with surgery and Botox, cover the gray, practice memory aids assiduously, but there is no way to avoid the internal sense of loss and the sadness that accompanies old age—sorrow that's made exponentially worse by a culture that glorifies youth and sells it so relentlessly. (49)

The picture is not all bleak; I find deep sources of hope in women's ability to support one another and their ability to hone their relational skills to make their worlds more comfortable. Typically, women's strengths and virtues like care have taken second place to those associated with men's. So we need to claim our strengths and name our virtues and not let them be regularly subordinated. Why should climbing a mountain be esteemed more than catching our neighbor if she falls (Ruddick 1999)?

Throughout this book, I have touched upon ways in which old women, and old people more generally, can resist the imposition of negative stereotyping at the same time that we do not try to deny the fact of aging itself. I have maintained that while we have considerable room to fight cultural constructions of age, all possibilities are not open to us since our bodies, or at least most of our bodies, have changed in ways that are not modifiable, at least short of a complete makeover. I have also argued that absent the underlying conditions such as economic and other forms of security, our ability to make choices about our lives will be constrained. Physical, cognitive, and/or financial limitations may render the long-awaited chance to be free to live as we wish an unrealizable hope for many of us.

While I will do whatever I can to stay as healthy as possible, I will continue to speak as freely and as often as I can about the physicality of aging and the opportunities nonetheless to live well and fully, albeit not without occasional longing for what can be no more. I think we have another task—to present ourselves as we want to be seen. I need to practice walking into that "hip" store in a way that suggests I belong there as much as the twenty-five-year-olds and to be respected as a potential customer. Through my actions, I want to demonstrate that I have control over the way I expect to be perceived.

I have great hope for the communities of which we are a part, which are sometimes communities of resistance. The task is nothing short of reconstructing old age. In such communities, not only can we challenge identities that others impose on us, but we can redefine what it means to live a good and worthy life—for us and others like us. "A morally significant life is built on bricolage, not on a master narrative" (Holstein, Parks, and Waymack 2011, 68). We can also think of the much-mentioned concept of empowerment not as a contrast with powerlessness but rather as a dialectic between strength and weakness that focuses on the "interplay between a woman's consciousness and body, her spirit and her flesh, her strengths and weaknesses, her abilities and disabilities, her life and eventual death" (Morell

2003, 80). To repeat what I said earlier, we can only make this a better place to be old if we see it as a complex story not reducible to dichotomous poles. To guide the development of this dialectic is to help women cultivate the "demanding arts of acceptance, adjustment, and appreciation" (Wendell 1999, 146).

References

Aaron, H. 2011. "Social Security Reconsidered." *National Tax Journal* 64 (2, part 1): 385–414.
———. 2013. "Progressives and the Safety Net." *Democracy Journal*, no. 17 (winter), http://www.democracyjournal.org/27/progressives-and-the-safety-net.php.
Abel, E. 1991. *Who Cares for the Elderly: Public Policy and the Experiences of Adult Daughters*. Philadelphia, PA: Temple University Press.
Achenbaum, A. 1986. *Social Security: Visions and Revisions*. New York: Cambridge University Press.
Administration on Aging. 2012. A Profile of Older Americans: 2012. http://www.aoa.gov/Aging_Statistics/Profile/2012/docs/2012profile.pdf.
Agich, G. 1990. "Reassessing Autonomy in Long-Term Care." *Hastings Center Report* 20 (6): 12–17.
———. 1995. "Actual Autonomy and Long-Term Care Decision Making." In *Long-Term Care Decisions: Ethical and Conceptual Dimensions*, edited by L. McCullough and N. Wilson, 113–36. Baltimore, MD: Johns Hopkins University Press.
———. 2003. *Dependence and Autonomy in Old Age*. New York: Cambridge University Press.
Anderson, J. 1983. "Conference on Aging Rigged." *Sumter Daily Item*, March 8, 8.
Andrews, M. 1999. "The Seductiveness of Agelessness." *Ageing and Society* 19: 301–18.
———. 2000. "Ageful and Proud." *Ageing and Society* 20: 791–95.
Angell, M. 2012. "May Doctors Help You Die?" *New York Review of Books*, October 11.
Angus, J., and P. Reeve. 2006. "Ageism: A Threat to 'Aging Well' in the 21st Century." *Journal of Applied Gerontology* 25: 137–52.
Anti-Aging Task Force. 2006. *Ageism in America*. New York: International Longevity Center.
Aries, P. 1981. *The Hour of Our Death*. New York: Oxford University Press.
Aristotle. 1962. *Nicomachean Ethics*. Translated with an introduction and notes by Martin Oswald. New York: Macmillan.
Aronson, J. 1990. "Women's Perspectives on Informal Care of the Elderly: Public Ideology and Personal Experience of Giving and Receiving Care." *Ageing and Society* 10: 61–84.
———. 2002. "Elderly People's Accounts of Home Care Rationing: Missing Voices in Long-Term Care Policy Debates." *Ageing and Society* 22 (4): 399–418.
Atchley, R. 1987. *Aging: Continuity and Change*. Belmont, CA: Wadsworth.
———. 1999. Continuity and adaption in aging. Baltimore: Johns Hopkins University Press.

Aujoulat, I., R. Marcolongo, L. Bonadiman, and A. Deccache. 2008. "Reconsidering Patient Empowerment in Chronic Illness: A Critique of Models of Self-Efficacy and Bodily Control." *Social Science and Medicine* 66: 1228–39.

Baars, J. 2006. "Beyond Neomodernism, Antimodernism, and Postmodernism: Basic Categories for Contemporary Critical Gerontology." In *Aging, Globalization and Inequality: The New Critical Gerontology*, edited by J. Baars, D. Dannefer, and C. Phillipson, 17–42. Amityville, NY: Baywood.

Bakewell, S. 2010. *How to Live; or, a Life of Montaigne*. New York: Other Press.

Baltes, P., and M. Baltes. 1990. *Successful Aging: Perspectives from the Behavioral Sciences*. Cambridge: Cambridge University Press.

Barker, P. 1983. *Union Street*. New York: Ballantine.

Bartky, S. 1999. "Unplanned Obsolescence: Some Reflections on Aging." In *Mother Time: Women, Aging, and Ethics*, edited by M. U. Walker, 61–74. Lanham, MD: Rowman & Littlefield.

Bartlett, B. 2007. "'Starve the Beast': Origins and Development of a Budgetary Metaphor." *Independent Review* 12: 5–26.

Bass, S., and F. Caro. 2001. "Productive Aging: A Conceptual Framework." In *Productive Aging: Concepts and Challenges*, edited by N. Morrow-Howell, J. Hinterlong, and M. Sherraden, 37–78. Baltimore, MD: Johns Hopkins University Press.

Bass, S., F. Caro, and Y.-P. Chen, eds. 1993. *Achieving a Productive Aging Society*. Westport, CT: Auburn House.

Bauman, Z. 1992. *Mortality, Immortality and Other Life Strategies*. Stanford, CA: Stanford University Press.

Beauvoir, Simone de. 1973. *The Coming of Age*. Translated by Patrick O'Brian. New York: Warner.

Beck, U. 2002. *Risk Society: Toward a New Modernity*. London: Sage.

Becker, G. 1997. *Disrupted Lives: How People Create Meaning in a Chaotic World*. Berkeley: University of California Press.

Becker, G., and E. Newsome. 2005. "Resilience in the Face of Serious Illness among Chronically Ill African Americans in Later Life." *Journals of Gerontology Series B, Psychological Sciences and Social Sciences* 60 (4): S214–S223.

Benhabib, S. 1992. *Situating the Self: Gender, Community and Postmodernism in Contemporary Ethics*. New York: Routledge.

Berger, J. 2005. "Patients' Interests in Their Family Members' Well-Being: An Overlooked Fundamental Consideration in Substituted Judgment." *Journal of Clinical Ethics* 16: 3–10.

Bernard, D. 1996. "Chronic Illness and the Dynamics of Hoping." In *Chronic Illness: From Experience to Policy*, edited by K. Toombs, D. Bernard, and R. Carson. Bloomington: Indiana University Press.

Bernard, M., and V. Harding Davies. 1999. "Our Ageing Selves: Reflections on Growing Older." In *Women and Ageing: Changing Identities, Challenging Myths*, edited by M. Bernard, J. Phillips, L. Machin, and V. Harding Davies, 58–73. London: Routledge.

Bernard, M., J. Phillips, L. Machin, and V. Harding Davies. 2000. *Women and Aging: Changing Identities, Challenging Myths*. London: Routledge.

Bernstein, N. 2014. "Pitfalls Seen in a Turn to Privately Run Long-Term Care. *New York Times*, March 6, A1. http://www.nytimes.com/2014/03/07/nyregion/pitfalls-seen-in-tennessees-turn-to-privately-run-long-term-care.html.

Bernstein, R. 1992. *The New Constellation: The Ethical-Political Horizons of Modernity/Postmodernity*. Cambridge, MA: MIT Press.

Biggs, S. 1997. "Choosing Not to Be Old? Masks, Bodies, and Identity Management in Later Life." *Ageing and Society* 17: 553–70.

———. 2001. "Toward a Critical Narrativity: Stories of Aging in Contemporary Social Policy." *Journal of Aging Studies* 15: 303–16.

———. 2004. "Age, Gender, Narratives, and Masquerades." *Journal of Aging Studies* 18: 45–58.

Biggs, S., C. Phillipson, A.-M. Money, and R. Leach. 2006. "The Age-Shift: Observations on Social Policy, Ageism and the Dynamics of the Adult Lifecourse." *Journal of Social Work Practice* 20 (3): 239–50.

Binstock, R. 1983. "The Aged as Scapegoat." *Gerontologist* 23: 136–43.

———. 1992. "The Oldest Old and 'Intergenerational Equity.'" In *The Oldest Old*, edited by R. Suzman, D. Villis, and K. Manton, 394–418. New York: Oxford University Press.

———. 2000. "Older People and Voting Participation: Past and Future." *Gerontologist* 40: 18–31.

———. 2010. "From Compassionate Ageism to Intergenerational Conflict?" *Gerontologist* 50 (5): 574–85.

———. 2012. "Older Voters and the 2010 Election: Implications for 2012 and Beyond." *Gerontologist* 52 (3): 408–17.

Binstock, R., and S. Post, eds. 1992. *Too Old for Health Care? Controversies in Medicine, Law, Economics and Ethics*. Baltimore: Johns Hopkins University Press.

Blackhall, L, S. Murphy, G. Frank, V. Michel, and S. Azeb. 1995. "Ethnicity and Attitudes toward Patient Autonomy." *Journal of the American Medical Association* 274: 820–25.

Blahous, C., and R. Reischauer. 2013. *A Summary of the 2012 Annual Reports*. Social Security Administration. http://www.ssa.gov/oact/trsum/index.html.

Blaikie, A. 1999. *Ageing and Popular Culture*. Cambridge: Cambridge University Press.

Blustein, J. 2004. "Integrating Medicine and the Family: Toward a Coherent Ethic of Care." In *The Cultures of Caregiving: Conflict and Common Ground among Families, Health Professionals, and Policy Makers*, edited by C. Levine and T. Murray, 127–46. Baltimore, MD: Johns Hopkins University Press.

Blythe, R. 1979. *The View in Winter*. New York: Harcourt Brace Jovanovich.

Board of the Treasury. 2012. *The 2012 Annual Report of the Board of Trustees of the Federal Old Age and Survivors Insurance and Federal Disability Insurance Trust Funds*. http://www.socialsecurity.gov/oact/TR/2012/tr2012.pdf.

Bordo, S. 1993. *Unbearable Weight*. Berkeley: University of California Press.

Bradley, D., and C. Longino. 2001. "How Older People Think about Images of Aging in Advertising and the Media." *Generations* 25 (3): 17–21.

Braithwaite, Y. 2002. "Reducing Ageism." In *Ageism: Stereotyping and Prejudice against Older People*, edited by T. Nelson, 311–38 . Cambridge, MA: MIT Press.

Brandsen, C. 2006. "A Public Ethics of Care: Implications for Long-Term Care." In *Socializing Care: Feminist Ethics and Public Issues*, edited by M. Hamington and D. Miller, 205–26. Lanham, MD: Rowman & Littlefield.

Braun, U., R. Beyeth, M. Ford, and L. McCullough. 2007. "Voices of African-American, Caucasian, and Hispanic Surrogates on the Burden of End of Life Decision-Making." *Journal of General Internal Medicine* 23 (3): 267–74.

Breheny, M., and C. Stephens. 2012. "Negotiating a Moral Identity in the Context of Later Life Care." *Journal of Aging Studies* 26: 438–47.

Brennan, S. 2009. "Feminist Ethics and Everyday Inequalities." *Hypatia* 24 (1): 141–59.

Brink, S. 2009. "Bunny's Last Days: When Living Will Isn't Enough." *Kaiser Health News*, March 5. http://kaiserhealthnews.org/news/when-living-will-isnt-enough.

Brooks, A. 2004. "'Under the Knife and Proud of It: ' An Analysis of the Normalization of Cosmetic Surgery." *Critical Sociology* 30: 207–39.

Brown, R. 2014. "Parsing Ambition." In *A Story Larger Than My Own: Women Writers Look Back on Their Lives and Careers*, edited by J. Burroway, 42–51. Chicago: University of Chicago Press.

Bruner, J. 1990. *Acts of Meaning*. Cambridge, MA: Harvard University Press.

Bubeck, D. 2002. "Justice and the Labor of Care." In *The Subject of Care: Feminist Perspectives in Dependency*, edited by E. F. Kittay and E. Feder, 160–85. Lanham, MD: Rowman & Littlefield.

Buhler-Wilkerson, K. 2007. "Care of the Chronically Ill: An Unresolved Dilemma in Health Policy for the United States." *Milbank Quarterly* 85 (4): 611–39.

Burroway, J., ed. 2014. *A Story Larger Than My Own: Women Writers Look Back on Their Lives and Careers*. Chicago: University of Chicago Press.

Bury, M. 1991. "The Sociology of Chronic Illness: A Review of Research and Prospects." *Sociology of Health and Illness* 13: 451–68.

Butler, K. 2014. *Knocking on Heaven's Door: The Path of a Better Way of Death*. New York Scribner.

Butler, R. 1969. "Age-ism: Another Form of Bigotry." *Gerontologist* 9: 243–46.

———. 1975. *Why Survive? Being Old in America*. New York: Harper & Row.

Butler, R., and M. Lewis. 1976. *Sex after Sixty: A Guide for Men and Women in Their Later Years*. New York: Harper & Row.

Butler, S., and P. Germanis. 1983. "Achieving a 'Leninist Strategy.'" *Cato Journal* 3 (2): 547–56.

Byock, I. 2003. "Rediscovering Community at the Core of the Human Condition and Social Covenant." *Hastings Center Report Special Supplement* 33: S40–S41.

Bytheway, B. 1995. *Ageism*. Bristol, UK: Open University Press.

Calasanti, T. 2004. "New Directions in Feminist Gerontology: An Introduction." *Journal of Aging Studies* 18: 1–8.

———. 2005. "Ageism, Gravity, and Gender: Experience of Aging Bodies." *Generations* 29 (3): 8–12.

———. 2006. "Gender and Old Age: Lessons from Spousal Care Work." In *Age Matters: Realigning Feminist Thought*, edited by T. Calasanti and K. Slevin, 269–94. New York: Routledge.

———. 2007. "Bodacious Berry, Potency Wood and the Aging Monster: Gender and Age Relations in Anti-aging Ads." *Social Forces* 86 (1): 335–55.

———. 2008. "A Feminist Confronts Ageism." *Journal of Aging Studies* 22: 152–57.

Calasanti, T., and K. Slevin. 2001. *Gender, Social Inequalities, and Aging*. Walnut Creek, CA: AltaMira.

———, eds. 2006. *Age Matters: Realigning Feminist Thinking*. New York: Routledge.

Calasanti, T., K. Slevin, and N. King. 2006. "Ageism and Feminism: From 'Et Cetera' to Center." *NWSA Journal* 18 (9): 13–30.

Callahan, D. 1987. *Setting Limits: Medical Goals in an Aging Society*. New York: Simon & Schuster.

———. 1988. "Families as Caregivers: The Limits of Morality." *Archives of Physical Medicine and Rehabilitation* 69: 323–28.

———. 1995. "Once Again, Reality." *Hastings Center Report* 25: S33–S37.

Campbell, A., and R. King. 2010. "Social Security: Political Resilience in the Face of Conservative Strides. In *The New Politics of Old Age*, 2nd ed., edited by R. Hudson, 233–53. Baltimore, MD: Johns Hopkins University Press.

Campbell, A., and K. Morgan. 2005. "Financing the Welfare State: Elite Politics and the Decline of the Social Insurance Model in America." *Studies in American Political Development* 19: 173–195.

Carpenter, Z. 2013. "CEOs with Massive Retirement Fortunes Push Social Security Cuts." *Nation.* http://www.thenation.com/blog/177251/ceos-massive-retirement-fortunes-push-social-security-cuts.

Carr, D., and K. Komp, eds. 2011. *Gerontology in the Era of the Third Age.* New York: Springer.

Carson, L. 2013. "HUD Housing Programs at Risk Locally and across the Nation." *San Francisco Bay View*, January 26.

Centers for Disease Control and Prevention. 2012. "Chronic Diseases and Health Promotions." http://www.cdc.gov/chronicdisease/overview/index.htm.

Centers for Medicare and Medicaid Services. 2012. Chronic Conditions among Medicare Beneficiaries. Chartbook: 2012 Edition. http://www.cms.gov/Research-Statistics-Data-and-Systems/Statistics-Trends-and-Reports/Chronic-Conditions/Downloads/2012Chartbook.pdf.

Chapman, A. 2004. "Ethical Implications of Prolonged Lives." *Theology Today* 60 (4): 479–96.

Charmaz, K. 1983. "Loss of Self: A Fundamental Form of Suffering in the Chronically Ill." *Sociology of Health and Illness* 5: 168–95.

———— 1987. "Struggling for a Self: Identity Levels in the Chronically Ill." *Research in the Sociology of Health Care* 6: 283–321.

————. 1995. "The Body, Identity, and Self: Adapting to Impairment." *Sociological Quarterly* 36 (4): 657–80.

————. 2006. "Measuring Pursuits, Marking Self: Meaning Construction in Chronic Illness." *International Journal of Qualitative Studies on Health and Well-Being* 1 (1): 27–37.

Chen, P. 2007. *Final Exam: A Surgeon's Reflections on Mortality.* New York: Vintage.

Chivers, S. 2003. *From Old Woman to Older Woman: Contemporary Culture and Women's Narratives.* Columbus: Ohio State University Press.

Chrisler, J. C., and L. Ghiz. 1993. "Body Image Issues of Older Women." In *Faces of Women and Aging*, edited by N. Davis, E. Cole, and E. Rothblum, 67–76. New York: Haworth.

Christakis, N. 1991. "Too Quietly into the Night." *British Medical Journal* 337: 326.

Churchill, L. 2002. "What Ethics Can Contribute to Health Policy." In *Ethical Dimensions of Health Policy*, edited by M. Danis, C. Clancy, L. and Churchill, 51–64. New York: Oxford University Press.

Clark, D. 2002. "Between Hope and Acceptance: The Medicalization of Dying." *British Medical Journal* 324: 904–7.

Clayman, J., and B. Seidman. 1981. "Letter to the Editor: A Questionable Resolution on Social Security." *New York Times*, December 17. http://www.nytimes.com/1981/12/17/opinion/l-a-questionable-resolution-on-social-security-136200.html.

Clement, G. 1996. *Care, Autonomy and Justice: Feminism and the Ethics of Care.* Boulder, CO: Westview.

Clift, E. 2008. *Two Weeks of Life: A Memoir of Love, Death, and Politics.* New York: Basic.

Cohen, E. 2001. The Complex Nature of Ageism: What Is It? Who Does It? Who Perceives It?" *Gerontologist* 41 (5): 576–77.

Cole, T. 1986. "Introduction." In *What Does It Mean to Grow Old? Reflections from the Humanities*, edited by T. Cole and S. Gadow, 3–8. Durham, NC: Duke University Press.

————. 1992. *The Journey of Life: A Cultural History of Aging in America.* New York: Cambridge University Press.

———. 1995. Introduction to *The Oxford Book of Aging*, edited by T. R. Cole and M. G. Winkler, 3–12. New York: Oxford University Press.

———. 1995. "What Have We 'Made' of Aging?" *Journals of Gerontology Series B, Psychological Sciences and Social Sciences* 50B (6): S341–S343.

Cole, T., and S. Gadow, eds. 1986. *What Does It Mean to Grow Old? Reflections from the Humanities*. Durham, NC: Duke University Press.

Collins, G. 2009. *When Everything Changed: The Amazing Journey of American Women from 1960 to the Present*. New York: Little, Brown.

Collopy, B. 1988. "Autonomy in Long-Term Care: Some Crucial Distinctions." *Gerontologist* 28 (Suppl.): 10–17.

Coupland, J. 2009. "Time, the Body and the Reversibility of Ageing: Commodifying the Decade." *Ageing and Society* 29: 953–76.

Crawford. R. 2004. "Risk Ritual and the Management of Control and Anxiety in Medical Culture." *Health (London)* 10 (4): 401–10.

Crawford Shearer, N., J. Fleury, and P. Reed. 2009. "The Rhythm of Health in Older Women with Chronic Illness." *Research and Theory for Nursing Practice* 23 (2): 148–60.

Croft, S. 1986. "Women Caring and the Recasting of Need: A Feminist Reappraisal." *Critical Social Policy* 6: 23.

Cruikshank, M. 2009. *Learning to Be Old: Gender, Culture, and Aging*, 2nd ed. Lanham, MD: Rowman & Littlefield.

Cruz-Saco, M. 2010. "Intergenerational Solidarity." In *Intergenerational Solidarity: Strengthening Economic and Social Ties*, edited by M. Cruz-Saco and S. Zelenev, 9–34. New York: Palgrave Macmillan.

Crystal, S., and D. Shea. 1990. "Cumulative Advantage, Cumulative Disadvantage, and Inequality among Older People." *Gerontologist* 39 (4): 437–43.

Cuddy, A., and S. Fiske. 2002. "Doddering but Dear: Process, Content, and Function in Stereotyping of Older Persons." In *Ageism: Stereotyping and Prejudice against Older People*, edited by T. Nelson, 3–26. Cambridge, MA: MIT Press.

Cuddy, A., M. Norton, and S. Fiske. 2005. "The Old Stereotype: The Pervasiveness and Persistence of the Elderly Stereotype." *Journal of Social Issues* 61: 267–85.

Dannefer, D. 2003. "Cumulative Advantage/Disadvantage and the Life Course: Cross-Fertilizing Age and Social Science Theory." *Journals of Gerontology Series B, Psychological Sciences and Social Sciences* 58 (6): S327–S337.

Degenholtz, H., Y. Rhee, and R. Arnold. 2004. "Brief Communication: The Relationship between Having a Living Will and Dying in Place." *Annals of Internal Medicine* 141 (2): 113–17.

DeLamater, J. 2011. "Sexual Expression in Later Life: A Review and Synthesis." CDE Working Paper 2011–08. Center for Demography and Ecology, University of Wisconsin, Madison.

Dillaway, H., and M. Byrnes. 2009. "Reconsidering Successful Aging: A Call for Renewed and Expanded Academic Critiques and Conceptualizations." *Journal of Applied Gerontology* 28: 702–22.

Dionne, E. J. 2012. *Our Divided Political Heart: The Battle for the American Idea in an Age of Discontent*. New York: Bloomsbury.

Diprose, R. 1995. "The Body Biomedical Ethics Forgets." In *Troubled Bodies: Critical Perspectives on Postmodernism, Medical Ethics, and the Body*, edited by P. Komesaroff, 202–21. Durham, NC: Duke University Press.

Dodds, S. 2000. "Choice and Control in Feminist Bioethics." In *Relational Autonomy: Feminist Perspectives on Autonomy, Agency and the Social Self*, edited by C. Mackenzie and N. Stoljar, 213–35. New York: Oxford University Press.

———. 2007. "Depending on Care: Recognition of Vulnerability and the Social Contribution of Care Provision." *Bioethics* 21 (9): 500–510.

Douard, J. 1996. "Disability and the Persistence of the "Normal." In *Chronic Illness: From Experience to Policy*, edited by S. K. Toombs, D. Barnard, and R. Carson, 154–75. Bloomington: Indiana University Press.

Drought, T., and B. Koenig. 2002. "'Choice' in End-of-Life-Decision Making: Researching Fact or Fiction?" *Gerontologist* 42 (Special Issue III): 114–28.

Dubler, N. 2005. "Conflict and Consensus at the End of Life." *Improving End of Life Care: Why Has It Been So Difficult? Hastings Center Report Special Report* 35 (6): S19–S25.

Duffy, M. 2005. "Labor Inequalities: Challenges for Feminists Conceptualizing Care at the Intersections of Gender, Race, and Class." *Gender and Society* 19 (1): 66–82.

Dula, A. 1994. "African-Americans' Suspicion of the Healthcare System Is Justified. What Can We Do about It?" *Cambridge Quarterly of Healthcare Ethics* 3 (3): 347–57.

Dumas, A., S. Laberge, and S. Straka. 2005. "Older Women's Relations to Bodily Appearance: The Embodiment of Social and Biological Conditions of Existence." *Ageing and Society* 25: 883–902.

Dunn, P., S. Tolle, A. Moss, and J. Black. 2007. "The POLST Paradigm: Respecting the Wishes of Patients and Families." *Annals of Long-Term Care* 15 (9): 33–40.

Edsall, Thomas B. 2013. The War on Entitlements. *New York Times*, March 6. http://opinionator.blogs.nytimes.com/2013/03/06/the-war-on-entitlements.

Ekherdt, D. J. 1996. "'The Busy Ethic': Moral Continuity between Work and Retirement." *Gerontologist* 26 (3): 239–44.

Ellington, S., and J. Fuller. 2003. "A Good Death? Finding the Balance between the Interests of Patients and Caregivers." In *Ethics and Community-Based Elder Care*, edited by M. Holstein and P. Mitzen, 200–208. New York: Springer.

Elliott, C. 2003. *Better Than Well: American Medicine Meets the American Dream*. New York: Norton.

Ells, C., M. Hunt, and J. Chambers-Evans. 2011. "Relational Autonomy as an Essential Component of Patient-Centered Care. *International Journal of Feminist Approaches to Bioethics* 4 (2): 79–101.

Engster, D. 2007. *The Heart of Justice: Care Ethics and Political Theory*. New York: Oxford University Press.

Ephron, N. 2011. *I Feel Bad about My Neck and Other Thoughts on Being a Woman*. New York: Knopf.

Estes, C., and Associates. 2001. *Social Policy and Aging: A Critical Perspective*. Thousand Oaks, CA: Sage.

Estes, C., S. Biggs, and C. Phillipson. 2003. *Social Theory, Social Policy and Ageing: A Critical Introduction*. London: Open University Press.

Estes, C., and E. Binney. 1991. "The Biomedicalization of Aging: Dangers and Dilemmas." In *Critical Perspectives on an Aging Society: The Political and Moral Economy of Growing Old*, edited by M. Minkler and C. Estes, 117–34. Amityville, NY: Baywood.

Estes, C., T. O'Neill, and H. Hartmann. 2012. *Breaking the Social Security Glass Ceiling: A Proposal to Modernize Women's Benefits*. Washington, DC: Institute for Women's Policy Research, National Committee to Preserve Social Security and Medicare and the NOW Foundation.

Fahey, C., and M. Holstein. 1993. "Toward a Philosophy of the Third Age." In *Voices and Visions: Toward a Critical Gerontology*, edited by T. Cole, W. A. Achenbaum, P. Jakobi, and R. Kastenbaum, 241–56. New York: Springer.

Faircloth, C. 2003. "Different Bodies and the Paradox of Aging: Locating Aging Bodies in Images and Everyday Experience." In *Aging Bodies: Images and Everyday Experiences*, edited by C. Faircloth, 1–28. Walnut Creek, CA: AltaMira.

Fairlie, H. 1988. "Talkin' 'bout My Generation: Government Assistance to Those over 65 and the Pampered Lifestyle." *New Republic*, March 28, 19–22.

Falcus, S. 2012. "Unsettling Ageing in Three Novels by Pat Barker." *Ageing and Society* 32: 1382–98.

Featherstone, M., and M. Hepworth. 1989. "Ageing and Old Age: Reflections on the Postmodern Lifecourse." In *Becoming and Being Old: Social Approaches to Later Life*, edited by B. Bytheway, 143–57. London: Sage.

———. 1991. "The Mask of Aging and the Postmodern Lifecourse." In *The Body: Social Processes and Cultural Theory*, edited by M. Featherstone, M. Hepworth, and B. Turner, 371–89. London: Sage.

Fegerlin, A. and C. Schneider. 2004. "Enough: The Failure of the Living Will." *Hastings Center Report* 34 (2): 30–42.

Feinberg, L., S. Reinhard, A. Houser, and R. Choula. 2011. *Valuing the Invaluable, 2011 Update: The Growing Contributions and Costs of Family Caregiving*. Washington, DC: AARP Public Policy Institute.

Ferguson, A. 1995. "Feminist Communities and Moral Revolution." *Feminism and Community*, edited by P. Weiss and M. Friedman, 367–97. Philadelphia, PA: Temple University Press.

Fey-Yensan, N., L. McCormick, and C. English. 2002. "Body Image and Weight Preoccupation in Older Women: A Review." *Healthy Weight Journal* 16 (5): 68–71.

Fine, M. 2007. *A Caring Society? Care and the Dilemmas of Human Service in the Twenty-First Century*. New York: Palgrave Macmillan.

Fine, M., and C. Glendinning. 2005. "Dependence, Independence or Interdependence? Revisiting the Concepts of 'Care' and 'Dependency.'" *Ageing and Society* 25 (4): 601–21.

Fineman, M. 1999. "Cracking the Foundational Myths: Independence, Autonomy, and Self-Sufficiency." *American University Journal of Gender, Social Policy, and the Law* 8 (1): 13–29.

Fins, J. 1999. "Commentary: From Contract to Covenant in Advance Care Planning." *Journal of Law, Medicine, and Ethics* 27: 46–51.

Fins, J., B. Maltby, E. Friedmann, M. Greene, K. Norris, R. Adelman, and I. Byock. 2005. "Contracts, Covenants, Care Planning: An Empirical Study of the Moral Obligations of Patient and Proxy." *Journal of Pain and Symptom Management* 29 (1): 55–68.

Fiore, R., and H. Lindemann Nelson, eds. 2003. *Recognition, Responsibility, and Rights*. Lanham, MD: Rowman & Littlefield.

Flanagan, O. 1991. *Varieties of Moral Personality: Ethics and Psychological Realism*. Cambridge, MA: Harvard University Press.

Flatt, M. A., R. A. Settersten Jr., R. Ponsaran, and J. R. Fishman. 2013. "Are 'Anti-aging Medicine' and 'Successful Aging' Two Sides of the Same Coin? Views of Anti-aging Practitioners." *Journals of Gerontology Series B, Psychological Sciences and Social Sciences* 68 (6): 944–55.

Foley, K. 2005. "The Past and Future of Palliative Care." *Improving End of Life Care: Why Has It Been So Difficult? Hastings Center Report, Special Report* 35 (6): S42–S46.

Foucault, M. 1973. *The Birth of the Clinic: An Archaeology of Medical Perception.* New York: Pantheon.

Fox, R. W., and T. J. Lears, eds. 1993. *The Power of Culture: Critical Essays in American History.* Chicago: University of Chicago Press.

Fraser, Nancy. 1989. *Unruly Practices: Power, Discourse and Gender in Contemporary Social Theory.* Minneapolis: University of Minnesota Press.

Freedman, M. 1999. *Primetime: How Baby Boomers Will Revolutionize Retirement and Transform America.* New York: PublicAffairs.

Freund, P. 2001. "Bringing Society into the Body." *Theory and Society* 17 (6): 839–64.

Friedan, B. 1963. *The Feminine Mystique.* New York: W.W. Norton.

———. 1994. *The Fountain of Age.* New York: Simon & Schuster.

Furman, F. 1997. *Facing the Mirror: Old Women and Beauty Shop Culture.* New York: Routledge.

———. 1999. "There Are No Old Venuses: Older Women's Responses to Their Aging Bodies." In *Mother Time: Women, Aging, and Ethics*, edited by M. U. Walker, 7–22. Lanham, MD: Rowman & Littlefield.

Galston, W. 2012. *The Long-Term Is Now.* Washington, DC: Brookings.

Garner, D., ed. 1999. *Fundamentals of Feminist Gerontology.* New York: Haworth.

Genevay, B. 2011. "Choosing Time, Purpose, and Meaning in Old Age." *Aging Today* 32 (6): 20.

Genova, L. 2007. *Still Alice.* iUniverse.

Gergen, K., and M. Gergen. 2000. "The New Aging: Self Construction and Social Values." In *The Evolution of the Aging Self: The Social Impact on the Aging Process*, edited by K. W. Schaie and J. Hendricks, 281–306. New York: Springer.

Gerstel, N., and K. McGonagle. 1999. "Job Leaves and the Limits of the Family and Medical Leave Act." *Work and Occupations* 26 (4): 510–34.

Ghilarducci, T. 2007. "Pressures on Retirement Income Security." *Public Policy and Aging Report* 17 (2): 8–12.

Gibson, D. 1996. "Broken Down by Age and Gender: 'The Problem of Old Women' Redefined." *Gender and Society* 10 (4): 443–48.

Giddens, A. 1998. *The Third Way: The Renewal of Social Democracy.* Cambridge: Cambridge University Press.

Gilens, M., and B. Page. 2014. "Testing Theories of American Politics: Elites, Interest Groups, and Average Citizens." *Perspectives on Politics* 12 (3): 564–81.

Gilleard, C., and P. Higgs. 2000. *Cultures of Aging: Self, Citizen and the Body.* London: Prentice-Hall.

———. 2002. "The Third Age: Class, Cohort or Generation?" *Ageing and Society* 22: 369–82.

———. 2010. "Aging without Agency: Theorizing the Fourth Age." *Aging and Mental Health* 14: 121–28.

———. 2011. "Ageing Abjection and Embodiment in the Fourth Age." *Journal of Aging Studies* 25 (2): 135–42.

Gillick, M. 2006. *The Denial of Aging: Perpetual Youth, Eternal Life, and Other Dangerous Fantasies.* Cambridge, MA: Harvard University Press.

Gilligan, C. 1982. *In a Different Voice: Psychological Theory and Women's Development.* Cambridge: Cambridge University Press.

Gillon, S. 2004. *Boomer Nation: The Largest and Richest Generation and How It Changed America.* New York: Free Press.

Glenn, E. N. 2000. "Creating a Caring Society." *Contemporary Sociology* 29 (1): 84–94.

————. 2010. *Forced to Care: Coercion and Caregiving in America.* Cambridge, MA: Harvard University Press.

Goldsteen, M., R. Houtepen, I. Proot, H. Abu-Saad, C. Spreeuwenberg, and G. Widdershoven. 2006. "What Is a Good Death? Terminally Ill Patients Dealing with Normative Expectations around Death and Dying." *Patient Education and Counseling* 64: 378–86.

Goleman, D. 2013. "Rich People Just Care Less." *New York Times*, October 5. http://opinionator.blogs.nytimes.com/2013/10/05/rich-people-just-care-less.

Gonyea, J. 1994. "The Paradox of the Advantaged Elder and the Feminization of Poverty." *Social Work* 39 (1): 35–41.

Gonyea, J., and N. Hooyman. 2005. "Reducing Poverty among Older Women: Social Security Reform and Gender Equity." *Families in Society: The Journal of Contemporary Social Services* (special issue) 86 (3): 338–46.

Gooberman-Hill, R., S. Ayis, and S. Ebrahim. 2003. "Understanding Long-Standing Illness among Older People." *Social Science and Medicine* 56: 2555–64.

Gordon, S. 2013. "Physician-Assisted Suicide Rarely Used, Study Finds." *U.S. News and World Report*, April 10. http://health.usnews.com/health-news/news/articles/2013/04/10/physician-assisted-suicide-program-rarely-used-study-finds.

Gott, M. 2006. "Sexual Health and the New Aging." *Age and Ageing* 35: 106–7.

Gott, M., and S. Hinchliff. 2003. "How Important Is Sex in Later Life? The Views of Older People." *Social Science and Medicine* 56 (6): 1617–28.

Gottfried, H., ed. 1996. *Feminism and Social Change.* Urbana: University of Illinois Press.

Gould, D. 2004. "Family Caregivers and the Health Care System: Findings from a National Survey." In *The Cultures of Caregiving: Conflict and Common Ground among Families, Health Professionals, and Policymakers*, edited by C. Levine and T. Murray, 15–34. Baltimore, MD: Johns Hopkins University Press.

Greenberg. J., J. Schimel, and A. Mertens. 2002. "Ageism: Denying the Face of the Future." In *Ageism: Stereotyping and Prejudice against Older Persons*, edited by T. Nelson, 27–48. Cambridge, MA: MIT Press.

Grefe, D. 2011. "Combating Ageism with Narrative and Intergroup Contact: Possibilities of Intergenerational Connections." *Pastoral Psychology* 60: 99–105.

Grenier, A. 2005. "The Contextual and Social Locations of Older Women's Experiences of Disability and Decline." *Journal of Aging Studies* 19 (2): 131–46.

Grenier, A., and J. Hanley. 2007. "Older Women and 'Frailty': Gendered and Embodied Resistance." *Current Sociology* 55 (2): 211–28.

Grogan, C., and C. Andrews. 2010. "The Politics of Aging within Medicaid." In *The New Politics of Old Age Policy*, 2nd ed., edited by R. Hudson, 275–306. Baltimore, MD: Johns Hopkins University Press.

Gross, J. 2007. "Study Finds Higher Costs for Caregivers of Elderly." *New York Times*, November 19. http://www.nytimes.com/2007/11/19/us/caregiver.html.

Grumbach, D. 1991. *Coming into the End Zone: A Memoir.* New York: Norton.

Guillemin, J. 1995. "Planning to Die." In *Where Medicine Fails*, 5th ed., edited by C. Weaver and A. Strauss, 73–80. New Brunswick, NJ: Transaction.

Gullette, M. M. 1997. *Declining to Decline: Cultural Combat and the Politics of Midlife.* Charlottesville: University of Virginia Press.

————. 2004. *Aged by Culture.* Chicago: University of Chicago Press.

————. 2011. *Agewise: Fighting the New Ageism in America.* Chicago: University of Chicago Press.

Haber, C. 1983. *Beyond Sixty-Five: The Dilemma of Old Age in America's Past.* New York: Cambridge University Press.

————. 2002. "Anti-Aging: Why Now? A Historical Framework for Understanding the Contemporary Enthusiasm." *Generations* 25 (4): 9–14.

Haber, C., and B. Gratton. 1994. *Old Age and the Search for Security*. Bloomington: University of Indiana Press.

Hacker, J. 2004. "Privatizing Risk without Privatizing the Welfare State: The Hidden Politics of Social Policy Retrenchment in the United States." *American Political Science Review* 98 (2): 243–60.

————. 2007. "'The Great Risk Shift': Issues for Aging and Public Policy." In *Public Policy and Aging Report* 17 (2): 1, 3–7.

Hajjar, I. 2002. "Age-Related Bias in the Management of Hypertension: A National Survey of Physicians' Opinions on Hypertension in Elderly Adults." *Journals of Gerontology Series A, Biological Sciences and Medical Sciences* 57: M487–91.

Halberg, I. R. 2004. "Death and Dying from Old People's Point of View: A Literature Review." *Aging Clinical and Experimental Research* 16: 87–103.

Hamington, M., and D. Miller, eds. 2006. *Socializing Care: Feminist Ethics and Public Issues*. Lanham, MD: Rowman & Littlefield.

Harding, S., ed. 2003. *The Feminist Standpoint Theory Reader: Intellectual and Political Controversies*. New York: Routledge.

Hardwig, J. 2009. "Going to Meet Death: The Art of Dying in the Twenty-First Century." *Hastings Center Report* 39: 37–45.

Harper, S. 1997. "Constructing Later Life/Constructing the Body: Some Thoughts from Feminist Theory." In *Critical Approaches to Aging and Later Life*, edited by A. Jamieson, S. Harper, and C. Victor, 160–72. Buckingham: Open University Press.

Harrington Meyer, M. 1996. "Making Claims as Workers or Wives: The Distribution of Social Security Benefits." *American Sociological Review* 61 (3): 449–65.

————. 2000. *Care and Equality: Introducing a New Family Politics*. New York: Knopf.

————. 2010. "Shifting Risk and Responsibility: The State and Inequality in Old Age." In *The New Politics of Old Age*, 2nd ed., edited by R. Hudson, 42–63. Baltimore, MD: Johns Hopkins University Press.

Harrington Meyer, M., and C. Estes. 2009. "A New Social Security Agenda." *Public Policy and Aging Report* 19 (2): 7–12

Harris, B., and M. Kearney. 2013. "A Dozen Facts about America's Struggling Lower-Middle-Class." Policy paper, Hamilton Project, Brookings Institution. http://www.brookings.edu/research/reports/2013/12/12-facts-lower-middle-class.

Harrison, L., and S. Huntington, eds. 2000. *Culture Matters: How Values Shape Human Progress*. New York: Basic.

Hartmann, H. 2012. "Can Boomer Women Afford to Retire?" Washington, D.C. Institute for Women's Policy Research. Available at http://www.iwpr.org/publications/pubs/can-boomer-women-afford-to-retire.

Hartmann, H., and A. English. 2009. "Older Women's Retirement Security: A Primer." *Journal of Women, Politics and Policy* 30: 109–40.

Hartmann, H., J. Hayes, and R. Drago. 2011. "Social Security Especially Vital to Women and People of Color, Men Increasingly Reliant. D494. Washington, DC: Institute for Women's Policy Research.

Harvey, D. 2006. "Neoliberalism as Creative Destruction." *Geografiska Annaler: Series B, Human Geography* 88 (2): 145–58.

Hatch, L. 2005. "Gender and Ageism." *Generations* 29 (Fall): 19–24.

Havighurst, R. 1961. "Successful Aging." *The Gerontologist* 1 (1): 8–13.

Hawkins, N., P. Ditto, J. Danks, and W. Smucker. 2005. "Micromanaging Death: Process Preferences, Values, and Goals in End-of-Life Medical Decision-Making." *Gerontologist* 45: 107–17.

Hayes, C. 2012. *Twilight of the Elites: America after Meritocracy*. New York: Crown.

Hayflick, L. 1994. *How and Why We Age*. New York: Ballantine.

Hayward, M., T. Miles, E. Crimmins, and Y. Yang. 2000. "The Significance of Socioeconomic Status in Explaining the Racial Gap in Chronic Health Conditions." *American Sociological Review* 65 (6): 910–30.

Healy, S. 1999. "Growing to Be an Old Woman: Aging and Ageism." In *Worlds of Difference: Inequality in the Aging Experience*, edited by E. Stoller and R. Gibson. Thousand Oaks, CA: Pine Forge.

Heilbrun, C. 1997. *The Last Gift of Time: Life beyond Sixty*. New York: Ballantine.

Henchoz, K., S. Cavalli, and M. Girardin. 2008. "Health Perception and Health Status in Advanced Old Age: A Paradox of Association." *Journal of Aging Studies* 22: 282–90.

Hepworth, M. 1995. "Positive Ageing: What Is the Message?" *The Sociology of Health Promotion* 175.

Herd, P. 2005. "Reforming a Breadwinner Welfare State: Gender, Race, Class and Social Security Reform." *Social Forces* 83 (4): 1365–93.

———. 2009. "The Two-Legged Stool: The Reconfiguration of Risk in Retirement Income Security." *Generations* 33 (3): 12–18.

———. 2002. "Carework: Invisible Civic Engagement." *Gender and Society* 16 (5): 665–88.

Herzlich, C., and J. Pierret. 1987. *Illness and Self in Society*. Baltimore, MD: Johns Hopkins University Press.

Hickman, S. 2005. "The POLST Paradigm: Respecting the Wishes of Patients and Families." *Annals of Long-Term Care* 15 (9): 33–40.

Hickman, S., B. Hammes, A. Moss, and S. Tolle. 2005. "Hope for the Future: Achieving the Original Intent of Advance Directives." *Hastings Center Report* 35 (6): S26–S30.

High, D. 1991. "A New Myth about Families of Older People." *Gerontologist* 31 (5): 611–18.

Hillyer, B. 1998. "The Embodiment of Old Women: Silences." *Frontiers: A Journal of Women's Studies* 19 (1): 48–60.

Hochschild, A. 1989. *Second Shift: Working Parents and the Revolution at Home*. New York: Viking.

Hoffmaster, B. 2006. "What Does Vulnerability Mean?" *Hastings Center Report* 36 (2): 38–45.

Hofmann, J., N. Wenger, R. Davis, et al. 1997. "Patient Preferences for Communication with Physicians about End-of-Life Decisions." *Annals of Internal Medicine* 127: 1–12.

Holstein, M. 1994. "Taking Next Steps: Gerontological Education, Research, and the Literary Imagination." *Gerontologist* 34 (6): 822–27.

———. 1997. "Reflections on Death and Dying." *Academic Medicine* 72 (10): 848–55.

———. 1999. "Home Care: A Case Study in Injustice." In *Mother Time: Women, Ethics and Aging*, edited by M. U. Walker, 227–44. Lanham, MD: Rowman & Littlefield.

———. 2001–2002. "A Feminist Perspective on Anti-aging Medicine." *Generations* 25 (4): 38–43.

———. 2006. "A Critical Reflection on Civic Engagement." *Public Policy and Agency Report* 16 (4): 1, 21–26.

———. 2007. "Long-Term Care, Feminism, and an Ethics of Solidarity." In *Challenges of an Aging Society: Ethical Dilemmas and Political Issues*, edited by R. Pruchno and M. Smyer, 157–74. Baltimore, MD: Johns Hopkins University Press.

————. 2010. "Ethics and Aging: Retrospectively and Prospectively." In *A Guide to Humanistic Studies in Aging: What Does It Mean to Grow Old?*, edited by T. Cole, R. Ray, and R. Kastenbaum, 244–70. Baltimore, MD: Johns Hopkins University Press.

Holstein, M., and T. Cole. 1995. "Long-Term Care: A Historical Reflection." In *Long-Term Care Decisions: Ethical and Conceptual Dimensions*, edited by L. McCoulough and N. Wilson, 15–34. Baltimore, MD: Johns Hopkins University Press.

Holstein, M., and J. Gubrium. 2000. *The Self We Live By*. New York: Oxford University Press.

Holstein, M., and M. Minkler. 2003. "Self, Society and the 'New Gerontology.'" *Gerontologist* 43 (6): 787–96.

————. 2007. "Critical Gerontology: Reflections for the 21st Century." In *Critical Perspectives on Ageing Societies*, edited by M. Bernard, 13–26. Bristol, UK: Policy Press.

Holstein, M., J. Parks, and M. Waymack. 2011. *Ethics, Aging and Society: The Critical Turn*. New York: Springer.

Hooyman, N. 1999. "Research on Older Women: Where Is Feminism?" *Gerontologist* 39 (1): 115–18.

Hooyman, N., and J. Gonyea. 1995. *Feminist Perspectives on Family Care: Politics for Gender Justice*. Thousand Oaks, CA: Sage.

Hopp, F., N. Thornton, L. Martin, and R. Zalenski. 2012. "Life Disruption, Life Continuation: Contrasting Themes in the Lives of African-American Elders with Advanced Heart Failure." *Social Work in Health Care* 51 (2): 149–72.

Horton, S., and J. Baker. 2008. "Understanding Seniors' Perceptions and Stereotypes of Aging." *Educational Gerontology* 34: 997–1017.

Horton, S., J. Baker, J. Cote, and J. Deakin. 2008. "Understanding Seniors' Perceptions and Stereotypes of Aging." *Educational Gerontology* 34: 997–1017.

Howarth, G. 1998. "'Just Live for Today': Living, Caring, Ageing and Dying." *Ageing and Society* 18: 673–89.

————. 2010a. "Analysis and Advocacy in Home- and Community-Based Care: An Approach in Three Parts." *Journal of Gerontological Social Work* 52: 3–20.

————. 2010b. "Theoretical Approaches to the Development of Aging Policy." In *The New Politics of Old Age Policy*, 2nd ed., edited by R. Hudson, 108–40. Baltimore, MD: Johns Hopkins University Press.

Hudson, R. 1999. "Conflict in Today's Aging Politics: New Population Encounters Old Ideology." *Social Science Review* 73 (3): 358–79.

————. 2007. "The Political Paradoxes of Thinking Outside the Life-Cycle Boxes." In *Challenges of an Aging Society: Ethics Dilemmas, Political Issues*, edited by R. Pruchno, R. and M. Smyer, 268–84. Baltimore, MD: Johns Hopkins University Press.

Hudson, R., and J. Gonyea. 2012. "Baby Boomers and the Shifting Political Construction of Old Age." *Gerontologist* 52 (2): 272–82.

Hung, L.-W., G. Kempen, and N. DeVries. 2010. "Cross-cultural Comparison between Academic Views and Lay Views of Healthy Aging: A Literature Review." *Ageing and Society* 30 (8): 1373–91.

Hurd, L. 1999. "'We're Not Old!' Older Women's Negotiation of Aging and Oldness." *Journal of Aging Studies* 13 (4): 419–39.

Hurd Clarke, L. 2001. "Older Women's Bodies and the Self: The Construction of Identity in Later Life. *CRSA/RCSA* 38 (4): 442–64.

————. 2011. *Facing Age: Women Growing Older in Anti-aging Culture*. Lanham, MD: Rowman & Littlefield.

Hurd Clarke, L., and E. Bennett. 2013. "'You Learn to Live with All the Things That Are Wrong with You': Gender and the Experience of Multiple Chronic Conditions in Later Life." *Ageing and Society* 33: 342–60.

Hurd Clarke, L., and M. Griffin. 2008. "Visible and Invisible Ageing: Beauty Work as a Response to Ageism." *Journal of Aging Studies* 28: 653–74.

Hurd Clarke, L., M. Griffin, and PACC Research Team. 2008. "Failing Bodies: Body Image and Multiple Chronic Conditions in Later Life." *Qualitative Health Research* 18: 1084–95.

Hurd Clarke, L., A. Korotchenko, and A. Bundon. 2012. "'The Calendar Is Just about Up': Older Adults with Multiple Chronic Conditions Reflect on Death and Dying." *Ageing and Society* 32 (8): 1399–1417.

Hutchins, L., J. Unger, J. Crowley, C. Coltman Jr., and K. Albain. 1999. "Underrepresentation of Patients 65 Years of Age or Older in Cancer-Treatment Trials." *New England Journal of Medicine* 341 (27): 2061–67.

Imel, S. 1996. *Older Workers: Myths and Realities*. Columbus, OH: ERIC Clearinghouse on Adult, Career and Vocational Education.

Institute for Women's Policy Research. June 2011. "Six Key Facts on Women and Social Security." Washington, DC: IWPR. http://www.wowonline.org/wp-content/uploads/2013/09/Living-Below-the-Line-Economic-Insecurity-and-Older-Americans-Women-Sept-2013.pdf.

Jacobs, R. 2002. "The Narrative Integration of Personal and Collective Identity in Social Movements." In *Narrative Impact: Social and Cognitive Foundations*, edited by M. Green, J. Strange, and T. Brock, 205–28. Mahwah, NJ: Erlbaum.

Jacoby, S. 2011. *Never Say Die: The Myth and Marketing of the New Old Age*. New York: Pantheon.

Jaggar, A. 1989. "Love and Knowledge: Emotion in Feminist Epistemology." *Inquiry: An Interdisciplinary Journal of Philosophy* 32 (2): 151–76.

Jennings, B., D. Callahan, and A. Caplan. 1988. "Ethical Challenges of Chronic Illness." *Hastings Center Report* 18 (1): S1–S6.

Johnson, H. 1982. "Three Perspectives on the 1981 White House Conference on Aging." *Gerontologist* 22 (2): 125–26.

Johnson, R., and J. Mutchler. 2013. "The Emergence of a Positive Gerontology: From Disengagement to Social Involvement." *Gerontologist* doi:10.1093/geront/gnt099.

Jönson, H. 2013. "We Will Be Different! Ageism and the Temporal Construction of Old Age." *Gerontologist* 53 (2): 198–204.

Kahn, R. 2002. "Guest Editorial on 'Successful Aging and Well-Being': Self-Related with Rowe and Kahn." *Gerontologist* 42 (6): 725–26.

Kane, R. 2001. "Long-Term Care and a Good Quality of Life: Bringing Them Closer Together." *Gerontologist* 41 (3): 293–304.

Kane, R., and R. Kane. 2005. "Ageism in Healthcare and Long-Term Care." *Generations* 29 (3): 49–54.

Karlawish, J. 2014. "Too Young to Die, Too Old to Worry." *New York Times*, September 21, SR5.

Katz, S. 2000. "Busy Bodies: Activity, Aging, and the Management of Everyday Life." *Journal of Aging Studies* 14 (2): 135–52.

———. 2001–2002. "Growing Older without Aging? Positive Aging, Anti-ageism, and Anti-aging." *Generations* 25 (4): 27–32.

Katz, S., and T. Calasanti. 2014. "Critical Perspectives on Successful Aging: Does It 'Appeal More Than It Illuminates'?" *Gerontologist*, doi: 10.1093/geront/gnu027.

Katz, S., and B. Marshall. 2003. "New Sex for Old: Lifestyle, Consumerism, and the Ethics of Aging Well." *Journal of Aging Studies* 17: 3–16.

Kaufman, S. 1987. *The Ageless Self: Sources of Meaning in Late Life*. New York: New American Library.

Kaufman, S. 1988a. "Illness, Biography, and the Interpretation of Self Following a Stroke." *Journal of Aging Studies* 2: 217–27.

———. 1988b. "Toward a Phenomenology of Boundaries in Medicine: Chronic Illness in Case of Stroke." *Medical Anthropology Quarterly* 2 (4): 338–54.

———. 2000. "Senescence, Decline, and the Quest for a Good Death: Contemporary Dilemmas and Historical Antecedents." *Journal of Aging Studies* 14 (1): 1–23.

———. 2002. "A Community Hospital Experience and Meaning at the End of Life." *Gerontologist* 42 (Suppl. 3): 34–39.

———. 2006. *. . . And a Time to Die: How American Hospitals Shape the End of Life*. Chicago: University of Chicago Press.

———. 2009. "Making Longevity in an Aging Society: Linking Ethical Sensibility and Medicare Spending." *Medical Anthropology* 28: 317–25.

———. 2010. "The Age of Reflexive Longevity." In *A Guide to Humanistic Studies in Aging: What Does It Mean to Grow Old?* edited by T. Cole, R. Ray, and R. Kastenbaum, 225–241. Baltimore, MD: Johns Hopkins University Press.

Kaufman, S., and L. Fjord. 2011. "Medicine, Ethics, and Reflexive Longevity: Governing Time and Treatment in an Aging Society." *Medical Anthropology Quarterly* 25 (2): 209–31.

Kaufman, S., J. Shim, and A. Russ. 2004. "Revisiting the Biomedicalization of Aging: Clinical Trends and Ethical Challenges." *Gerontologist* 44: 731–38.

Kaye, H. 2009. "Death and Us." *Society* 46: 237–39.

Kessler, E.-M., K. Rakoczy, and U. M. Staudinger. 2004. "The Portrayal of Older People in Prime Time Television Series: The Match with Gerontological Evidence." *Ageing and Society* 24 (4): 531–52.

Kingson, E., and N. Altman. 2011. "The Social Security Retirement Age(s) Debate: Perspectives and Consequences." In *Public Policy and Aging Report* 21 (2): 1–7.

Kingson, E., B. Hirshown, and J. Cornman. 1986. *Ties That Bind*. Washington, DC: Seven Locks.

Kingson, E., and J. Quadagno. 1995. "Social Security: Marketing Radical Reform." *Generations* 14 (3): 43–49.

Kite, M., and L. S. Wagner. 2002. "Attitudes toward Older Adults." In *Ageism: Stereotyping and Prejudice against Older People*, edited by T. Nelson, 129–62. Cambridge, MA: MIT Press.

Kittay, E. F. 1999. *Love's Labor: Essays on Women, Equality, and Dependency*. New York: Routledge.

Kittay, E. F., and E. Feder. 2002. *The Subject of Care: Feminist Perspectives on Dependency*. Lanham, MD: Rowman & Littlefield.

Kitwood, T. 1993. "Toward a Theory of Dementia Care: The Interpersonal Process." *Ageing and Society* 13 (1): 51–67.

Kitwood, T., and K. Bredin. 1992. "A New Approach to the Evaluation of Dementia Care." *Journal of Advances in Health and Nursing Care* 1 (5): 41–60.

Klein, E. 2011. "What the Social Security Trust Fund Is Worth." *Washington Post*, March 11. http://voices.washingtonpost.com/ezra-klein/2011/03/what_the_social_security_trust.html.

Kleinman, A. 1988. *The Illness Narratives: Suffering, Healing, and the Human Condition*. New York: Basic.

———. 1993. "What Is Specific to Western Medicine?" In *Companion Encyclopedia of the History of Medicine*, vol. 1, edited by W. F. Bynum and R. Porter, 15–23. London: Routledge.

Krakauer, E., C. Crenner, and K. Fox. 2002. "Barriers to Optimum End-of-Life Care for Minority Patients." *Journal of the American Geriatrics Society* 50: 182–90.

Kristof, N. 2014. "She Gets No Respect: Sexism Persists Even among the Enlightened." *New York Times*, June 12, A31.

Krugman, P. 2010. "Attacking Social Security." *New York Times*, August 16, A19. http://www.nytimes.com/2010/08/16/opinion/16krugman.html.

———. 2011. "Life, Death and Deficits." *New York Times*, November 15. http://www.nytimes.com/2012/11/16/opinion/life-death-and-deficits.html.

———. 2014. "Secret Deficit Lovers." *New York Times*, October 10, A23.

Krysl, M. 2014. "Passing It On." In *A Story Larger Than My Own: Women Writers Look Back on Their Lives and Careers*, edited by J. Burroway, 94–103. Chicago: University of Chicago Press.

Kübler-Ross, E. 1970. *On Death and Dying*. London: Tavistock.

Kuhn, M., with C. Long and L. Quinn. 1991. *No Stone Unturned: The Life and Times of Maggie Kuhn*. New York: Ballantine.

Kuttner, R. 2012. "Greedy Geezers, Reconsidered." *American Prospect*, December 3. http://www.prospect.org/article/greedy-geezers-reconsidered.

Ladimer, B. 1993. "Colette: Rewriting the Script for the Aging Woman." In *Ageing and Gender in Literature: Studies in Creativity*, edited by A. Wyatt-Brown and J. Rossen, 242–57. Charlottesville: University of Virginia Press.

Lakoff, G. 1996. *Moral Politics: What Conservatives Know That Liberals Don't*. Chicago: University of Chicago Press.

Lamb, S. 2014. "'Permanent Personhood or Meaningful Decline': Toward a Critical Anthropology of Successful Aging." *Journal of Aging Studies* 29: 41–52.

Lane, C. 2013. "Pandering to Seniors over Social Security." *Washington Post*, December 4. http://www.washingtonpost.com/opinions/charles-land-is-boosting-social-security-thethg-course2113/12/04/3b2a444e-5d02-11e3-95c2-13623eb2b0e1_print.html.

Lasch, C. 1979. *Culture of Narcissism: American Life in an Age of Diminished Expectations*. New York: Norton.

Laslett, P. 1991. *A Fresh Map of Life: The Emergence of the Third Age*. Cambridge, MA: Harvard University Press.

Laws, G. 1995. "Understanding Ageism: Lessons from Feminism and Postmodernism." *Gerontologist* 35 (1): 112–18.

Laz, C. 2003. "Age Embodied." *Journal of Aging Studies* 17: 503–19.

Lebacqz, K. 1995. "Feminism." In *The Encyclopedia of Bioethics*, edited by W. T. Reich. New York: Simon & Schuster.

Leibovitch, M. 2013. *This Town: Two Parties and a Funeral, Plenty of Valet Parking in American's Gilded Capital.* New York: Blue Rider Press.

Letter of Experts Opposed to Cuts in Social Security Benefits. 2011. http://strengthensocialsecurity.org/letter-of-experts-opposed-to-cuts-in-social-security.

Levitsky, S. 2010. "Caregiving and the Construction of Political Claims for Long-Term Care Policy Reform. In *The New Politics of Old Age*, 2nd ed., edited by R. Hudson, 208–30. Baltimore, MD: Johns Hopkins University Press.

Lewis, D., K. Medvedev, and D. Seponski. 2011. "Awakening to the Desires of Older Women: Deconstructing Ageism within Fashion Magazines." *Journal of Aging Studies* 25: 101–109.

Liao, M. 2006. "The Right of Children to Be Loved." *Journal of Political Philosophy* 14 (4): 420–40.

Lieberman, T. 2013. "The Enduring Myth of the Greedy Geezer." *Columbia Journalism Review*, March 14. http://www.cjr.org/united_states_project/the_enduring_myth_of_the_greed.php?.

Lindau, S., P. Schumm, E. Laumann, W. Levinson, C. O'Muircheartaigh, and L. Waite. 2007. "A Study of Sexuality and Health among Older Adults in the United States." *New England Journal of Medicine* 357: 762–74.

Lindemann, H. 2006. *An Invitation to Feminist Ethics*. New York: McGraw-Hill.

Lindemann Nelson, H. 1999. "Stories of My Old Age." In *Mother Time: Women, Aging, and Ethics*, edited by M. U. Walker, 75–96. Lanham, MD: Rowman & Littlefield.

———. 2001. *Damaged Identities, Narrative Repair*. Ithaca, NY: Cornell University Press.

Liptak, A. 2014. "Kagan Says Her Path to Supreme Court Was Made Smoother by Ginsburg's." *New York Times*, February 11, A14.

Lively, P. 1998. *Spiderweb: A Novel*. New York: Viking.

———. 2012. *How It All Began: A Novel*. New York: Viking.

Lloyd, L. 2004. "Mortality and Morality: Ageing and the Ethics of Care." *Ageing and Society* 24 (2): 235–56.

———. 2006. "A Caring Profession? The Ethics of Care and Social Work with Older People." *British Journal of Social Work* 3 (7): 1171–85.

Lloyd, L., M. Calnan, A. Cameron, J. Seymour, and R. Smith. 2014. "Identity in the Fourth Age: Perseverance, Adaptation and Maintaining Dignity." *Ageing and Society* 34 (1): 1–19.

Lo, B. 1995. "Improving Care at the End of Life: Why Is It So Hard?" *JAMA* 274 (20): 1634–36.

Long, J,. J. Ickovics, T. Gill, and R. Horwitz. 2002. "Social Class and Mortality in Older Women." *Journal of Clinical Epidemiology* 55 (10): 952–58.

Lowrey, A. 2012. "Tax Breaks and Savings Play a Role in Budget Talks." *New York Times*, November 26, A19.

Lugones, M. 1987. "Playfulness, 'World'-Travelling, and Loving Perception." *Hypatia* 2 (2): 3–20.

Lugones, M., and E. Spellman. 1983. "Have We Got a Theory for You! Feminist Theory, Cultural Imperialism, and the Demand for the Woman's Voice." *Women Studies International Forum* 6 (6): 573–81.

Lynn, J. 2005. "Living Long in Fragile Health: The New Demographics Shape End of Life Care." *Improving Care at the End of Life: Why Has It Been So Difficult? Hastings Center Special Report* 35: S14–S18.

MacDonald, B., with C. Rich. 1991. *Look Me in the Eye: Old Women, Aging, and Ageism*, 2nd ed. San Francisco: Spinsters Ink.

Mackenzie, C. 2000. "Imagining Oneself Otherwise." In *Relational Autonomy: Feminist Perspectives on Autonomy, Agency, and the Social Self*, edited by C. Mackenzie and N. Stoljar, 124–50. New York: Oxford University Press.

Mackenzie, C., and J. Scully. 2007. "Moral Imagination, Disability and Embodiment." *Journal of Applied Philosophy* 24 (4): 335–51.

Mackenzie, C., and N. Stoljar, eds. 2000. *Relational Autonomy: Feminist Perspectives on Autonomy, Agency, and the Social Self*. New York: Oxford University Press.

MacRae, H. 2010. "Managing Identity While Living with Alzheimer's Disease." *Qualitative Health Research* 20: 293–305.

Madoff, R. 2014. "A Better Way to Encourage Charity." *New York Times*, October 5, A23. http://www.nytimes.com/2014/10/06/opinion/a-better-way-to-encourage-charity.html.

Margalit, A. 1996. *The Decent Society*. Cambridge, MA: Harvard University Press.

Marks, N., and. J. May. 1997. *Family Caregiving: Contemporary Trends and Issues*. NSFH Working Paper no. 78. Center for Demography and Ecology, University of Wisconsin, Madison.

Markus, M. 1987. "Women, Success and Civil Society: Submission to, or Subversion of, the Achievement Principle." In *Feminism as Critique*, edited by S. Benhabib and D. Cornell, 96–110. Minneapolis: University of Minnesota Press.

Marshall, B. 2011. "The Graying of 'Sexual Health': A Critical Research Agenda." *Canadian Review of Sociology* 48 (4): 390–413.

———. 2012. "Medicalization and the Refashioning of Age-Related Limits on Sexuality." *Journal of Sex Research* 49 (4): 337–43.

Marshall, P. 1995. "The SUPPORT Study: Who's Talking?" Special supplement, *Hastings Center Report* 25: S11.

Martensen, R. 2011. "Words Matter: How 'EOL' Rhetoric Undermines Good Palliative Care." Hastings Center Bioethics Forum, January 21. http://www.thehastingscenter.org/ Bioethicsforum/Post.aspx?id=5109.

Martinson, M. 2006–2007. "Opportunities or Obligations? Civic Engagement and Older Adults." *Generations* 30 (4): 59–65.

Martinson, M., and J. Halperin. 2011. "Ethical Implications of the Promotion of Elder Volunteerism: A Critical Perspective." *Journal of Aging Studies* 25: 427–35.

Martinson, M., and M. Minkler. 2006. "Civic Engagement and Older Adults: A Critical Perspective." *Gerontologist* 46: 318–24.

Mashaw, J. 2005. "Social Insurance and the American Social Contract." In *In Search of Retirement Security*, edited by T. Ghilarducci, A. Ooms, J. Palmer, and C. Hill, 95–102. New York: Century Press.

Maslow, A. 1943. "A Theory of Human Motivation." *Psychological Review* 50: 370–96.

Mayhard, M., H. Afshar, M. Franks, and S. Wray. 2008. *Women in Later Life: Exploring "Race" and Ethnicity*. Berkshire, UK: Open University Press.

McCorkle, J. 2013. *Life after Life*. Chapel Hill, NC: Algonquin Books of Chapel Hill.

McGhee, H. 2012. "Millennials and the American Dream." Presentation at Chicago Humanities Festival, Chicago, IL.

McHugh, K. 2000. "The 'Ageless Self'? Emplacement of Identities in Sun-Belt Retirement Communities." *Journal of Aging Studies* 14 (1): 103–14.

———. 2003. "Three Faces of ageism: Society, Image and Place." *Ageing and Society* 23 (2): 165–85.

McIntyre, G. 2012. "Chained CPI: A Hidden Benefit Cut Targeting the Most Vulnerable." *Aging Today* 18 (1). http://www.nsclc.org/wp-content/uploads/2012/01/ATv33n1-McIntyre. pdf.

McLaughlin, S., C. Connell, S. Heerings, L. Li, and J. S. Roberts. 2009. "Successful Aging in the United States: Prevalence Estimates from a National Sample of Older Adults." *Journals of Gerontology Series B, Psychological Sciences and Social Sciences* 65 (2): 216–26.

McMullin, J. A., and E. D. Berger. 2006. "Gendered Ageism/Age(ed) Sexism. The Case of Unemployed Older Workers." In *Age Matters: Realigning Feminist Thought*, edited by T. Calasanti and K. Slevin, 201–24. New York: Routledge.

McMullin, J. A., and J. Cairney. 2004. "Self-Esteem and the Intersection of Age, Class, and Gender." *Journal of Aging Studies* 18: 75–90.

MetLife Mature Market Institute. 1999. *The MetLife Juggling Act Study: Balancing Caregiving with Work and the Costs Involved*. New York: Metropolitan Life Insurance Company. http:// www.caregiving.org/data/jugglingstudy.pdf.

————. 2011. *The MetLife Study of Caregiving Costs to Working Caregivers: Double Jeopardy for Baby Boomers Caring for Their Parents*. New York: Metropolitan Life Insurance Company. https://www.metlife.com/mmi/research/caregiving-cost-working-caregivers. html#key%20findings.

Meyer, M., and C. Estes. 2009. "A New Social Security Agenda." *Public Policy and Aging Report* 19 (2): 7–12.

Meyers, D. 1989. *Self, Society, and Personal Choice*. New York: Columbia University Press.

————. 1994. *Subjection and Subjectivity: Psychoanalytic Feminism and Moral Philosophy*. New York: Routledge.

————. 1997a. "Emotion and Heterodox Moral Perception: An Essay in Moral Social Psychology." In *Feminists Rethink the Self*, edited by D. Meyers, 197–218. Boulder, CO: Westview.

————. 1997b. *Feminists Rethink the Self*. Boulder, CO: Westview.

————. 1999. "Miroir, Memoire, Mirage: Appearance, Aging, and Women." In *Mother Time: Women, Aging, and Ethics*, edited by M. U. Walker, 23–44. Lanham, MD: Rowman & Littlefield.

————. 2001. "Social Groups and Individual Identity: Individuality, Agency, and Theory." In *Feminists Doing Ethics*, edited by P. DesAustels and J. Waugh, 35–44. Lanham, MD: Rowman & Littlefield.

————. 2002. *Gender in the Mirror: Cultural Imagery and Women's Agency*. New York: Oxford University Press.

————. 2003. "Frontiers of Individuality: Embodiment and Relationships in Cultural Context. *History and Theory* 42 (2): 271–85.

Miller, N. 1999. "The Marks of Time." In *Figuring Age: Women, Bodies, Generations*, edited by K. Woodward, 3–19. Bloomington: Indiana University Press.

Minichiello, V., J. Browne, and H. Kendig. 2000. "Perceptions and Consequences of Ageism: Views of Older People." *Ageing and Society* 20: 253–78.

Minkler, M. 1990. "Aging and Disability: Behind and beyond the Stereotypes." *Journal of Aging Studies* 4 (3): 245–60.

————. 1991. "Gold in Gray: Reflections on Business's Discovery of the Elderly Market." In *Critical Perspectives on Aging: The Political and Moral Economy of Growing Old*, edited by M. Minkler and C. Estes. Amityville, NY: Baywood.

————. 1996. "Critical Perspectives on Ageing: New Challenges for Gerontology." *Ageing and Society* 16: 467–87.

Minkler, M., and C. Estes, eds. 1991. *Critical Perspectives on Aging: The Political and Moral Economy of Growing Old*. Amityville, NY: Baywood.

————. 1999. *Critical Gerontology: Perspectives from Political and Moral Economy*. Amityville, NY: Baywood.

Minkler, M., and P. Fadem. 2002. "'Successful Aging': A Disability Perspective." *Journal of Disability Policy Studies* 12: 229–35.

Minkler, M., E. Fuller-Thompson, and J. Guralnick. 2006. "Gradient of Disability across the Socioeconomic Spectrum in the United States." *New England Journal of Medicine* 355 (7): 695–703.

Minkler, M., and M. Holstein. 2008. "From Civil Rights to . . . Civic Engagement? Concerns of Two Older Critical Gerontologists about a 'New Social Movement' and What It Portends." *Journal of Aging Studies* 22: 196–204.

Minow, M. 1990. *Making All the Difference: Inclusion, Exclusion and American Law*. Ithaca, NY: Cornell University Press.

Minnich, E. K. 1990. *Transforming Knowledge*. Philadelphia, PA: Temple University Press.

Mishler, E. 1984. *The Discourse of Medicine: Dialectics of Medical Interviews*. Norwood, NJ: Ablex.

Moody, H. R. 1988. "From Informed Consent to Negotiated Consent." *Gerontologist* 28 (Suppl.): 64–70.

———. 1994. *Aging: Concepts and Controversies*. Thousand Oaks, CA: Pine Forge Press.

———. 2009. "Aging, Generational Opposition, and the Future of the Family." In *Challenges of an Aging Society*, edited by R. Pruchno and M. Smyer, 175–89. Baltimore, MD: Johns Hopkins University Press.

Morell, C. 2003. "Empowerment and Long-Living Women: Return to the Rejected Body." *Journal of Aging Studies* 17: 69–85.

Morgan, K. P. 2003. "Women and the Knife: Cosmetic Surgery and the Colonization of Women's Bodies." In *The Politics of Women's Bodies*, 2nd ed., edited by R. Weitz, 164–83. New York: Oxford University Press.

Morrow-Howell, N. 2000. *Productive Engagement of Older Adults: Effects on Well-Being* (CSD Report 00-27). St. Louis, MO: Washington University, Center for Social Development.

Morrow-Howell, N., J. Hinterlong, and M. Sherraden, eds. 2001. *Productive Aging: Concepts and Challenges*. Baltimore, MD: Johns Hopkins University Press.

Morton, B. 1998. *Starting Out in the Evening*. New York: Berkley Books.

Mueller-Johnson, K., M. P. Toglia, C. D. Sweeney, and S. J. Ceci. 2007. "The Perceived Credibility of Older Adults as Witnesses and Its Relation to Ageism." *Behavioral Sciences and the Law* 25: 355–75.

Muller, C., and O. Volkov. 2009. "Older Women: Work and Caregiving in Conflict?" *Social Work in Health Care* 48: 665–95.

Munnell, A. H. 2004. "Why Are So Many Older Women Poor?" *Just the Facts on Retirement Issues* (April), Center for Retirement Research, Boston College.

Murray, T., and B. Jennings. 2005. "The Quest to Reform End of Life Care. Rethinking Assumptions and Setting New Directions: Why Has It Been So Difficult?" *Hasting Center Special Report* 35 (6): S52–S57.

Mutchler, J., and J. Burr. 2009. "Boomer Diversity and Well-Being: Race, Ethnicity, and Gender." In *Boomer or Bust? Economic and Political Issues of the Graying Society*, edited by R. Hudson, 123–46. Westport, CT: Praeger.

Mykytyn, C. 2008. "Medicalizing the Optimal: Anti-aging Medicine and the Quandary of Intervention." *Journal of Aging Studies* 22: 313–21.

Myles, J., and J. Quadagno. 2000. "Envisioning a Third Way: The Welfare State in the Twenty-First Century." *Contemporary Sociology* 29 (1): 156–67.

National Academy of Social Insurance. 2014. Hard Choices on Social Security: Survey Finds Most Americans Would Pay More to Fix Its Finances and Improve Benefits. Washington, DC: NASI, press release.

Nelson, H. L. 1999. *An Invitation to Feminist Ethics*. Boston: McGraw-Hill.

Nelson, L. 1999. "Death's Gender." In *Mother Time: Women, Aging, and Ethics*, edited by M. U. Walker, 113–32. Lanham, MD: Rowman & Littlefield.

Nelson, T., ed. 2002. *Ageism: Stereotyping and Prejudice against Older People*. Cambridge, MA: MIT Press.

———. 2005. "Ageism: Prejudice against Our Feared Future Self." *Journal of Social Issues* 61 (2): 207–21.

Nettleson, S., and J. Watson, eds. 1998. *The Body in Everyday Life*. London: Routledge.

Nolan, M., J. Sood, J. Kub, and D. Sulmasy. 2005. "When Patients Lack Capacity: The Roles That Patients with Terminal Diagnoses Would Choose for Their Physicians and Loved Ones in Making Medical Decisions." *Journal of Pain and Symptom Management* 30: 342–53.

Nussbaum, M. 2002. "The Future of Feminist Liberalism." In *The Subject of Care: Feminist Perspectives on Dependency*, edited by E. F. Kittay and E. Feder, 186–214. Lanham, MD: Rowman & Littlefield.

Obama, B. 2013. The Defining Challenge of Our Time: Obama Goes All in on Income Inequality and Upward Mobility." Washington, DC: Center for American Progress, December 4.

Oberg, P., and L. Tornstam. 1999. "Body Images among Men and Women of Different Ages." *Ageing and Society* 19 (5): 629–44.

Olsen, T. 1995. *Tell Me a Riddle*. New Brunswick, NJ: Rutgers University Press. Originally published in 1961.

O'Rand, A. 1996. "The Precious and the Precocious: Understandoing Cumulative Disadvantage and Cumulative Advantage over the Life Course." *Gerontologist* 36 (2): 230–38.

O'Rand, A., and K. Shuey 2007. "Gender and the Devolution of Pension Risks in the US." *Current Sociology* 55: 287–304. http://csi.sagepub.com/content/55/2/287.

Ovrebo, B., and M. Minkler. 1996. "The Lives of Older Women: Perspective from Political Economy and the Humanities." In *Voices and Visions: Toward a Critical Gerontology*, edited by T. Cole, A. Achenbaum, P. Jakobi, and R. Kastenbaum, 289–308. New York: Springer.

Packer, G. 2013. *The Unwinding: An Inner History of the New America*. New York: Farrar, Straus and Giroux.

Park, E., and M. Broaddus. 2013. "Ryan Block Grants Would Cut Medicaid by Nearly One-Third by 2023 and More after that." Washington, DC: Center on Budget and Policy Priorities, March 26.

Parks, J. 2000. "Why Gender Matters in the Euthanasia Debate: On Decisional Capacity and the Rejection of Women's Death Requests." *Hastings Center Report* 30: 30–36.

———. 2003. *No Place Like Home? Feminist Ethics and Home Health Care*. Bloomington: University of Indiana Press.

Pastan, L. 2014. "Old Woman or Nearly So Myself: An Essay in Poems." In *A Story Larger Than My Own: Women Writers Look Back on Their Lives and Careers*, edited by J. Burroway, 137–46. Chicago: University of Chicago Press.

Pasupathi, M., and C. Lockenhoff. 2002. "Ageist Behavior." In *Ageism: Stereotyping and Prejudice against Older People*, edited by T. Nelson, 201–46. Cambridge, MA: MIT Press.

PBS Frontline. 2010. *Facing Death*. Written, produced, and directed by Miri Navasky and Karen O'Connor. Aired November 23. http://www.pbs.org/wgbh/pages/frontline/facing-death.

Pearlman, S. 1993. "Late Mid-Life Astonishment: Disruptions to Identity and Self-Esteem." In *Faces of Women and Aging*, edited by N. Davis, E. Cole, and E. Rothblum, 1–12. New York: Routledge.

Peterson, P. 1996. "Will America Grow Up before It Grows Old?" *Atlantic Monthly* (May), 55–86.

Pew Research Center. 2011. "The Generation Gap and the 2012 Election." Pew Research Center for People and the Press. http://www.people-press.org/2011/11/03/the-generation-gap-and-the-2012-election-3.

Phillipson, C. 1998. *Reconstructing Old Age: New Agendas in Social Theory and Practice*. London: Sage.

Phillipson, C., and A. Walker, eds. 1986. *Ageing and Social Policy: A Critical Assessment*. Aldershot, UK: Gower.

Polivka, L. 2012. "Growing Neo-liberal Threat to the Economic Security of Workers and Retirees." *Gerontologist* 52 (1): 133–43.

Polivka, L., and C. Estes. 2009. "The Economic Meltdown and Old Age Politics." *Generations* 33 (3): 56–62.

Porter, E. 2013. "Inequality in America: The Data Is Sobering." *New York Times*, July 31. http://www.nytimes.com/2013/07/31/business/economy/in-us-an-inequality-gap-of-sobering-breadth.html.

Post, S. 1995. *The Moral Challenge of Alzheimer Disease*. Baltimore, MD: Johns Hopkins University Press.

Post, S., and R. Binstock. 2004. *The Fountain of Youth: Cultural, Scientific, and Ethical Perspectives on a Biomedical Goal*. New York: Oxford University Press.

Prohaska, A., and J. Zipp. 2011. "Gender Inequality and the Family and Medical Leave Act." *Journal of Family Issues* 32: 1425–48.

Purcell, P. 2009. Income of Americans Aged 65 and Older, 1968–2008. Washington, DC: Congressional Research Service.

Putnam, M. 2002. "Linking Aging Theory and Disability Models: Increasing the Potential to Explore Aging with Physical Impairment." *Gerontologist* 42 (6): 799–806.

Putnam, R. 1995. "Bowling Alone: America's Declining Social Capital." *Journal of Democracy* 6 (1): 65–78.

Putney, N. M., V. L. Bengtson, and M. A. Wakeman. 2007. "The Family and the Future: Challenges, Prospects, and Resilience." In *Challenges of an Aging Society: Ethical Dilemmas, Political Issues*, edited by R. A. Pruchno and M. A. Smyer, 117–55. Baltimore, MD: Johns Hopkins University Press.

Quadagno, J. 1988. *The Transformation of Old Age Security: Class and Politics in the American Welfare State*. Chicago: University of Chicago Press.

———. 1990. "Generational Equity and the Politics of the Welfare State." *International Journal of Health Services* 20 (4): 631–49.

———. 1996. "Social Security and the Myth of the Entitlement 'Crises.'" *Gerontologist* 36 (3): 391–99.

———. 1999. "Creating the Capital Investment Welfare State: The New American Exceptionalism." *American Sociological Review* 64: 1–11.

Quadagno, J., and J. Pederson. 2012. "Has Support for Social Security Declined? Attitudes toward the Public Pension Scheme in the USA, 2000 and 2010." *International Journal of Social Welfare* 21: S88–S100.

Queniart, A., and M. Charpentier. 2012. "Older Women and Their Representations of Old Age: A Qualitative Analysis." *Ageing and Society* 32 (6): 983–1007.

Quill, T. 1991. "Death and Dignity. A Case of Individualized Decision Making." *New England Journal of Medicine* 324: 691–94.

Radley, A. 1989. "Style, Discourse and Constraint in Adjusting to Chronic Illness." *Sociology of Health and Illness* 11 (3): 230–52.

Ralph, N., T. Mielenz, H. Parton, A.-M. Flatley, and L. Thorpe. 2013. "Multiple Chronic Conditions and Limitations in Activities of Daily Living in a Community-Based Sample of Older Adults in New York City, 2009." *Preventing Chronic Disease* 10: 130159. doi:10.5888/pcd10.130159.

Rappaport, A. 2008. Facts about Women, Old Age and Retirement. Chicago: meeting handout.

Rawls, J. 1972. *A Theory of Justice*. Cambridge, MA: Harvard University Press.

Ray, R. 1996. "A Postmodern Perspective on Feminist Gerontology." *Gerontologist* 36 (5): 674–80.

———. 1999. "Researching to Transgress: The Need for Critical Feminism in Gerontology." In *Fundamentals of Feminist Gerontology*, edited by D. Garner, 171–84. New York: Haworth.

———. 2004. "Toward the Croning of Feminist Gerontology." *Journal of Aging Studies* 18 (1): 109–21.

———. 2006. "The Personal as Political: The Legacy of Betty Friedan." In *Age Matters: Realigning Feminist Thinking*, edited by T. Calasanti and K. Slevin, 21–45. New York: Routledge.

———. 2007. "Narratives as Agents of Social Change: A New Direction for Narrative Gerontologists." In *Critical Perspectives on Ageing Societies*, edited by M. Bernard and T. Scharf, 59–72. Bristol, UK: Policy Press.

———. 2008. *Endnotes: An Intimate Look at the End f Life*. New York: Columbia University Press.

Reich, R. 2001. "We Are All Third-Agers Now." *American Prospect*. http://www.prospect.org/article/we-are-all-third-agers-now.

———. 2010. *Aftershock: The New Economics and America's Future*. New York: Knopf.

———. 2011. "The Limping Middle Class." *New York Times*. http://www.nytimes.com/2011/09/04/opinion/sunday/jobs-will-follow-a-strengthening-of-the-middle-class.html.

Reilly, S. 2006. "Transforming Aging: The Civic Engagement of Adults 55+." *Public Policy and Aging Report* 16 (4): 1, 3–7.

Reinhard, S., C. Levine, and S. Samis. 2012. *Home Alone: Family Caregivers Providing Complex Chronic Care*. Washington, DC: AARP; New York: United Hospital Fund.

Reischer, E., and K. Koo. 2004. "The Body Beautiful: Symbolism and Agency in the Social World." *Annual Review of Anthropology* 33: 297–317.

Reker, G., and P. Wong. 1988. "Aging as an Individual Process: Toward a Theory of Personal Meaning." In *Emergent Theories of Aging*, edited by J. Birren and V. Bengston, 214–46. New York: Springer.

Reno, V., T. Bethell, and E. Walker. June 2011. "Social Security Beneficiaries Face 19% Cut; New Revenue Can Restore Balance." *Social Security Brief*. Washington, DC: National Academy of Social Insurance.

Reyes-Ortiz, C. 1997. "Letter to the Editor: Physicians Must Confront Ageism." *Academic Medicine* 72 (10): 831.

Rice, D. 2011. House and Senate Funding Bills Risk Loss of Rental Assistance for Thousands of Low-Income Families. Washington, DC: Center on Budget and Policy Priorities.

Ridgeway, C. 2011. *Framed by Gender: How Gender Inequality Persists in the Modern World*. New York: Oxford University Press.

Ridgeway, C., and S. Corell. 2000. "Limiting Gender Inequality through Interaction: The End(s) of Gender." *Contemporary Sociology* 29: 110–20.

Rieff, T. 1966. *The Triumph of the Therapeutic: Use of Faith after Freud*. New York: Harper & Row.

Roberto, K., C. Gigliotti, and E. Husser. 2004. "Older Women's Experiences with Multiple Health Conditions: Daily Challenges and Care Practices." *Health Care for Women International* 26: 672–692.

Roberto, K., and B. McCann. 2011. "Everyday Health and Identity Management among Older Women with Chronic Health Conditions." *Journal of Aging Studies* 25: 94–100.

Robertson, A. 1999. "Beyond Apocalyptic Demography: Toward a Moral Economy of Interdependence." In *Critical Gerontology: Perspectives from Political and Moral Economy*, edited by M. Minkler and C. Estes, 75–90. Amityville, NY: Baywood.

Robinson, T., B. Gustafson, and M. Popovich. 2008. "Perceptions of Negative Stereotypes of Older People in Magazine Advertisements: Comparing the Perceptions of Older Adults and College Students." *Ageing and Society* 28 (2): 233–51.

Rodgers, D. 2011. *The Age of Fracture*. Cambridge, MA: Harvard University Press.

Rosen, R. 2000. *The World Split Open: How the Modern Women's Movement Changed America*. New York: Viking.

Rosenbaum, J. R. 2010. "When You Least Expect It." *Hastings Center Report* 40 (1): 7–8.

Rosenfeld, S. 2013. "Unless Social Security Is Expanded with Increased Funding, We Face an Unprecedented Crisis of Millions of Baby Boomers in Poverty." *Alternet*. http://www.alternet.org/print/economy/new-impetus-modernizing-and-expanding-social-security.

Ross, L. F. 2006. "And a Time to Die: How American Hospitals Shape End of Life." *Journal of the National Medical Association* 98: 461–62.

Rowe, J., and R. Kahn. 1987. "Human Aging: Usual and Successful." *Science* 237: 263–71.

———. 1998. *Successful Aging*. New York: Pantheon.

Rozario, P., and D. Derienzis. 2009. "'So Forget How Old I Am!' Examining Age Identities in the Face of Chronic Illness." *Sociology of Health and Illness* 31 (4): 540–53.

Rubenstein, R. L. 2002. "The Third Age." In *Challenges of the Third Age: Meaning and Purpose in Later Life*, edited by R. Weiss and S. Bass, 29–40. New York: Oxford University Press.

Rubin, L. 2007. *60 on Up: The Truth about Aging in the Twenty-First Century*. Boston: Beacon.

Rubin, L., C. Nemeroff, and N. Russo. 2004. "Exploring Feminist Women's Body Consciousness." *Psychology of Women Quarterly* 28: 27–37.

Ruddick, S. 1999. "The Virtues of Age." In *Mother Time: Women, Aging and Ethics*, edited by M. U. Walker, 45–60. Lanham, MD: Rowman & Littlefield.

Ruether, R. R. 1986. *Women-Church: Theology and Practice of Feminist Liturgical Communities.* San Francisco: Harper & Row.

Russell, R. 2001. "In Sickness and in Health." *Journal of Aging Studies* 15: 351–67.

Sabat, S., L. Napolitano, and H. Fath. 2004. "Barriers to the Construction of a Valued Social Identity: A Case Study of Alzheimer's Disease." *American Journal of Alzheimer's Disease and Other Dementias* 19: 177–85.

Said, E. 1982. *The Text, the World, the Critic.* Cambridge, MA: Harvard University Press.

Samuelson, R. 2013. "America's Clash of Generations Is Inevitable." *Washington Post*, December 8. http://www.washingtonpost.com/opinions/robert-samuelson-americas-clash-of-generations-is-inevitable/2013/12/08/e4810416-5ea0-11e3-be07-006c776266ed_story.html.

Sarton, M. 1989. *After the Stroke: A Journal.* New York: W.W. Norton.

Scannell, K. 2006. "An Aging Un-American." *New England Journal of Medicine* 355 (14): 1415–17.

Scherrer, K. 2009. "Images of Sexuality and Aging in the Gerontological Literature." *Sexuality Research and Social Policy* 6 (4): 5–12.

Schoeni, R., V. Freedman, and L. Martin. 2008. "Why Is Late-Life Disability Declining?" *Milbank Quarterly* 86 (1): 47–89.

Schulz, J., and R. Binstock. 2006. *Aging Nation: The Economics and Politics of Growing Old in America.* Westport, CT: Praeger.

Scott-Maxwell, F. 1968. *Measure of My Days*. New York: Penguin.

Seavey, D. 2005. "Family Care and Paid Care: Separate Worlds or Common Ground?" *Better Jobs Better Care Issue Brief No. 5.* Washington, DC: Institute for the Future of Aging Services.

Segal, L. 2013. *Out of Time: The Pleasures and Perils of Aging.* London: Verso.

Settersten, R., Jr. 2007. "10 Reasons Why Shake-Ups in the Life Course Should Change Approaches to Old-Age Policies." *Public Policy and Aging Report* 17 (3): 1, 21–27.

Sheehy, G. 2006. *Sex and the Seasoned Woman: Pursuing the Passionate Life*. New York: Ballantine.

Shelton, A. 2013. "Key Facts about Women and Social Security." AARP Fact Sheet 288. Washington, DC: AARP Public Policy Institute.

Shem, S. 1978. *The House of God*. New York: Dell.

Shields, V., with D. Heineken. 2002. *Measuring Up: How Advertising Affects Self-Image*. Philadelphia: University of Pennsylvania Press.

Silver, A. 1999. "Aging Fairly: Feminist and Disability Perspectives on Intergenerational Justice." In *Mother Time: Women, Aging, and Ethics*, edited by M. U. Walker, 203–26. Lanham, MD: Rowman & Littlefield.

Silver, M. 2013. *Mary Coin*. New York: Penguin.

Silverman, M., J. Nutini, D. Musa, N. Schoenberg, N., and S. Albert. 2009. "Is It Half Full or Half Empty? Affective Responses to Chronic Illness." *Journal of Cross-Cultural Gerontology* 24: 291–306.

Slevin, K. 2010. "If I Had Lots of Money I'd Have a Body Makeover: Managing the Aging Body." *Social Forces* 88 (3): 1003–20.

Smith, H. 2012. *Who Stole the American Dream?* New York: Random House.

Sobchack, V. 1999. "Scary Women, Cosmetic Surgery, and Special Effects." In *Figuring Age: Women, Bodies, and Generations*, edited by K. Woodward, 200–211. Bloomington: Indiana University Press.

Solimeo, S. 2008. "Sex and Gender in Older Adults' Experience of Parkinson's Disease." *Journals of Gerontology Series B, Psychological Sciences and Social Sciences* 63: S42–S48.

Stiglitz, J. 2012. *The Price of Inequality: How Today's Divided Society Endangers Our Future*. New York: Norton.

Stone, D. 1999. "Care and Trembling." *American Prospect* 43 (March–April): 61–67.

———. 2000. "Why We Need a Care Movement." *Nation*, March 13.

Strauss, M. 2003. "The Role of Recognition in the Formation of Self-Understanding." In *Recognition, Responsibility, and Rights*, edited by R. Fiore and H. Lindemann Nelson, 37–52. Lanham, MD: Rowman & Littlefield.

Strengthen Social Security. 2013. Social Security Does Not Add a Single Penny to the Federal Deficit. http://www.strengthensocialsecurity.org/sites/default/files/Social-Security-and-Deficit-Fact-Sheet_FINAL_1.14.2013.pdf.

Svihula, J., and C. Estes. 2007. "Social Security Politics: Ideology and Reform." *Journals of Gerontology Series B, Psychological Sciences and Social Sciences* 62 (2): S79–S89.

Syme, M. 2014. "The Evolving Concept of Older Adult Sexual Behavior and Its Benefits." *Generations* 38 (1): 35–41.

Taylor, C. 1994. *Sources of the Self*. Cambridge, MA: Harvard University Press.

Teifer, L. 2002. "Beyond the Medical Model of Women's Sexual Problems: A Campaign to Resist the Promotion of 'Female Sexual Dysfunction.'" *Sexual and Relationship Therapy* 17 (2): 127–35.

Teno, J., A. Grunier, Z. Schwartz, A. Nanda, and T. Wetle. 2007. "Association between Advance Directives and Quality of End-of-Life Care: A National Study." *Journal of the American Geriatrics Society* 55: 189–94.

Thorne, S., J. McCormick, and E. Carty. 1997. "Deconstructing the Gender Neutrality of Chronic Illness and Disability." *Health Care for Women International* 18 (1): 1–16.

Toombs, K. 1992. "The Body in Multiple Sclerosis: A Patient's Perspective." *The Body in Medical Thought and Practice* 43: 127–37.

————. 1995. "The Lived Experience of Disability." *Human Studies* 18 (1): 9–23.

Toombs, K. 1995. "Sufficient unto the Day: A Life with Multiple Sclerosis." In *Chronic Illness: From Experience to Policy*, edited by K. Toombs, D. Barnard, and R. Carson, 3–23. Bloomington; Indiana University Press.

Toombs, K., D. Bernard, and R. Carson, eds. 1996. *Chronic Illness: From Experience to Policy*. Bloomington: Indiana University Press.

Tronto, J. 1993. *Moral Boundaries: A Political Argument for an Ethics of Care*. New York: Routledge.

————. 2006. "Vicious Circles of Privatized Care." In *Socializing Care: Feminist Ethics and Public Issues*, edited by M. Hamington and D. Miller, 3–26. Lanham, MD: Rowman & Littlefield.

Tucker, J. V., V. P. Reno, and T. N. Bethell. n.d. *Strengthening Social Security: What Do Americans Want?* Washington, D.C: National Academy of Social Insurance. http://www.nasi.org/sites/default/files/research/What_Do_Americans_Want.pdf.

Tunaley, J. R., S. Walsh, and P. Nicolson. 1999. "'I'm Not Bad for My Age': The Meaning of Body Size and Eating in the Lives of Older Women." *Ageing and Society* 19 (6): 741–59.

Turner, B. 1995. "Aging and Identity: Some Reflections on the Somatization of the Self. In *Images of Aging: Cultural Representations of Later Life*, edited by M. Feathestone and A. Wernick, 245–60. London, UK: Routledge.

Twigg, J. 2004. "The Body, Gender, and Age: Feminist Insights in Social Gerontology." *Journal of Aging Studies* 18: 59–73.

————. 2006. *The Body in Health and Social Care*. London: Palgrave.

————. 2008. "Clothing, Aging and Me—Routes to Research." *Journal of Aging Studies* 22: 158–62.

United States Senate Special Committee on Aging. 2003. Statement of Daniel Perry, executive director of the Alliance for Aging Research before the Senate Special Committee on Aging on May 19, 2003. Ageism in the health care system: Short shrifting seniors. Washington, DC: U.S. Government Printing Office.

Vares, T. 2009. "Reading the 'Sexy Oldie': Gender, Age(ing) and Embodiment." *Sexualities* 12 (4): 503–24.

Wakabayashi, C., and K. Donato. 2006. "Does Caregiving Increase Poverty among Women in Later Life? Evidence from the Health and Retirement Survey." *Journal of Health and Social Behavior* 47 (3): 258–74.

Walby, S. 2011. *The Future of Feminism*. Cambridge: Polity.

Walker, A. 2012. "The New Ageism." *Political Quarterly* 83 (4): 812–19.

Walker, M. U. 1998a. *Moral Understandings: A Feminist Study in Ethics*. New York: Routledge.

————. 1998b. "Unnecessary Identities: Representational Practices and Moral Recognition." In *Moral Understandings: A Feminist Study in Ethics*, 177–200. New York: Routledge.

————. 1999a. "Getting out of Line: Alternatives to Life as a Career." In *Mother Time: Women, Aging, and Ethics*, edited by M. U. Walker, 97–111. Lanham, MD: Rowman & Littlefield.

————. 1999b. Introduction. In *Mother Time: Women, Aging, and Ethics*, edited by M. Walker, 1–6. Lanham, MD: Rowman & Littlefield.

————. 1999c. *Mother Time: Women, Aging, and Ethics*. Lanham, MD: Rowman & Littlefield.

————. 2006. "Reconstructing Moral Relation after Wrongdoing." In *Socializing Care: Feminist Ethics and Public Issues*, edited by M. Hamington and D. Miller, 145–62. Lanham, MD: Rowman & Littlefield.

Waxman, B. F. 2010. "Literary Texts and Literary Critics Team Up against Ageism." In *A Guide to Humanistic Studies in Aging*, edited by T. Cole, R. Ray, and R. Kastenbaum, 83–104. Baltimore: Johns Hopkins University Press.

Weinberg, J. 1999. "Caregiving, Age and Class in the Skeleton of the Welfare State: 'And Jill Came Tumbling After . . .'" In *Critical Gerontology: Perspectives from Political and Moral Economy*, edited by M. Minkler and C. Estes, 257–74. Amityville, NY: Baywood.

Weiss, S. 2014. "The Elements of Style." *New York Times Book Review*, October 5, 16.

———. 1999. "Old Women out of Control: Some Thoughts on Aging, Ethics, and Psychosomatic Medicine." In *Mother Time: Women, Ethics, and Aging*, edited by M. U. Walker, 133–50. Lanham, MD: Rowman & Littlefield.

Wendell, S. 1992. "Toward a Feminist Theory of Disability." In *Feminist Perspectives in Medical Ethics*, edited by H. Bequart Holmes and M. Purdy, pp. 63–81. Bloomington: Indiana University Press.

Werner, A., L. W. Isaksen, and K. Malterud. 2004. "'I Am Not the Kind of Woman Who Complains of Everything': Illness Stories on Self and Shame in Women with Chronic Pain." *Social Science and Medicine* 59 (5): 1035–45.

Whitbourne, S., and J. Sneed. 2002a. "Identity Processes in Adulthood: Theoretical Methods and Challenges." *Identity* 2 (1): 29–45.

———. 2002b. "The Paradox of Well-Being, Identity Processes, and Stereotype Threat: Ageism and Its Potential Relationships to the Self in Later Life." In *Ageism: Stereotyping and Prejudice against Older People*, edited by T. Nelson, 247–76. Cambridge, MA: MIT Press.

White, J., and J. Tronto. 2004. "Political Practices of Care: Needs and Rights." *Ratio Juris* 17 (4): 425–53.

Wider Opportunities for Women. 2013. Living Below the Line: Economic Insecurity and Older Americans. No. 2: Women (September). Washington, DC:WOW. http://www.wowonline. org/wp-content/uploads/2013/09/Living-Below-the-Line-Economic-Insecurity-and-Older-Americans-Women-Sept-2013.pdf.

Williams, G. 1984. "The Genesis of Chronic Illness: Narrative Re-construction." *Sociology of Health and Illness* 6: 175–200.

Williamson, J., and D. Watts-Roy. 1999. "Framing the Generational Equity Debate." In *The Generational Equity Debate*, edited by E. J. Williamson, E. Kingson, and D. Watts-Roy, 3–37. New York: Columbia University Press.

Winerip, M. 2013. "Three Men, Three Ages. Which Do You Like?" *New York Times*, July 22.

Winterich, J. 2007. "Aging, Femininity, and the Body: What Appearance Changes Mean to Women with Age." *Gender Issues* 24: 51–69.

Winzelberg, G., L. Hanson, and J. Tulsky. 2009. "Beyond Autonomy: Diversifying End-of-Life Decision-Making Approaches to Serve Patients and Families. *Journal of the American Geriatrics Society* 53: 1046–50.

Wolf, N. 1991. *The Beauty Myth: How Images of Beauty Are Used against Women*. New York: Morrow.

Wolf, S. 1996. "Gender and Death: Physician-Assisted Suicide and Euthanasia." In *Feminism and Bioethics: Beyond Reproduction*, edited by S. Wolf, 282–317. New York: Oxford University Press.

Woodward, K. 1991. *Aging and Its Discontents: Freud and Other Fictions*. Bloomington: Indiana University Press.

———, ed. 1999a. *Figuring Age: Women, Bodies, Generations*. Bloomington: Indiana University Press.

———. 1999. "Introduction." In *Figuring Age: Women, Bodies, Generations*, edited by K. Woodward, ix–xxix. Bloomington: Indiana University Press.

————. 2002. "Against Wisdom: The Social Politics of Anger and Aging." *Cultural Critique* 51: 186–218.

Young, I. M. 1990. *Justice and the Politics of Difference*. Princeton: Princeton University Press.

Young, M., and T. Schuller. 1991. *Life after Work: The Arrival of the Ageless Society*. London: HarperCollins. Cited in Blaikie, A. 1999. *Aging and Popular Culture*. Cambridge: Cambridge University Press.

Index

Aaron, Henry, 186
academy, and resistance to ageism, 253–255
acceptance of aging: appearance alteration and, 59; overview, 2; young women and, 16
acceptance of old age: importance of, 15–17, 58; stereotypes, 16
The Acorn, 25
activism: feminism, 240. *See also* advocacy; long-term care activism; resistance to ageism
activity, in new aging, 97
acute illness, 120
advance care planning: overview, 213–216; problems with, 213–216, 227; revisited, 227
advertising: appearance alteration and, 55–56; for retirement communities, 101, 252; sex in old age and, 100–101
advocacy: caregiver, 171; recommendations for Social Security, 177, 178, 180, 200, 201. *See also* organizations, advocacy
Affordable Care Act, 151, 218
AGE. *See* Americans for Generational Equity
age and gender: inequality and, 3, 250; literature on, 17; OWL's strategy linking, 240. *See also* ageism
age grading, 70–71

ageism: age relations and, 66–67, 84; arts, culture and, 85–86; bodily markers, stereotyping and, 69–70; clinical trials, 73; clothing and, 76; deconstructing, 84–87; definition, 66–67; denial of age and, 63, 80–83; difference and, 84–85; everyday life and, 70–72; familiar, 64–65; fourth age and, 138; humiliation and, 71; identity, social recognition and, 78–80; inequality and, 66, 77, 78; in-groups and, 84; Mayslake women and, 29–30, 73, 81; of media, 76; new, 92; new aging and, 3, 111; normalization of, 67–69; other sites of, 76–77; overview, 63–64, 87–89, 254; patronizing speech and, 29, 71, 72, 73; politics and, 77–78; public policy and, 77–78; retirement communities and, 70, 71; sexism, new aging and, 3; third age and, 138; women's aging bodies and, 20; work and, 75–76; younger selves and, 2, 46; young people and, 67. *See also* resistance to ageism; societal ageism; stereotypes, of old age
ageism, and professional encounters: long-term care, 74; medical care, 72–73; overview, 72; social services, 74–75
agelessness: denial of age and, 82; successful aging and, 99
age-related changes: to bodies, 46; new aging and, 103

age-related changes, to women's bodies,
40; to older women's bodies, 41,
43–44. *See also* women's aging bodies
age relations: ageism and, 66–67, 84;
dimensions of, 66
age-studies scholars. *See* gerontology
Agich, George, 74, 140, 236
aging: facts and myths of, 86; literature on
gender and, 17; responses, 1–2;
younger selves and, 2; *See also specific
topics*
Alzheimer's disease: fourth age and, 137,
139; social identity and, 139
Americans for Generational Equity (AGE),
181
Andrews, Molly, 2, 83
Angell, Marcia, 219
Angelou, Maya, 16
anger, in resistance to ageism, 88
anti-aging interventions: new aging and,
98–103, 109; women's conversations
about, 47–48
appearance, conversations about, 48–49
appearance alteration: acceptance of aging
and, 59; advertising and, 55–56; in
identity management, 51–52, 54; mask
of aging and, 51–52, 54. *See also*
cosmetic surgery
Aristotle, 104
arts: ageism and, 85–86; stereotypes of old
age and, 85–86
Audrey, 25, 246; gleanings, 31, 32;
overview, 28. *See also* Mayslake
women
austerity politics: deficit reduction and, 11;
Medicaid and, 13; Medicare and, 13;
neoliberalism and, 258; retirement
security and, 195; Social Security and,
13, 14; women and, 12–14
autonomy, 120; chronic illness and, 127,
140–141; rethinking, 168. *See also*
independence
autonomy competence, 41–42, 45

baby boomers, 94
Bakewell, Sarah, 229
Barker, Pat, 135–136
Bartky, Sandra, 80, 244
Bass, Scott, 91

Beatles, 147
Bernard, Miriam, 17
Bernstein, Richard, 9, 157
Biggs, Simon, 51
Binstock, Robert, 110
biological body, 43–44
biomedicine, and chronic illness, 127–129
Blaikie, Andrew, 44, 121, 236
body: age-related changes, 46; biological,
43–44; bodily markers, stereotyping
and ageism, 69–70; complex
understanding of, 40–42;
constructionist and material views of,
40–42; culture and, 40; how bodies
matter, 44–46; moral importance of, 45;
politics and, 46; self and, 38. *See also*
women's bodies
body consciousness: of girls, 37
body reflections: on anti-aging
interventions, 55; on appearance
alteration, 55–56; overview, 54–56;
personal, 56–57
bottom-up talk, 115
Bowles, Erskine, 13
Brown, Iva, 63, 65, 78, 254
Brown, Rosellen, 15–16
Brown, Sherrod, 256
Bruner, Jerome, 126
Butler, Robert, 66, 94, 99
Butler, Stuart, 181

Calasanti, Toni, 17, 189
Callahan, Daniel, 73, 225
cancer, and death, 207–210
caregivers: advocacy, 171. *See also* family
caregivers; women caregivers
caregiving: gender inequality and, 150,
152, 154–159, 254; as private and
public responsibility, 154–157; society
and, 147. *See also* family caregivers;
women caregivers
caregiving's dystopic future: class and,
150, 152, 153; contingency of care,
independence and, 152–154;
essentialism, women caregivers and
choice, 157–159; financial and
structural contributions, 160; gender
inequality, 150, 152, 154–159;
impoverished commitment to care,

151–152; independence and, 152–154, 161; inequality, 148–149, 150, 152; neoliberalism and, 148, 149, 153, 156; overview, 22, 147–151, 173–174; private and public responsibility in, 154–157; rethinking long-term care policy, practice and ethics, 165; summary of, 161–162; in 2034, 162–165

caregiving's dystopic future, alternatives to: barriers to, 169; making real choices possible, 169–173; moving toward remedies, 167–168; overview, 165–167, 173–174; rethinking autonomy, 168

Carol, 25, 26, 83, 244; gleanings, 28–29, 32; overview, 27–28. *See also* Mayslake women

ceremonies, and women's counterstories, 248

chained CPI, 191–192

Chen, Pauline, 219

chronically ill women: culture, meaning and impairment, 121–122; fiction and, 135; overview, 21, 117–119, 142; reflection on lessons learned, 141–142. *See also* chronic illness

chronic illness: acute illness compared to, 120; class and, 121, 135; as enabling, 137–138; ethical dimensions of, 140–141; fourth age and, 21, 118–119, 136–139; gender and, 121, 129–130; inequality and, 121; neoliberalism and, 129–130; overview, 120–121; personal responsibility and, 159; race and, 121; third age and, 21, 136–139. *See also* disability

chronic illness, and identity: core ideas, 119–120; experiencing chronic illness, 122–124; meaning and, 124–125; overview, 21, 117–119. *See also* chronic illness narratives

chronic illness, in context: autonomy, 127, 140–141; cultural norms, 126–127; gender, 129–130; independence, 127; overview, 125–126; professional cultures of biomedicine and social services, 127–129

chronic illness narratives: overview, 119, 130–132; self and, 119

chronic illness narrative themes: gender, 132–133; learning from texts, 134–136; overview, 132

civic engagement, 96

Clarke, Laura Hurd, 47, 52, 55

class: caregiving's dystopic future and, 150, 152, 153; chronic illness and, 121, 135; identity management and, 53, 54; Mayslake women and, 25, 28–29; women's bodies and, 39

Clift, Eleanor, 217

clothing, and ageism, 76

COLA. *See* cost-of-living adjustment

Cole, Thomas, 18, 106, 136

collective responsibility, 7

common good: recovery of, 251–255; young people and, 251

community: human dependency and, 251–252; individualism and, 8, 20, 44, 93, 251; recovery of, 251–255; of resistance, 261. *See also* retirement communities

community-based long term care: Medicaid and, 160. *See also* caregiving's dystopic future

complex interventions, 205, 213, 215–216; reversing normalization of, 224–227

conceptual frameworks. *See* frameworks, personal and conceptual

conservatism: on aging, 259; new, 255, 256. *See also* neoliberalism

constructionist view of body, 40–42

consumer culture: body and, 40; new aging and, 101, 102; resistance to ageism and, 254

Consumer Price Index (CPI), 191–192

context, in old age: critical gerontology and, 8–10; feminism and, 8–10; neoliberalism and, 11–15; new aging's birth and social, cultural, political, 92–95; understanding social, political and cultural, 10–17

context, of chronic illness. *See* chronic illness, in context

cosmetic surgery, 48

cost-of-living adjustment (COLA), 184, 185, 191, 192, 193, 200

counterstories. *See* women's counterstories
CPI. *See* Consumer Price Index
critical gerontology: context in old age
and, 8–10; frameworks of feminism
and, 8–10
crone, 249
Cruikshank, Margaret, 17, 88, 248
cultural context, in old age: neoliberalism
and, 11–15; new aging's birth and,
92–95; overview, 10–17
cultural imagery, 241
culture: ageism and, 85–86; body and, 40;
chronic illness and cultural norms,
126–127; conversation about death and
dying, 229; impairment, meaning and,
121–122; narratives and, 126; new
aging and, 92; stereotypes of old age
and, 85–86. *See also* consumer culture
culture of medicine: advance care planning
and, 219–220; biomedicine and chronic
illness, 127–129

The Daily Show, 68
death: from cancer, 207–210; cultural
conversation about, 229; with dignity,
213; good, 205, 213, 216, 219;
physician aid in dying, 218–219. *See
also* dying; end-of-life
de Beauvoir, Simone, 89
deficit reduction, 255; austerity and, 11;
Obama's commission on, 13, 183;
Social Security and, 22–23, 175, 183,
184, 185, 190, 192, 194
DeLamater, John, 99
dementia: identity and, 139. *See also*
Alzheimer's disease
denial of age: ageism and, 63, 80–83;
agelessness and, 82; resistance to
ageism and, 80, 81–82, 87; stereotypes
of old age and, 81, 83; strategies, 63,
64, 80–83; youthfulness and, 82, 83.
See also acceptance of old age
difference: ageism and, 84–85; resistance
to ageism and, 87
Dionne, E. J., 93, 94
disability, 121; exclusion and, 131;
inequality and, 121; normalcy and, 123;
society and, 42. *See also* chronic illness

dying: cultural conversation about, 229.
See also death
dying at home: identity preservation and,
222–224; Medicaid and, 223; Medicare
and, 223, 224; overview, 222–224, 258.
See also hospice
dystopic future of caregiving. *See*
caregiving's dystopic future

economy: disadvantaged status of women,
240; freedom and women's economic
security, 261; inequality and economic
insecurity, 256; recession and
retirement security, 196. *See also*
deficit reduction
Edsall, Thomas, 178
Elder Standard, 22
elites: neoliberalism and, 11–12, 13–14,
255; Social Security and, 23, 183–184,
196. *See also* privileged people
Elliott, Carl, 102
embodied selves, 19, 42, 45
embodied women, 19, 38, 42, 45, 55
employers, and retirement security,
188–189
end-of-life: relationships and, 228;
storytelling at, 210, 221. *See also* death
end-of-life care: complex interventions,
205, 213, 215–216, 224–227;
contemporary medicine and, 212; from
contract to covenant, 228; cultural
conversation about death and dying,
229; culture of medicine and, 219–220;
hospice and palliative care, 216–218;
imagining death and, 210–212;
individual treatment choices and, 214;
lessons learned, 212–213; overview, 23,
205–207, 229–230, 258; physician aid
in dying, 218–219; POLST, 228; social
support in, 210; Susan and, 207–210,
221, 222; systems design approach,
225–226. *See also* advance care
planning
end-of-life care, and identity preservation:
advance care planning revisited, 227;
dying at home, 222–224; overview,
220–222; reversing normalization of
complex interventions, 224–227
Ephron, Nora, 47

equity: debate and generational inequities, 78; generational, 176, 177, 181. *See also* inequality

essentialism, and women caregivers, 157–159

ethics: chronic illness and, 140–141; rethinking long-term care, 165; retirement security as moral necessity, 197–199

evasion of aging: costs of, 1–2. *See also* denial of age

experiential body, 38

Faircloth, Christopher, 40

Fairlie, Henry, 181

Family and Medical Leave Act (FMLA), 152, 250

family caregivers: long-term care by, 150–151, 154, 161. *See also* caregiving's dystopic future

feeling old, 113; old as you feel, 63

feminism, 3, 7; activism, 240; age-studies scholars, 241; context in old age and, 8–10; frameworks of critical gerontology and, 8–10; gerontologists, 48, 241; inequality and, 4; literature about women and aging, 19; second-wave, 239, 240, 245; waves of, 239, 240; women's stories and, 239

The Feminine Mystique (Friedan), 245–246

fiction, about chronically ill women, 135–136

finance: caregiving's dystopic future and, 160. *See also* economy

FMLA. *See* Family and Medical Leave Act

Foucault, M., 40

fourth age: ageism and, 138; Alzheimer's disease and, 137, 139; chronic illness and, 21, 118–119, 136–139; overview, 136–137; third age and, 21, 136–139

frameworks, personal and conceptual: critical gerontology and feminism, 8–10; moral perception, 6–7; personal, 7; worrisome issues, 8

Frank, Elsie, 10

freedom: of Mayslake women, 32, 106, 108; new aging and, 260; old age and, 260; retirement and, 197; women's

economic security and, 261

Friedan, Betty, 245

Frontline, 212

Furman, Frida Kerner, 19, 44, 48, 58, 243, 248

gender: chronic illness and, 121, 129–130; chronic illness narratives and, 132–133. *See also* age and gender

gender inequality: age and, 3, 250; caregiving and, 150, 152, 154–159, 254; persistence of, 67; privileged people and, 255; resistance to ageism and, 255; retirement security and, 189–190, 195; Social Security and, 189, 191

generations: equity, 176, 177, 181; inequities and equity debate, 78; intergenerational approach in resistance to ageism, 249–251; warfare between, 246–247

Genevay, Bonnie, 220–221

Genova, Lisa, 139

Germanis, Peter, 181

gerontology: critical, 8–10; feminism and, 8–10, 48, 241

Gilleard, Chris, 14

Gillick, Muriel, 99

Ginsburg, Ruth Bader, 79

girls, and body consciousness, 37

Glenn, Evelyn Nakano, 153, 155

good death, 205, 213, 216, 219

good life, and new aging, 103, 104, 105–106

grandmother role, 79

gray hair, 47–48, 242

Gray Panthers, 10, 23

greedy geezers, 182

Grumbach, Doris, 18, 44, 50

Guillemin, Jeanne, 212

Gullette, Margaret, 6, 18, 69, 240

health optimization, and new aging, 98–103, 105

health promotion: inequality and, 46; new aging and, 105

Heilbrun, Carolyn, 5, 18–19, 44, 106

Hendricks, Jon, 96

Heschel, Abraham Joshua, 34

Higgs, Paul, 14
Hoffmaster, Barry, 216, 227
hospice, 208; overview, 216–218
Hudson, Robert, 12, 181, 197
human: dependency and community,
    251–252; meaning to human life,
    119–120

identity: ageism, social recognition and,
    78–80; as continuous, 254; core ideas,
    119–120; dementia and, 139; meaning
    and, 120; narratives and, 120, 130–131;
    relationships and, 120; social, 139. *See
    also* chronic illness, and identity; end-
    of-life care, and identity preservation;
    self
identity management: appearance
    alteration in, 51–52, 54; approaches,
    52–53; class and, 53, 54; mask of aging
    as, 51–52; of Mayslake women, 53–54;
    overview, 51–54; women's aging
    bodies and, 51–54, 60
ideology: resistance to ageism and,
    255–257; Social Security and, 175–178
illness: acute, 120. *See also* chronic illness
impairment: culture, meaning and,
    121–122; overview of chronic,
    120–121. *See also* chronic illness
independence: caregiving's dystopic future
    and, 152–154, 161; chronic illness and,
    127; contingency of care and, 152–154;
    myth of, 153; wise, 125. *See also*
    autonomy
individualism, 15, 44; community and, 8,
    20, 44, 93, 251; new aging and, 93, 107;
    society and, 95; women's counterstories
    and, 246
inequality, 198; age, gender and, 3, 250;
    ageism and, 66, 77, 78; caregiving's
    dystopic future and, 148–149, 150, 152;
    chronic illness and, 121; disability and,
    121; economic security and, 256;
    feminism and, 4; health promotion and,
    46; new aging and, 91, 107, 108, 110;
    old women and, 237; pensions and,
    195; privileged people and, 183–184;
    retirement security and, 195–196;
    Social Security and, 176, 185; women's
    bodies and starting, 44; women's

retirement security and, 200. *See also*
    class; gender inequality
in-groups: ageism and, 84; stereotypes and,
    84
Institute for Women's Policy Research
    (IWPR), 240
interventions, medical. *See* complex
    interventions
IWPR. *See* Institute for Women's Policy
    Research

Jacoby, Susan, 18, 81
Jan, 25, 47; gleanings, 31–32; overview,
    26. *See also* Mayslake women
Julie's International Salon, 243

Kahn, Robert, 95, 104
Katz, Stephen, 97
Kaufman, Sharon, 46
Kleinman, Arthur, 133
Krugman, Paul, 185, 191
Kuhn, Maggie, 10, 23, 242

Lane, Charles, 189
Laslett, Peter, 137
Laws, Glenda, 63
Laz, Cheryl, 41, 47
Lebacqz, Karen, 115
Lee, 25; gleanings, 30–31, 32; overview,
    27. *See also* Mayslake women
Lee, Spike, 68
Let's Face It, 243
Lewis, Myrna, 99
Lieberman, Trudy, 190
Life after Life (McCorkle), 136
literature, about women and aging:
    feminist, 19; gender in, 17; overview,
    17–19
Lively, Penelope, 50
long-term care: ageism and, 74; by family,
    150–151, 154, 161; Medicaid and, 151,
    172; public engagement and, 172–173;
    publicizing reality of, 170–171;
    rethinking policy, practice and ethics
    of, 165; by women caregivers,
    150–151, 154–159. *See also*
    caregiving's dystopic future;
    community-based long term care

long-term care activism: caregiver advocacy, 171; public engagement, 172–173; young people and, 172–173

Lynn, Joanne, 225

Marshall, Barbara, 108

Martin, Trayvon, 68

Mary, 25, 26, 71–72, 73; gleanings, 31; overview, 26–27. *See also* Mayslake women

mask of aging, 48; appearance-alteration and, 51–52, 54; as identity management, 51–52

material view of body, 40–42

Mayslake, overview, 26, 33

Mayslake women, 243–244, 252; ageism and, 29–30, 73, 81; class and, 25, 28–29; freedom of, 32, 106, 108; gleanings, 28–33; identity management of, 53–54; overview, 25–34; politics of, 33; as proud old women, 242; young people and, 30, 31, 31–32, 33; *See also specific Mayslake women*

McCorkle, Jill, 136

McHugh, Kevin, 88

meaning: chronic illness and, 124–125; to human life, 119–120; identity and, 120; impairment, culture and, 121–122

media: ageism of, 76; new aging and, 101; representations of women in, 76

Medicaid: austerity politics and, 13; community-based long term care and, 160; dying at home and, 223; long-term care and, 151, 172; nursing homes and, 160, 224

medical care: ageism and, 72–73. *See also* end-of-life care; long-term care

medical interventions, for aging, 40

Medicare: austerity politics and, 13; dying at home and, 223, 224

medicine: advance care planning and culture of, 219–220; chronic illness and culture of biomedicine, 127–129; end-of-life care and contemporary, 212

Meyers, Diana, 6, 41, 242

millennials, 246–247, 248, 249, 251, 259; long-term care activism and, 172–173. *See also* young people

Miller, Nancy, 57

Moody, Harry (Rick), 18

morality: importance of body, 45; retirement security as moral necessity, 197–199

moral perception, 6–7, 14

Morton, Brian, 229

narratives: culture and, 126; identity and, 120, 130–131. *See also* chronic illness narratives; stories

National Commission on Social Security Reform, 182

negative stereotypes of old age, 16; new aging and, 95; resisting, 261

Nelson, Hilde Lindemann, 87, 125, 244

Nelson, Todd, 64

neoliberalism: austerity politics and, 258; caregiving's dystopic future and, 148, 149, 153, 156; chronic illness and, 129–130; context in old age and, 11–15; elites and, 11–12, 13–14, 255; new aging and, 92, 93, 110, 256; overview, 255; pensions and, 203; retirement and, 12, 13, 14; Social Security and, 12, 13, 14, 184–185, 256; women and, 12–14

new aging, 11, 80; activity in, 97; ageism and, 3, 111; age-related changes and, 103; alternatives to, 112–113; anti-aging and, 98–103, 109; birth and social, cultural, political context, 92–95; consumer culture and, 101, 102; critique, claims and counterclaims, 103–112; culture and, 92; discovery and flourishing of, 95–98; expansion of, 98–103; freedom and, 260; good life and, 103, 104, 105–106; health optimization and, 98–103; health promotion and, 105; individualism and, 93, 107; inequality and, 91, 107, 108, 110; media and, 101; negative connotations of old and, 260; negative stereotypes of old age and, 95; neoliberalism and, 92, 93, 110, 256; overview, 3, 20–21, 91–93, 114–116; sex and, 98–103, 108–109; sexism, ageism and, 3; women's counterstories and, 245–246; work and, 96–97. *See also* new old age new old age, 2; overview, 20–21, 91–93. *See also* new aging

1980s: old people and, 12; Social Security turning point, 180–183; women and, 12

normalcy: ageism's normalization, 67–69; cultural norms and chronic illness, 126–127; disability and, 123; normalized stereotypes of old age, 67; reversing normalization of complex interventions, 224–227

nursing homes, 208; Medicaid and, 160, 224

Obama, Barack, 13, 183, 198

Obamacare. *See* Affordable Care Act

old: new aging and negative connotations of, 260; reclaiming meaning of, 259; as you feel, 63

old age: freedom and, 260; learning to be old, 59–60; loss and, 80; overview, 15; themes, 4–5; *See also specific topics*

old age research: methodological departures, 5; overview, 5

Older Women's League (OWL), 240, 247

old people: in clinical trials, 73; as greedy geezers, 182; loss of status of, 86; 1980s and, 12; young people and, 67, 248

old women: inequality and, 237; overview, 3, 235–237; in today's society, 235. *See also* proud old women

Olsen, Tillie, 221–222

organizations, advocacy: examples of, 240–241; resistance to ageism, 240–241, 249–251, 256

OWL. *See* Older Women's League

palliative care, 216–218, 223

PAS. *See* physician-assisted suicide

Pastan, Linda, 2

Patient Self-Determination Act (1994), 215

patronizing speech: ageism and, 29, 71, 72, 73; as flattering, 72; overview, 71

pensions, 201; defined benefit, 183, 189, 195; defined contribution, 189, 193, 195; inequality and, 195; neoliberalism and, 203; Social Security and private, 197. *See also* Social Security

personal framework, 7

personal responsibility, and chronic illness, 159

Peterson, Peter, 182

Phillipson, Chris, 255

physician aid in dying, 218–219

physician-assisted suicide (PAS), 218–219

physician orders for life-sustaining treatment (POLST), 228

policy: ageism and public, 77–78; resistance to ageism and, 255–259; rethinking long-term care, 165

political context, in old age, 10–17; new aging's birth and, 92–95

politics: ageism and, 77–78; body and, 46; of Mayslake women, 33; of retirement security, 202; of Social Security, 202. *See also* austerity politics; neoliberalism

Polivka, Larry, 14

POLST. *See* physician orders for life-sustaining treatment

positive active aging, 111

positive aging, 112, 113

Post, Stephen, 139

privileged people: gender inequality and, 255; inequality and, 183–184; on retirement security, 183–184, 196. *See also* elites

productive aging, 20, 91, 96–97, 112. *See also* new aging

professions: chronic illness and professional cultures, 127–129. *See also* ageism, and professional encounters

progressives, 18, 81; and Social Security proposals, 185, 186, 199–201

proud old women: impediments to, 39; learning to be, 59, 60, 88–89, 242; Mayslake women as, 242

public: engagement and long-term care, 172–173; policy and ageism, 77–78; resistance to ageism, 253–255; responsibility for caregiving, 154–157

Quill, Timothy, 219

race: chronic illness and, 121; Social Security and, 191

Rainsford, Charlotte, 50

Rawls, John, 110, 196
Ray, Ruth, 4, 6, 18, 25, 249
Reagan, Ronald, 180, 182
recession, and retirement security, 196
Red Hat Society, 248
relationships: end-of-life and, 228; identity and, 120
resistance to ageism, 52–53, 58, 60; from academy to public realm, 253–255; advocacy organizations and, 240–241, 256; anger in, 88; basic tools of, 258; communities of, 261; consumer culture and, 254; denial of age and, 80, 81–82, 87; difference and, 87; gender inequality and, 255; intergenerational and organizational approaches, 249–251; lessons from foremothers, 240–241; life stories, 241–244; moving policy forward, 257–259; overview, 23, 237–238, 259–261; policy, ideology and state, 255–257; possible paths to change, 239–240; power of collective counterstories, 244–249; recommendations for, 87–89; recovery of common good and community, 251–255; societal ageism and, 87
responsibility: caregiving as private and public, 154–157; chronic illness and personal, 159; collective, 7
retirement: freedom and, 197; neoliberalism and, 12, 13, 14; savings and economic recession, 196
retirement communities: advertising for, 101, 252; ageism and, 70, 71; caring, 252–253. *See also* Mayslake
retirement security: austerity and, 195; economic recession and, 196; employers and, 188–189; gender inequality in, 189–190, 195; individual savings and, 183; inequality and, 195–196; as moral necessity, 197–199; overview, 22–23, 175–179, 202–204; politics of, 202; privileged perspective on, 183–184, 196; proposals, 199–201; real crisis, 195–197; social justice and, 201–202, 247. *See also* pensions; Social Security; women's retirement security
Ridgeway, Cecilia, 67, 80, 157
Robertson, Ann, 153

Rodgers, Daniel, 93, 95
Rosenbaum, Julie Rothstein, 212
Rowe, Jack, 94, 95
Rubin, Lillian, 18, 44, 58, 101, 106–107, 107, 110, 215, 227, 260–261
Ruddick, Sarah, 113, 125, 236

Schiavo, Terri, 216
Scott-Maxwell, Florida, 44, 122, 136, 137
second-wave feminism, 239, 240, 245–246
Segal, Lynne, 18, 70, 111, 260
self: body and, 38; chronic illness narratives and, 119; embodied, 19, 42, 45. *See also* identity; women's selves; younger selves
Settersten, Richard, 107–108, 256
seventy, as new fifty, 16
sex in old age, 3; advertising and, 100–101; new aging and, 98–103, 108–109
sexism, ageism and new aging, 3
Sheehy, Gail, 99
Shem, Samuel, 72
Shields, Laurie, 240
Silver, Marisa, 64
Simpson, Alan, 13, 183
Slevin, Kathleen, 17, 189
social action, 8
social context, in old age, 10–17; new aging's birth and, 92–95
social identity, 139
social justice: retirement security and, 201–202, 247; Social Security and, 201–202
social media, and women's counterstories, 247–248
social recognition, ageism and identity, 78–80
Social Security, 9, 29, 198, 199; austerity politics and, 13, 14; background, 179; challenges to, 176, 180–183; elites and, 23, 183–184, 196; ideological struggle over, 175–178; inequality and, 176, 185; neoliberalism and, 12, 13, 14, 184–185, 256; overview, 22–23, 178–179, 202–204; politics of, 202; private pensions and, 197; race and, 191; social justice and, 201–202; sowing doubt about, 177; turning point (1980s), 180–183; young people and,

181, 203, 251

Social Security problem: deconstructing crises and proposed solutions, 190–195, 203; deficit and, 22–23, 175, 183, 184, 185, 190, 192, 194; gender inequality, 189, 191; generational equity framing, 176, 177, 181; overview, 175, 175–179, 187–188

Social Security proposals and remedies, 176, 178; benefit reductions, 178, 179, 182, 185–186, 200; chained CPI and, 191–192; COLA and, 184, 185, 191, 192, 193, 200; current reform, 185–186; deconstructing crises and, 190–195, 203; entitlement reform, 185–186, 190, 199–201; investment income taxes, 200, 201–202, 203; lifting cap, 177, 178; means-testing, 194; moderate or rational, 184, 185; neoliberal, 184–185, 256; overview, 178–179, 199, 202–204, 257; payroll tax raises, 177, 199–200, 203; privatization, 177, 178, 181, 185, 193, 199, 203; progressive, 185, 186, 199–201; raising retirement age, 177, 184, 191, 192; retirement security and entitlement reform, 199–201; revenue increases, 199; social justice and, 201–202; spousal death benefits, 200; three dominant positions, 184–185; women caregivers and, 200

social services: ageism and, 74–75; chronic illness and professional culture of, 127–129

social support, in end-of-life care, 210

societal ageism, 16, 65; resistance to ageism and, 87

society: caregiving and, 147; disability and, 42; individualism and, 95; old women in today's, 235; women's conversations about their bodies and, 49. *See also* caregiving's dystopic future

Solimeo, Samantha, 132, 133

Sommers, Tish, 200, 240

Sotomayor, Sonia, 172, 239

sources, 5

status, old people's loss of, 86

stereotypes: incongruent information about, 86; in-groups and, 84

stereotypes, of old age, 2, 17; acceptance of, 16; arts, culture and, 85–86; bodily markers, ageism and, 69–70; denial of age and, 81, 83; disconfirming, 86; grandmother role, 79; normalized, 67. *See also* ageism; negative stereotypes of old age

Stewart, Jon, 68–69, 88, 89

stories: end-of-life and telling, 210, 221. *See also* narratives; women's stories

successful aging: agelessness and, 99; discovery and flourishing of, 95–98; expansion of, 98–103; overview, 91–93. *See also* new aging

Susan, 207–210, 221, 222

Taylor, Charles, 124

Tell Me a Riddle, 221–222

terror management, 85

texts, about chronically ill women, 134–136

themes: overview, 4–5. *See also* chronic illness narrative themes

third age, 11; ageism and, 138; chronic illness and, 21, 136–139; fourth age and, 21, 136–139

Toombs, Kay, 122, 124

top-down thinking, 115

Union Street (Barker), 135

voluntarism, 94, 96–97

Walker, Alan, 77

Walker, Margaret Urban, 74, 105–106

wheelchairs, and alteration of perceptions, 123–124

Wider Opportunities for Women (WOW), 240

wise independence, 125

women: acceptance of aging and young, 16; austerity politics and, 12–14; economic status of, 240; media and representations of, 76; neoliberalism and, 12–14; 1980s and, 12; in positions of power, 239. *See also* Mayslake women

women caregivers: essentialism, choice and, 157–159; long-term care by,

150–151, 154–159; overview, 258; Social Security proposals and, 200. *See also* caregiving's dystopic future

women in late life. *See* old women

women's aging bodies: ageism and, 20; age-related changes to, 41, 43–44; biological body, 43–44; constructed and material views of body and, 40–42; how bodies matter, 44–46; identity management, 51–54, 60; overview, 19–20, 37–40, 58–60; reflections on, 54–57; women's conversations about their, 47–51; women's selves and, 58. *See also* age-related changes, to women's bodies

women's bodies: class and, 39; embodied, 19, 38, 42, 45, 55; starting inequality and, 44; women's conversations about their, 47–51. *See also* women's aging bodies

women's conversations, about their bodies: about anti-aging interventions, 47–48; overview, 47–51; about social expectations, 49; about their appearance, 48–49

women's counterstories: ceremonies and, 248; collective, 244–249; individualism and, 246; moving stories outward, 247–249; new aging and, 245–246; overview, 244; power of collective, 244–249; social media and, 247–248

women's economic security: freedom and, 261; inequality and, 256. *See also* women's retirement security

women's retirement security: challenge of, 186–189; disadvantaged status analysis, 189–190; inequality and, 200; overview, 22–23, 175–179. *See also* retirement security; Social Security

women's selves: embodied selves, 19, 42, 45; inner and outer, 38; women's aging bodies and, 58. *See also* younger selves

women's stories: claiming our voices, 241–244; feminism and, 239; life stories, 241–244; moving stories outward, 247–249. *See also* women's counterstories

Woodward, Kathleen, 18, 88, 240

work: ageism and, 75–76; new aging and, 96–97

worrisome issues, 8

WOW. *See* Wider Opportunities for Women

Young, Iris Marion, 14

younger selves: ageism and, 2, 46; aging and, 2

young people: ageism and, 67; common good and, 251; long-term care activism and, 172–173; Mayslake women and, 30, 31, 31–32, 33; old people and, 67, 248; Social Security and, 181, 203, 251. *See also* generations

young women, and acceptance of aging, 16

youthfulness, and denial of age, 82, 83

Zimmerman, George, 68

About the Author

Martha Holstein has spent forty-one years working in the field of aging both in the community and in academia. At Loyola University, she has taught health care ethics while at the University of Chicago, she teaches aging and health policy. She also works on long-term care policy at the Health and Medicine Policy Research Group in Chicago. For many years she was the associate director of the American Society on Aging and a research scholar at the Park Ridge Center for the Study of Health, Faith and Ethics. She has published widely in academic journals and books, is coauthor of the recent work *Ethics, Aging, and Society: The Critical Turn*, written with two Loyola colleagues, and the coeditor of several books including *Ethics in Community-Based Elder Care*.